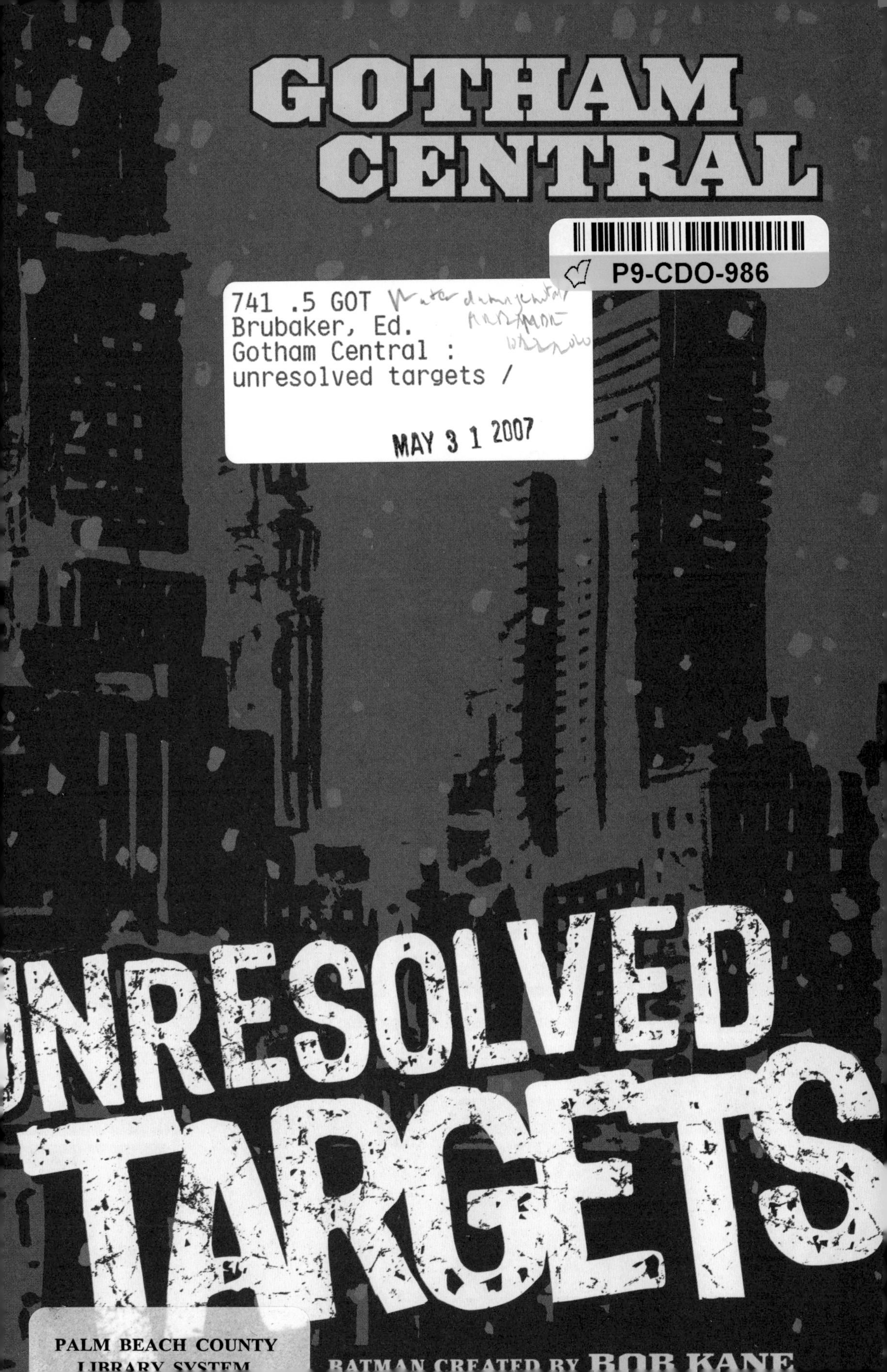

GOTHAM CENTRAL

UNRESOLVED TARGETS

BATMAN CREATED BY BOB KANE

GOTHAM CENTRAL: UNRESOLVED TARGETS
Published by DC Comics. Cover, introduction and
compilation copyright © 2006 DC Comics. All Rights Reserved.
Originally published in single magazine form in GOTHAM
CENTRAL 12-15, 19-22. Copyright © 2003, 2004 DC Comics.
All Rights Reserved. All characters, their distinctive
likenesses and related elements featured in this publication
are trademarks of DC Comics. The stories, characters and
incidents featured in this publication are entirely fictional.
DC Comics does not read or accept unsolicited submissions
of ideas, stories or artwork.
DC Comics, 1700 Broadway, New York, NY 10019.
A Warner Bros. Entertainment Company.
Printed in Canada. First Printing.
ISBN: 1-56389-995-7
ISBN 13: 978-1-5638-9995-9
Cover illustration by Michael Lark.
Publication design by Amie Brockway-Metcalf.

GOTHAM CITY POLICE

**CAPTAIN
MAGGIE SAWYER**
First shift commander;
formerly head of Metropolis
Special Crimes Unit.

**SGT. VINCENT
DEL ARRAZIO**
First shift
second-in-command;
partner of Joely Bartlett.

**DETECTIVE
ANDI KASINSKY**
Partner of Eric Cohen.

**DETECTIVE
JOSEPHINE "JOSIE
MAC" MacDONALD**
Has the distinction of being
the first MCU officer selected
after Jim Gordon's retirement.

SECOND SHIFT →

LT. DAVID CORNWELL
Second shift commander.

**SGT. JACKSON
"SARGE" DAVIES**
Second shift co-second-in-
command; partner of Crowe.

LT. RON PROBSON
Second shift co-second-in-
command.

**DETECTIVE
TREY HARTLEY**
Partner of Josh Azeveda.

**DETECTIVE
NATE PATTON**
Partner of Romy Chandler.

POLICE SUPPORT →

**COMMISSIONER
MICHAEL AKINS**
Former commissioner for
Gateway City, replaced
James W. Gordon.

EPARTMENT, MAJOR CRIMES UNIT

**DETECTIVE
CRISPUS ALLEN**
Partner of Renee Montoya.

**DETECTIVE
JOELY BARTLETT**
Partner of Vincent
Del Arrazio.

**DETECTIVE
TOMMY BURKE**
Partner of
Dagmar Procjnow.

**DETECTIVE
ERIC COHEN**
Partner of Andi Kasinsky.

**DETECTIVE 2ND GRADE
RENEE MONTOYA**
Partner of Crispus Allen.

**DETECTIVE
DAGMAR PROCJNOW**
Partner of Tommy Burke.

**FIRST
SHIFT**
←

**DETECTIVE
JOSH AZEVEDA**
Partner of Trey Hartley.

**DETECTIVE
ROMY CHANDLER**
Partner of Nate Patton.

DETECTIVE CROWE
Partner of Sarge Davies.

**DETECTIVE
MARCUS DRIVER**
Last MCU officer to be select-
ed by former Commissioner
James W. Gordon.

JIM CORRIGAN
GCPD crime scene
investigator.

NORA FIELDS
City coroner.

JAMES W. GORDON
Former Gotham City police
commissioner, and 20-year
veteran of the force. Currently
teaches criminology at
Gotham University.

STACY
Receptionist; only person
permitted to operate the
Bat-signal.

GOTHAM CENTRAL

SOFT TARGETS

**ED BRUBAKER
& GREG RUCKA**
WRITERS

**MICHAEL LARK
& STEFANO GAUDIANO**
ARTISTS

LEE LOUGHRIDGE COLORIST

CLEM ROBINS LETTERER

MICHAEL LARK ORIGINAL SERIES COVERS

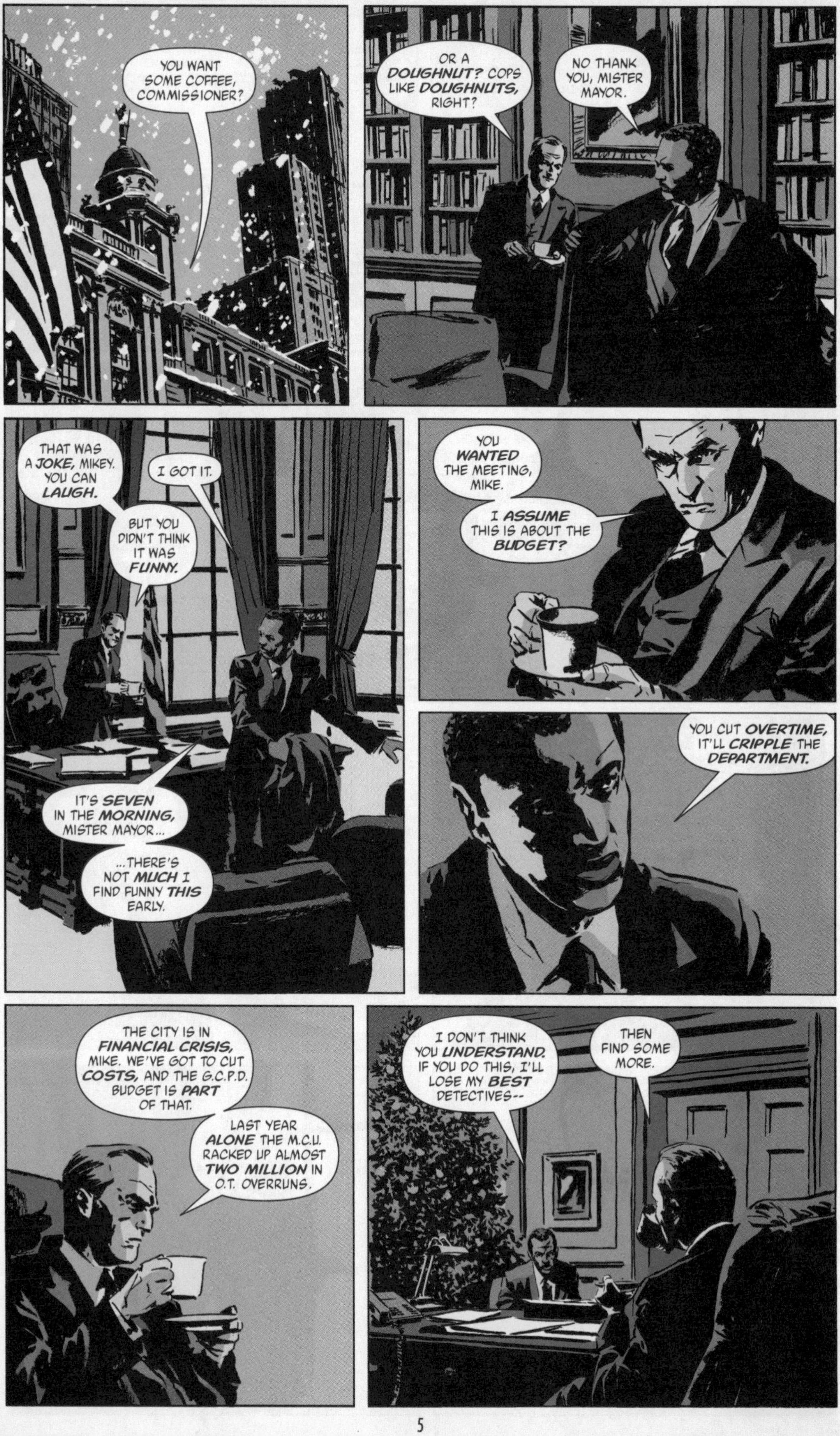
YOU WANT SOME COFFEE, COMMISSIONER?
OR A DOUGHNUT? COPS LIKE DOUGHNUTS, RIGHT?
NO THANK YOU, MISTER MAYOR.
THAT WAS A JOKE, MIKEY. YOU CAN LAUGH.
I GOT IT.
BUT YOU DIDN'T THINK IT WAS FUNNY.
IT'S SEVEN IN THE MORNING, MISTER MAYOR...
...THERE'S NOT MUCH I FIND FUNNY THIS EARLY.
YOU WANTED THE MEETING, MIKE.
I ASSUME THIS IS ABOUT THE BUDGET?
YOU CUT OVERTIME, IT'LL CRIPPLE THE DEPARTMENT.
THE CITY IS IN FINANCIAL CRISIS, MIKE. WE'VE GOT TO CUT COSTS, AND THE G.C.P.D. BUDGET IS PART OF THAT.
LAST YEAR ALONE THE M.C.U. RACKED UP ALMOST TWO MILLION IN O.T. OVERRUNS.
I DON'T THINK YOU UNDERSTAND. IF YOU DO THIS, I'LL LOSE MY BEST DETECTIVES--
THEN FIND SOME MORE.

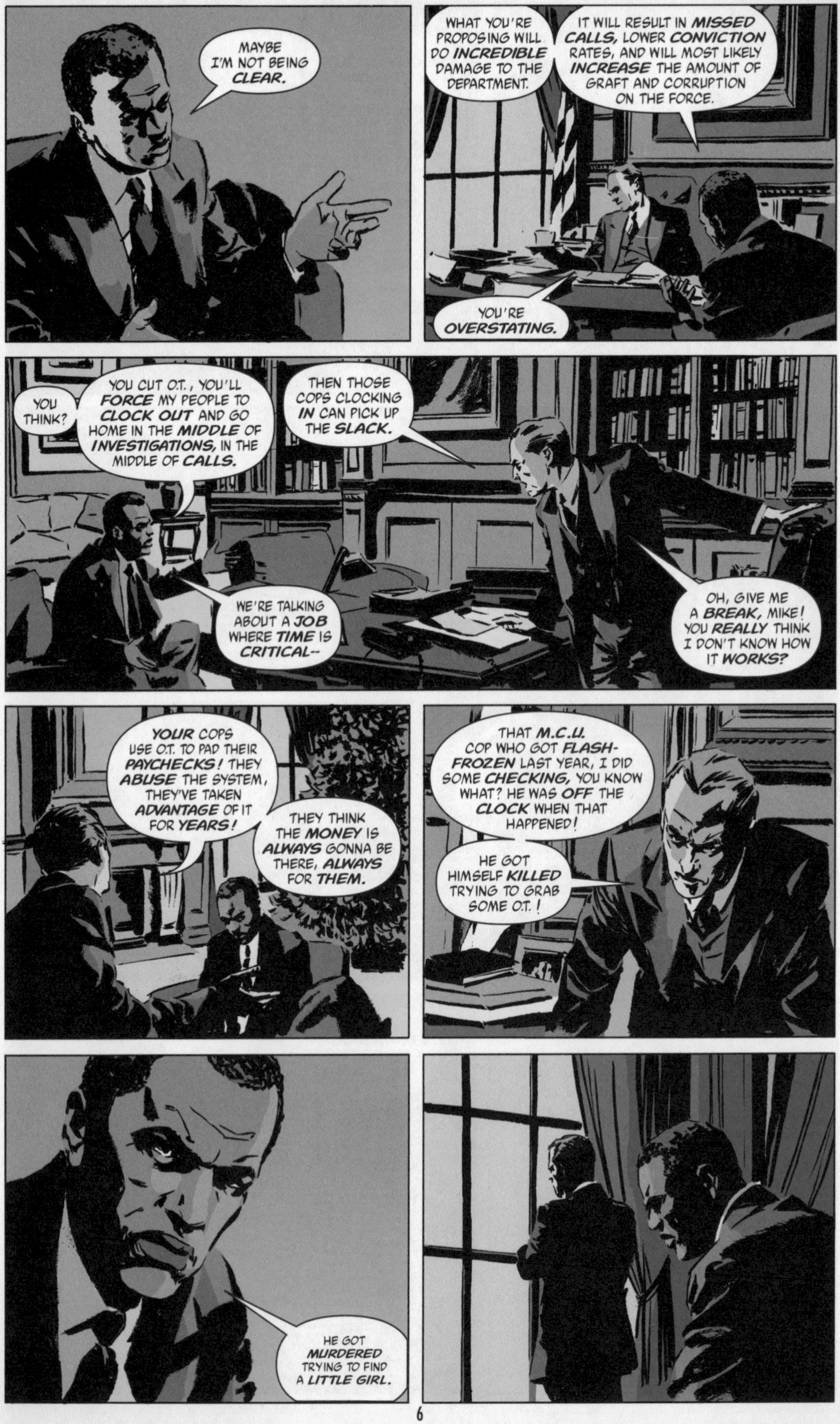
MAYBE I'M NOT BEING CLEAR.
WHAT YOU'RE PROPOSING WILL DO INCREDIBLE DAMAGE TO THE DEPARTMENT.
IT WILL RESULT IN MISSED CALLS, LOWER CONVICTION RATES, AND WILL MOST LIKELY INCREASE THE AMOUNT OF GRAFT AND CORRUPTION ON THE FORCE.
YOU'RE OVERSTATING.
YOU THINK?
YOU CUT O.T., YOU'LL FORCE MY PEOPLE TO CLOCK OUT AND GO HOME IN THE MIDDLE OF INVESTIGATIONS, IN THE MIDDLE OF CALLS.
THEN THOSE COPS CLOCKING IN CAN PICK UP THE SLACK.
WE'RE TALKING ABOUT A JOB WHERE TIME IS CRITICAL--
OH, GIVE ME A BREAK, MIKE! YOU REALLY THINK I DON'T KNOW HOW IT WORKS?
YOUR COPS USE O.T. TO PAD THEIR PAYCHECKS! THEY ABUSE THE SYSTEM, THEY'VE TAKEN ADVANTAGE OF IT FOR YEARS!
THEY THINK THE MONEY IS ALWAYS GONNA BE THERE, ALWAYS FOR THEM.
THAT M.C.U. COP WHO GOT FLASH-FROZEN LAST YEAR, I DID SOME CHECKING, YOU KNOW WHAT? HE WAS OFF THE CLOCK WHEN THAT HAPPENED!
HE GOT HIMSELF KILLED TRYING TO GRAB SOME O.T.!
HE GOT MURDERED TRYING TO FIND A LITTLE GIRL.

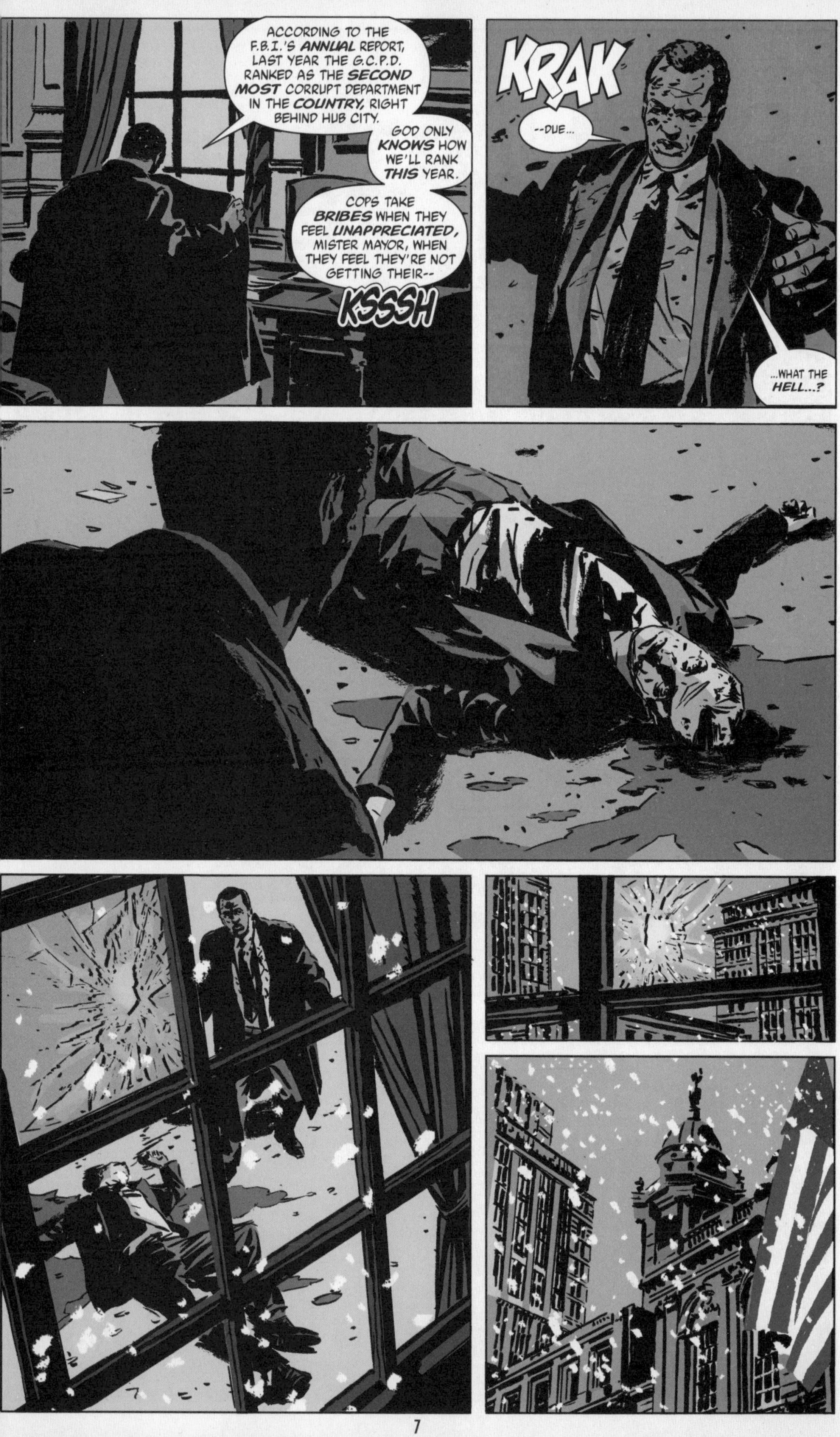
ACCORDING TO THE F.B.I.'S **ANNUAL** REPORT, LAST YEAR THE G.C.P.D. RANKED AS THE **SECOND MOST** CORRUPT DEPARTMENT IN THE **COUNTRY,** RIGHT BEHIND HUB CITY.
GOD ONLY **KNOWS** HOW WE'LL RANK **THIS** YEAR.
COPS TAKE **BRIBES** WHEN THEY FEEL **UNAPPRECIATED,** MISTER MAYOR, WHEN THEY FEEL THEY'RE NOT GETTING THEIR--
KSSSH
KRAK
--DUE...
...WHAT THE **HELL...?**

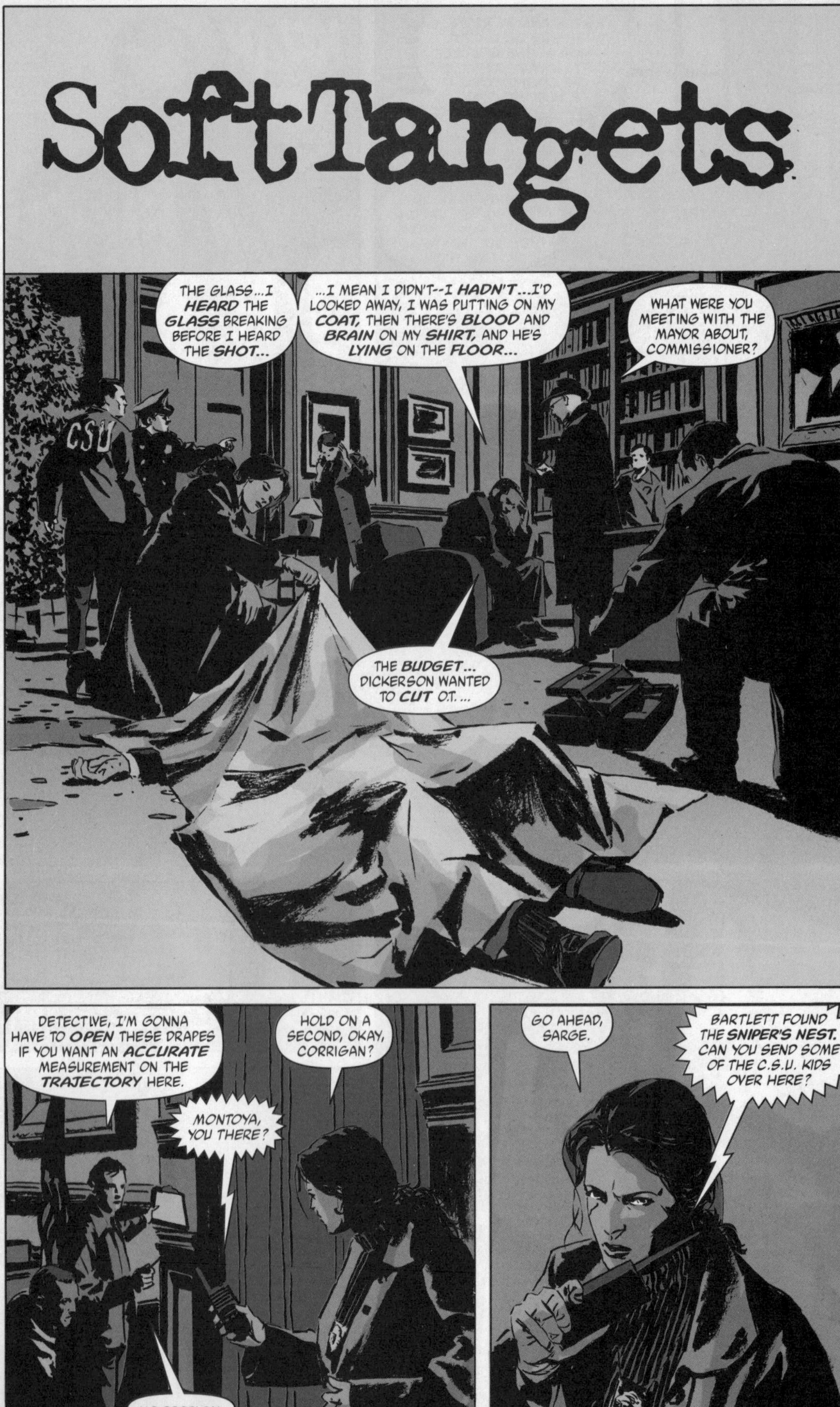
Soft Targets
THE GLASS...I HEARD THE GLASS BREAKING BEFORE I HEARD THE SHOT...
...I MEAN I DIDN'T--I HADN'T...I'D LOOKED AWAY, I WAS PUTTING ON MY COAT, THEN THERE'S BLOOD AND BRAIN ON MY SHIRT, AND HE'S LYING ON THE FLOOR...
WHAT WERE YOU MEETING WITH THE MAYOR ABOUT, COMMISSIONER?
THE BUDGET... DICKERSON WANTED TO CUT O.T. ...
CSU
DETECTIVE, I'M GONNA HAVE TO OPEN THESE DRAPES IF YOU WANT AN ACCURATE MEASUREMENT ON THE TRAJECTORY HERE.
HOLD ON A SECOND, OKAY, CORRIGAN?
MONTOYA, YOU THERE?
NO PROBLEM.
GO AHEAD, SARGE.
BARTLETT FOUND THE SNIPER'S NEST. CAN YOU SEND SOME OF THE C.S.U. KIDS OVER HERE?

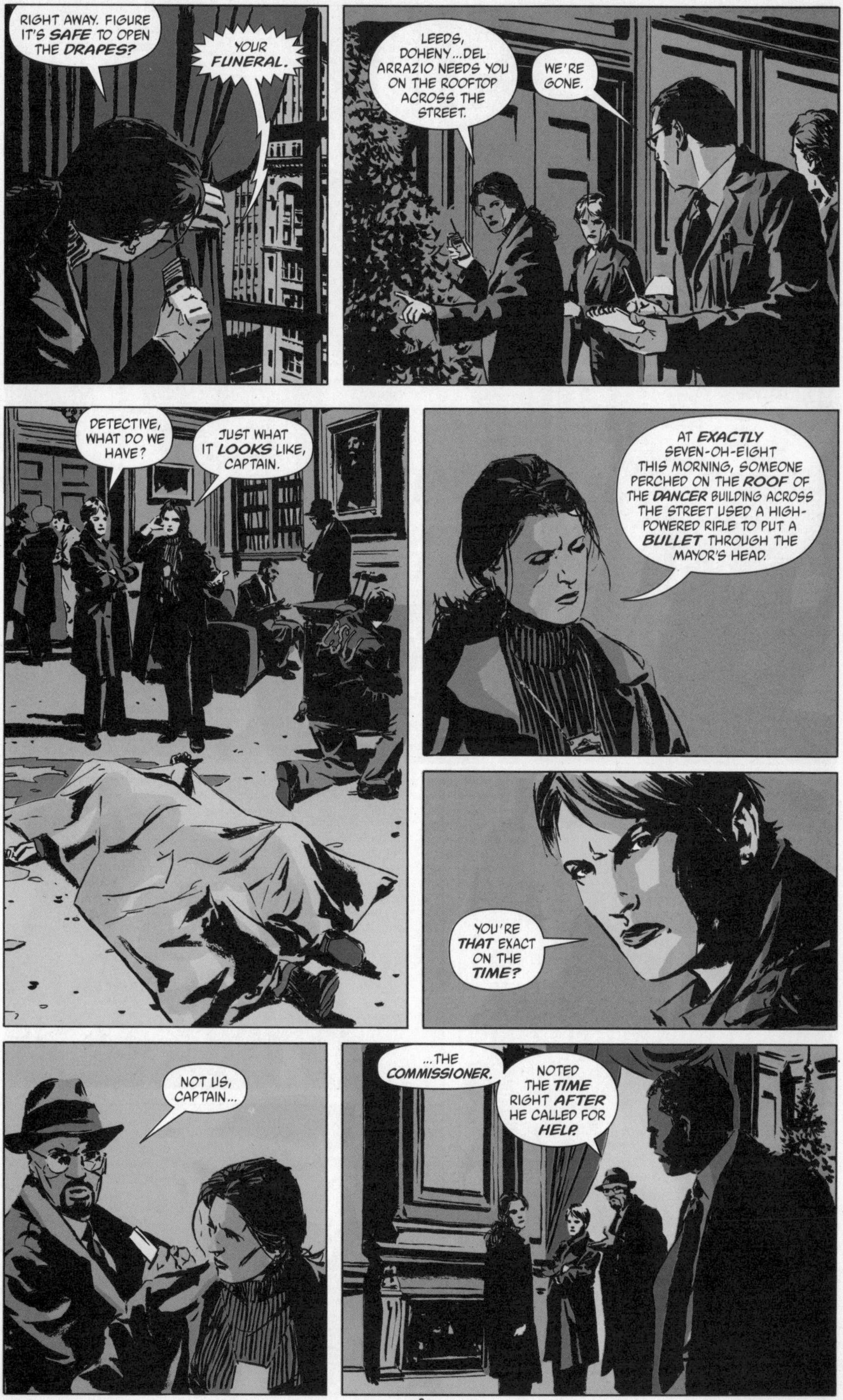

RIGHT AWAY. FIGURE IT'S SAFE TO OPEN THE DRAPES?
YOUR FUNERAL.
LEEDS, DOHENY...DEL ARRAZIO NEEDS YOU ON THE ROOFTOP ACROSS THE STREET.
WE'RE GONE.
DETECTIVE, WHAT DO WE HAVE?
JUST WHAT IT LOOKS LIKE, CAPTAIN.
AT EXACTLY SEVEN-OH-EIGHT THIS MORNING, SOMEONE PERCHED ON THE ROOF OF THE DANCER BUILDING ACROSS THE STREET USED A HIGH-POWERED RIFLE TO PUT A BULLET THROUGH THE MAYOR'S HEAD.
YOU'RE THAT EXACT ON THE TIME?
NOT US, CAPTAIN...
...THE COMMISSIONER.
NOTED THE TIME RIGHT AFTER HE CALLED FOR HELP.

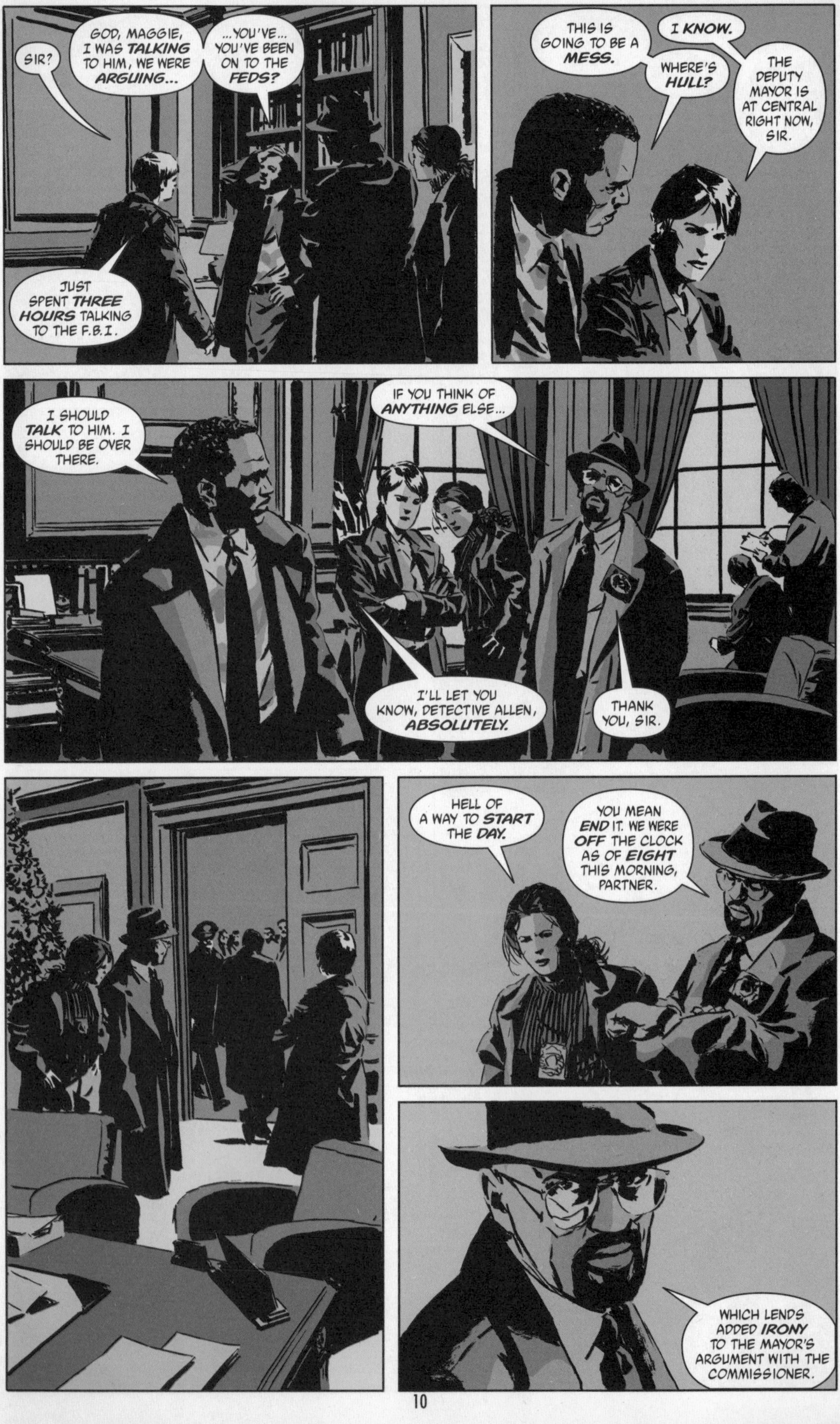
SIR?
GOD, MAGGIE, I WAS TALKING TO HIM, WE WERE ARGUING...
...YOU'VE... YOU'VE BEEN ON TO THE FEDS?
JUST SPENT THREE HOURS TALKING TO THE F.B.I.
THIS IS GOING TO BE A MESS.
I KNOW.
WHERE'S HULL?
THE DEPUTY MAYOR IS AT CENTRAL RIGHT NOW, SIR.
I SHOULD TALK TO HIM. I SHOULD BE OVER THERE.
IF YOU THINK OF ANYTHING ELSE...
I'LL LET YOU KNOW, DETECTIVE ALLEN, ABSOLUTELY.
THANK YOU, SIR.
HELL OF A WAY TO START THE DAY.
YOU MEAN END IT. WE WERE OFF THE CLOCK AS OF EIGHT THIS MORNING, PARTNER.
WHICH LENDS ADDED IRONY TO THE MAYOR'S ARGUMENT WITH THE COMMISSIONER.

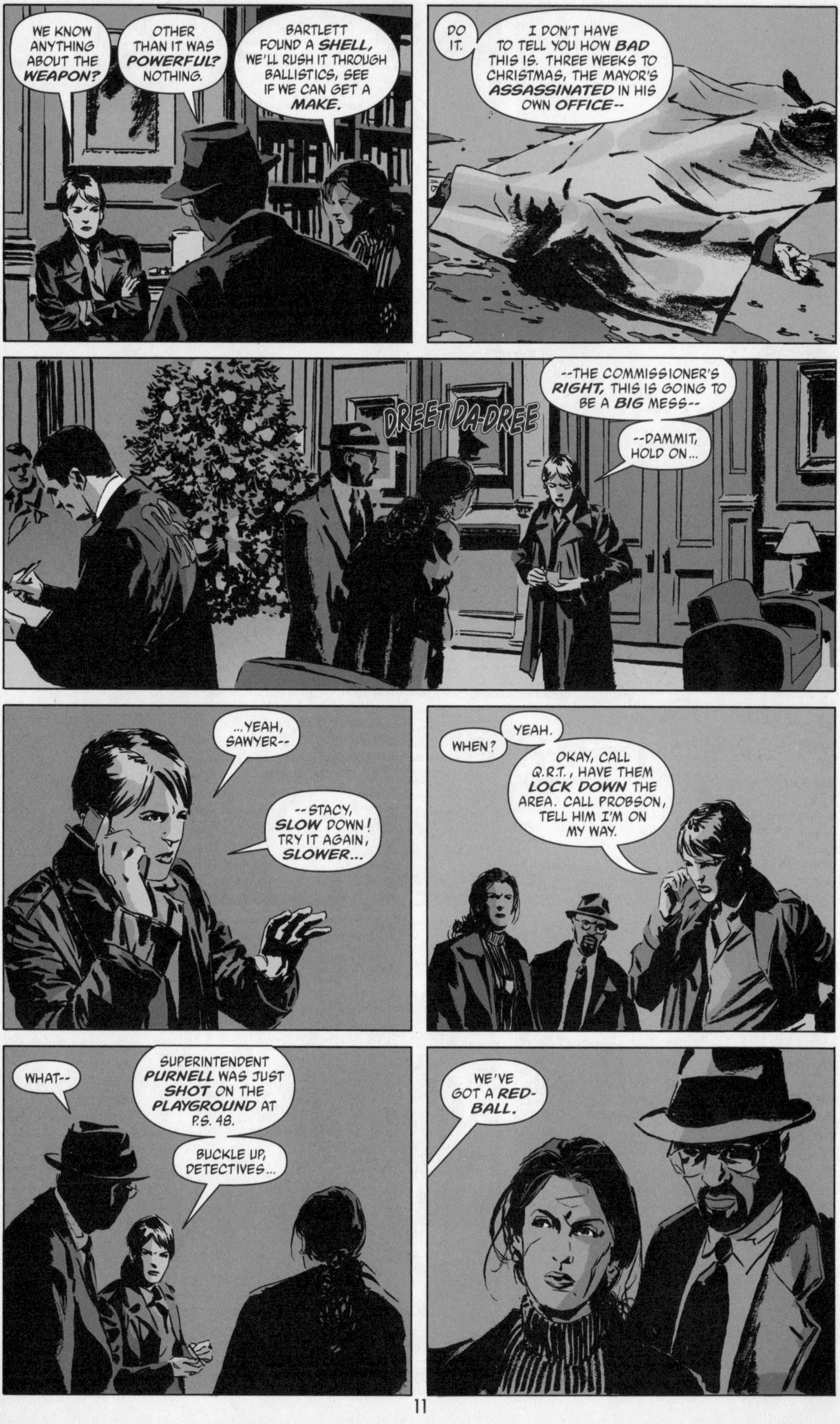
WE KNOW ANYTHING ABOUT THE WEAPON?
OTHER THAN IT WAS POWERFUL? NOTHING.
BARTLETT FOUND A SHELL, WE'LL RUSH IT THROUGH BALLISTICS, SEE IF WE CAN GET A MAKE.
DO IT.
I DON'T HAVE TO TELL YOU HOW BAD THIS IS. THREE WEEKS TO CHRISTMAS, THE MAYOR'S ASSASSINATED IN HIS OWN OFFICE--
DREET DA-DREE
--THE COMMISSIONER'S RIGHT, THIS IS GOING TO BE A BIG MESS--
--DAMMIT, HOLD ON...
...YEAH, SAWYER--
--STACY, SLOW DOWN! TRY IT AGAIN, SLOWER...
WHEN?
YEAH.
OKAY, CALL Q.R.T., HAVE THEM LOCK DOWN THE AREA. CALL PROBSON, TELL HIM I'M ON MY WAY.
WHAT--
SUPERINTENDENT PURNELL WAS JUST SHOT ON THE PLAYGROUND AT P.S. 48.
BUCKLE UP, DETECTIVES...
WE'VE GOT A RED-BALL.

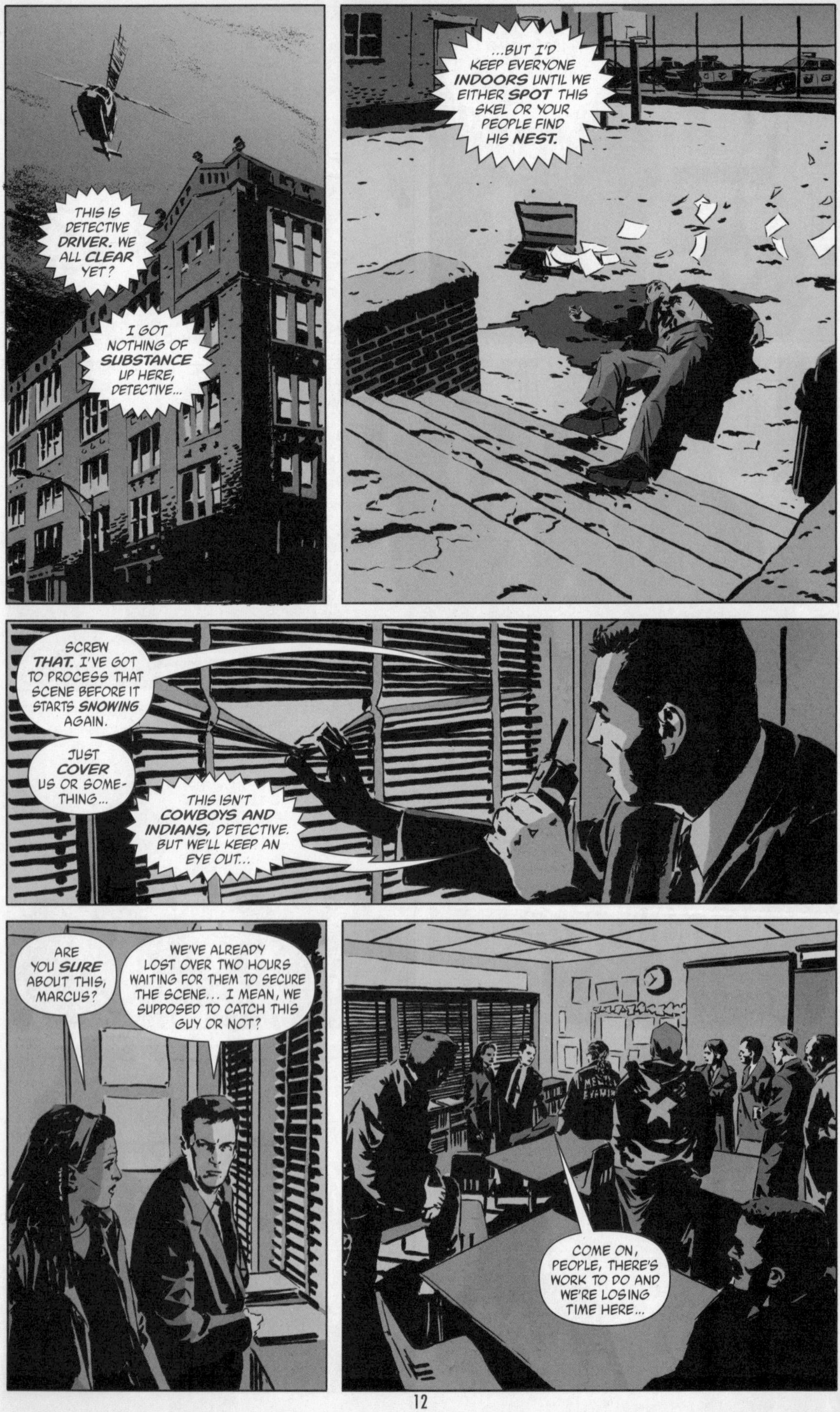
THIS IS DETECTIVE DRIVER. WE ALL CLEAR YET?
I GOT NOTHING OF SUBSTANCE UP HERE, DETECTIVE...
...BUT I'D KEEP EVERYONE INDOORS UNTIL WE EITHER SPOT THIS SKEL OR YOUR PEOPLE FIND HIS NEST.
SCREW THAT. I'VE GOT TO PROCESS THAT SCENE BEFORE IT STARTS SNOWING AGAIN.
JUST COVER US OR SOME-THING...
THIS ISN'T COWBOYS AND INDIANS, DETECTIVE. BUT WE'LL KEEP AN EYE OUT...
ARE YOU SURE ABOUT THIS, MARCUS?
WE'VE ALREADY LOST OVER TWO HOURS WAITING FOR THEM TO SECURE THE SCENE... I MEAN, WE SUPPOSED TO CATCH THIS GUY OR NOT?
COME ON, PEOPLE, THERE'S WORK TO DO AND WE'RE LOSING TIME HERE...

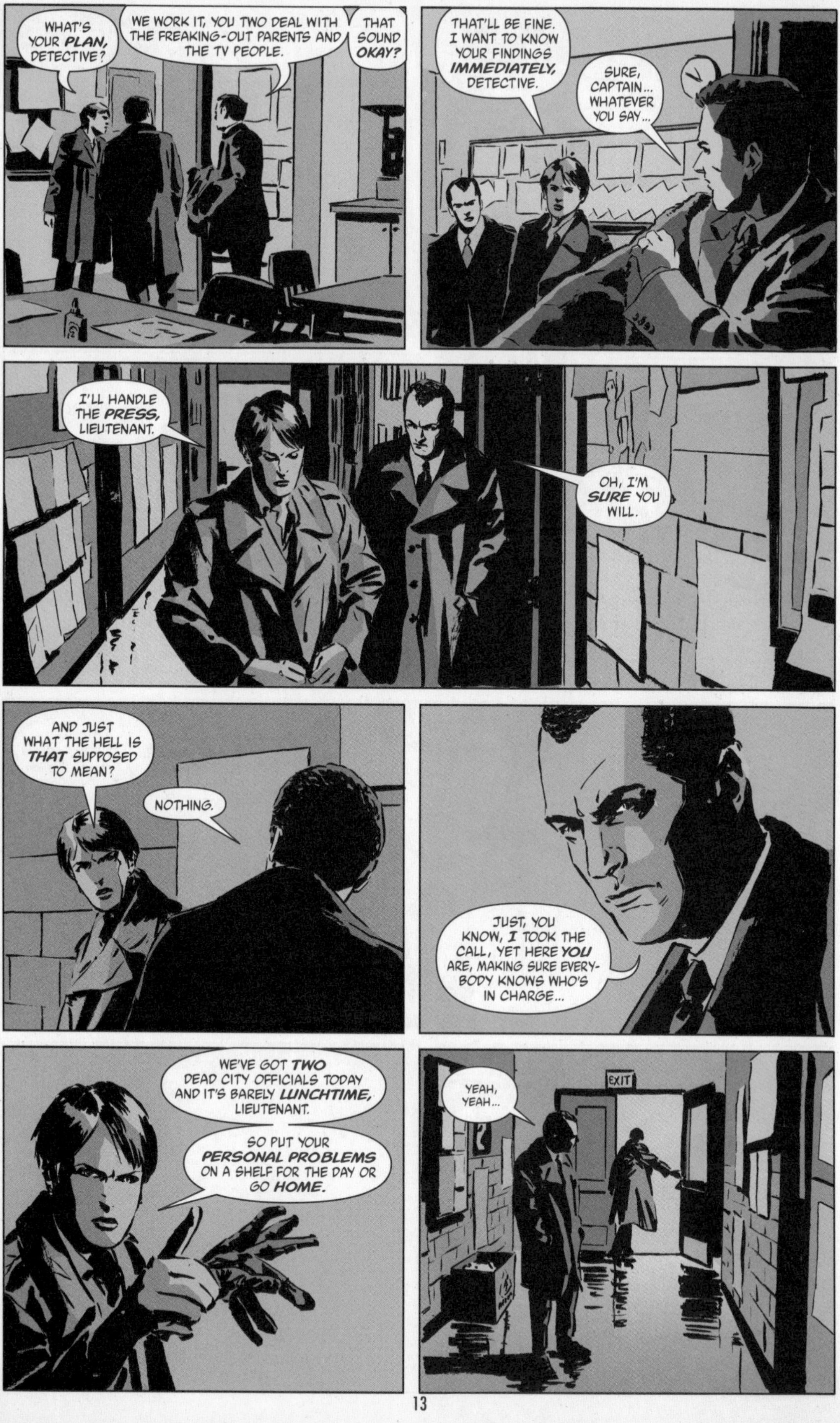
WHAT'S YOUR PLAN, DETECTIVE?
WE WORK IT, YOU TWO DEAL WITH THE FREAKING-OUT PARENTS AND THE TV PEOPLE.
THAT SOUND OKAY?
THAT'LL BE FINE. I WANT TO KNOW YOUR FINDINGS IMMEDIATELY, DETECTIVE.
SURE, CAPTAIN... WHATEVER YOU SAY...
I'LL HANDLE THE PRESS, LIEUTENANT.
OH, I'M SURE YOU WILL.
AND JUST WHAT THE HELL IS THAT SUPPOSED TO MEAN?
NOTHING.
JUST, YOU KNOW, I TOOK THE CALL, YET HERE YOU ARE, MAKING SURE EVERYBODY KNOWS WHO'S IN CHARGE...
WE'VE GOT TWO DEAD CITY OFFICIALS TODAY AND IT'S BARELY LUNCHTIME, LIEUTENANT.
SO PUT YOUR PERSONAL PROBLEMS ON A SHELF FOR THE DAY OR GO HOME.
YEAH, YEAH...
EXIT

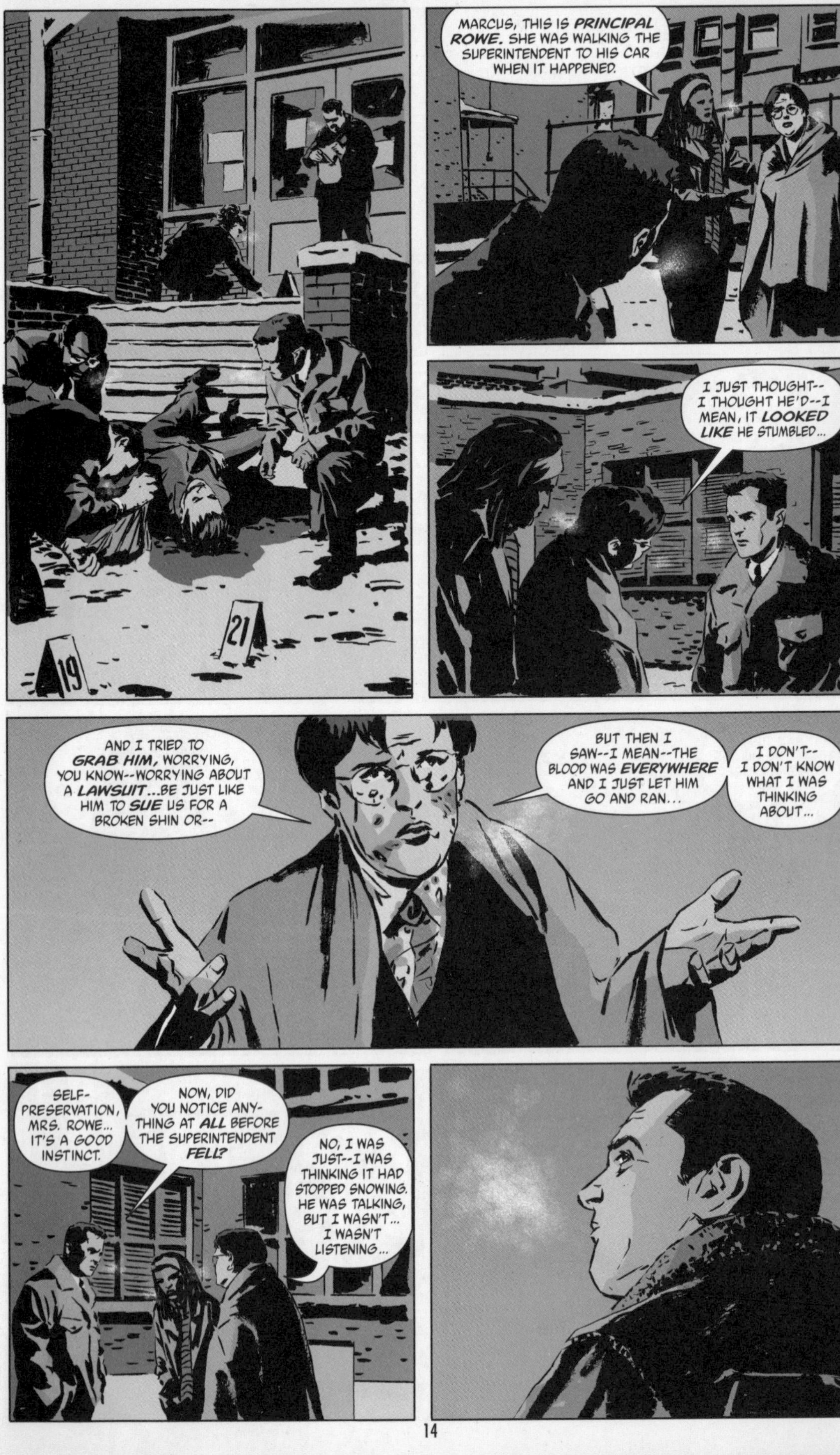
MARCUS, THIS IS PRINCIPAL ROWE. SHE WAS WALKING THE SUPERINTENDENT TO HIS CAR WHEN IT HAPPENED.
I JUST THOUGHT-- I THOUGHT HE'D--I MEAN, IT LOOKED LIKE HE STUMBLED...
AND I TRIED TO GRAB HIM, WORRYING, YOU KNOW--WORRYING ABOUT A LAWSUIT...BE JUST LIKE HIM TO SUE US FOR A BROKEN SHIN OR--
BUT THEN I SAW--I MEAN--THE BLOOD WAS EVERYWHERE AND I JUST LET HIM GO AND RAN...
I DON'T-- I DON'T KNOW WHAT I WAS THINKING ABOUT...
SELF-PRESERVATION, MRS. ROWE... IT'S A GOOD INSTINCT.
NOW, DID YOU NOTICE ANYTHING AT ALL BEFORE THE SUPERINTENDENT FELL?
NO, I WAS JUST--I WAS THINKING IT HAD STOPPED SNOWING. HE WAS TALKING, BUT I WASN'T... I WASN'T LISTENING...
19
21

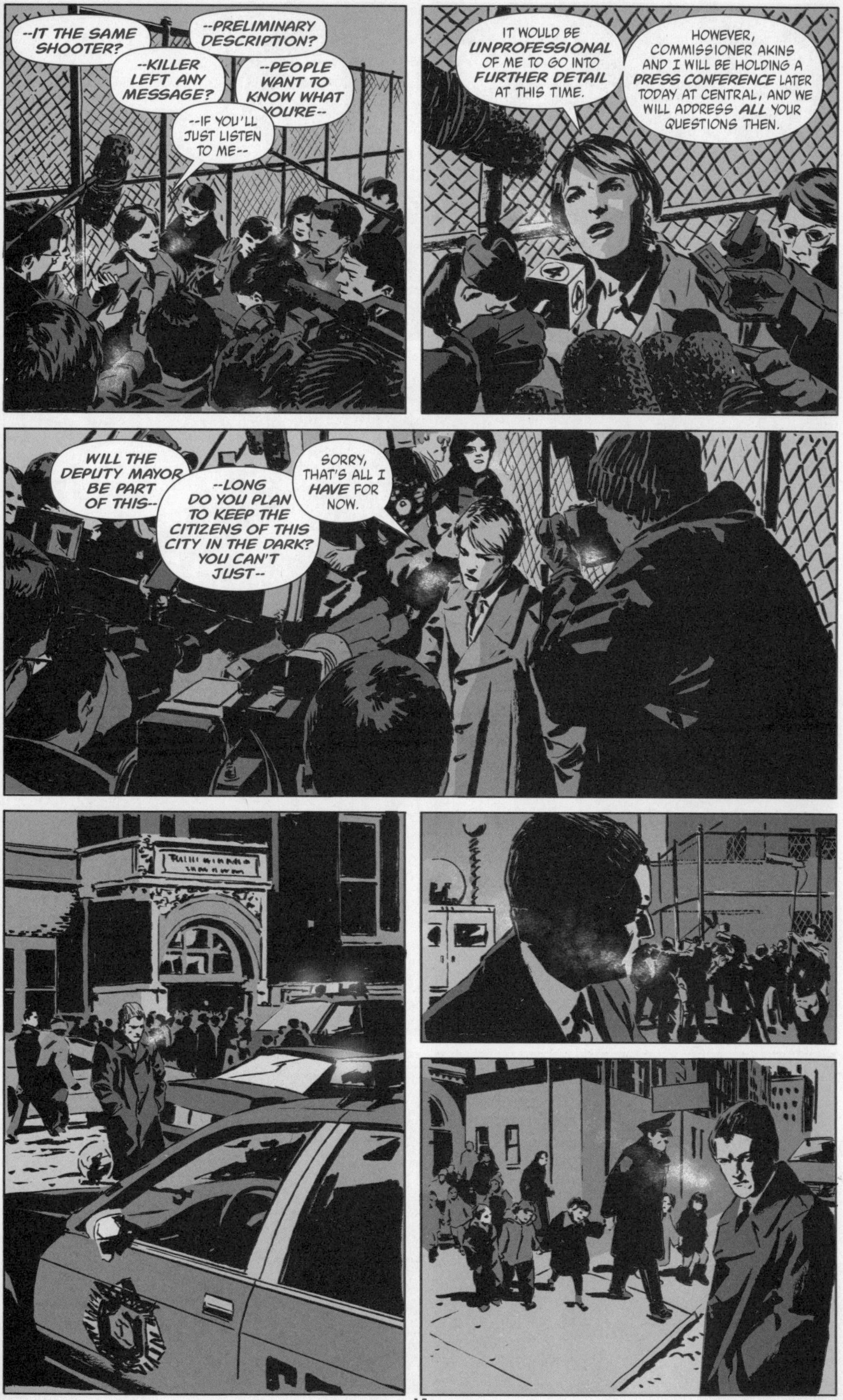
--IT THE SAME SHOOTER?
--PRELIMINARY DESCRIPTION?
--KILLER LEFT ANY MESSAGE?
--PEOPLE WANT TO KNOW WHAT YOU'RE--
--IF YOU'LL JUST LISTEN TO ME--
IT WOULD BE UNPROFESSIONAL OF ME TO GO INTO FURTHER DETAIL AT THIS TIME.
HOWEVER, COMMISSIONER AKINS AND I WILL BE HOLDING A PRESS CONFERENCE LATER TODAY AT CENTRAL, AND WE WILL ADDRESS ALL YOUR QUESTIONS THEN.
WILL THE DEPUTY MAYOR BE PART OF THIS--
--LONG DO YOU PLAN TO KEEP THE CITIZENS OF THIS CITY IN THE DARK? YOU CAN'T JUST--
SORRY, THAT'S ALL I HAVE FOR NOW.

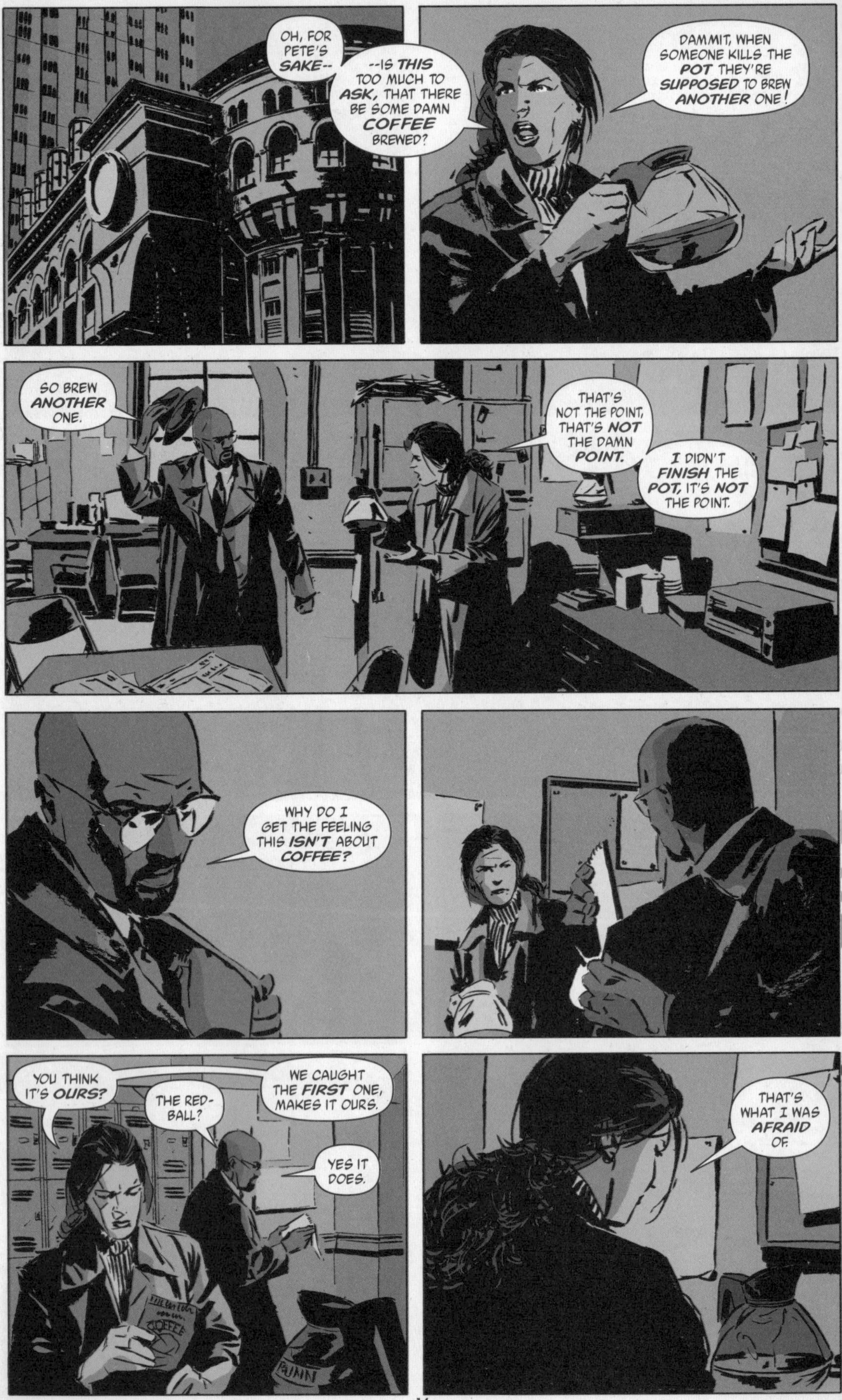
OH, FOR PETE'S SAKE--
--IS THIS TOO MUCH TO ASK, THAT THERE BE SOME DAMN COFFEE BREWED?
DAMMIT, WHEN SOMEONE KILLS THE POT THEY'RE SUPPOSED TO BREW ANOTHER ONE!
SO BREW ANOTHER ONE.
THAT'S NOT THE POINT, THAT'S NOT THE DAMN POINT.
I DIDN'T FINISH THE POT, IT'S NOT THE POINT.
WHY DO I GET THE FEELING THIS ISN'T ABOUT COFFEE?
YOU THINK IT'S OURS?
THE RED-BALL?
WE CAUGHT THE FIRST ONE, MAKES IT OURS.
YES IT DOES.
THAT'S WHAT I WAS AFRAID OF.

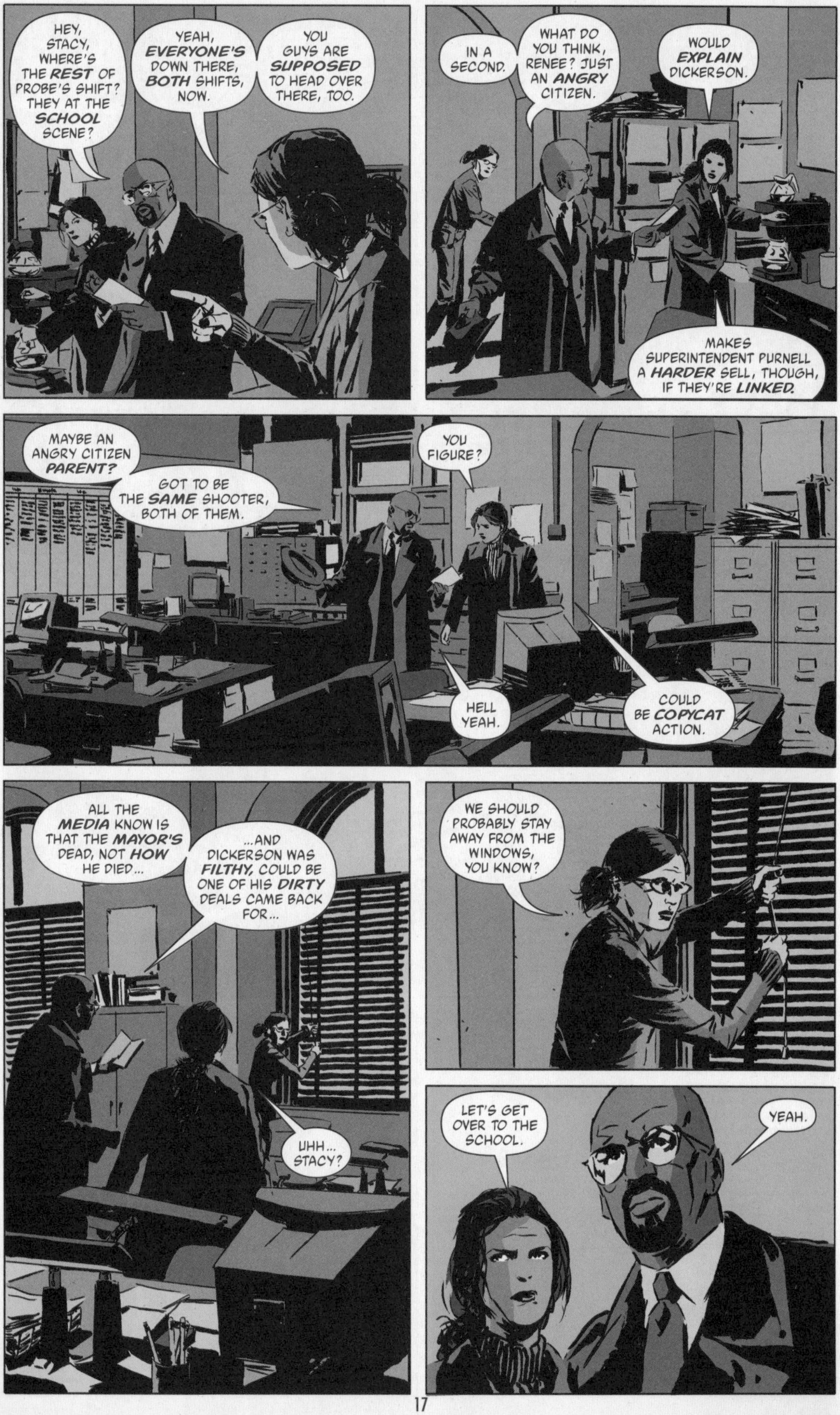
HEY, STACY, WHERE'S THE REST OF PROBE'S SHIFT? THEY AT THE SCHOOL SCENE?
YEAH, EVERYONE'S DOWN THERE, BOTH SHIFTS, NOW.
YOU GUYS ARE SUPPOSED TO HEAD OVER THERE, TOO.
IN A SECOND.
WHAT DO YOU THINK, RENEE? JUST AN ANGRY CITIZEN.
WOULD EXPLAIN DICKERSON.
MAKES SUPERINTENDENT PURNELL A HARDER SELL, THOUGH, IF THEY'RE LINKED.
MAYBE AN ANGRY CITIZEN PARENT?
GOT TO BE THE SAME SHOOTER, BOTH OF THEM.
YOU FIGURE?
HELL YEAH.
COULD BE COPYCAT ACTION.
ALL THE MEDIA KNOW IS THAT THE MAYOR'S DEAD, NOT HOW HE DIED...
...AND DICKERSON WAS FILTHY, COULD BE ONE OF HIS DIRTY DEALS CAME BACK FOR...
UHH... STACY?
WE SHOULD PROBABLY STAY AWAY FROM THE WINDOWS, YOU KNOW?
LET'S GET OVER TO THE SCHOOL.
YEAH.

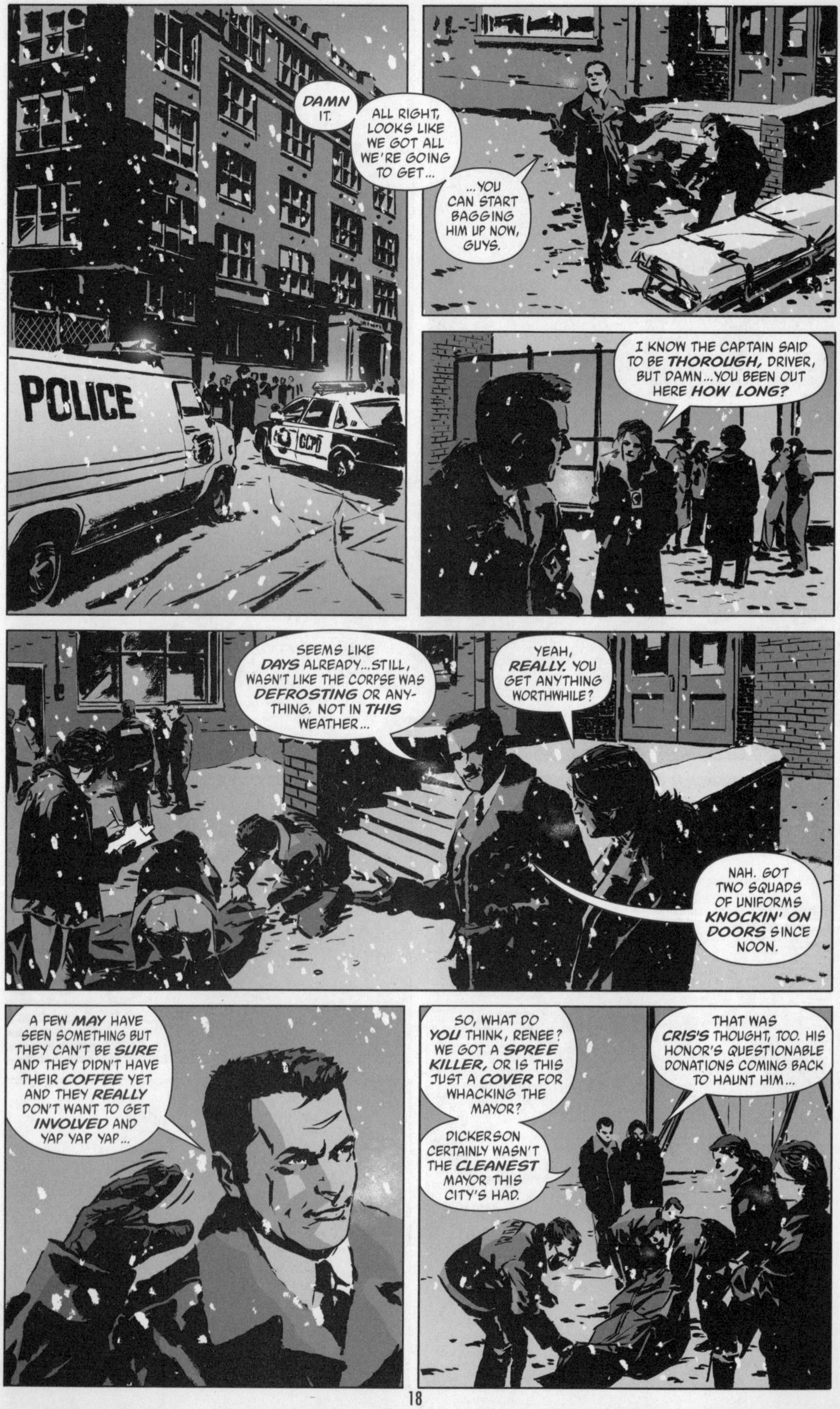
DAMN IT.
POLICE
GCPD
ALL RIGHT, LOOKS LIKE WE GOT ALL WE'RE GOING TO GET...
...YOU CAN START BAGGING HIM UP NOW, GUYS.
I KNOW THE CAPTAIN SAID TO BE THOROUGH, DRIVER, BUT DAMN...YOU BEEN OUT HERE HOW LONG?
SEEMS LIKE DAYS ALREADY...STILL, WASN'T LIKE THE CORPSE WAS DEFROSTING OR ANY-THING. NOT IN THIS WEATHER...
YEAH, REALLY. YOU GET ANYTHING WORTHWHILE?
NAH. GOT TWO SQUADS OF UNIFORMS KNOCKIN' ON DOORS SINCE NOON.
A FEW MAY HAVE SEEN SOMETHING BUT THEY CAN'T BE SURE AND THEY DIDN'T HAVE THEIR COFFEE YET AND THEY REALLY DON'T WANT TO GET INVOLVED AND YAP YAP YAP...
SO, WHAT DO YOU THINK, RENEE? WE GOT A SPREE KILLER, OR IS THIS JUST A COVER FOR WHACKING THE MAYOR?
DICKERSON CERTAINLY WASN'T THE CLEANEST MAYOR THIS CITY'S HAD.
THAT WAS CRIS'S THOUGHT, TOO. HIS HONOR'S QUESTIONABLE DONATIONS COMING BACK TO HAUNT HIM...

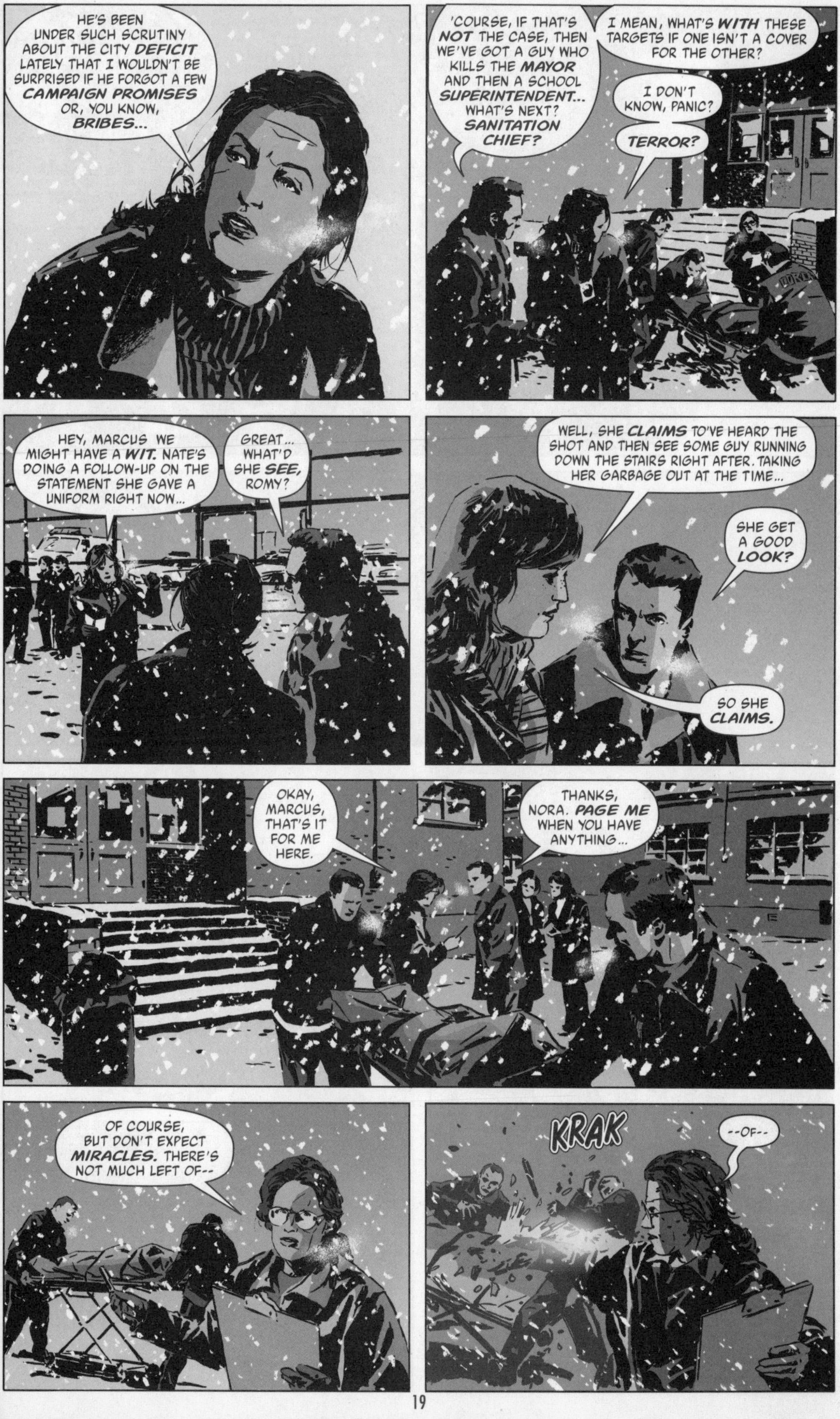
HE'S BEEN UNDER SUCH SCRUTINY ABOUT THE CITY DEFICIT LATELY THAT I WOULDN'T BE SURPRISED IF HE FORGOT A FEW CAMPAIGN PROMISES OR, YOU KNOW, BRIBES...
'COURSE, IF THAT'S NOT THE CASE, THEN WE'VE GOT A GUY WHO KILLS THE MAYOR AND THEN A SCHOOL SUPERINTENDENT... WHAT'S NEXT? SANITATION CHIEF?
I MEAN, WHAT'S WITH THESE TARGETS IF ONE ISN'T A COVER FOR THE OTHER?
I DON'T KNOW, PANIC?
TERROR?
HEY, MARCUS WE MIGHT HAVE A WIT. NATE'S DOING A FOLLOW-UP ON THE STATEMENT SHE GAVE A UNIFORM RIGHT NOW...
GREAT... WHAT'D SHE SEE, ROMY?
WELL, SHE CLAIMS TO'VE HEARD THE SHOT AND THEN SEE SOME GUY RUNNING DOWN THE STAIRS RIGHT AFTER. TAKING HER GARBAGE OUT AT THE TIME...
SHE GET A GOOD LOOK?
SO SHE CLAIMS.
OKAY, MARCUS, THAT'S IT FOR ME HERE.
THANKS, NORA. PAGE ME WHEN YOU HAVE ANYTHING...
OF COURSE, BUT DON'T EXPECT MIRACLES. THERE'S NOT MUCH LEFT OF--
KRAK
--OF--

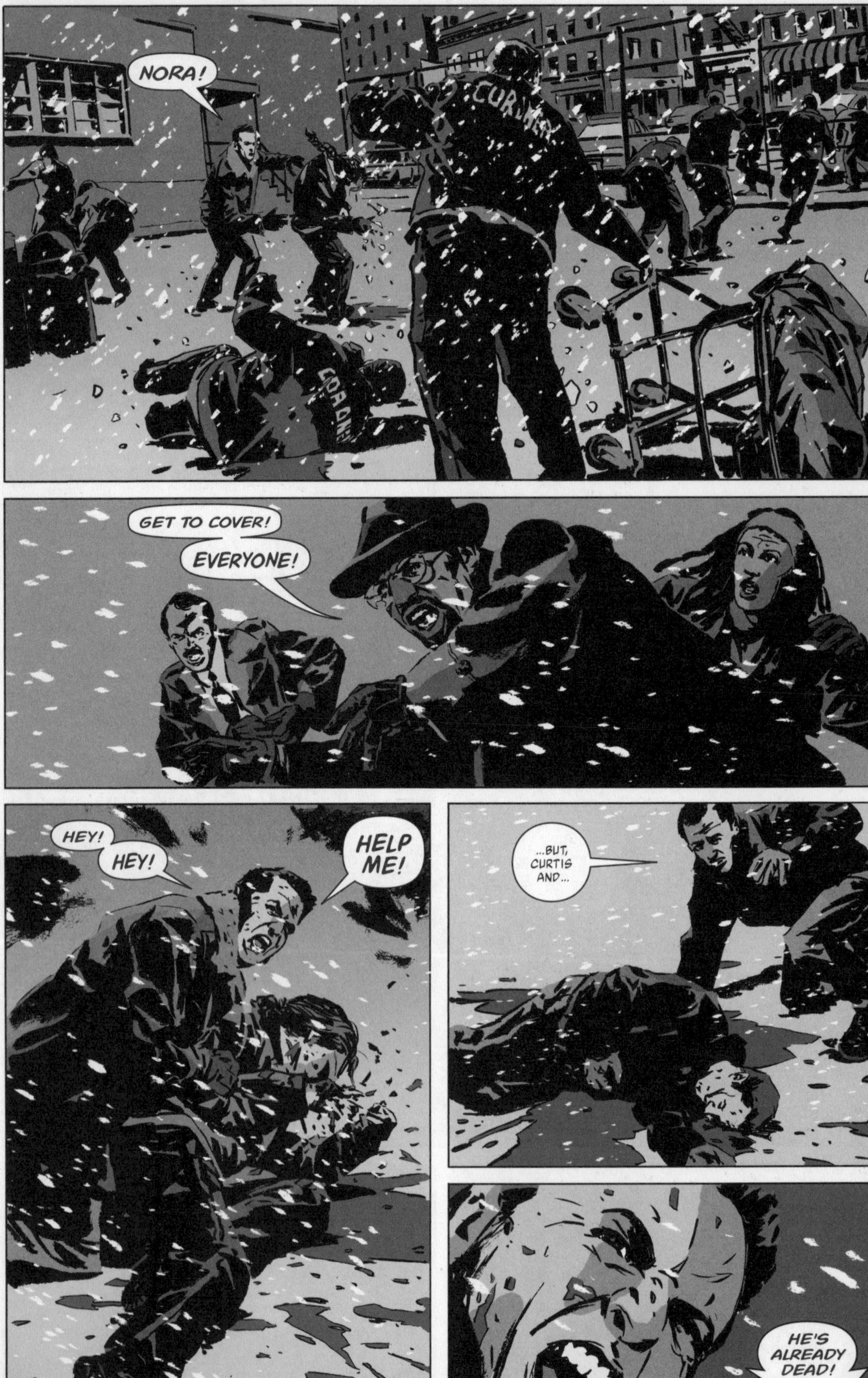
NORA!
GET TO COVER!
EVERYONE!
HEY!
HEY!
HELP ME!
...BUT, CURTIS AND...
HE'S ALREADY DEAD! HELP ME!

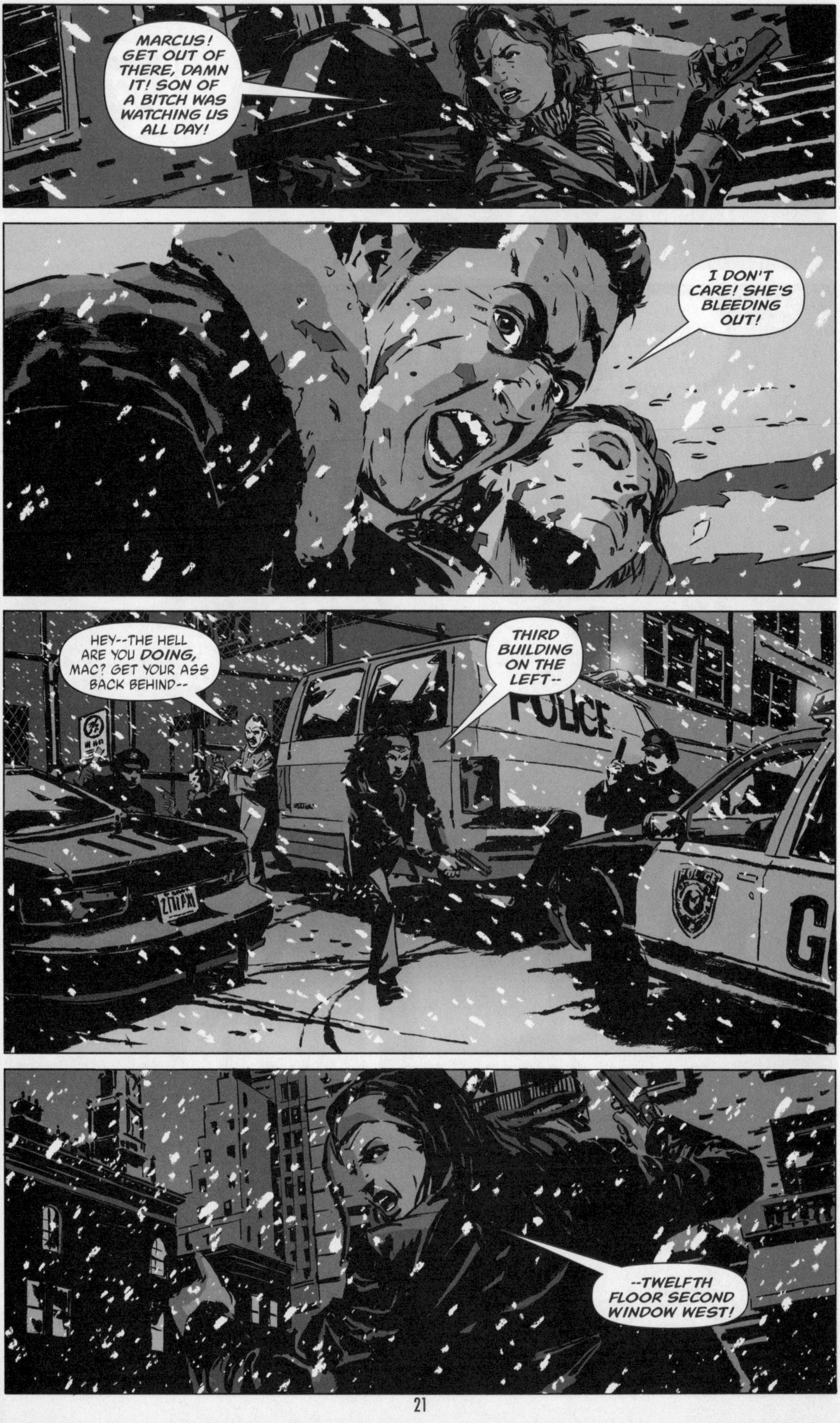
MARCUS! GET OUT OF THERE, DAMN IT! SON OF A BITCH WAS WATCHING US ALL DAY!
I DON'T CARE! SHE'S BLEEDING OUT!
HEY--THE HELL ARE YOU DOING, MAC? GET YOUR ASS BACK BEHIND--
THIRD BUILDING ON THE LEFT--
POLICE
--TWELFTH FLOOR SECOND WINDOW WEST!

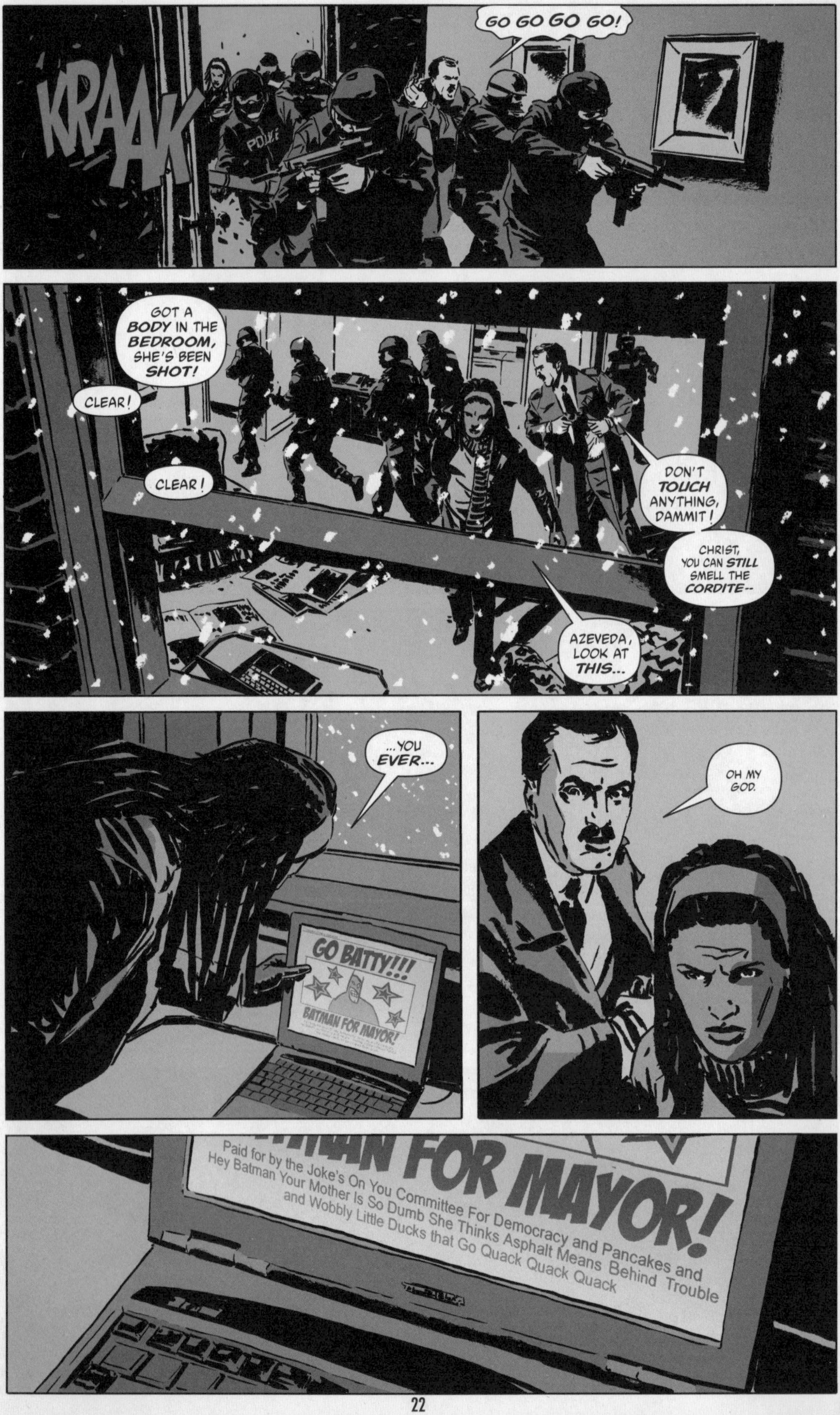
KRAAK
GO GO GO GO GO!
GOT A BODY IN THE BEDROOM, SHE'S BEEN SHOT!
CLEAR!
CLEAR!
DON'T TOUCH ANYTHING, DAMMIT!
CHRIST, YOU CAN STILL SMELL THE CORDITE--
AZEVEDA, LOOK AT THIS...
...YOU EVER...
GO BATTY!!!
BATMAN FOR MAYOR!
OH MY GOD.
...MAN FOR MAYOR!
Paid for by the Joke's On You Committee For Democracy and Pancakes and Hey Batman Your Mother Is So Dumb She Thinks Asphalt Means Behind Trouble and Wobbly Little Ducks that Go Quack Quack Quack

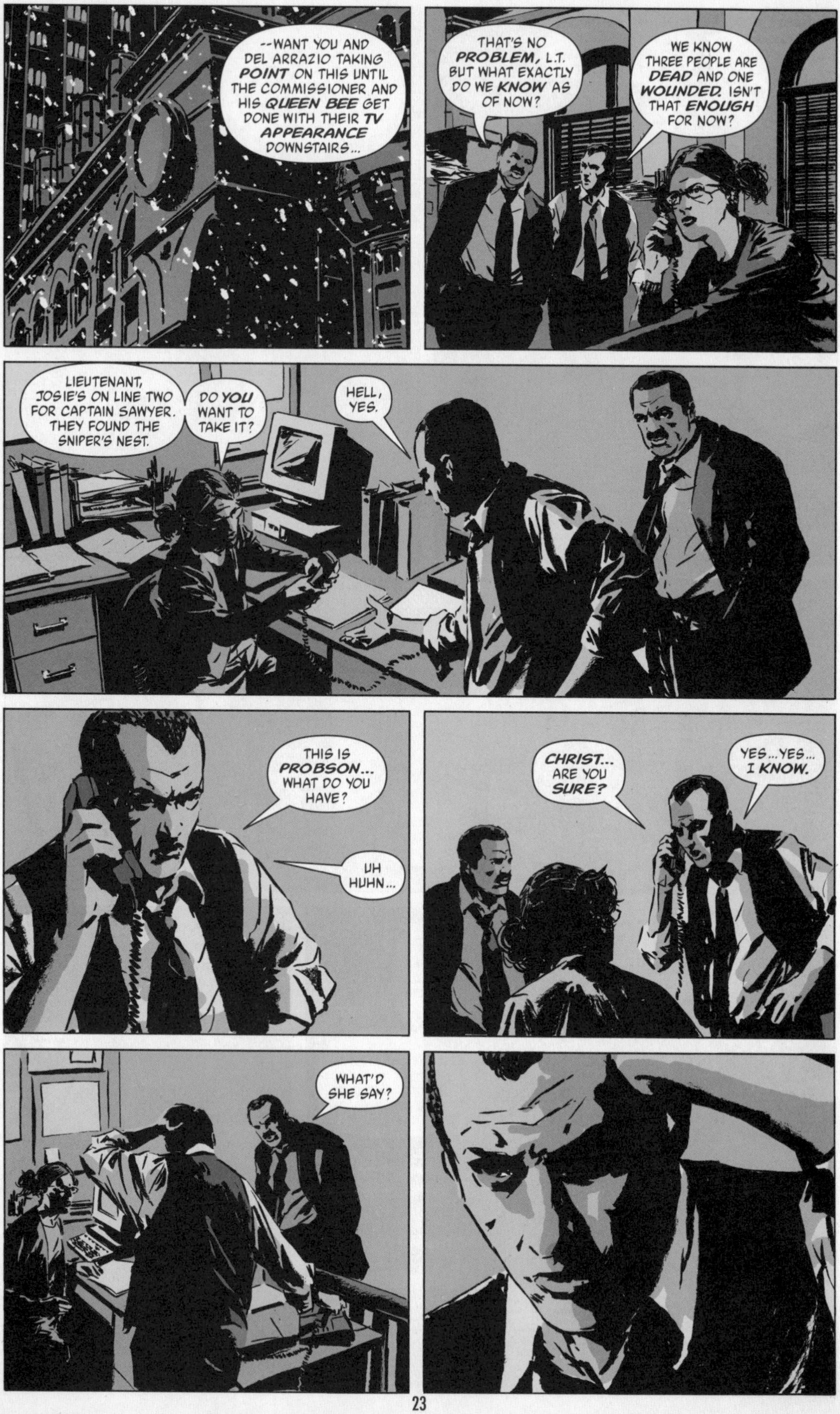
--WANT YOU AND DEL ARRAZIO TAKING POINT ON THIS UNTIL THE COMMISSIONER AND HIS QUEEN BEE GET DONE WITH THEIR TV APPEARANCE DOWNSTAIRS...
THAT'S NO PROBLEM, L.T. BUT WHAT EXACTLY DO WE KNOW AS OF NOW?
WE KNOW THREE PEOPLE ARE DEAD AND ONE WOUNDED. ISN'T THAT ENOUGH FOR NOW?
LIEUTENANT, JOSIE'S ON LINE TWO FOR CAPTAIN SAWYER. THEY FOUND THE SNIPER'S NEST.
DO YOU WANT TO TAKE IT?
HELL, YES.
THIS IS PROBSON... WHAT DO YOU HAVE?
UH HUHN...
CHRIST... ARE YOU SURE?
YES...YES... I KNOW.
WHAT'D SHE SAY?

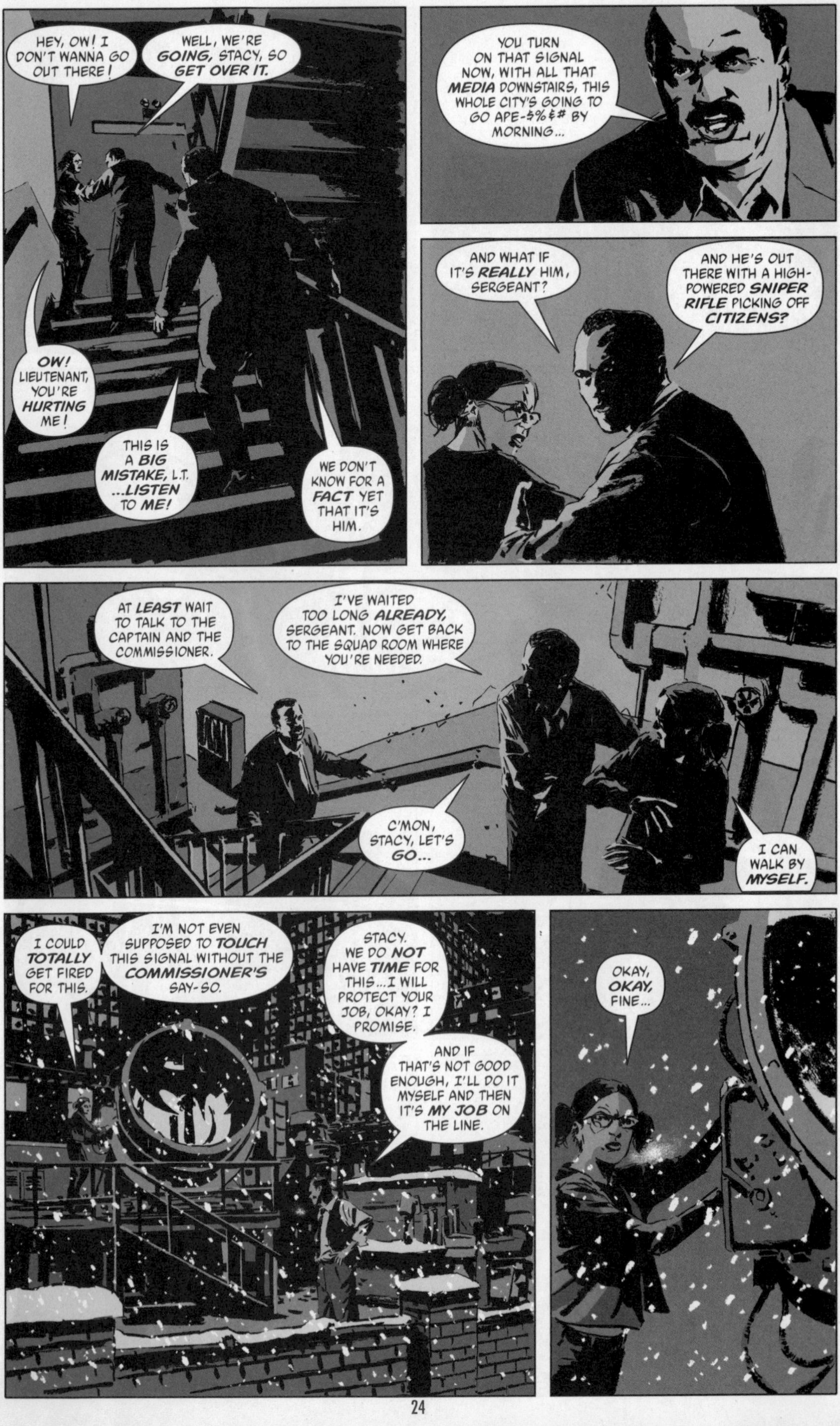
HEY, OW! I DON'T WANNA GO OUT THERE!
WELL, WE'RE **GOING,** STACY, SO **GET OVER IT.**
OW! LIEUTENANT, YOU'RE **HURTING** ME!
THIS IS A **BIG MISTAKE,** L.T. **...LISTEN** TO **ME!**
WE DON'T KNOW FOR A **FACT** YET THAT IT'S HIM.
YOU TURN ON THAT SIGNAL NOW, WITH ALL THAT **MEDIA** DOWNSTAIRS, THIS WHOLE CITY'S GOING TO GO APE-$%&# BY MORNING...
AND WHAT IF IT'S **REALLY** HIM, SERGEANT?
AND HE'S OUT THERE WITH A HIGH-POWERED **SNIPER RIFLE** PICKING OFF **CITIZENS?**
AT **LEAST** WAIT TO TALK TO THE CAPTAIN AND THE COMMISSIONER.
I'VE WAITED TOO LONG **ALREADY,** SERGEANT. NOW GET BACK TO THE SQUAD ROOM WHERE YOU'RE NEEDED.
C'MON, STACY, LET'S **GO...**
I CAN WALK BY **MYSELF.**
I COULD **TOTALLY** GET FIRED FOR THIS.
I'M NOT EVEN SUPPOSED TO **TOUCH** THIS SIGNAL WITHOUT THE **COMMISSIONER'S** SAY-SO.
STACY. WE DO **NOT** HAVE **TIME** FOR THIS... I WILL PROTECT YOUR JOB, OKAY? I PROMISE.
AND IF THAT'S NOT GOOD ENOUGH, I'LL DO IT MYSELF AND THEN IT'S **MY JOB** ON THE LINE.
OKAY, **OKAY,** FINE...

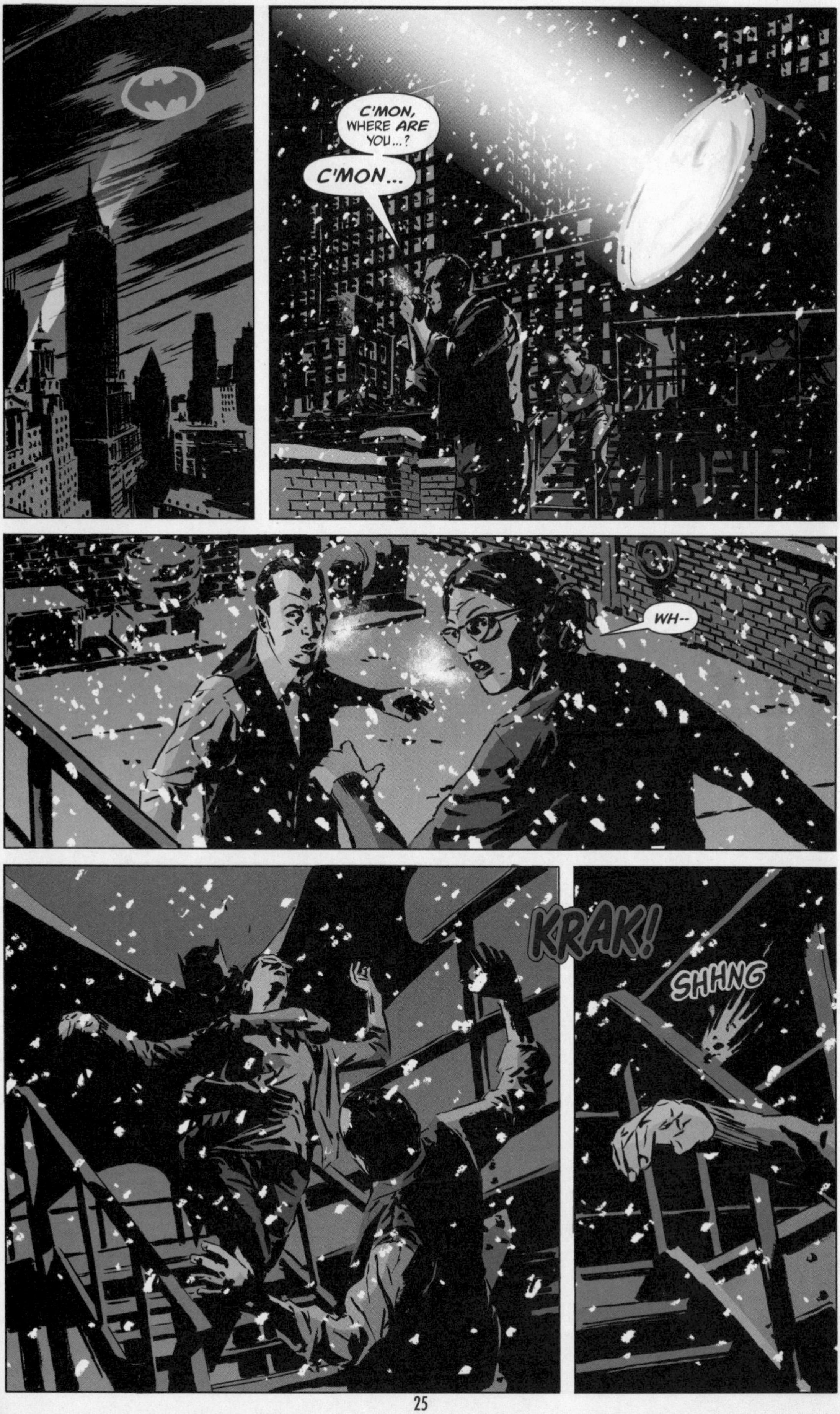
C'MON, WHERE ARE YOU...?
C'MON...
WH--
KRAK!
SHHNG

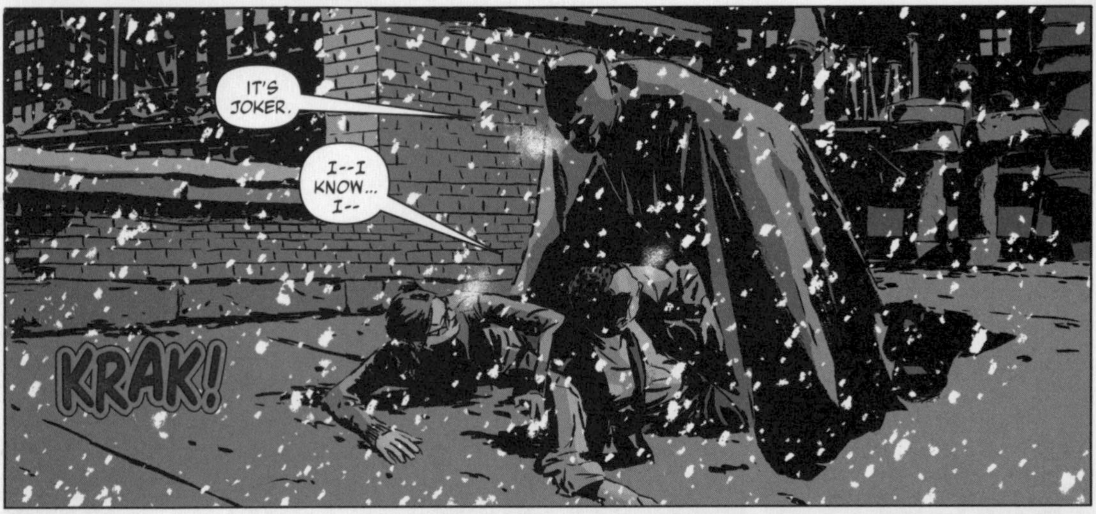
IT'S JOKER.
I--I KNOW... I--
KRAK!

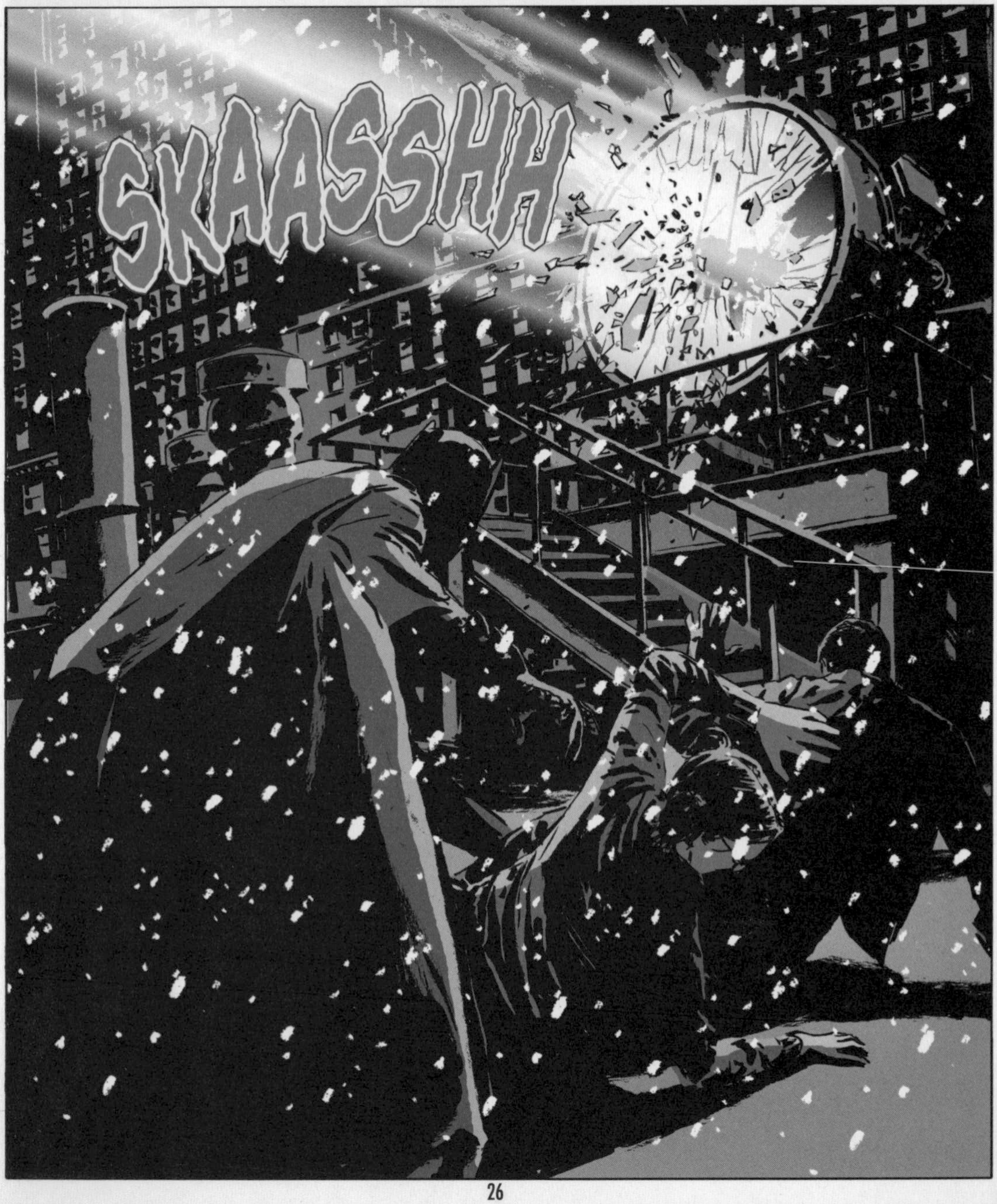
SKAASSHH

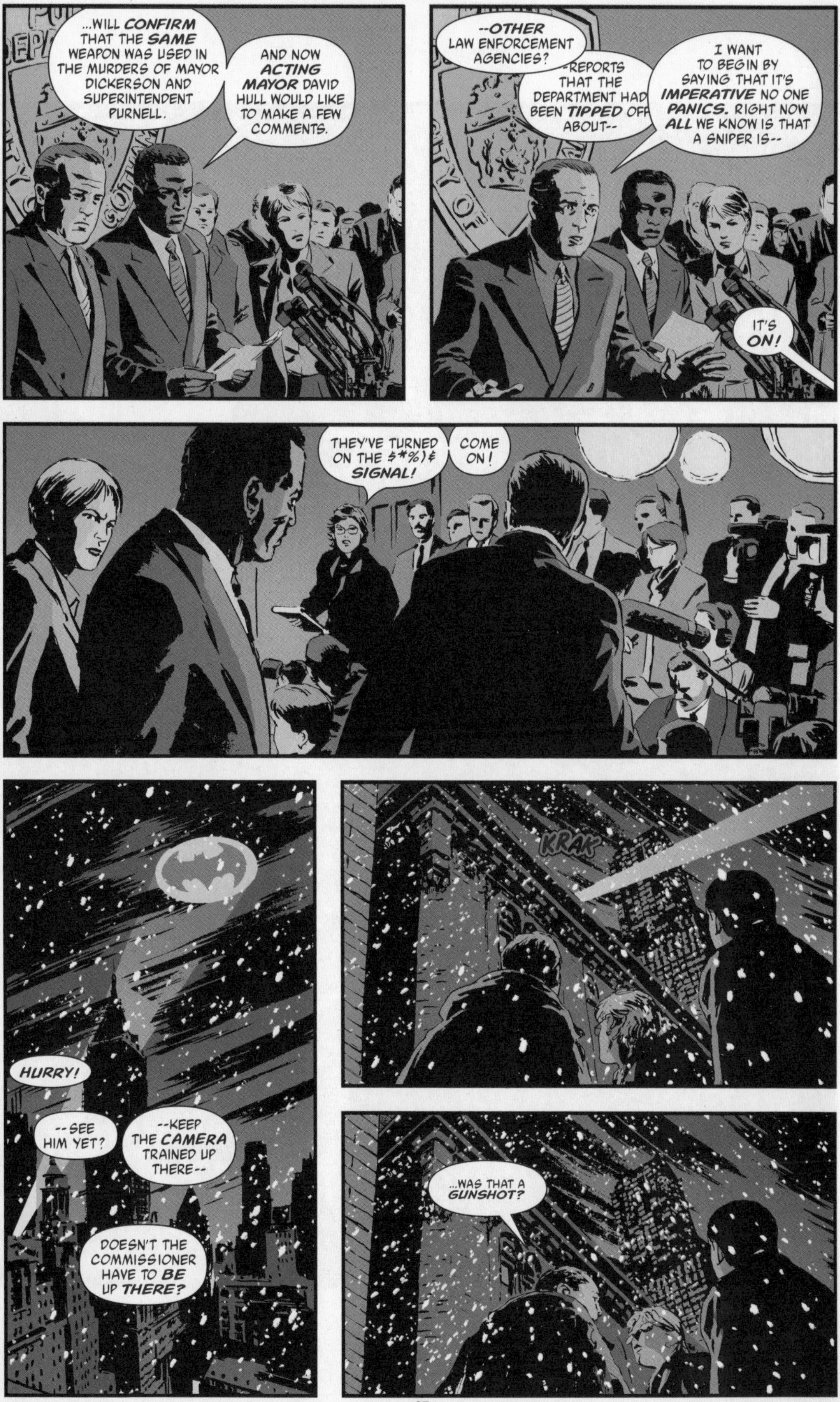
...WILL CONFIRM THAT THE SAME WEAPON WAS USED IN THE MURDERS OF MAYOR DICKERSON AND SUPERINTENDENT PURNELL.
AND NOW ACTING MAYOR DAVID HULL WOULD LIKE TO MAKE A FEW COMMENTS.
--OTHER LAW ENFORCEMENT AGENCIES?
-REPORTS THAT THE DEPARTMENT HAD BEEN TIPPED OFF ABOUT--
I WANT TO BEGIN BY SAYING THAT IT'S IMPERATIVE NO ONE PANICS. RIGHT NOW ALL WE KNOW IS THAT A SNIPER IS--
IT'S ON!
THEY'VE TURNED ON THE $*%)& SIGNAL!
COME ON!
HURRY!
--SEE HIM YET?
--KEEP THE CAMERA TRAINED UP THERE--
DOESN'T THE COMMISSIONER HAVE TO BE UP THERE?
KRAK
...WAS THAT A GUNSHOT?

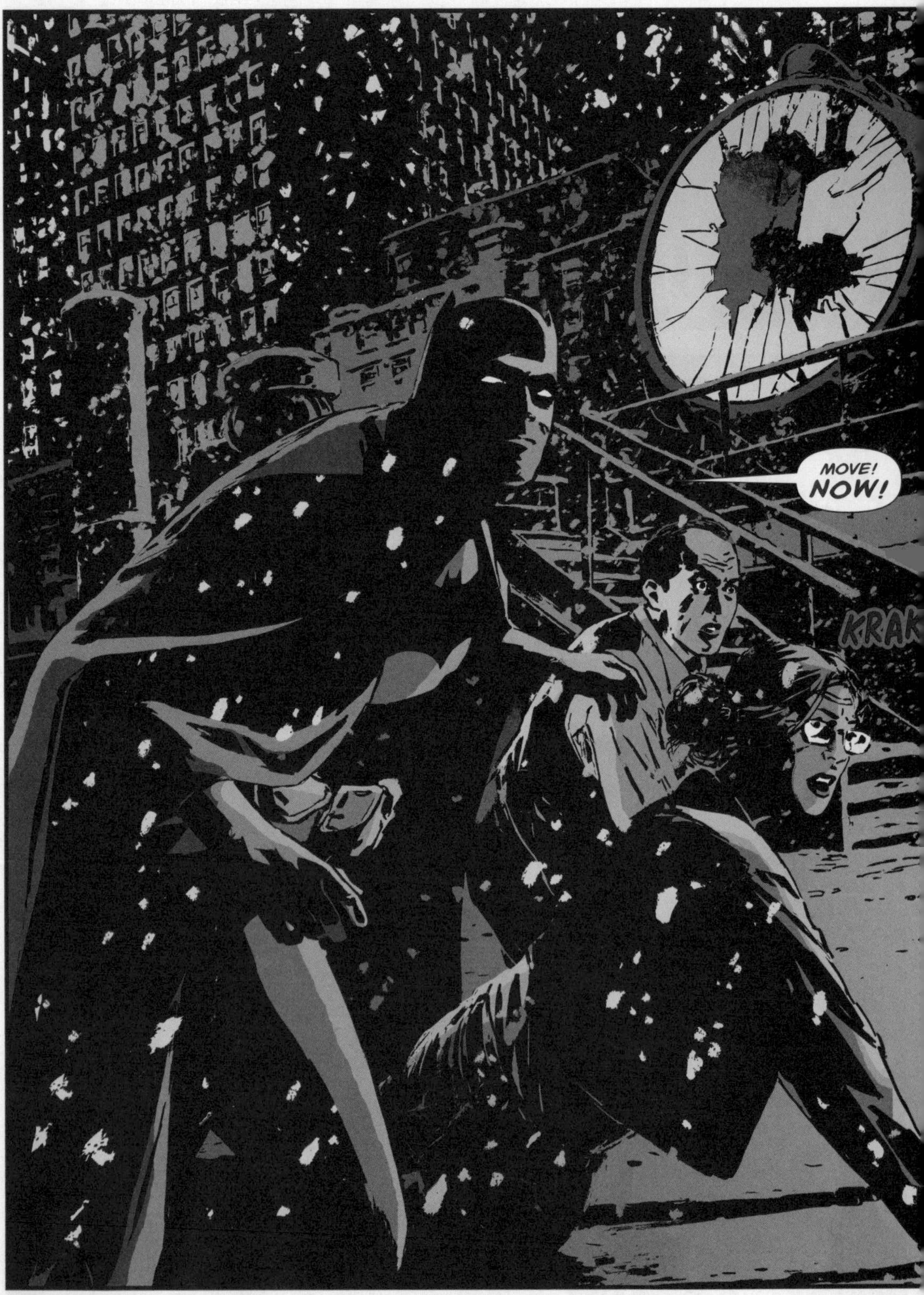
MOVE! NOW!
KRAK

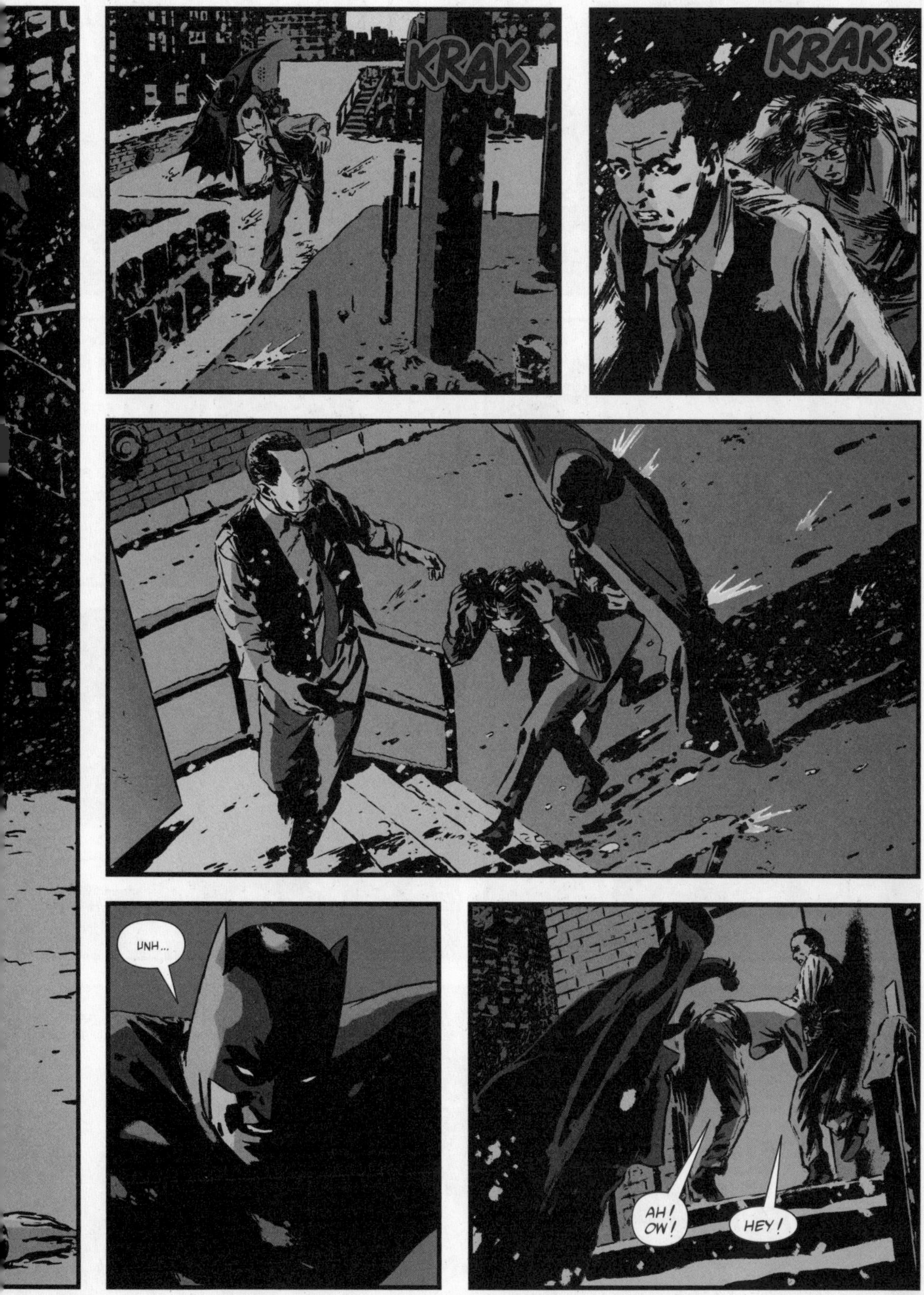
KRAK
KRAK
UNH...
AH! OW!
HEY!

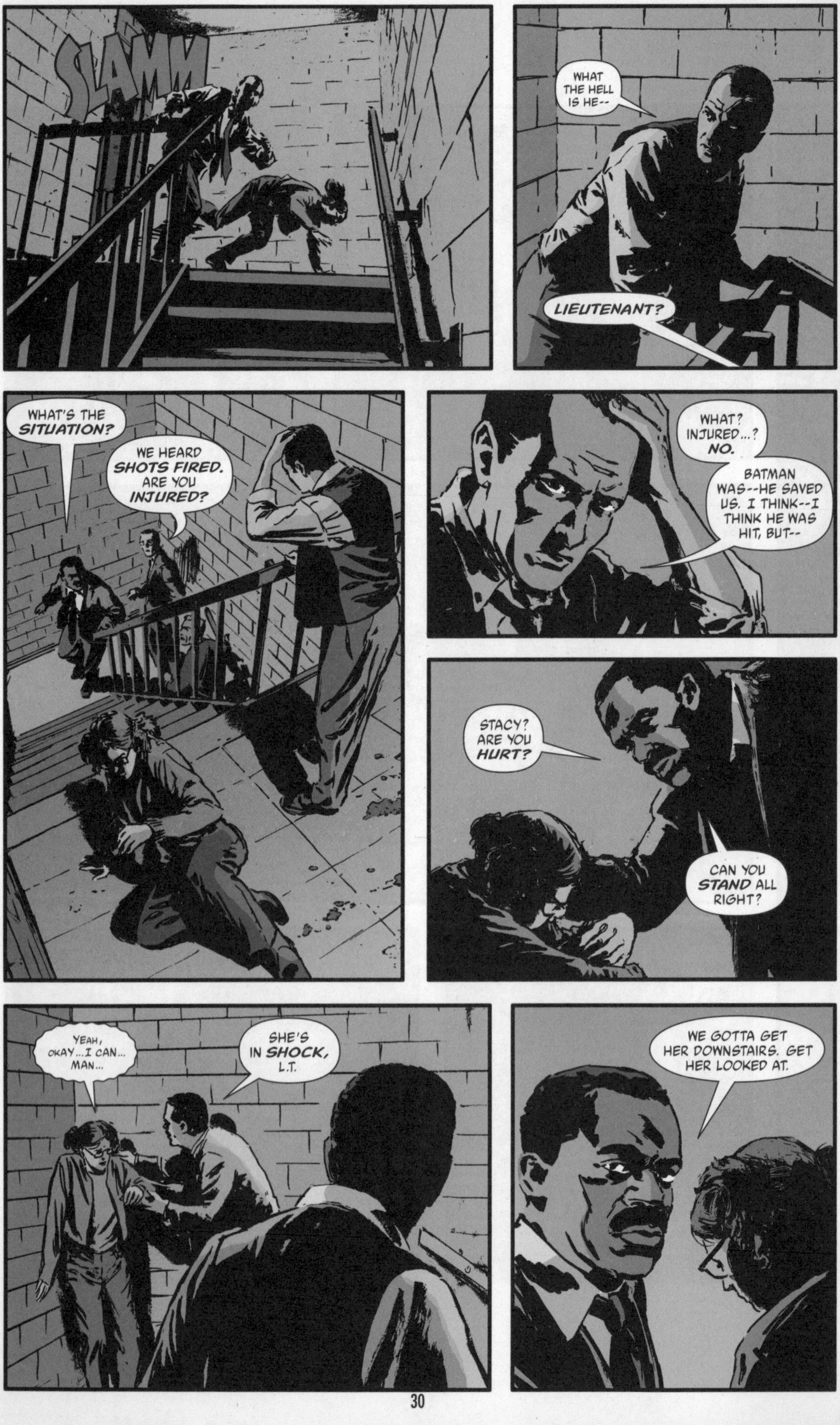
SLAMM
WHAT THE HELL IS HE--
LIEUTENANT?
WHAT'S THE SITUATION?
WE HEARD SHOTS FIRED. ARE YOU INJURED?
WHAT? INJURED...? NO.
BATMAN WAS--HE SAVED US. I THINK--I THINK HE WAS HIT, BUT--
STACY? ARE YOU HURT?
CAN YOU STAND ALL RIGHT?
YEAH, OKAY...I CAN... MAN...
SHE'S IN SHOCK, L.T.
WE GOTTA GET HER DOWNSTAIRS. GET HER LOOKED AT.

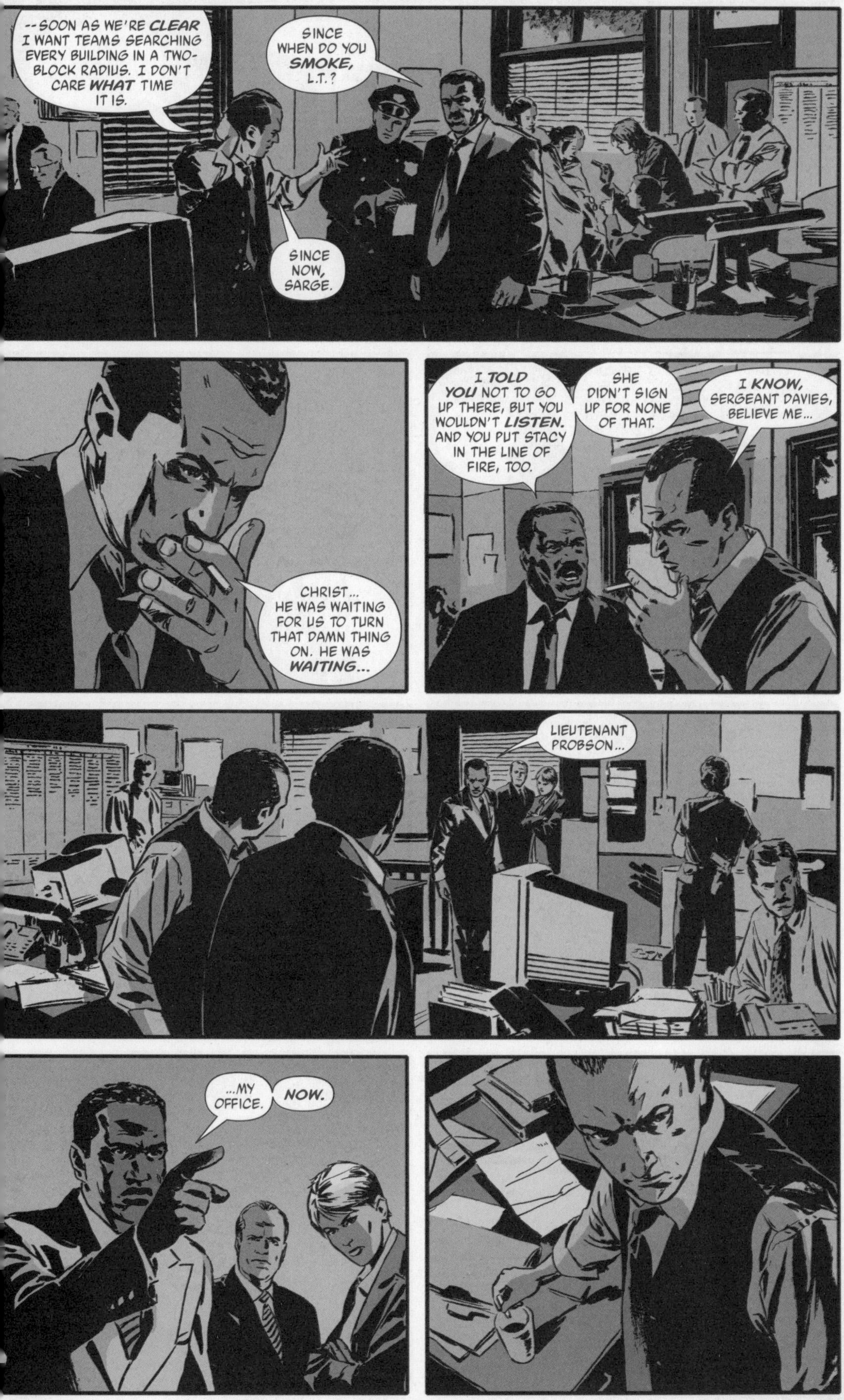
--SOON AS WE'RE CLEAR I WANT TEAMS SEARCHING EVERY BUILDING IN A TWO-BLOCK RADIUS. I DON'T CARE WHAT TIME IT IS.
SINCE WHEN DO YOU SMOKE, L.T.?
SINCE NOW, SARGE.
CHRIST... HE WAS WAITING FOR US TO TURN THAT DAMN THING ON. HE WAS WAITING...
I TOLD YOU NOT TO GO UP THERE, BUT YOU WOULDN'T LISTEN. AND YOU PUT STACY IN THE LINE OF FIRE, TOO.
SHE DIDN'T SIGN UP FOR NONE OF THAT.
I KNOW, SERGEANT DAVIES, BELIEVE ME...
LIEUTENANT PROBSON...
...MY OFFICE.
NOW.

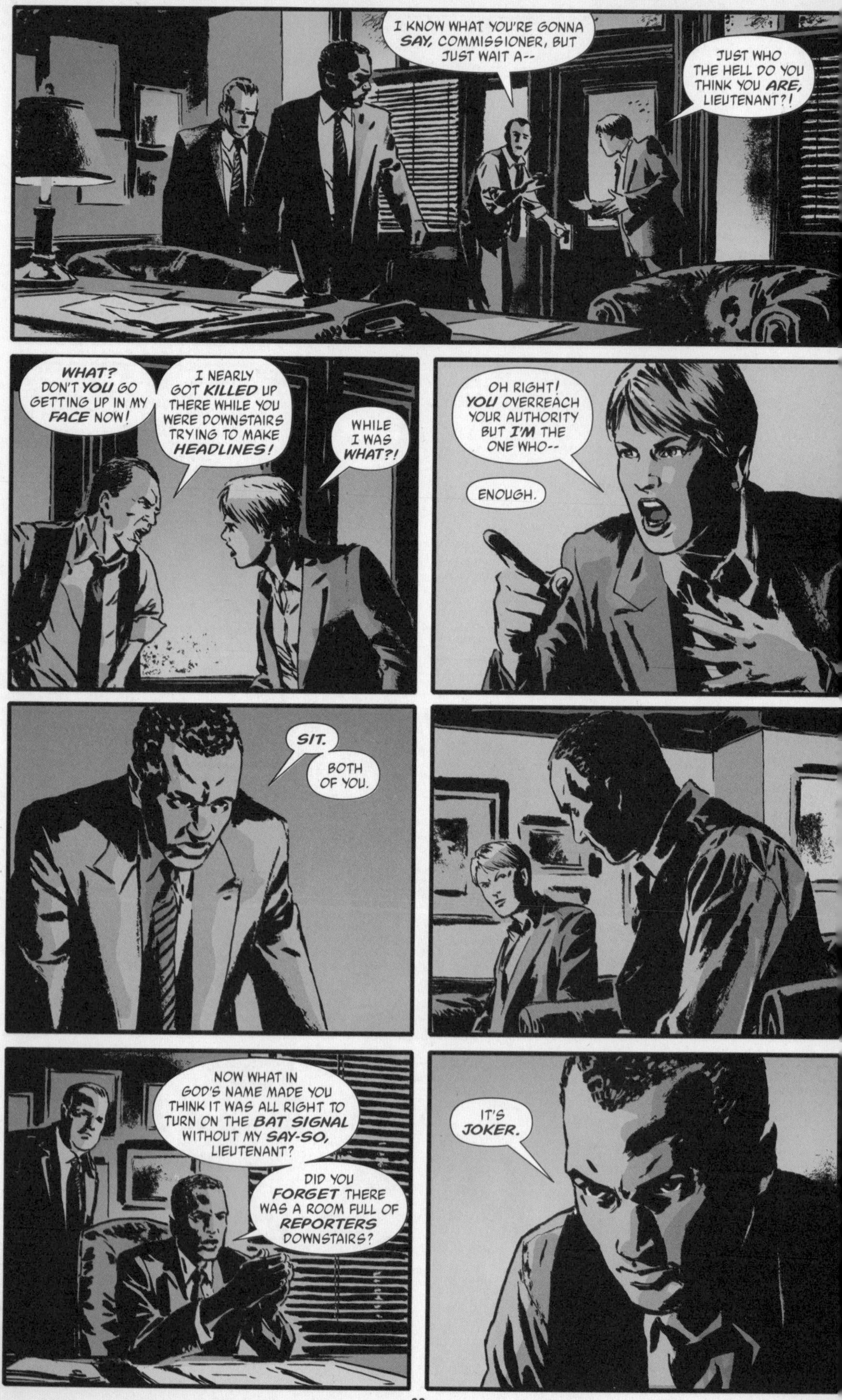
I KNOW WHAT YOU'RE GONNA SAY, COMMISSIONER, BUT JUST WAIT A--
JUST WHO THE HELL DO YOU THINK YOU ARE, LIEUTENANT?!
WHAT? DON'T YOU GO GETTING UP IN MY FACE NOW!
I NEARLY GOT KILLED UP THERE WHILE YOU WERE DOWNSTAIRS TRYING TO MAKE HEADLINES!
WHILE I WAS WHAT?!
OH RIGHT! YOU OVERREACH YOUR AUTHORITY BUT I'M THE ONE WHO--
ENOUGH.
SIT.
BOTH OF YOU.
NOW WHAT IN GOD'S NAME MADE YOU THINK IT WAS ALL RIGHT TO TURN ON THE BAT SIGNAL WITHOUT MY SAY-SO, LIEUTENANT?
DID YOU FORGET THERE WAS A ROOM FULL OF REPORTERS DOWNSTAIRS?
IT'S JOKER.

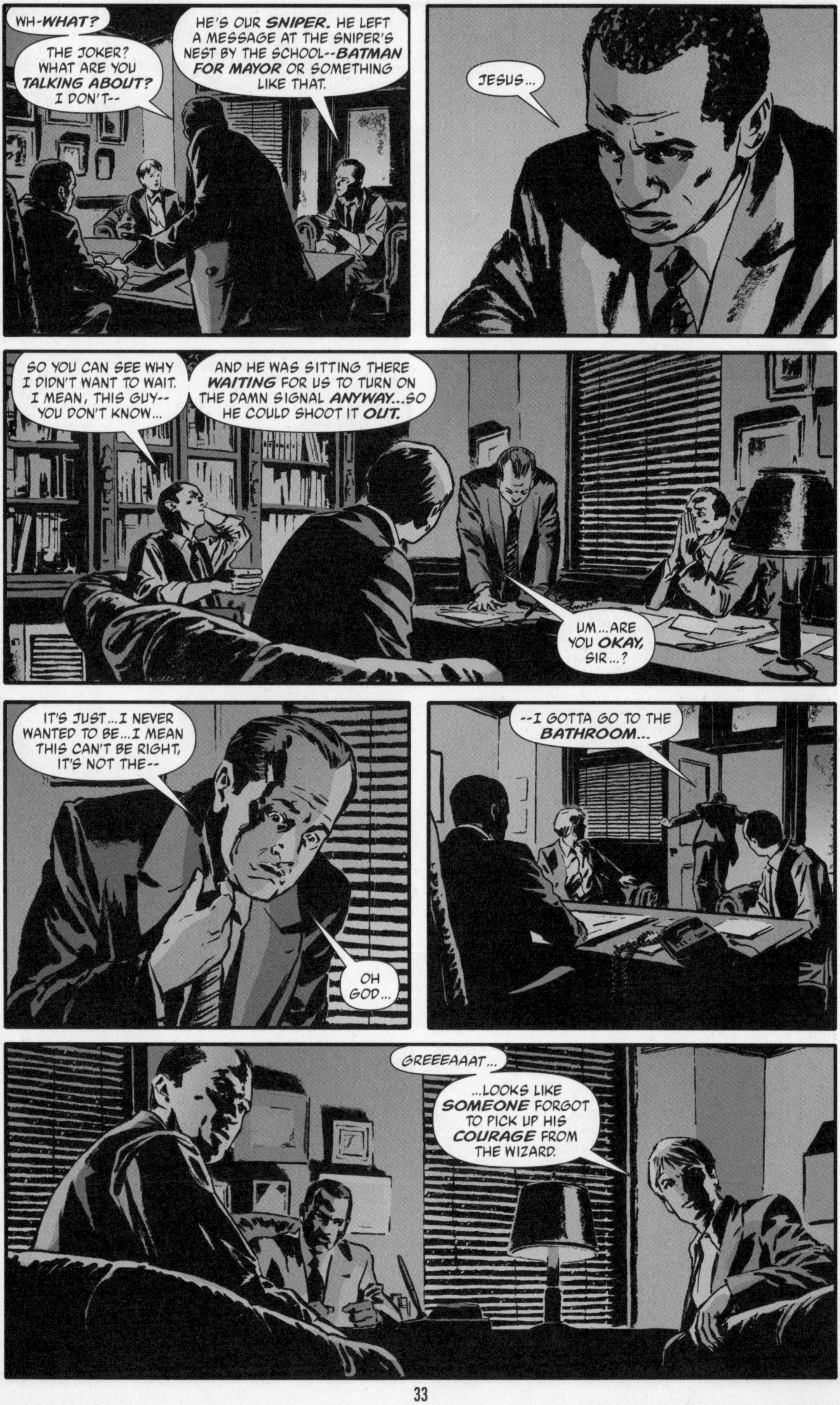

WH-WHAT?
THE JOKER? WHAT ARE YOU TALKING ABOUT? I DON'T--
HE'S OUR SNIPER. HE LEFT A MESSAGE AT THE SNIPER'S NEST BY THE SCHOOL--BATMAN FOR MAYOR OR SOMETHING LIKE THAT.
JESUS...
SO YOU CAN SEE WHY I DIDN'T WANT TO WAIT. I MEAN, THIS GUY-- YOU DON'T KNOW...
AND HE WAS SITTING THERE WAITING FOR US TO TURN ON THE DAMN SIGNAL ANYWAY...SO HE COULD SHOOT IT OUT.
UM...ARE YOU OKAY, SIR...?
IT'S JUST...I NEVER WANTED TO BE...I MEAN THIS CAN'T BE RIGHT, IT'S NOT THE--
OH GOD...
--I GOTTA GO TO THE BATHROOM...
GREEEAAAT...
...LOOKS LIKE SOMEONE FORGOT TO PICK UP HIS COURAGE FROM THE WIZARD.

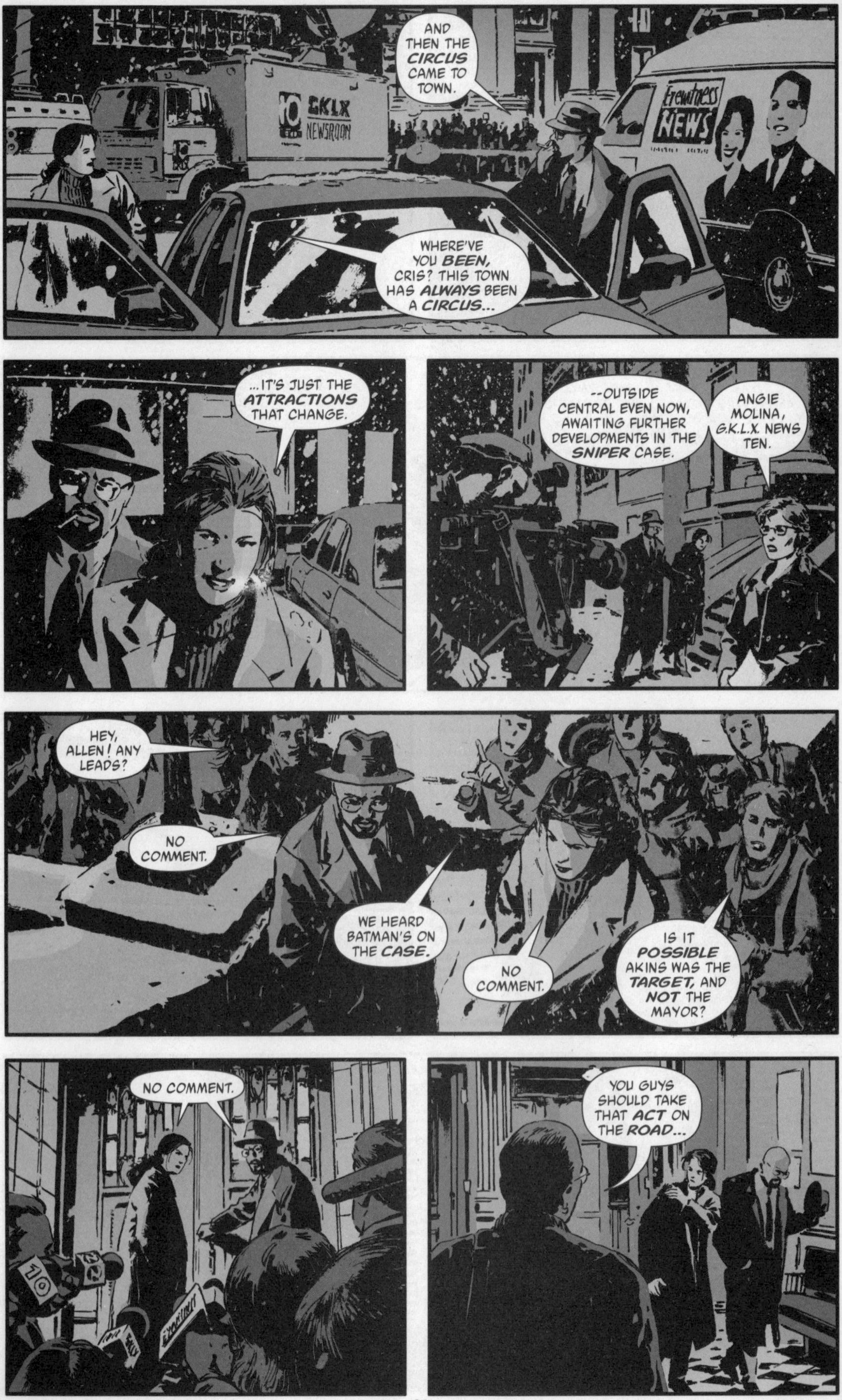
AND THEN THE CIRCUS CAME TO TOWN.
GKLX
NEWSROOM
Eyewitness NEWS
WHERE'VE YOU BEEN, CRIS? THIS TOWN HAS ALWAYS BEEN A CIRCUS...
...IT'S JUST THE ATTRACTIONS THAT CHANGE.
--OUTSIDE CENTRAL EVEN NOW, AWAITING FURTHER DEVELOPMENTS IN THE SNIPER CASE.
ANGIE MOLINA, G.K.L.X. NEWS TEN.
HEY, ALLEN! ANY LEADS?
NO COMMENT.
WE HEARD BATMAN'S ON THE CASE.
NO COMMENT.
IS IT POSSIBLE AKINS WAS THE TARGET, AND NOT THE MAYOR?
NO COMMENT.
YOU GUYS SHOULD TAKE THAT ACT ON THE ROAD...

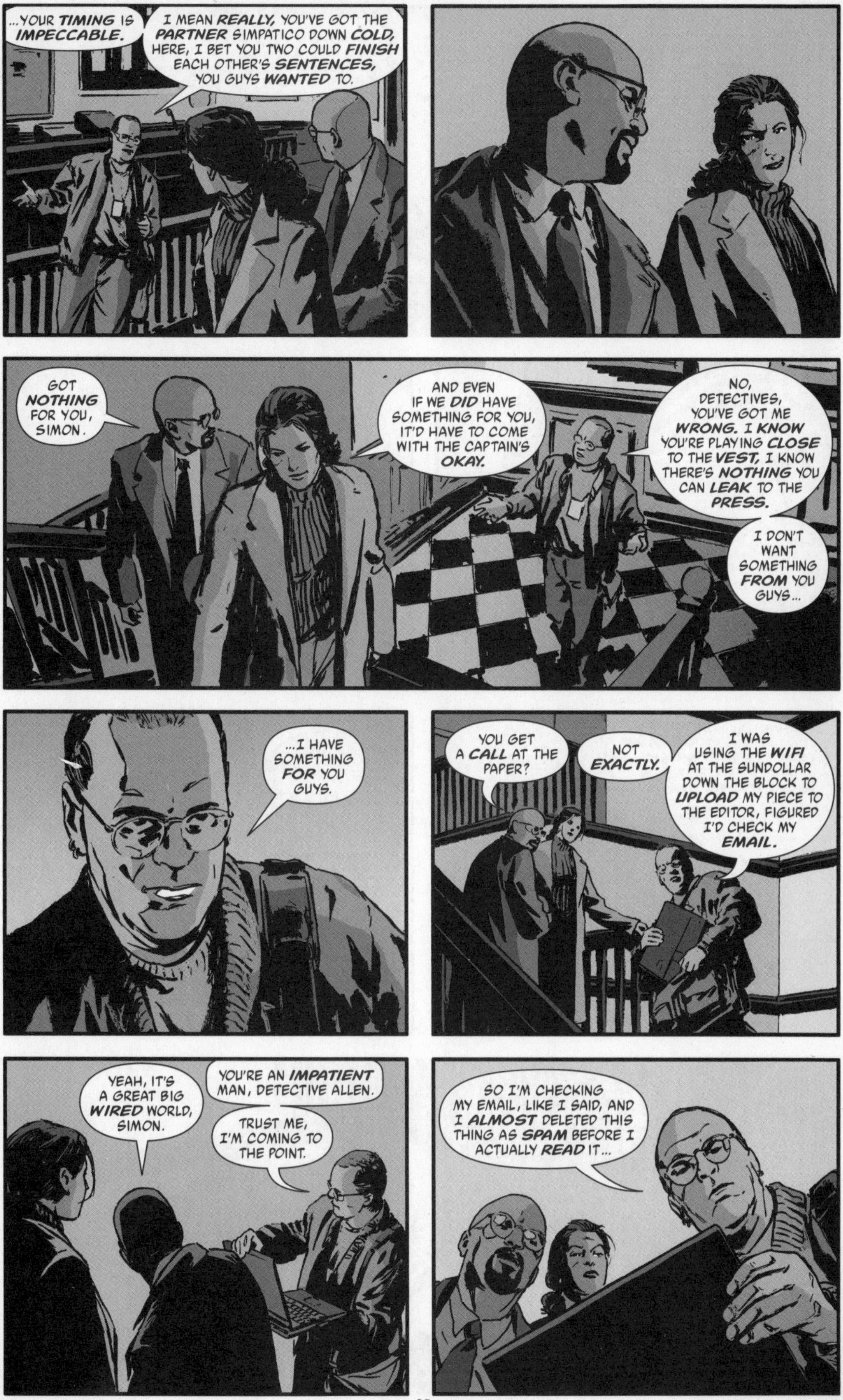
...YOUR TIMING IS IMPECCABLE.
I MEAN REALLY, YOU'VE GOT THE PARTNER SIMPATICO DOWN COLD, HERE, I BET YOU TWO COULD FINISH EACH OTHER'S SENTENCES, YOU GUYS WANTED TO.
GOT NOTHING FOR YOU, SIMON.
AND EVEN IF WE DID HAVE SOMETHING FOR YOU, IT'D HAVE TO COME WITH THE CAPTAIN'S OKAY.
NO, DETECTIVES, YOU'VE GOT ME WRONG. I KNOW YOU'RE PLAYING CLOSE TO THE VEST, I KNOW THERE'S NOTHING YOU CAN LEAK TO THE PRESS.
I DON'T WANT SOMETHING FROM YOU GUYS...
...I HAVE SOMETHING FOR YOU GUYS.
YOU GET A CALL AT THE PAPER?
NOT EXACTLY.
I WAS USING THE WIFI AT THE SUNDOLLAR DOWN THE BLOCK TO UPLOAD MY PIECE TO THE EDITOR, FIGURED I'D CHECK MY EMAIL.
YEAH, IT'S A GREAT BIG WIRED WORLD, SIMON.
YOU'RE AN IMPATIENT MAN, DETECTIVE ALLEN.
TRUST ME, I'M COMING TO THE POINT.
SO I'M CHECKING MY EMAIL, LIKE I SAID, AND I ALMOST DELETED THIS THING AS SPAM BEFORE I ACTUALLY READ IT...

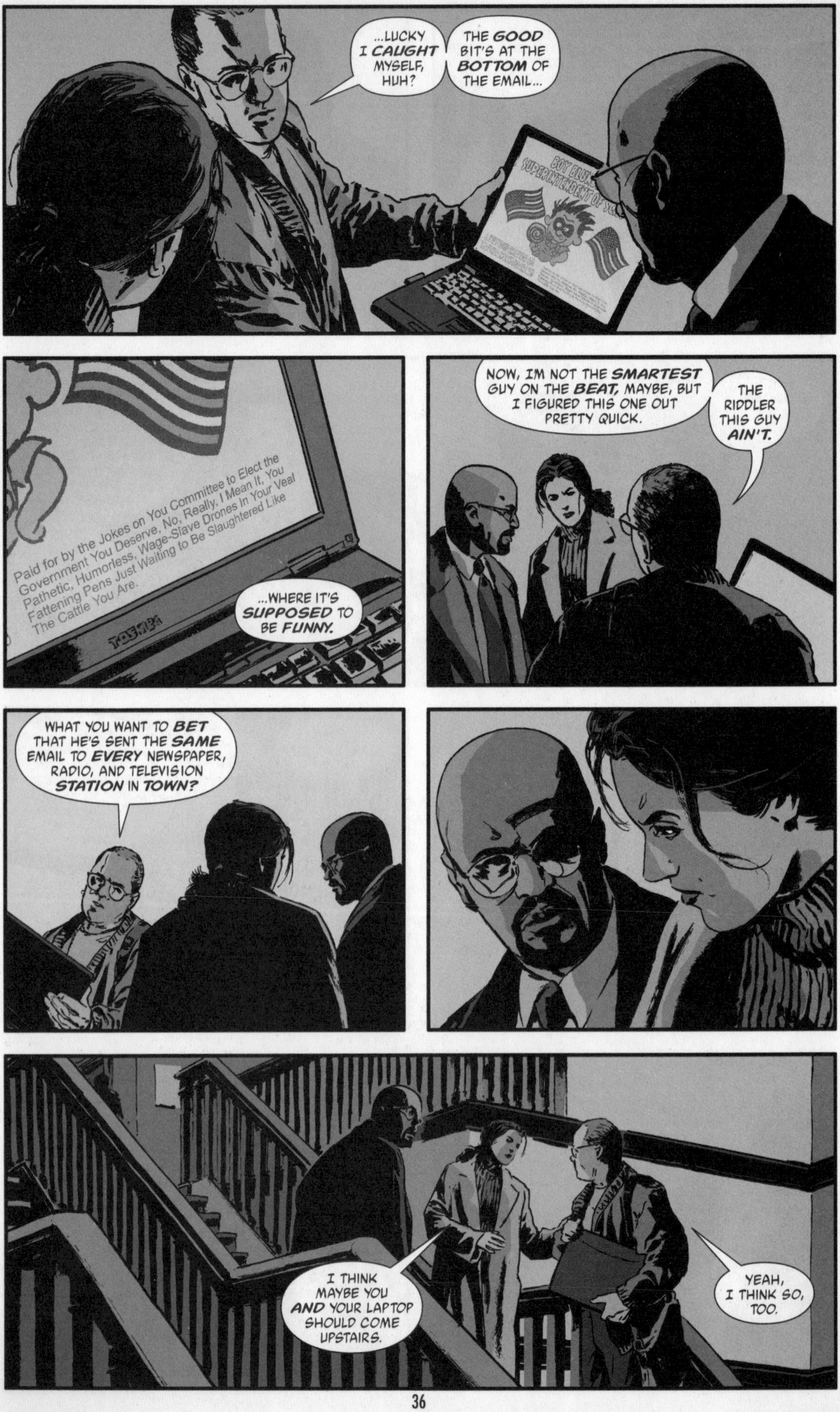

...LUCKY I CAUGHT MYSELF, HUH?
THE GOOD BIT'S AT THE BOTTOM OF THE EMAIL...
Paid for by the Jokes on You Committee to Elect the Government You Deserve, No, Really, I Mean It, You Pathetic, Humorless, Wage-Slave Drones In Your Veal Fattening Pens Just Waiting to Be Slaughtered Like The Cattle You Are.
...WHERE IT'S SUPPOSED TO BE FUNNY.
NOW, I'M NOT THE SMARTEST GUY ON THE BEAT, MAYBE, BUT I FIGURED THIS ONE OUT PRETTY QUICK.
THE RIDDLER THIS GUY AIN'T.
WHAT YOU WANT TO BET THAT HE'S SENT THE SAME EMAIL TO EVERY NEWSPAPER, RADIO, AND TELEVISION STATION IN TOWN?
I THINK MAYBE YOU AND YOUR LAPTOP SHOULD COME UPSTAIRS.
YEAH, I THINK SO, TOO.

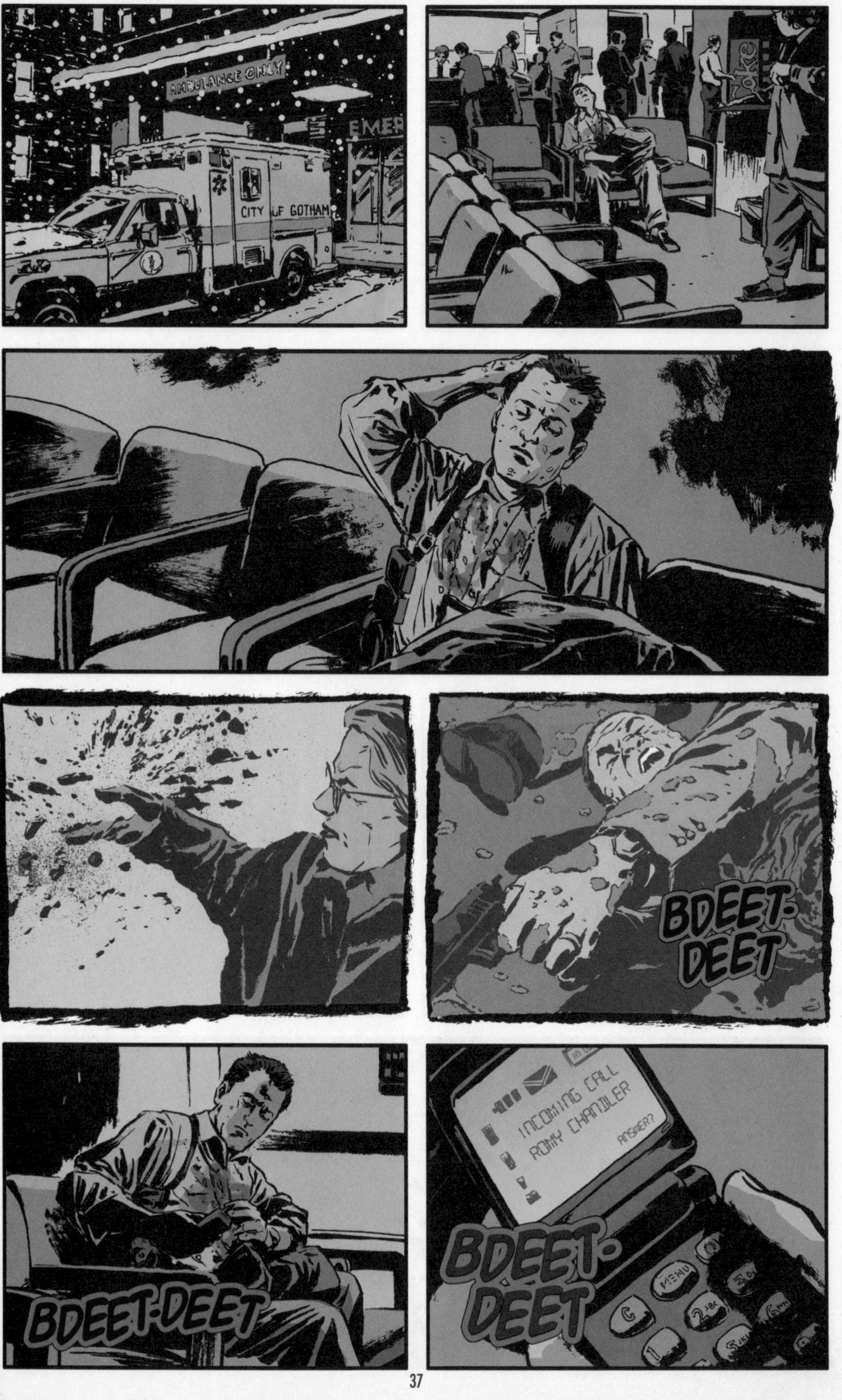
AMBULANCE ONLY
EMER
CITY OF GOTHAM
BDEET-DEET
BDEET-DEET
INCOMING CALL
ROMY CHANDLER
ANSWER?
BDEET-DEET

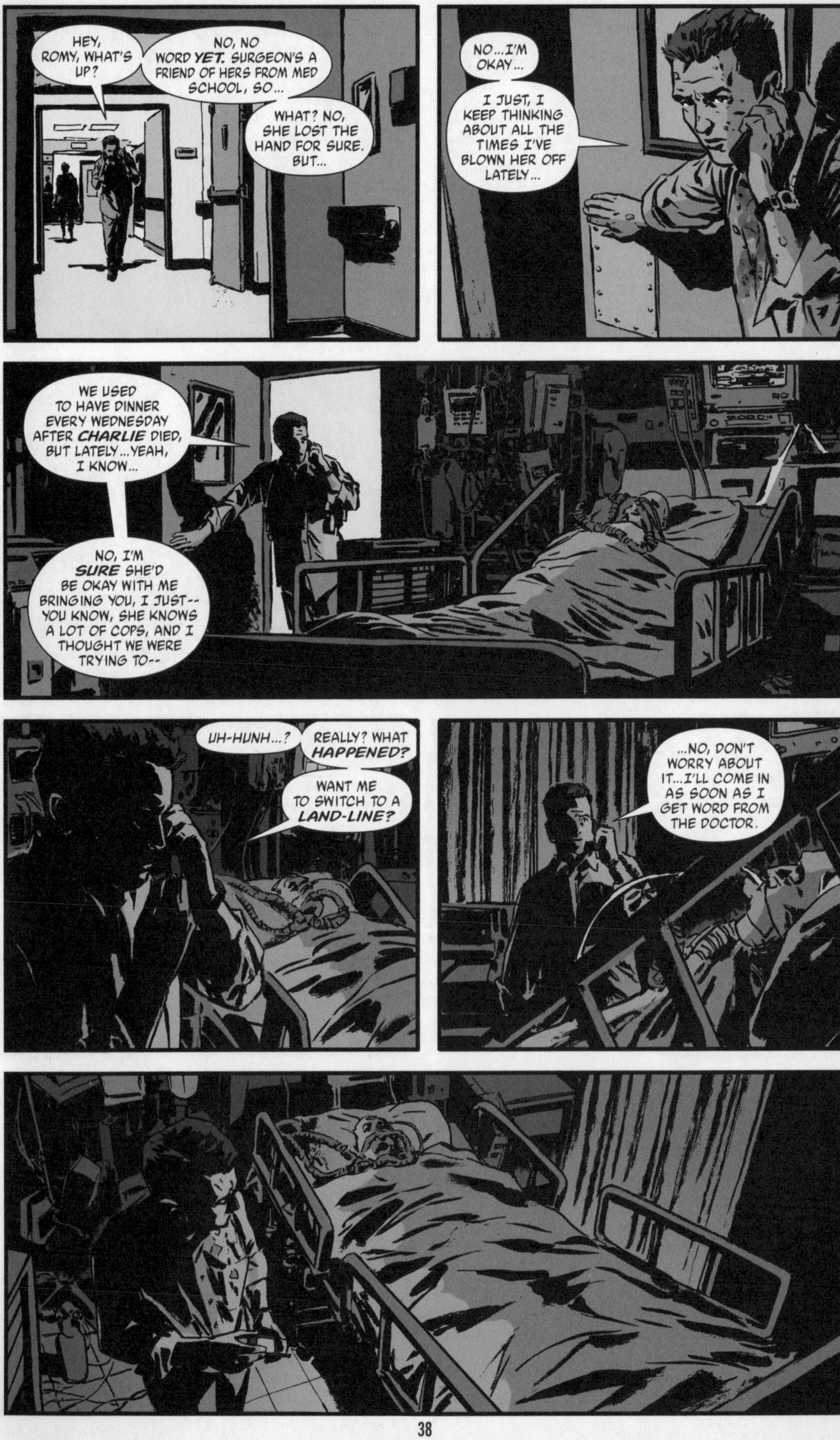
HEY, ROMY, WHAT'S UP?
NO, NO WORD YET. SURGEON'S A FRIEND OF HERS FROM MED SCHOOL, SO...
WHAT? NO, SHE LOST THE HAND FOR SURE. BUT...
NO...I'M OKAY...
I JUST, I KEEP THINKING ABOUT ALL THE TIMES I'VE BLOWN HER OFF LATELY...
WE USED TO HAVE DINNER EVERY WEDNESDAY AFTER CHARLIE DIED, BUT LATELY...YEAH, I KNOW...
NO, I'M SURE SHE'D BE OKAY WITH ME BRINGING YOU, I JUST-- YOU KNOW, SHE KNOWS A LOT OF COPS, AND I THOUGHT WE WERE TRYING TO--
UH-HUNH...?
REALLY? WHAT HAPPENED?
WANT ME TO SWITCH TO A LAND-LINE?
...NO, DON'T WORRY ABOUT IT...I'LL COME IN AS SOON AS I GET WORD FROM THE DOCTOR.

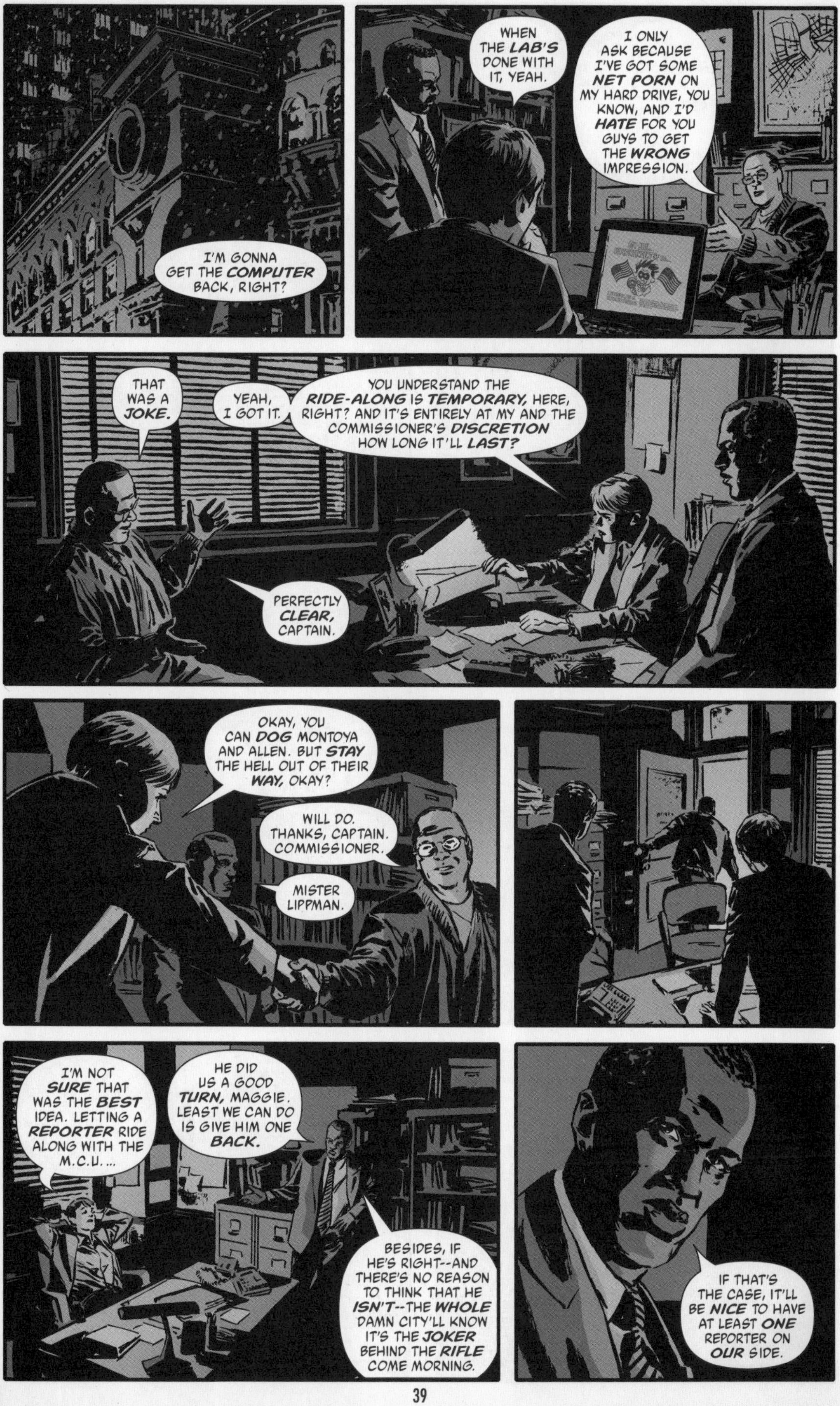
I'M GONNA GET THE COMPUTER BACK, RIGHT?
WHEN THE LAB'S DONE WITH IT, YEAH.
I ONLY ASK BECAUSE I'VE GOT SOME NET PORN ON MY HARD DRIVE, YOU KNOW, AND I'D HATE FOR YOU GUYS TO GET THE WRONG IMPRESSION.
THAT WAS A JOKE.
YEAH, I GOT IT.
YOU UNDERSTAND THE RIDE-ALONG IS TEMPORARY, HERE, RIGHT? AND IT'S ENTIRELY AT MY AND THE COMMISSIONER'S DISCRETION HOW LONG IT'LL LAST?
PERFECTLY CLEAR, CAPTAIN.
OKAY, YOU CAN DOG MONTOYA AND ALLEN. BUT STAY THE HELL OUT OF THEIR WAY, OKAY?
WILL DO. THANKS, CAPTAIN. COMMISSIONER.
MISTER LIPPMAN.
I'M NOT SURE THAT WAS THE BEST IDEA. LETTING A REPORTER RIDE ALONG WITH THE M.C.U. ...
HE DID US A GOOD TURN, MAGGIE. LEAST WE CAN DO IS GIVE HIM ONE BACK.
BESIDES, IF HE'S RIGHT--AND THERE'S NO REASON TO THINK THAT HE ISN'T--THE WHOLE DAMN CITY'LL KNOW IT'S THE JOKER BEHIND THE RIFLE COME MORNING.
IF THAT'S THE CASE, IT'LL BE NICE TO HAVE AT LEAST ONE REPORTER ON OUR SIDE.

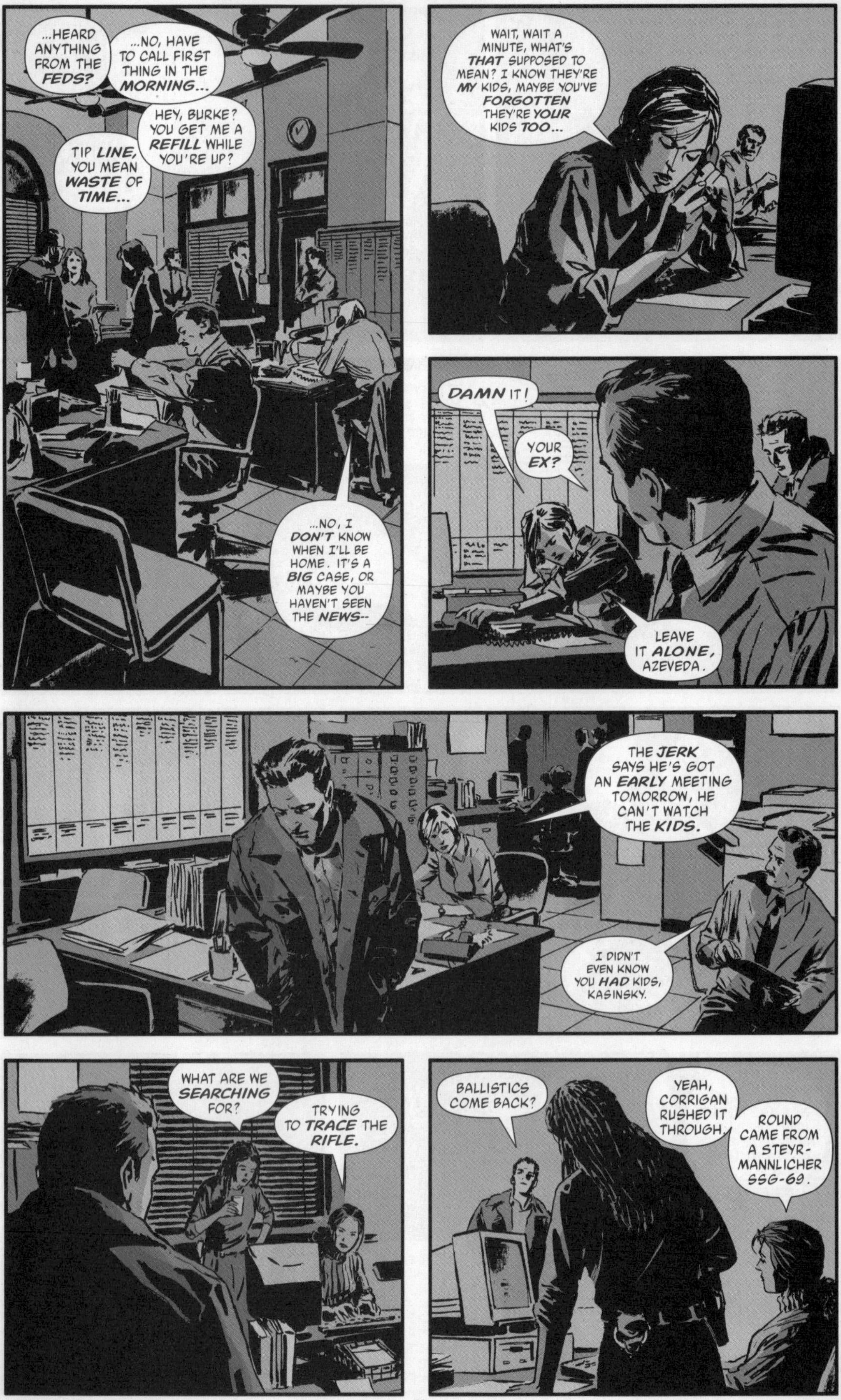
...HEARD ANYTHING FROM THE FEDS?
...NO, HAVE TO CALL FIRST THING IN THE MORNING...
HEY, BURKE? YOU GET ME A REFILL WHILE YOU'RE UP?
TIP LINE, YOU MEAN WASTE OF TIME...
...NO, I DON'T KNOW WHEN I'LL BE HOME. IT'S A BIG CASE, OR MAYBE YOU HAVEN'T SEEN THE NEWS--
WAIT, WAIT A MINUTE, WHAT'S THAT SUPPOSED TO MEAN? I KNOW THEY'RE MY KIDS, MAYBE YOU'VE FORGOTTEN THEY'RE YOUR KIDS TOO...
DAMN IT!
YOUR EX?
LEAVE IT ALONE, AZEVEDA.
THE JERK SAYS HE'S GOT AN EARLY MEETING TOMORROW, HE CAN'T WATCH THE KIDS.
I DIDN'T EVEN KNOW YOU HAD KIDS, KASINSKY.
WHAT ARE WE SEARCHING FOR?
TRYING TO TRACE THE RIFLE.
BALLISTICS COME BACK?
YEAH, CORRIGAN RUSHED IT THROUGH.
ROUND CAME FROM A STEYR-MANNLICHER SSG-69.

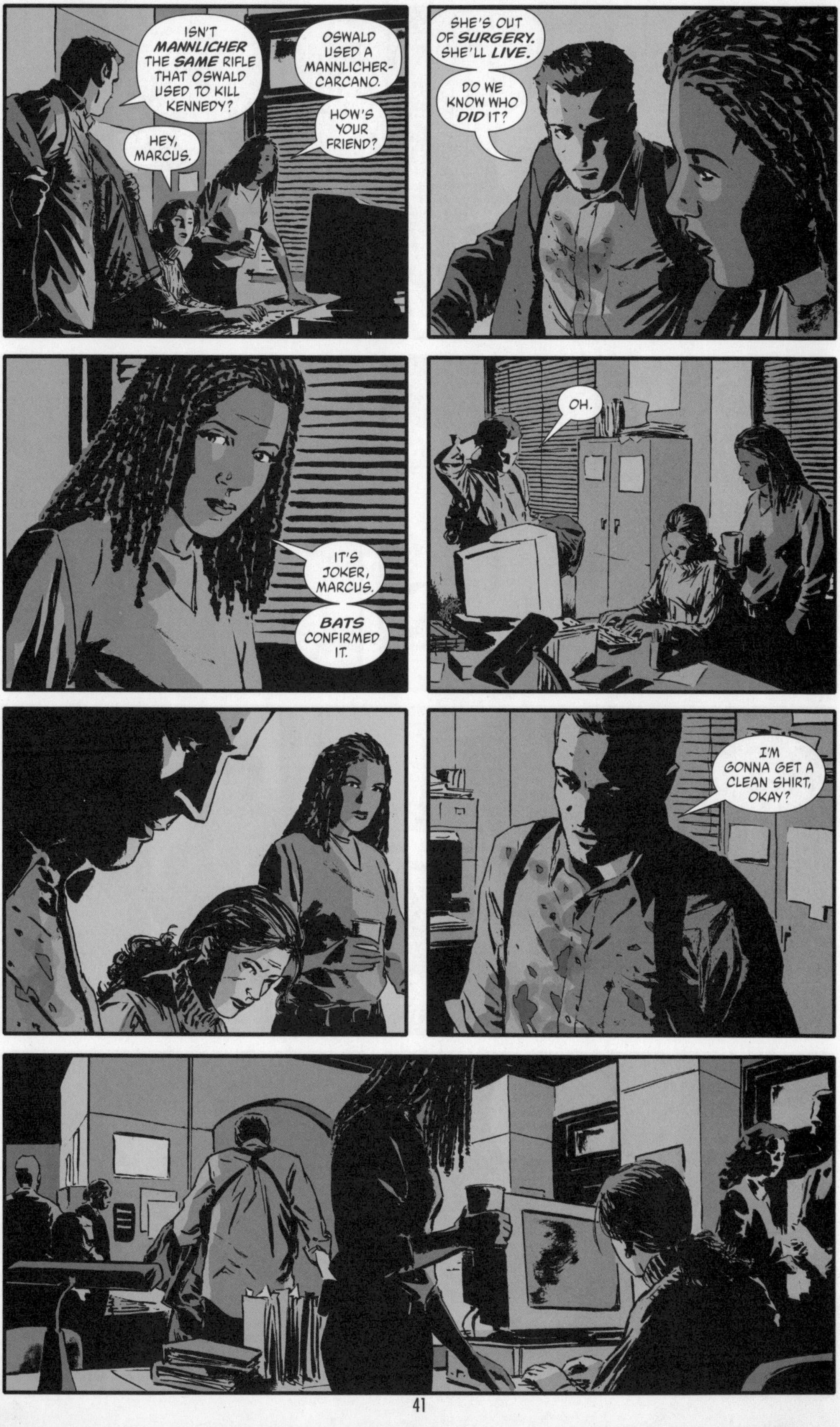
ISN'T MANNLICHER THE SAME RIFLE THAT OSWALD USED TO KILL KENNEDY?
OSWALD USED A MANNLICHER-CARCANO.
HEY, MARCUS.
HOW'S YOUR FRIEND?
SHE'S OUT OF SURGERY. SHE'LL LIVE.
DO WE KNOW WHO DID IT?
IT'S JOKER, MARCUS.
BATS CONFIRMED IT.
OH.
I'M GONNA GET A CLEAN SHIRT, OKAY?

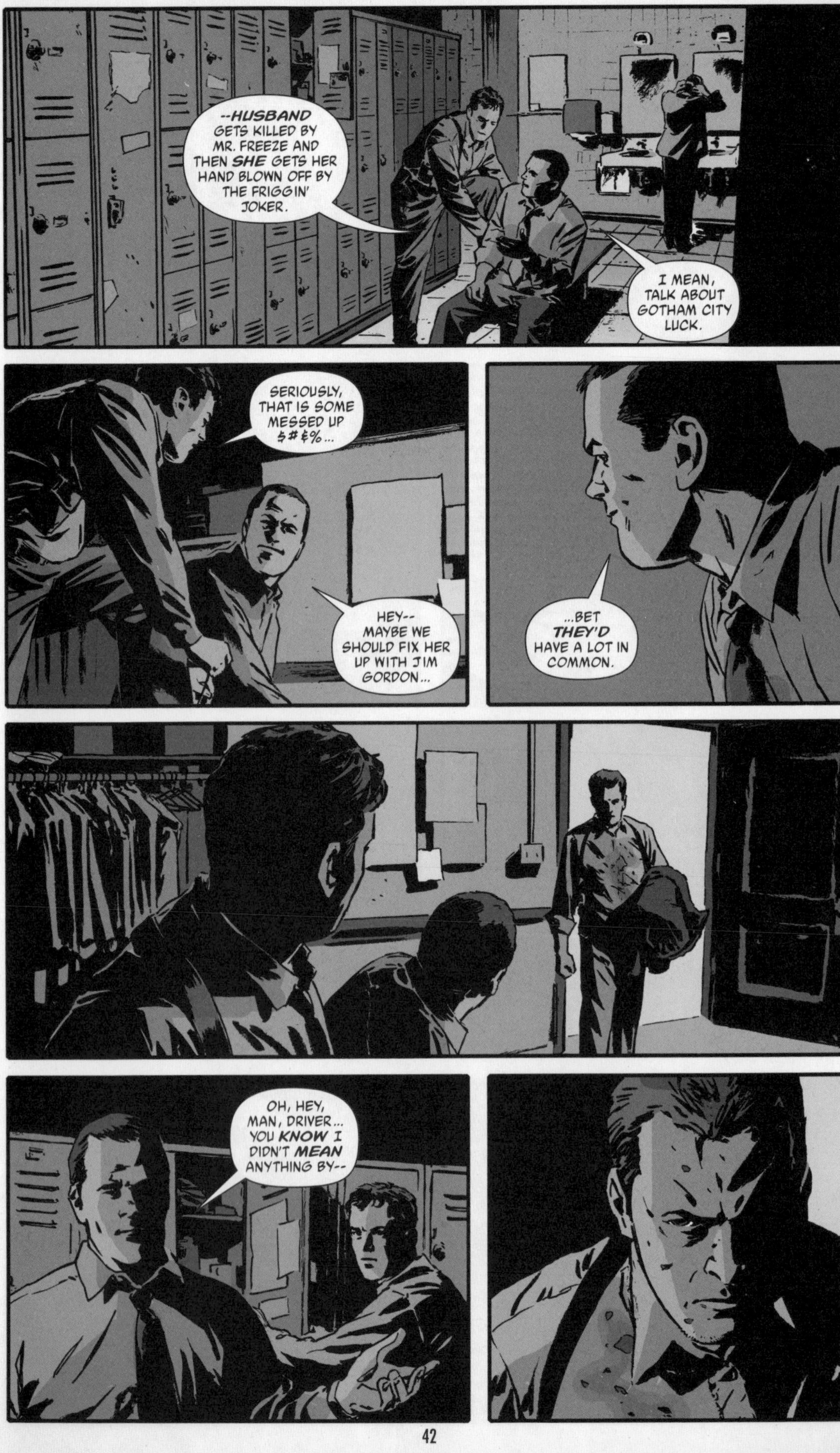
--HUSBAND GETS KILLED BY MR. FREEZE AND THEN SHE GETS HER HAND BLOWN OFF BY THE FRIGGIN' JOKER.
I MEAN, TALK ABOUT GOTHAM CITY LUCK.
SERIOUSLY, THAT IS SOME MESSED UP $#&%...
HEY-- MAYBE WE SHOULD FIX HER UP WITH JIM GORDON...
...BET THEY'D HAVE A LOT IN COMMON.
OH, HEY, MAN, DRIVER... YOU KNOW I DIDN'T MEAN ANYTHING BY--

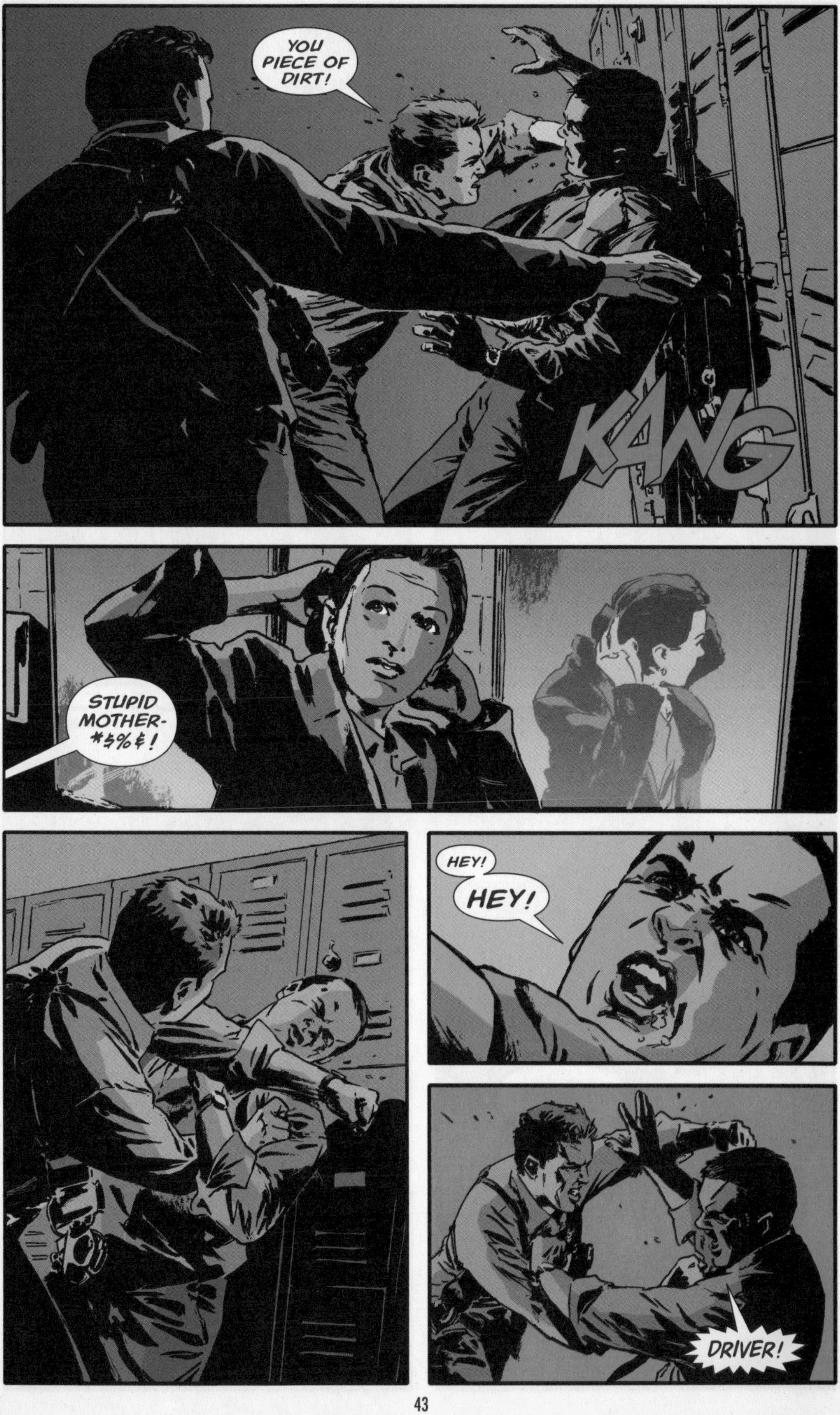
YOU PIECE OF DIRT!
KANG
STUPID MOTHER-*$%&!
HEY!
HEY!
DRIVER!

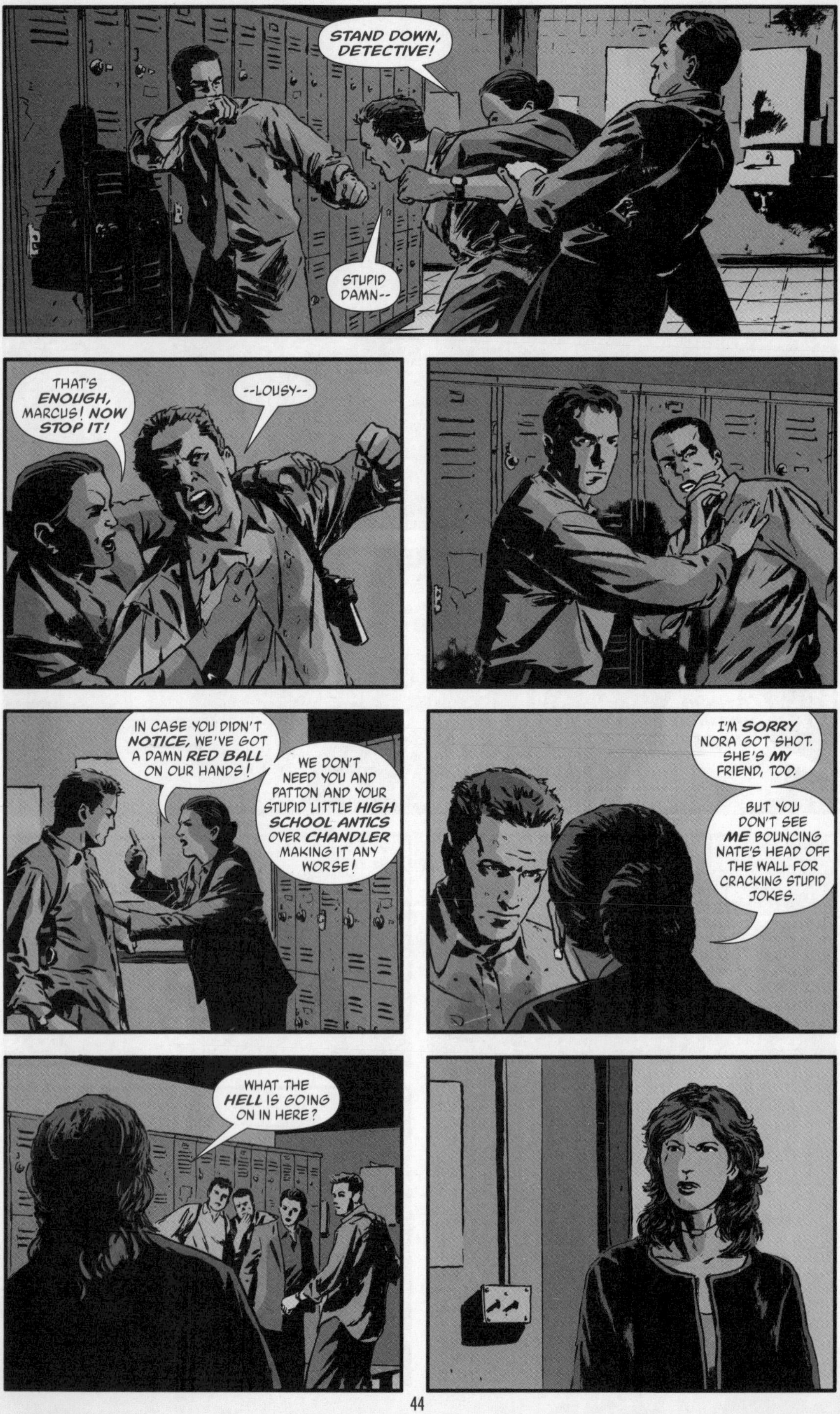
STAND DOWN, DETECTIVE!
STUPID DAMN--
THAT'S ENOUGH, MARCUS! NOW STOP IT!
--LOUSY--
IN CASE YOU DIDN'T NOTICE, WE'VE GOT A DAMN RED BALL ON OUR HANDS!
WE DON'T NEED YOU AND PATTON AND YOUR STUPID LITTLE HIGH SCHOOL ANTICS OVER CHANDLER MAKING IT ANY WORSE!
I'M SORRY NORA GOT SHOT. SHE'S MY FRIEND, TOO.
BUT YOU DON'T SEE ME BOUNCING NATE'S HEAD OFF THE WALL FOR CRACKING STUPID JOKES.
WHAT THE HELL IS GOING ON IN HERE?

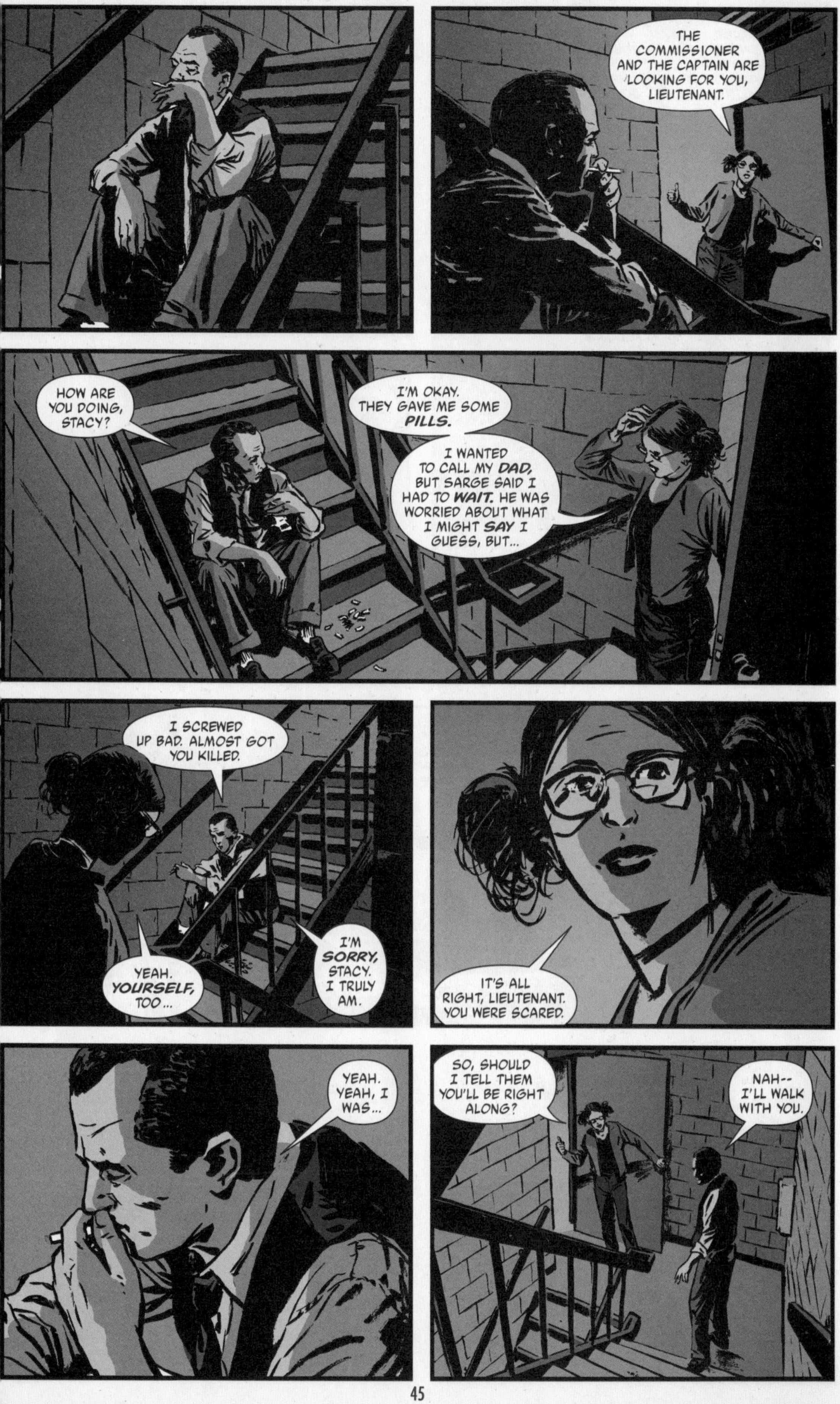
THE COMMISSIONER AND THE CAPTAIN ARE LOOKING FOR YOU, LIEUTENANT.
HOW ARE YOU DOING, STACY?
I'M OKAY. THEY GAVE ME SOME **PILLS.**
I WANTED TO CALL MY **DAD,** BUT SARGE SAID I HAD TO **WAIT.** HE WAS WORRIED ABOUT WHAT I MIGHT **SAY** I GUESS, BUT...
I SCREWED UP BAD. ALMOST GOT YOU KILLED.
YEAH. **YOURSELF,** TOO...
I'M **SORRY,** STACY. I TRULY AM.
IT'S ALL RIGHT, LIEUTENANT. YOU WERE SCARED.
YEAH. YEAH, I WAS...
SO, SHOULD I TELL THEM YOU'LL BE RIGHT ALONG?
NAH-- I'LL WALK WITH YOU.

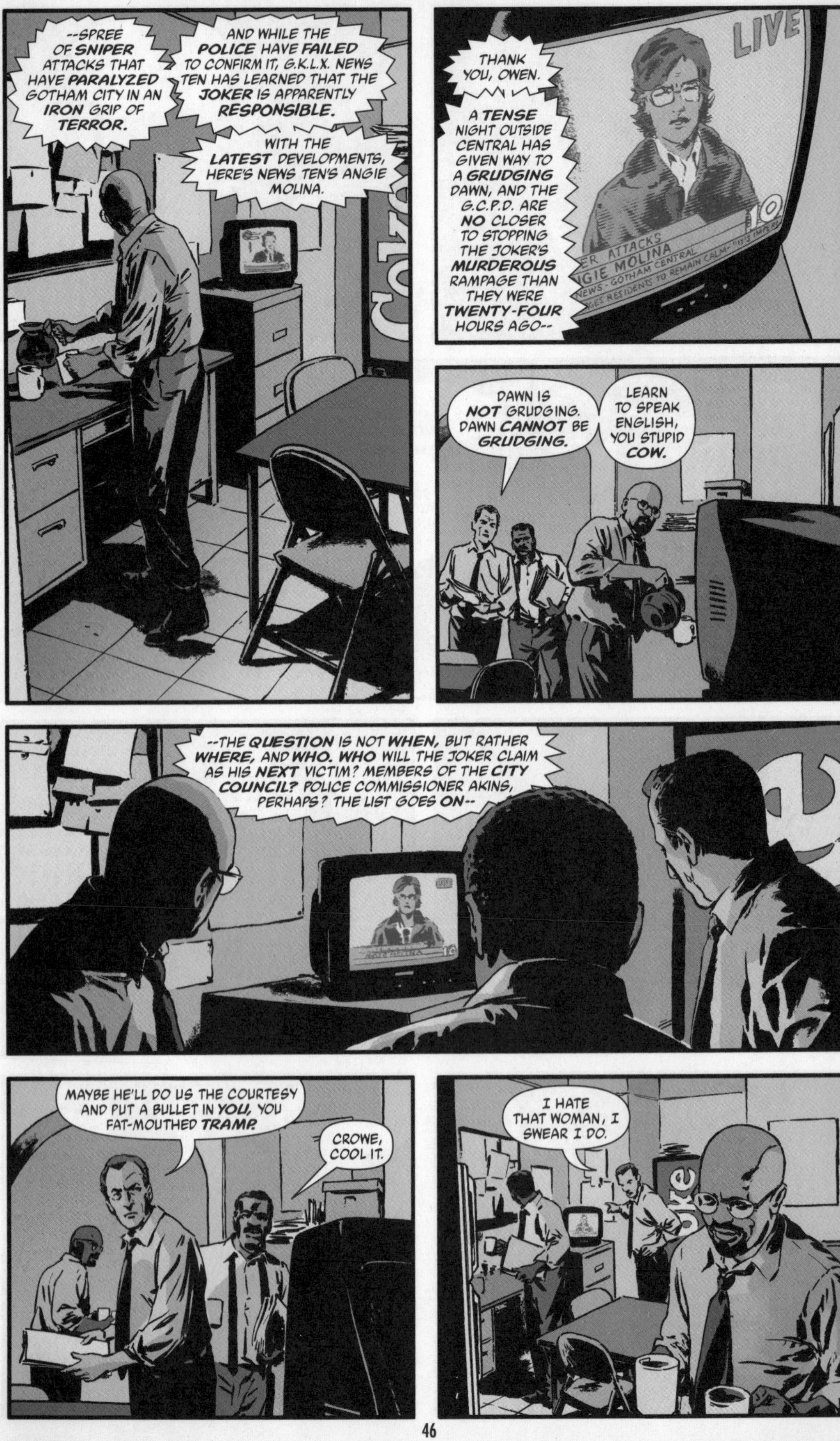
--SPREE OF SNIPER ATTACKS THAT HAVE PARALYZED GOTHAM CITY IN AN IRON GRIP OF TERROR.
AND WHILE THE POLICE HAVE FAILED TO CONFIRM IT, G.K.L.X. NEWS TEN HAS LEARNED THAT THE JOKER IS APPARENTLY RESPONSIBLE.
WITH THE LATEST DEVELOPMENTS, HERE'S NEWS TEN'S ANGIE MOLINA.
LIVE
THANK YOU, OWEN.
A TENSE NIGHT OUTSIDE CENTRAL HAS GIVEN WAY TO A GRUDGING DAWN, AND THE G.C.P.D. ARE NO CLOSER TO STOPPING THE JOKER'S MURDEROUS RAMPAGE THAN THEY WERE TWENTY-FOUR HOURS AGO--
DAWN IS NOT GRUDGING. DAWN CANNOT BE GRUDGING.
LEARN TO SPEAK ENGLISH, YOU STUPID COW.
--THE QUESTION IS NOT WHEN, BUT RATHER WHERE, AND WHO. WHO WILL THE JOKER CLAIM AS HIS NEXT VICTIM? MEMBERS OF THE CITY COUNCIL? POLICE COMMISSIONER AKINS, PERHAPS? THE LIST GOES ON--
MAYBE HE'LL DO US THE COURTESY AND PUT A BULLET IN YOU, YOU FAT-MOUTHED TRAMP.
CROWE, COOL IT.
I HATE THAT WOMAN, I SWEAR I DO.

...SNIPER RIFLE...

HEY, UH, CRIS?

YES?

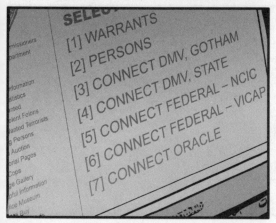

YOU EVER HEAR OF A *DATABASE* CALLED *ORACLE?*

GCPD

SELECT DATA SOURCE

[1] WARRANTS
[2] PERSONS
[3] CONNECT DMV, GOTHAM
[4] CONNECT DMV, STATE
[5] CONNECT FEDERAL – NCIC
[6] CONNECT FEDERAL – VICAP

SELECT

[1] WARRANTS
[2] PERSONS
[3] CONNECT DMV, GOTHAM
[4] CONNECT DMV, STATE
[5] CONNECT FEDERAL – NCIC
[6] CONNECT FEDERAL – VICAP
[7] CONNECT ORACLE

ISN'T THAT *INTERPOL?*

NO, THAT'S...

...I DON'T BELIEVE IT.

I'VE GOT THE *GUN.*

LINCOLN ARMS, 8820 NORTH CURZON, IN BURNLEY. STORE OWNED BY WILLIAM D. BROOKS.

I'M GONNA TELL THE CAPTAIN.

WE'RE GONNA WANT *BACKUP.*

YOU'RE TELLING *ME.*

GCPD
ORACLE SEARCH RESULTS:
STEYR-MANNLICHER SSG-69
SERIAL # SM S 09004344-2

AUTHORIZED DEALER:
BROOKS, WILLIAM D.
LINCOLN ARMS
8820 N. CURZON, BURNLEY.

WHERE'S JOKE-O?

RENEE!!

RENEE, GET *OVER* HERE, *NOW!*

WHAT--

IT'S *HIM,* HE'S GOT SOME KIND OF--

WHAT THE *HELL'S* HAPPENING WITH THE *COMPUTERS?*

UH, *GUYS?* I JUST GOT THIS *POP-UP* WINDOW--

IT'S *HIM,* HE'S *DOING* IT.

WAIT A *MINUTE,* HE'S IN OUR *SYSTEM?*

OH MY GOD.

IT'S SNIPER TIME!

WHO'S NEXT TO WEAR THE RED HALO?

03:12:06

SNIPER TIME!

IT'S A WEB-CAM, A *LIVE* IMAGE...

NEXT TO WEAR R HALO?

03:12:02

03:12:01

...HE'S *COUNTING* DOWN TO THE *NEXT* SHOT...

:11.59

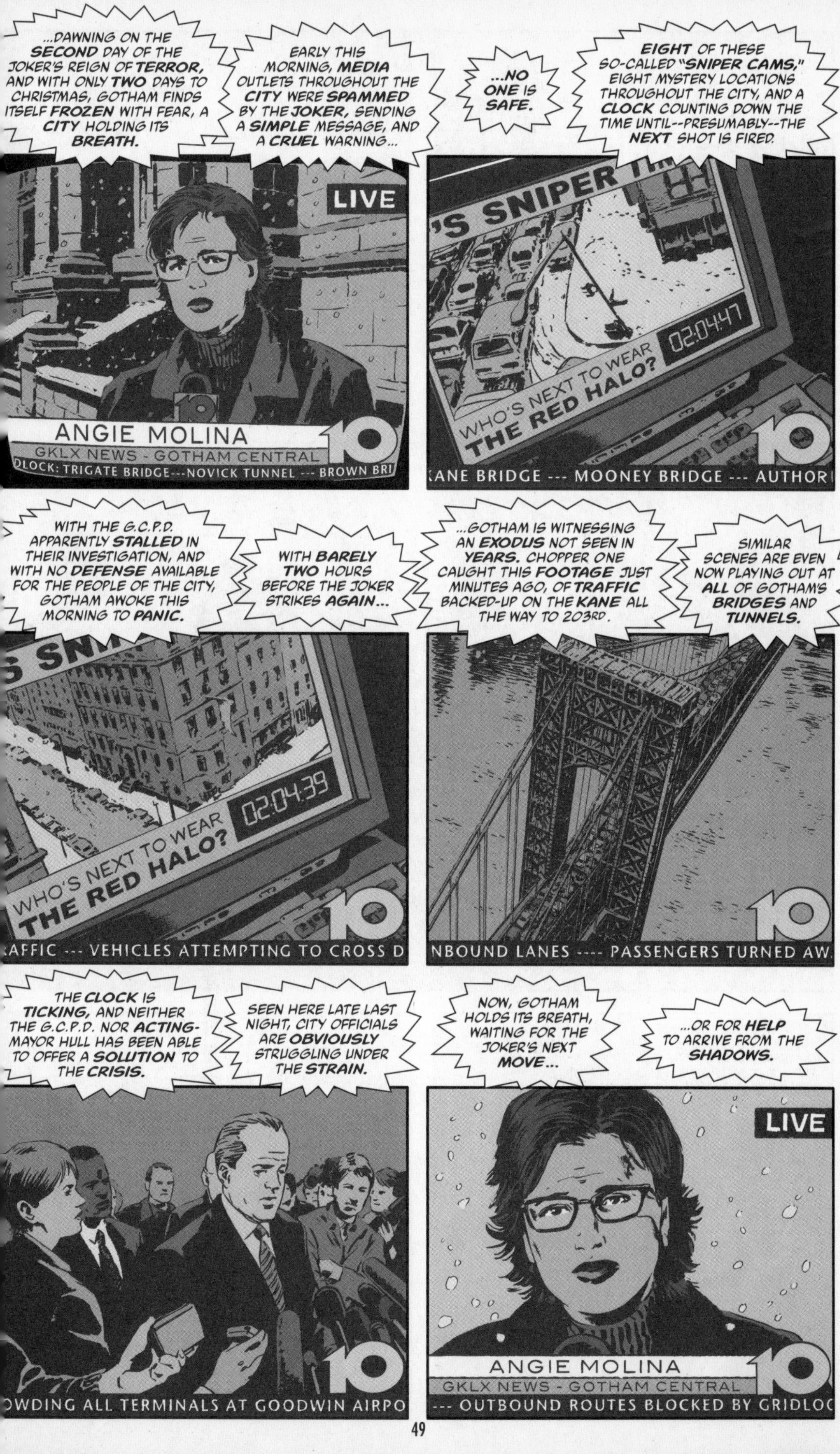

...DAWNING ON THE SECOND DAY OF THE JOKER'S REIGN OF TERROR, AND WITH ONLY TWO DAYS TO CHRISTMAS, GOTHAM FINDS ITSELF FROZEN WITH FEAR, A CITY HOLDING ITS BREATH.
EARLY THIS MORNING, MEDIA OUTLETS THROUGHOUT THE CITY WERE SPAMMED BY THE JOKER, SENDING A SIMPLE MESSAGE, AND A CRUEL WARNING...
...NO ONE IS SAFE.
EIGHT OF THESE SO-CALLED "SNIPER CAMS," EIGHT MYSTERY LOCATIONS THROUGHOUT THE CITY, AND A CLOCK COUNTING DOWN THE TIME UNTIL--PRESUMABLY--THE NEXT SHOT IS FIRED.
LIVE
ANGIE MOLINA
GKLX NEWS - GOTHAM CENTRAL
10
DLOCK: TRIGATE BRIDGE---NOVICK TUNNEL --- BROWN BRI
'S SNIPER
02:04:47
WHO'S NEXT TO WEAR THE RED HALO?
10
ANE BRIDGE --- MOONEY BRIDGE --- AUTHOR
WITH THE G.C.P.D. APPARENTLY STALLED IN THEIR INVESTIGATION, AND WITH NO DEFENSE AVAILABLE FOR THE PEOPLE OF THE CITY, GOTHAM AWOKE THIS MORNING TO PANIC.
WITH BARELY TWO HOURS BEFORE THE JOKER STRIKES AGAIN...
...GOTHAM IS WITNESSING AN EXODUS NOT SEEN IN YEARS. CHOPPER ONE CAUGHT THIS FOOTAGE JUST MINUTES AGO, OF TRAFFIC BACKED-UP ON THE KANE ALL THE WAY TO 203RD.
SIMILAR SCENES ARE EVEN NOW PLAYING OUT AT ALL OF GOTHAM'S BRIDGES AND TUNNELS.
'S SN
02:04:39
WHO'S NEXT TO WEAR THE RED HALO?
10
AFFIC --- VEHICLES ATTEMPTING TO CROSS D
10
NBOUND LANES ---- PASSENGERS TURNED AW
THE CLOCK IS TICKING, AND NEITHER THE G.C.P.D. NOR ACTING-MAYOR HULL HAS BEEN ABLE TO OFFER A SOLUTION TO THE CRISIS.
SEEN HERE LATE LAST NIGHT, CITY OFFICIALS ARE OBVIOUSLY STRUGGLING UNDER THE STRAIN.
NOW, GOTHAM HOLDS ITS BREATH, WAITING FOR THE JOKER'S NEXT MOVE...
...OR FOR HELP TO ARRIVE FROM THE SHADOWS.
10
OWDING ALL TERMINALS AT GOODWIN AIRPO
LIVE
ANGIE MOLINA
GKLX NEWS - GOTHAM CENTRAL
10
--- OUTBOUND ROUTES BLOCKED BY GRIDLOC

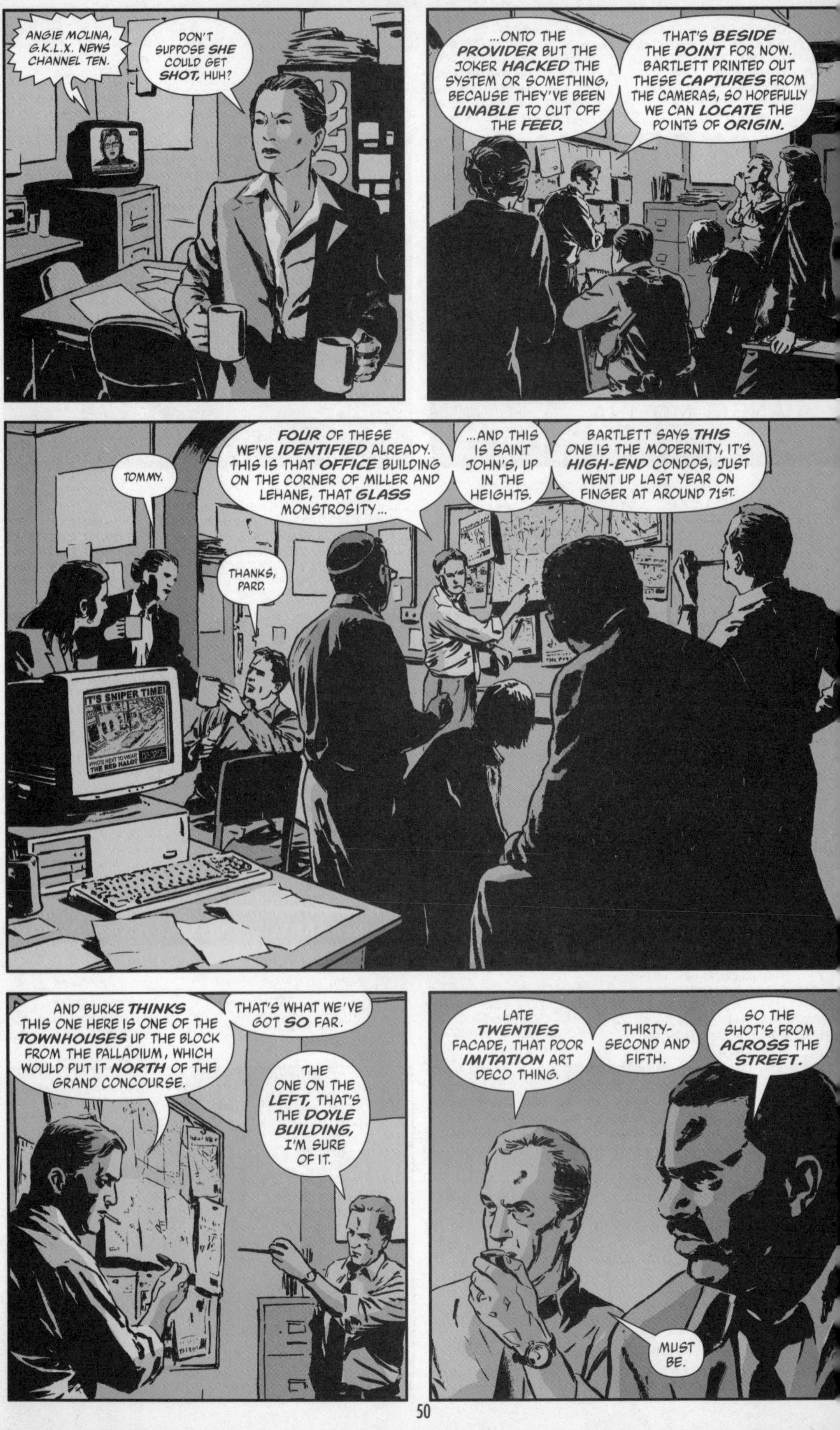
ANGIE MOLINA, G.K.L.X. NEWS CHANNEL TEN.
DON'T SUPPOSE SHE COULD GET SHOT, HUH?
...ONTO THE PROVIDER BUT THE JOKER HACKED THE SYSTEM OR SOMETHING, BECAUSE THEY'VE BEEN UNABLE TO CUT OFF THE FEED.
THAT'S BESIDE THE POINT FOR NOW. BARTLETT PRINTED OUT THESE CAPTURES FROM THE CAMERAS, SO HOPEFULLY WE CAN LOCATE THE POINTS OF ORIGIN.
TOMMY.
FOUR OF THESE WE'VE IDENTIFIED ALREADY. THIS IS THAT OFFICE BUILDING ON THE CORNER OF MILLER AND LEHANE, THAT GLASS MONSTROSITY...
...AND THIS IS SAINT JOHN'S, UP IN THE HEIGHTS.
BARTLETT SAYS THIS ONE IS THE MODERNITY, IT'S HIGH-END CONDOS, JUST WENT UP LAST YEAR ON FINGER AT AROUND 71ST.
THANKS, PARD.
IT'S SNIPER TIME!
WHO'S NEXT TO WEAR THE RED HALO?
AND BURKE THINKS THIS ONE HERE IS ONE OF THE TOWNHOUSES UP THE BLOCK FROM THE PALLADIUM, WHICH WOULD PUT IT NORTH OF THE GRAND CONCOURSE.
THAT'S WHAT WE'VE GOT SO FAR.
THE ONE ON THE LEFT, THAT'S THE DOYLE BUILDING, I'M SURE OF IT.
LATE TWENTIES FACADE, THAT POOR IMITATION ART DECO THING.
THIRTY-SECOND AND FIFTH.
SO THE SHOT'S FROM ACROSS THE STREET.
MUST BE.

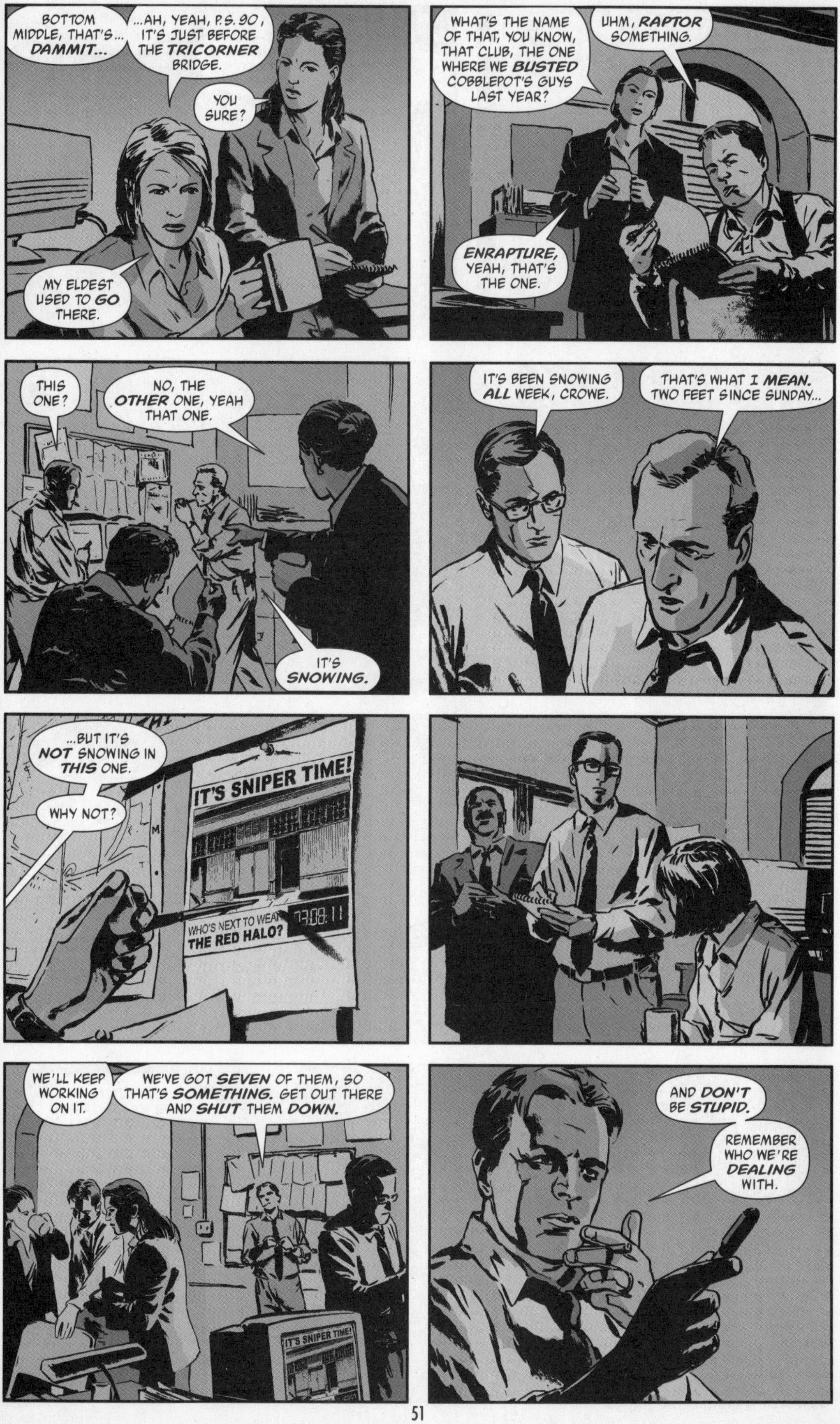
BOTTOM MIDDLE, THAT'S... DAMMIT...
...AH, YEAH, P.S. 90, IT'S JUST BEFORE THE TRICORNER BRIDGE.
YOU SURE?
MY ELDEST USED TO GO THERE.
WHAT'S THE NAME OF THAT, YOU KNOW, THAT CLUB, THE ONE WHERE WE BUSTED COBBLEPOT'S GUYS LAST YEAR?
UHM, RAPTOR SOMETHING.
ENRAPTURE, YEAH, THAT'S THE ONE.
THIS ONE?
NO, THE OTHER ONE, YEAH THAT ONE.
IT'S SNOWING.
IT'S BEEN SNOWING ALL WEEK, CROWE.
THAT'S WHAT I MEAN. TWO FEET SINCE SUNDAY...
...BUT IT'S NOT SNOWING IN THIS ONE.
WHY NOT?
IT'S SNIPER TIME!
WHO'S NEXT TO WEAR THE RED HALO?
73:08:11
WE'LL KEEP WORKING ON IT.
WE'VE GOT SEVEN OF THEM, SO THAT'S SOMETHING. GET OUT THERE AND SHUT THEM DOWN.
IT'S SNIPER TIME!
AND DON'T BE STUPID.
REMEMBER WHO WE'RE DEALING WITH.

IT'S SNIPER TIME

WHAT DO YOU THINK, COHEN, WAS I RIGHT OR WAS I RIGHT?

CLOSE... ALMOST...

O'S NEXT TO WEAR HALO?

03:06

...BUT NOT QUITE. THE ANGLE IS JUST A LITTLE OFF.

OKAY, GOT IT.

JUST A FRIGGIN' *CAMCORDER* UNDER HERE...

Boo Hoo Batly! Better Luck Next Time!

...AND ANOTHER OH-SO-*FUNNY* MESSAGE FOR THE *BAT*.

DETECTIVE THREE TO *CENTRAL*. NEGATIVE ON CAMERA ONE LOCATION. WE'VE GOT A MOUNTED CAMCORDER AND A LAPTOP.

POLICE

52

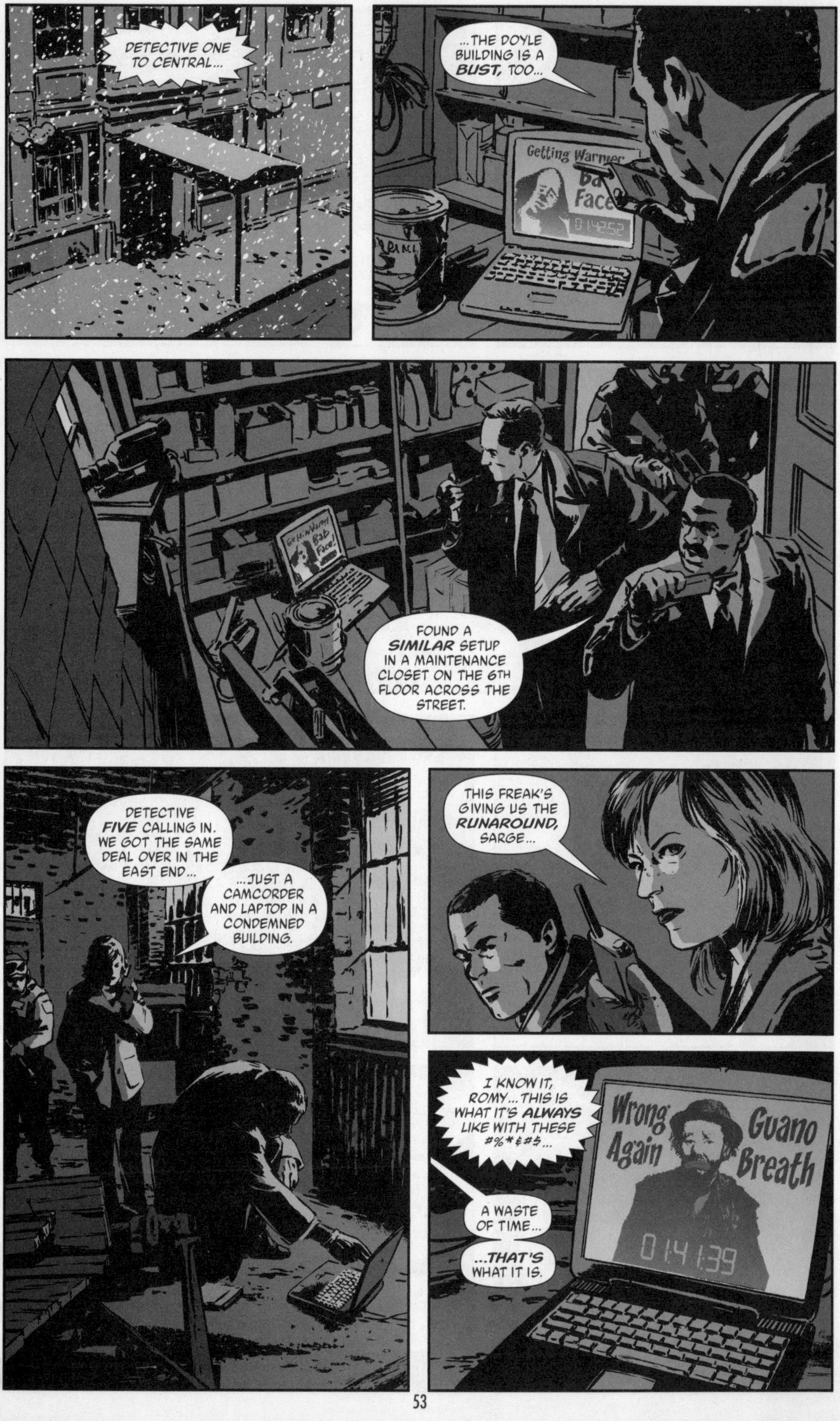
DETECTIVE ONE TO CENTRAL...
...THE DOYLE BUILDING IS A BUST, TOO...
Getting Warmer
FOUND A SIMILAR SETUP IN A MAINTENANCE CLOSET ON THE 6TH FLOOR ACROSS THE STREET.
DETECTIVE FIVE CALLING IN. WE GOT THE SAME DEAL OVER IN THE EAST END...
...JUST A CAMCORDER AND LAPTOP IN A CONDEMNED BUILDING.
THIS FREAK'S GIVING US THE RUNAROUND, SARGE...
I KNOW IT, ROMY... THIS IS WHAT IT'S ALWAYS LIKE WITH THESE #%*¢#$...
A WASTE OF TIME...
...THAT'S WHAT IT IS.
Wrong Again
Guano Breath
01:41:39

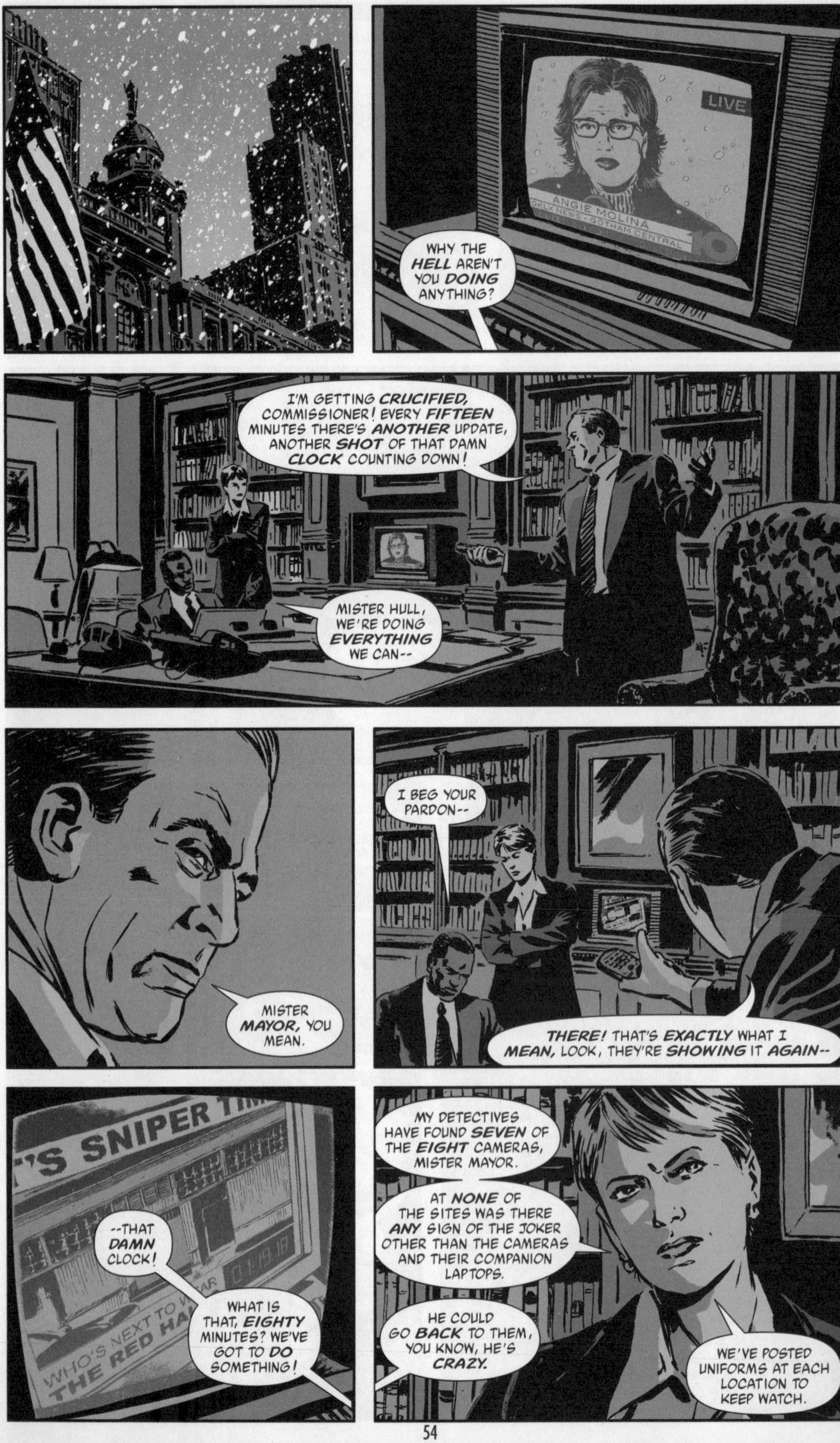
LIVE
ANGIE MOLINA
GKLX NEWS - GOTHAM CENTRAL
WHY THE HELL AREN'T YOU DOING ANYTHING?
I'M GETTING CRUCIFIED, COMMISSIONER! EVERY FIFTEEN MINUTES THERE'S ANOTHER UPDATE, ANOTHER SHOT OF THAT DAMN CLOCK COUNTING DOWN!
MISTER HULL, WE'RE DOING EVERYTHING WE CAN--
MISTER MAYOR, YOU MEAN.
I BEG YOUR PARDON--
THERE! THAT'S EXACTLY WHAT I MEAN, LOOK, THEY'RE SHOWING IT AGAIN--
'S SNIPER TI
WHO'S NEXT TO W
THE RED HA
--THAT DAMN CLOCK!
WHAT IS THAT, EIGHTY MINUTES? WE'VE GOT TO DO SOMETHING!
MY DETECTIVES HAVE FOUND SEVEN OF THE EIGHT CAMERAS, MISTER MAYOR.
AT NONE OF THE SITES WAS THERE ANY SIGN OF THE JOKER OTHER THAN THE CAMERAS AND THEIR COMPANION LAPTOPS.
HE COULD GO BACK TO THEM, YOU KNOW, HE'S CRAZY.
WE'VE POSTED UNIFORMS AT EACH LOCATION TO KEEP WATCH.

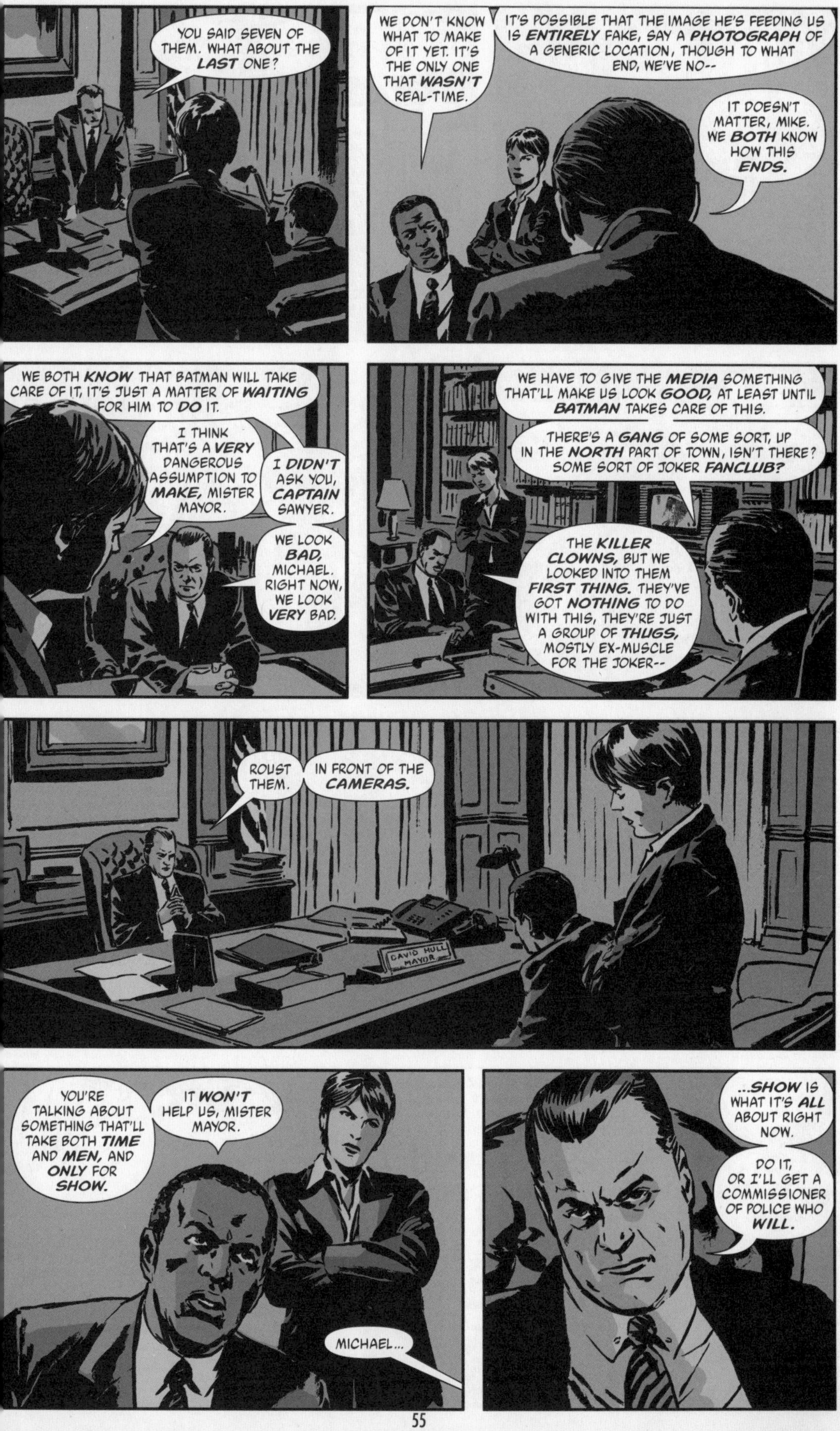

YOU SAID SEVEN OF THEM. WHAT ABOUT THE LAST ONE?
WE DON'T KNOW WHAT TO MAKE OF IT YET. IT'S THE ONLY ONE THAT WASN'T REAL-TIME.
IT'S POSSIBLE THAT THE IMAGE HE'S FEEDING US IS ENTIRELY FAKE, SAY A PHOTOGRAPH OF A GENERIC LOCATION, THOUGH TO WHAT END, WE'VE NO--
IT DOESN'T MATTER, MIKE. WE BOTH KNOW HOW THIS ENDS.
WE BOTH KNOW THAT BATMAN WILL TAKE CARE OF IT, IT'S JUST A MATTER OF WAITING FOR HIM TO DO IT.
I THINK THAT'S A VERY DANGEROUS ASSUMPTION TO MAKE, MISTER MAYOR.
I DIDN'T ASK YOU, CAPTAIN SAWYER.
WE LOOK BAD, MICHAEL. RIGHT NOW, WE LOOK VERY BAD.
WE HAVE TO GIVE THE MEDIA SOMETHING THAT'LL MAKE US LOOK GOOD, AT LEAST UNTIL BATMAN TAKES CARE OF THIS.
THERE'S A GANG OF SOME SORT, UP IN THE NORTH PART OF TOWN, ISN'T THERE? SOME SORT OF JOKER FANCLUB?
THE KILLER CLOWNS, BUT WE LOOKED INTO THEM FIRST THING. THEY'VE GOT NOTHING TO DO WITH THIS, THEY'RE JUST A GROUP OF THUGS, MOSTLY EX-MUSCLE FOR THE JOKER--
ROUST THEM.
IN FRONT OF THE CAMERAS.
DAVID HULL MAYOR
YOU'RE TALKING ABOUT SOMETHING THAT'LL TAKE BOTH TIME AND MEN, AND ONLY FOR SHOW.
IT WON'T HELP US, MISTER MAYOR.
MICHAEL...
...SHOW IS WHAT IT'S ALL ABOUT RIGHT NOW.
DO IT, OR I'LL GET A COMMISSIONER OF POLICE WHO WILL.

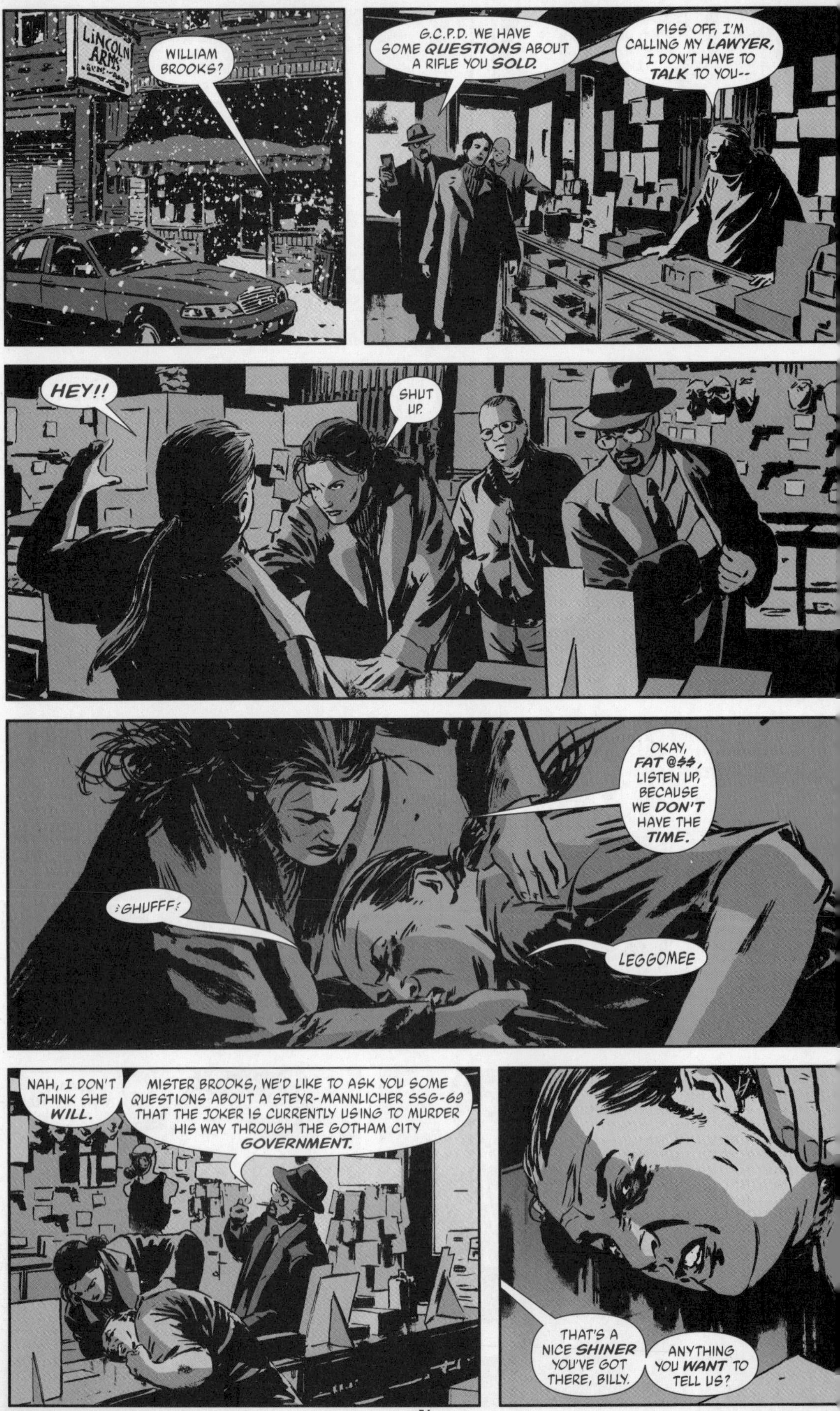
LINCOLN ARMS
WILLIAM BROOKS?
G.C.P.D. WE HAVE SOME QUESTIONS ABOUT A RIFLE YOU SOLD.
PISS OFF, I'M CALLING MY LAWYER, I DON'T HAVE TO TALK TO YOU--
HEY!!
SHUT UP.
OKAY, FAT @$$, LISTEN UP, BECAUSE WE DON'T HAVE THE TIME.
GHUFFF
LEGGOMEE
NAH, I DON'T THINK SHE WILL.
MISTER BROOKS, WE'D LIKE TO ASK YOU SOME QUESTIONS ABOUT A STEYR-MANNLICHER SSG-69 THAT THE JOKER IS CURRENTLY USING TO MURDER HIS WAY THROUGH THE GOTHAM CITY GOVERNMENT.
THAT'S A NICE SHINER YOU'VE GOT THERE, BILLY.
ANYTHING YOU WANT TO TELL US?

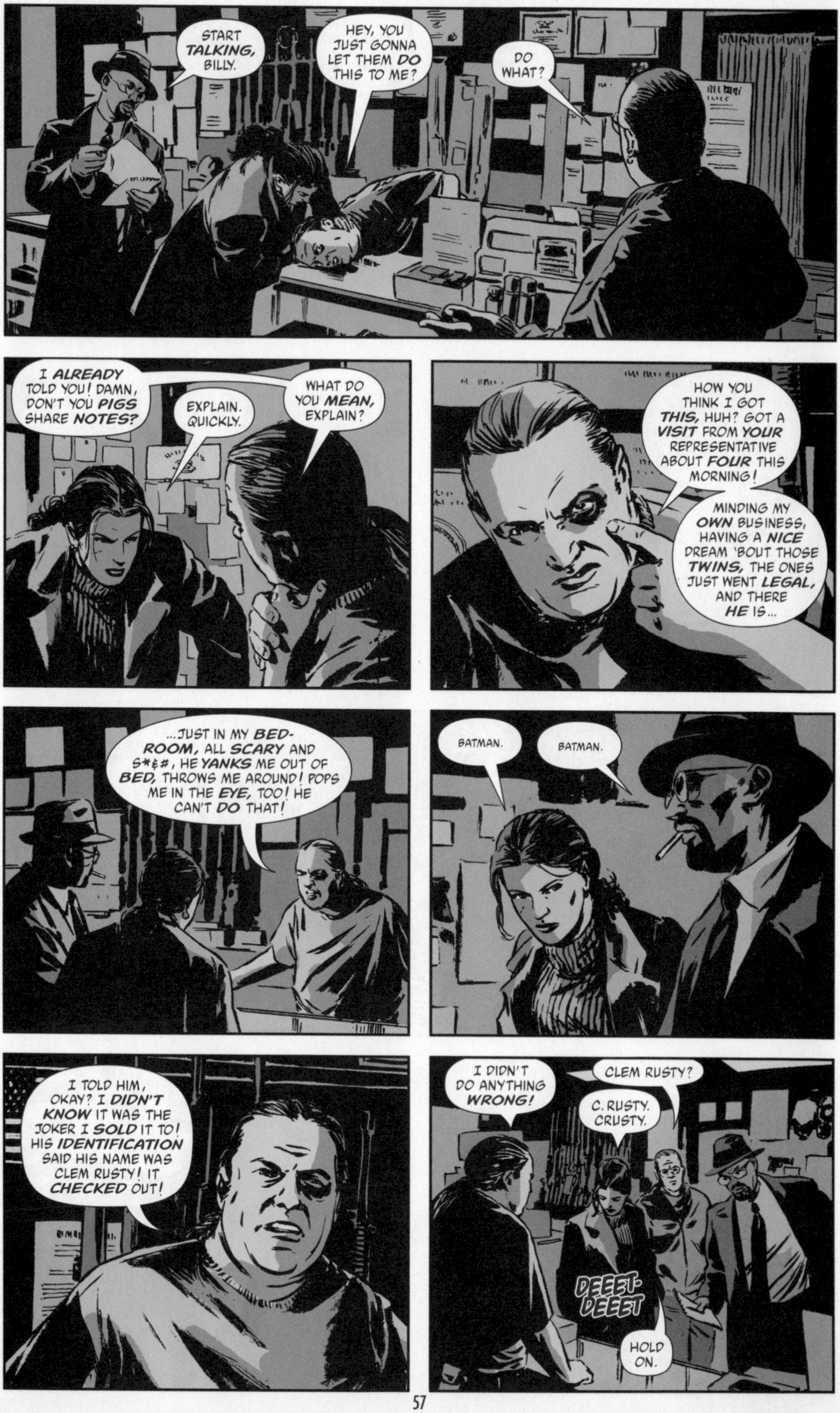
START TALKING, BILLY.
HEY, YOU JUST GONNA LET THEM DO THIS TO ME?
DO WHAT?
I ALREADY TOLD YOU! DAMN, DON'T YOU PIGS SHARE NOTES?
WHAT DO YOU MEAN, EXPLAIN?
EXPLAIN. QUICKLY.
HOW YOU THINK I GOT THIS, HUH? GOT A VISIT FROM YOUR REPRESENTATIVE ABOUT FOUR THIS MORNING!
MINDING MY OWN BUSINESS, HAVING A NICE DREAM 'BOUT THOSE TWINS, THE ONES JUST WENT LEGAL, AND THERE HE IS...
...JUST IN MY BED-ROOM, ALL SCARY AND S*&#, HE YANKS ME OUT OF BED, THROWS ME AROUND! POPS ME IN THE EYE, TOO! HE CAN'T DO THAT!
BATMAN.
BATMAN.
I TOLD HIM, OKAY? I DIDN'T KNOW IT WAS THE JOKER I SOLD IT TO! HIS IDENTIFICATION SAID HIS NAME WAS CLEM RUSTY! IT CHECKED OUT!
I DIDN'T DO ANYTHING WRONG!
CLEM RUSTY?
C. RUSTY. CRUSTY.
DEEET-DEEET
HOLD ON.

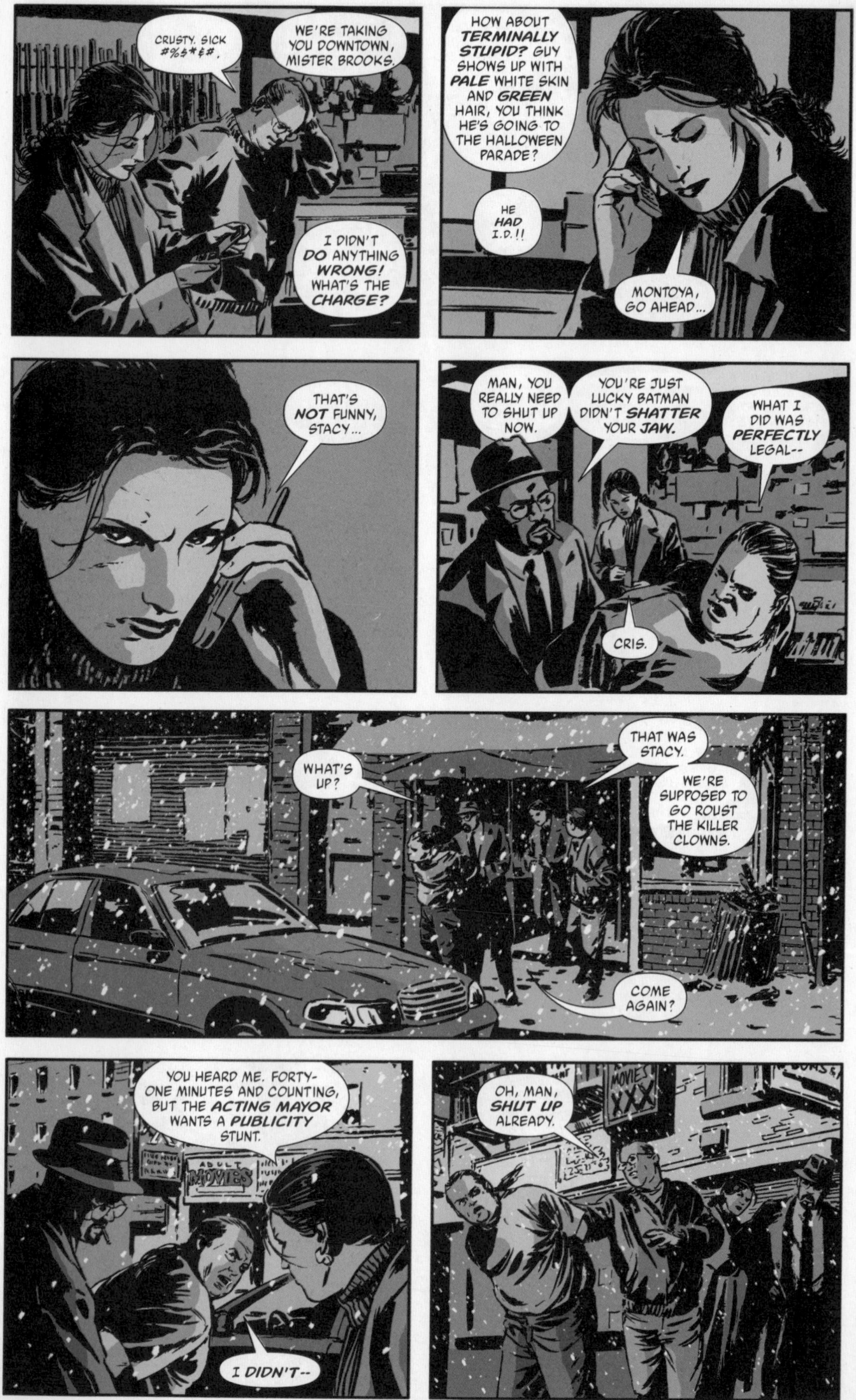
CRUSTY. SICK #%$*¢#.
WE'RE TAKING YOU DOWNTOWN, MISTER BROOKS.
I DIDN'T **DO** ANYTHING **WRONG!** WHAT'S THE **CHARGE?**
HOW ABOUT **TERMINALLY STUPID?** GUY SHOWS UP WITH **PALE** WHITE SKIN AND **GREEN** HAIR, YOU THINK HE'S GOING TO THE HALLOWEEN PARADE?
HE **HAD** I.D.!!
MONTOYA, GO AHEAD...
THAT'S **NOT** FUNNY, STACY...
MAN, YOU REALLY NEED TO SHUT UP NOW.
YOU'RE JUST LUCKY BATMAN DIDN'T **SHATTER** YOUR **JAW.**
WHAT I DID WAS **PERFECTLY** LEGAL--
CRIS.
WHAT'S UP?
THAT WAS STACY.
WE'RE SUPPOSED TO GO ROUST THE KILLER CLOWNS.
COME AGAIN?
YOU HEARD ME. FORTY-ONE MINUTES AND COUNTING, BUT THE **ACTING MAYOR** WANTS A **PUBLICITY** STUNT.
ADULT MOVIES
I DIDN'T--
OH, MAN, **SHUT UP** ALREADY.
MOVIES XXX

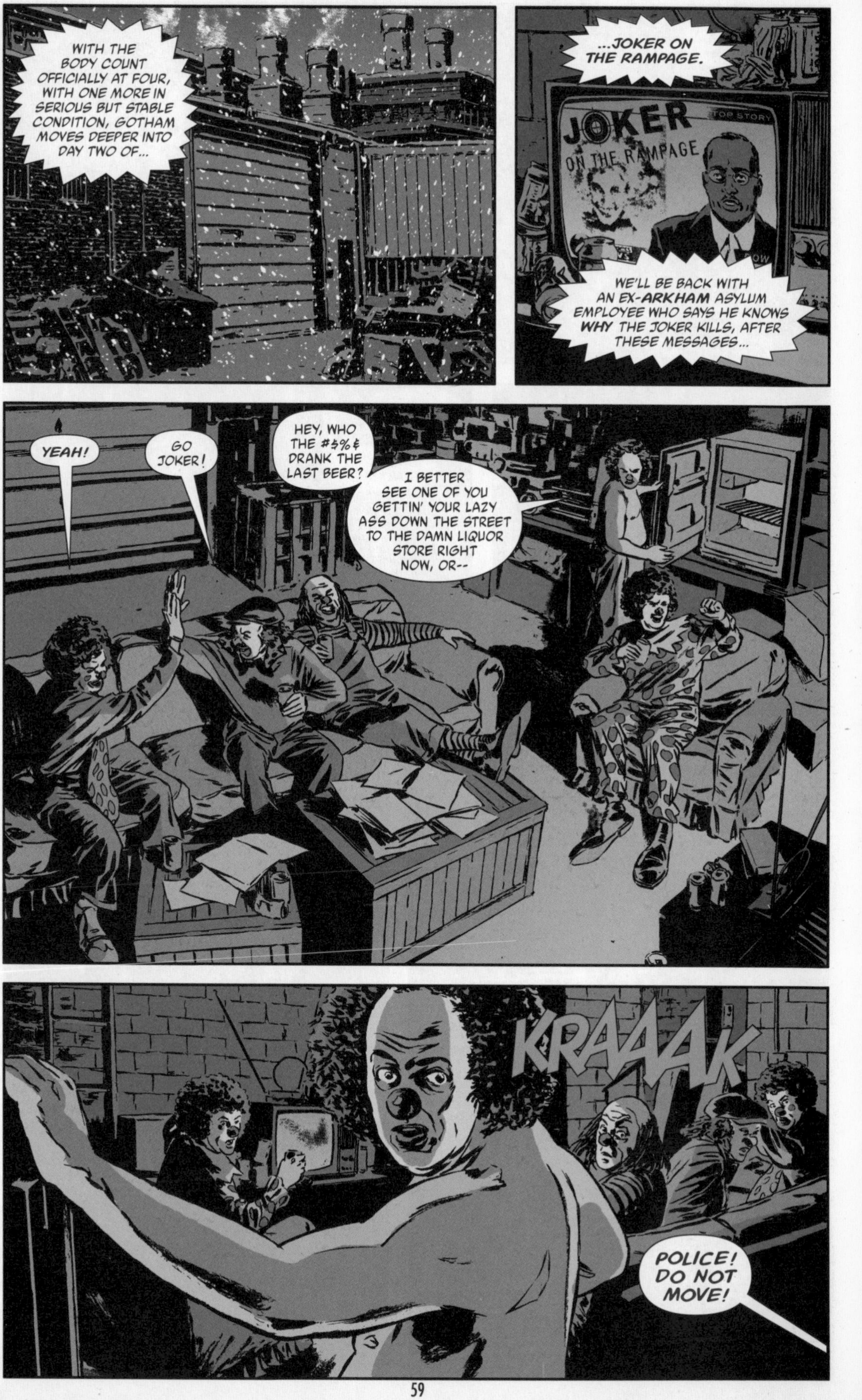
WITH THE BODY COUNT OFFICIALLY AT FOUR, WITH ONE MORE IN SERIOUS BUT STABLE CONDITION, GOTHAM MOVES DEEPER INTO DAY TWO OF...
...JOKER ON THE RAMPAGE.
JOKER
TOP STORY
ON THE RAMPAGE
WE'LL BE BACK WITH AN EX-ARKHAM ASYLUM EMPLOYEE WHO SAYS HE KNOWS WHY THE JOKER KILLS, AFTER THESE MESSAGES...
YEAH!
GO JOKER!
HEY, WHO THE #$%& DRANK THE LAST BEER?
I BETTER SEE ONE OF YOU GETTIN' YOUR LAZY ASS DOWN THE STREET TO THE DAMN LIQUOR STORE RIGHT NOW, OR--
KRAAAK
POLICE! DO NOT MOVE!

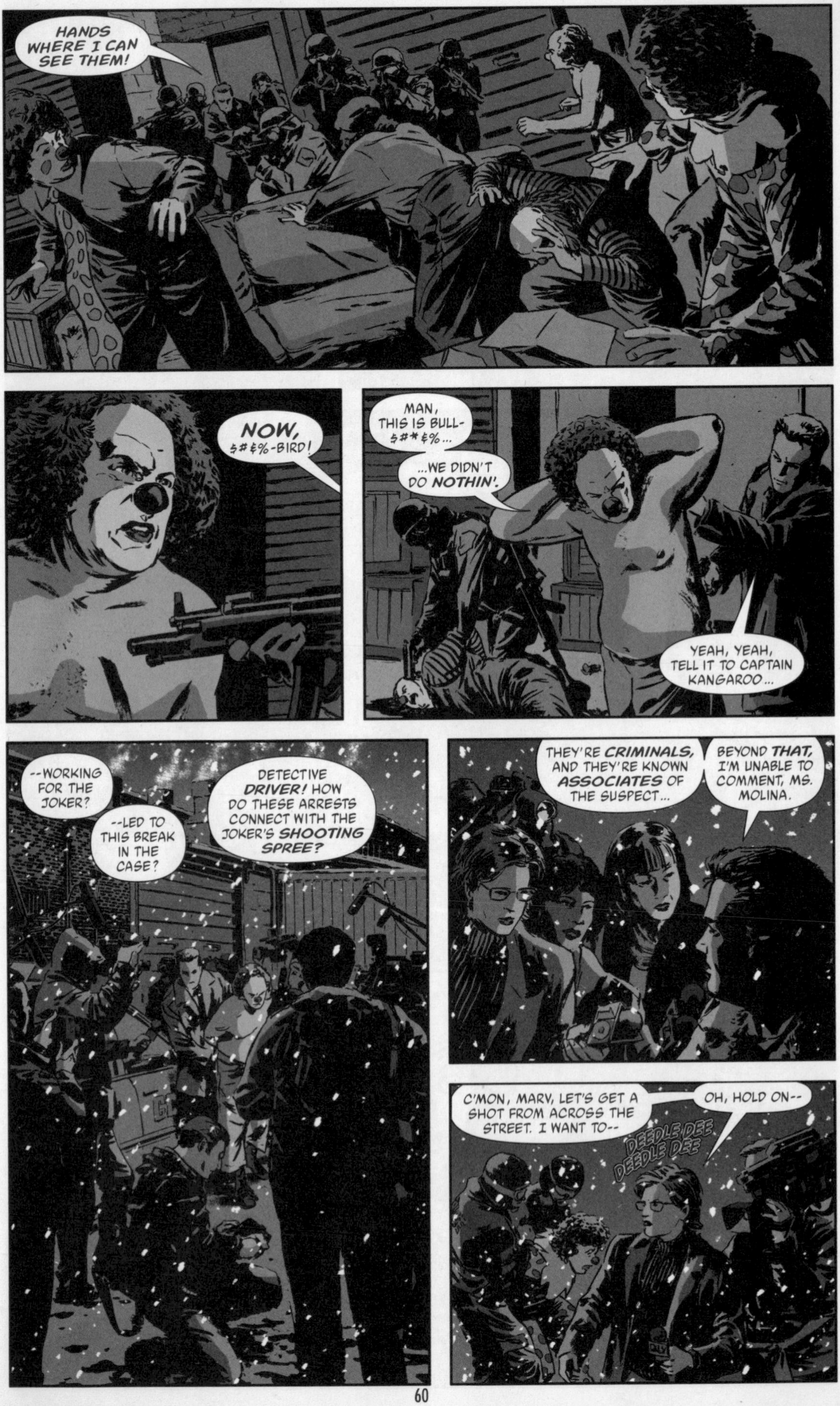

HANDS WHERE I CAN SEE THEM!
NOW, $#&%-BIRD!
MAN, THIS IS BULL-$#*&%...
...WE DIDN'T DO NOTHIN'.
YEAH, YEAH, TELL IT TO CAPTAIN KANGAROO...
--WORKING FOR THE JOKER?
--LED TO THIS BREAK IN THE CASE?
DETECTIVE DRIVER! HOW DO THESE ARRESTS CONNECT WITH THE JOKER'S SHOOTING SPREE?
THEY'RE CRIMINALS, AND THEY'RE KNOWN ASSOCIATES OF THE SUSPECT...
BEYOND THAT, I'M UNABLE TO COMMENT, MS. MOLINA.
C'MON, MARV, LET'S GET A SHOT FROM ACROSS THE STREET. I WANT TO--
DEEDLE DEE DEEDLE DEE
OH, HOLD ON--

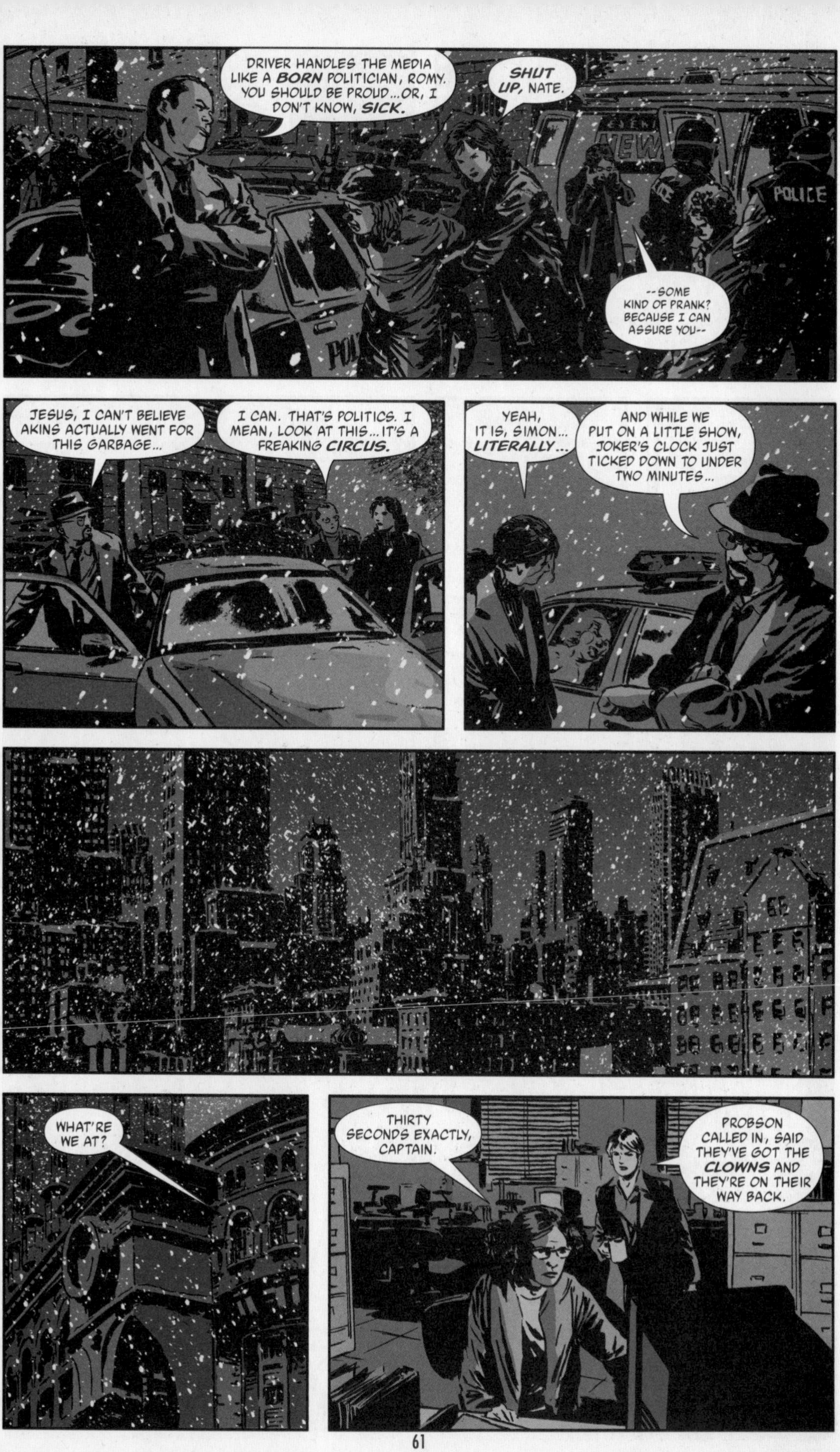
DRIVER HANDLES THE MEDIA LIKE A **BORN** POLITICIAN, ROMY. YOU SHOULD BE PROUD...OR, I DON'T KNOW, **SICK.**
SHUT UP, NATE.
NEWS
POLICE
--SOME KIND OF PRANK? BECAUSE I CAN ASSURE YOU--
JESUS, I CAN'T BELIEVE AKINS ACTUALLY WENT FOR THIS GARBAGE...
I CAN. THAT'S POLITICS. I MEAN, LOOK AT THIS...IT'S A FREAKING **CIRCUS.**
YEAH, IT IS, SIMON... **LITERALLY...**
AND WHILE WE PUT ON A LITTLE SHOW, JOKER'S CLOCK JUST TICKED DOWN TO UNDER TWO MINUTES...
WHAT'RE WE AT?
THIRTY SECONDS EXACTLY, CAPTAIN.
PROBSON CALLED IN, SAID THEY'VE GOT THE **CLOWNS** AND THEY'RE ON THEIR WAY BACK.

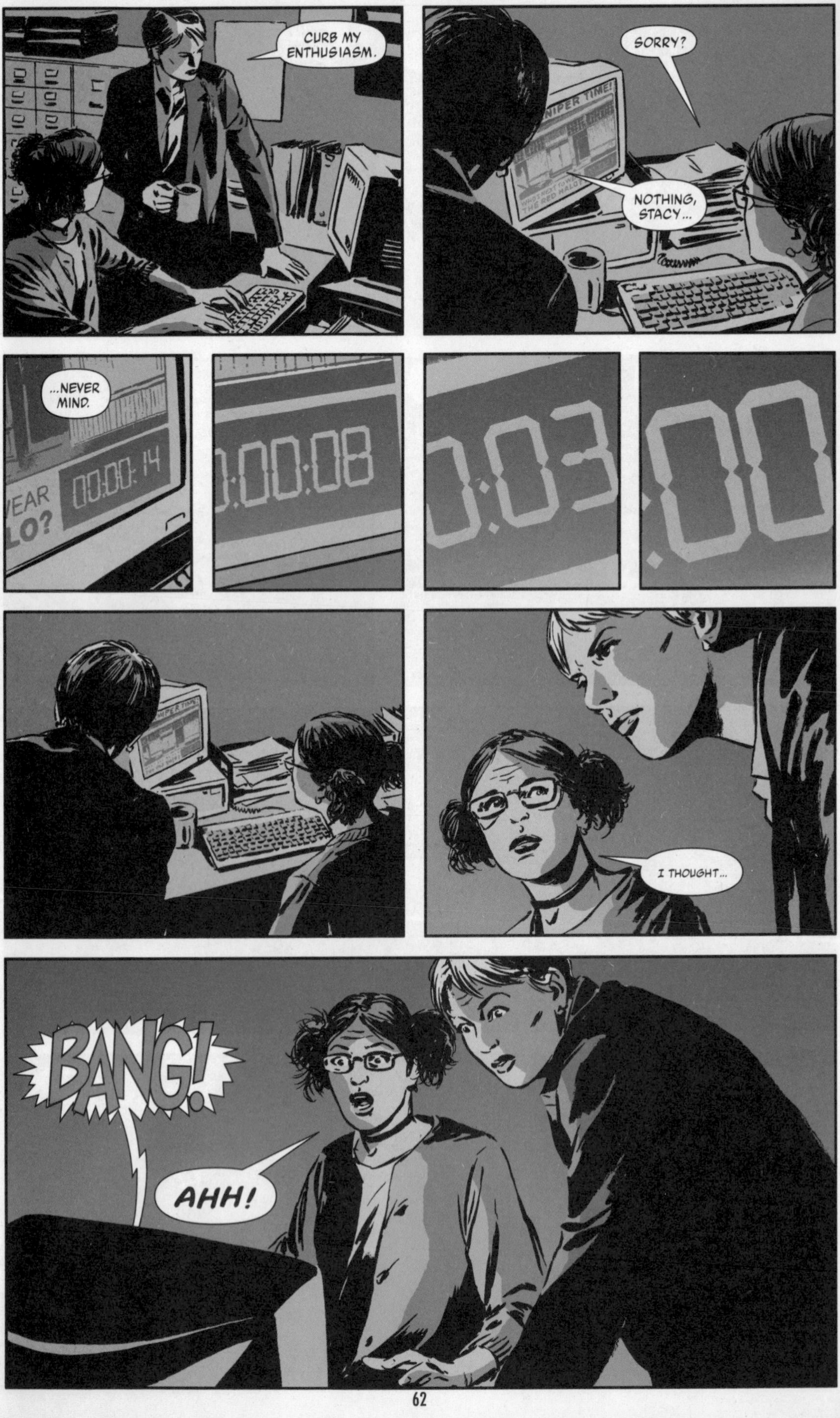
CURB MY ENTHUSIASM.
SORRY?
SNIPER TIME!
NOTHING, STACY...
...NEVER MIND.
00:00:14
0:00:08
0:03
:00
I THOUGHT...
BANG!
AHH!

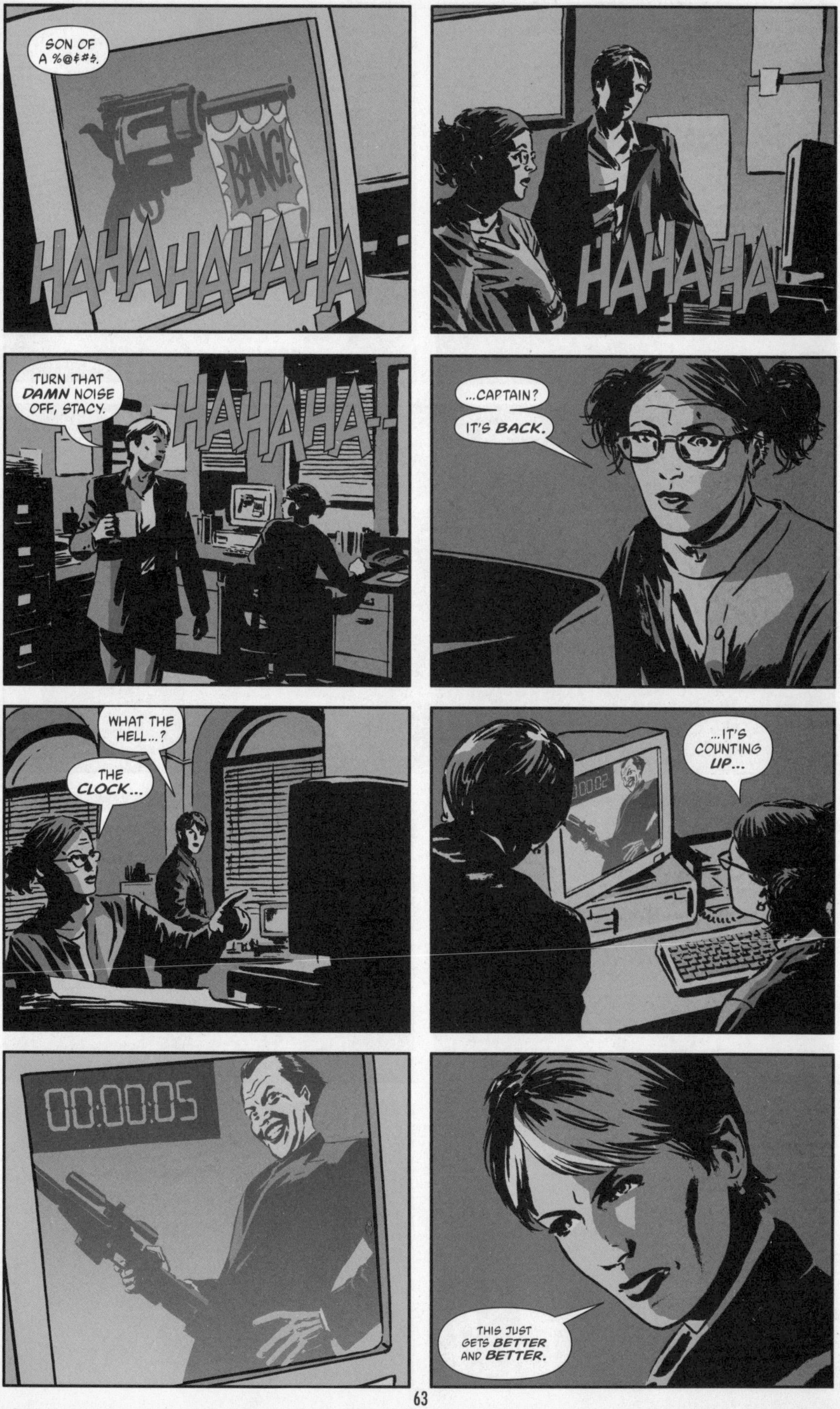
SON OF A %@¢#$.
HAHAHAHAHA
HAHAHA
TURN THAT DAMN NOISE OFF, STACY.
HAHAHA-
...CAPTAIN?
IT'S BACK.
WHAT THE HELL...?
THE CLOCK...
...IT'S COUNTING UP...
00:00:05
THIS JUST GETS BETTER AND BETTER.

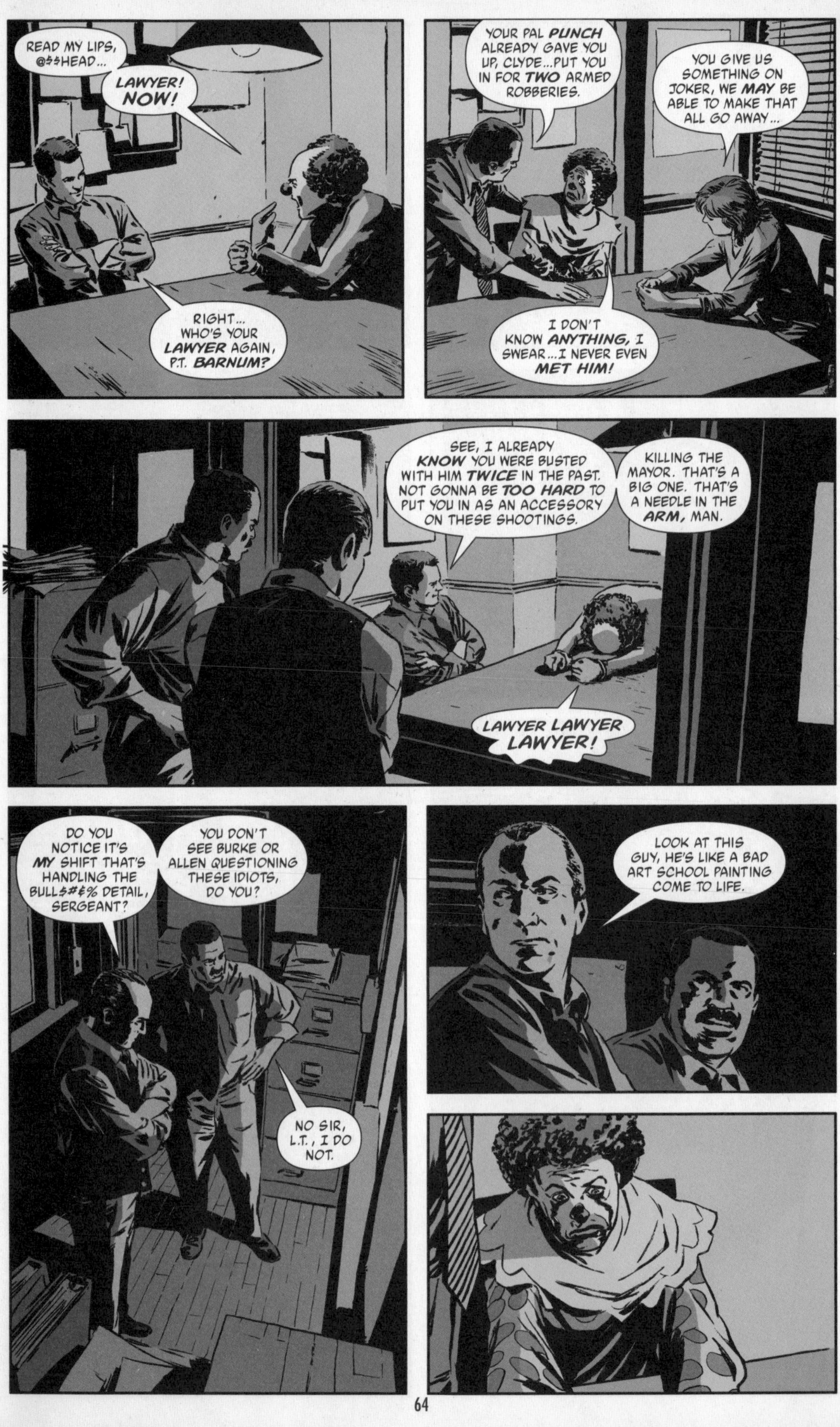
READ MY LIPS, @$$HEAD...
LAWYER! NOW!
RIGHT... WHO'S YOUR LAWYER AGAIN, P.T. BARNUM?
YOUR PAL PUNCH ALREADY GAVE YOU UP, CLYDE...PUT YOU IN FOR TWO ARMED ROBBERIES.
YOU GIVE US SOMETHING ON JOKER, WE MAY BE ABLE TO MAKE THAT ALL GO AWAY...
I DON'T KNOW ANYTHING, I SWEAR...I NEVER EVEN MET HIM!
SEE, I ALREADY KNOW YOU WERE BUSTED WITH HIM TWICE IN THE PAST. NOT GONNA BE TOO HARD TO PUT YOU IN AS AN ACCESSORY ON THESE SHOOTINGS.
KILLING THE MAYOR. THAT'S A BIG ONE. THAT'S A NEEDLE IN THE ARM, MAN.
LAWYER LAWYER LAWYER!
DO YOU NOTICE IT'S MY SHIFT THAT'S HANDLING THE BULL$#€% DETAIL, SERGEANT?
YOU DON'T SEE BURKE OR ALLEN QUESTIONING THESE IDIOTS, DO YOU?
NO SIR, L.T., I DO NOT.
LOOK AT THIS GUY, HE'S LIKE A BAD ART SCHOOL PAINTING COME TO LIFE.

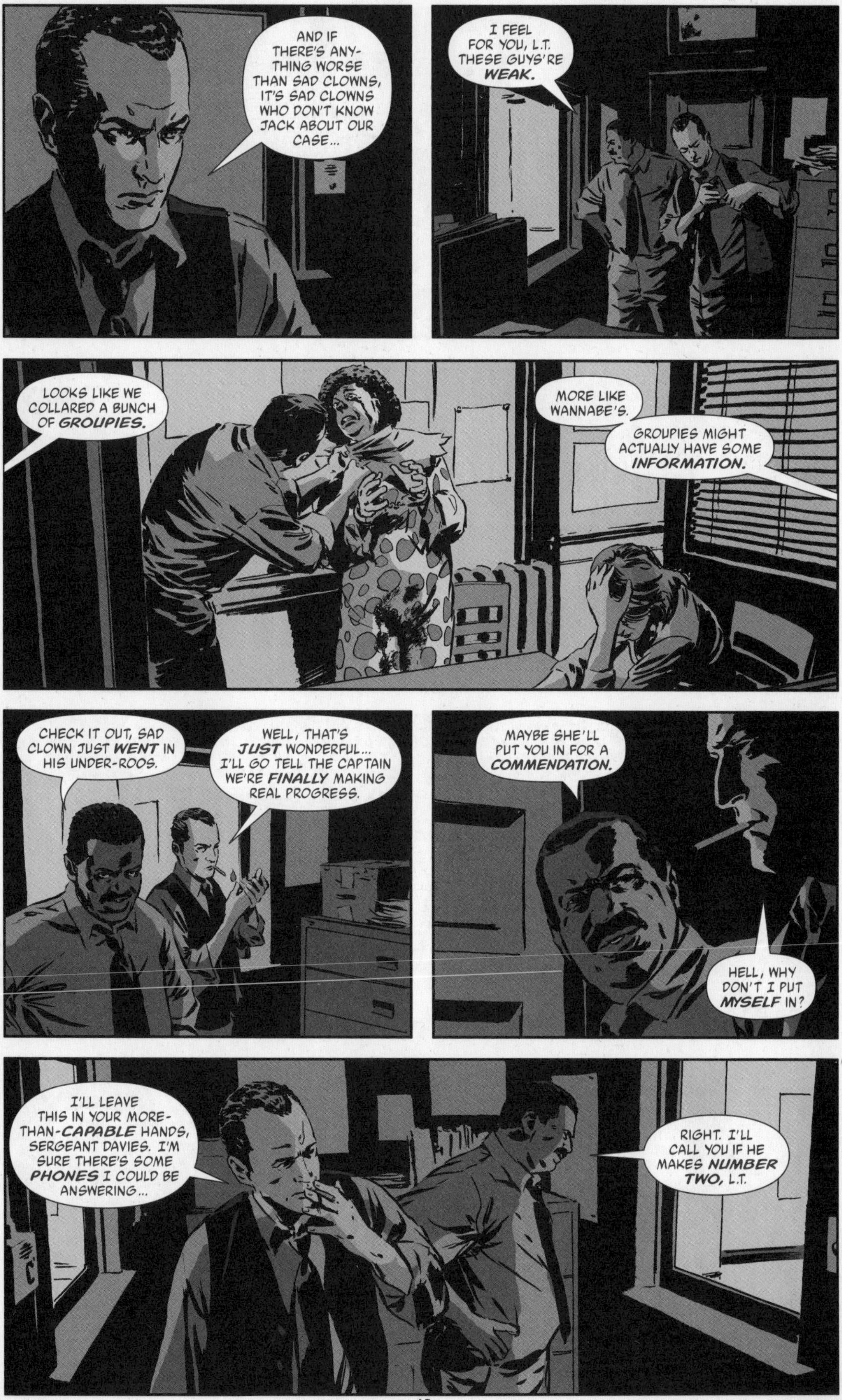
AND IF THERE'S ANY-THING WORSE THAN SAD CLOWNS, IT'S SAD CLOWNS WHO DON'T KNOW JACK ABOUT OUR CASE...
I FEEL FOR YOU, L.T. THESE GUYS'RE WEAK.
LOOKS LIKE WE COLLARED A BUNCH OF GROUPIES.
MORE LIKE WANNABE'S.
GROUPIES MIGHT ACTUALLY HAVE SOME INFORMATION.
CHECK IT OUT, SAD CLOWN JUST WENT IN HIS UNDER-ROOS.
WELL, THAT'S JUST WONDERFUL... I'LL GO TELL THE CAPTAIN WE'RE FINALLY MAKING REAL PROGRESS.
MAYBE SHE'LL PUT YOU IN FOR A COMMENDATION.
HELL, WHY DON'T I PUT MYSELF IN?
I'LL LEAVE THIS IN YOUR MORE-THAN-CAPABLE HANDS, SERGEANT DAVIES. I'M SURE THERE'S SOME PHONES I COULD BE ANSWERING...
RIGHT. I'LL CALL YOU IF HE MAKES NUMBER TWO, L.T.

...NO, I JUST DON'T THINK YOU SHOULD GO TO WORK, THAT'S ALL. IT'S NOT LIKE THE RESTAURANT'LL BE *BUSY* TONIGHT, DEE...

I STILL THINK YOU SHOULD GO. JUST TAKE THE *TRAIN,* FLY OUT OF A *DIFFERENT* AIRPORT...

...NO IDEA...NO, I MEAN, NOT UNTIL IT'S *OVER*...

...YES, I'M WEARING MY *VEST*...

...NOT UNTIL IT'S *OVER,* DORE, YOU KNOW THAT...

...NO, I'M *NOT* TRYING TO GET OUT OF SEEING YOUR PARENTS...

MAN, COHEN, YOU'RE SO *LUCKY* YOU'RE JEWISH. YOU DON'T HAVE TO DEAL WITH ALL THIS *CHRISTMAS* B.S. ...

THAT'S RIGHT, TOMMY, THAT *MORE* THAN MAKES UP FOR TWO *THOUSAND* PLUS YEARS OF *MURDER* AND *PERSECUTION.*

HEY, I WAS JUST *TALKING*--

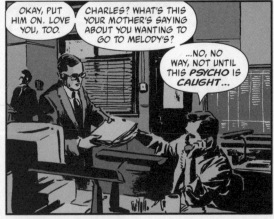

OKAY, PUT HIM ON. LOVE YOU, TOO.

CHARLES? WHAT'S THIS YOUR MOTHER'S SAYING ABOUT YOU WANTING TO GO TO MELODY'S?

...NO, NO WAY, NOT UNTIL THIS *PSYCHO* IS *CAUGHT*...

NO CHANGE?

NOTHING.

YOU SOUND *DISAPPOINTED,* SARGE.

TWO-PLUS HOURS, AND *NOTHING,* JOELY.

JOKE, VINCENT. JUST A *JOKE.*

NOT *FUNNY.*

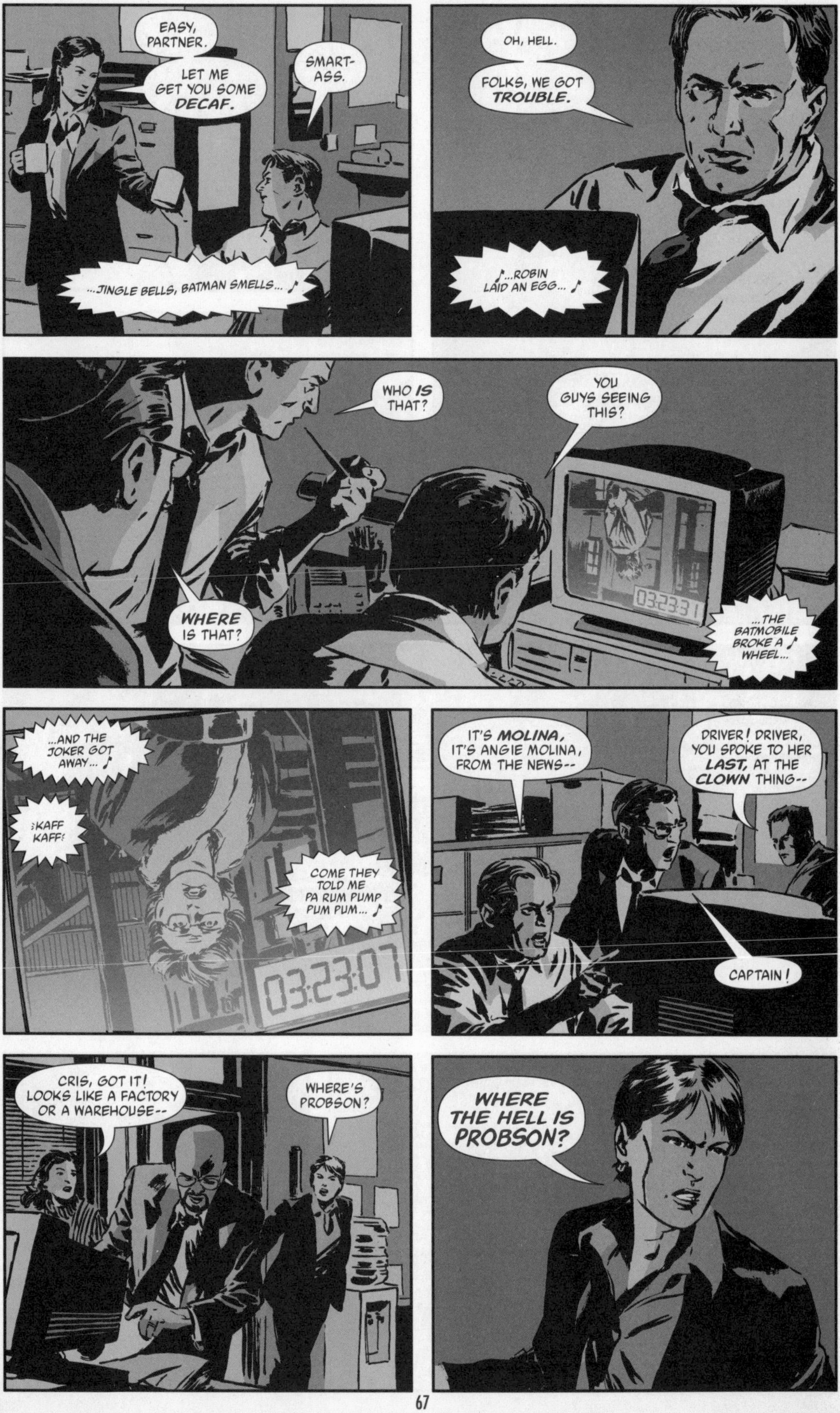
EASY, PARTNER.
LET ME GET YOU SOME DECAF.
SMART-ASS.
...JINGLE BELLS, BATMAN SMELLS... ♪
OH, HELL.
FOLKS, WE GOT TROUBLE.
♪...ROBIN LAID AN EGG... ♪
WHO IS THAT?
YOU GUYS SEEING THIS?
WHERE IS THAT?
03:23:31
...THE BATMOBILE BROKE A ♪ WHEEL...
...AND THE JOKER GOT AWAY... ♪
KAFF KAFF
COME THEY TOLD ME PA RUM PUMP PUM PUM... ♪
03:23:07
IT'S MOLINA, IT'S ANGIE MOLINA, FROM THE NEWS--
DRIVER! DRIVER, YOU SPOKE TO HER LAST, AT THE CLOWN THING--
CAPTAIN!
CRIS, GOT IT! LOOKS LIKE A FACTORY OR A WAREHOUSE--
WHERE'S PROBSON?
WHERE THE HELL IS PROBSON?

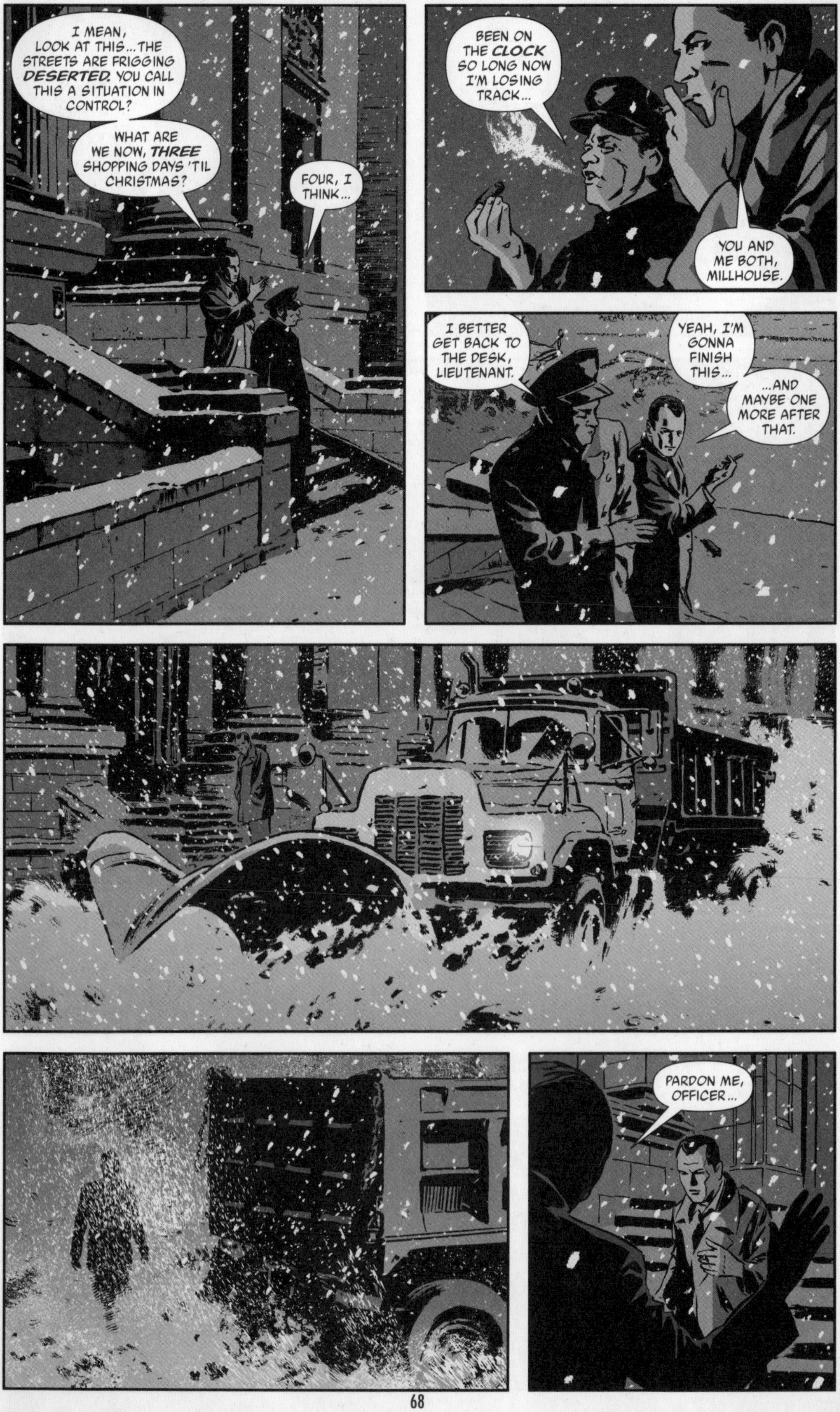
I MEAN, LOOK AT THIS... THE STREETS ARE FRIGGING DESERTED. YOU CALL THIS A SITUATION IN CONTROL?
WHAT ARE WE NOW, THREE SHOPPING DAYS 'TIL CHRISTMAS?
FOUR, I THINK...
BEEN ON THE CLOCK SO LONG NOW I'M LOSING TRACK...
YOU AND ME BOTH, MILLHOUSE.
I BETTER GET BACK TO THE DESK, LIEUTENANT.
YEAH, I'M GONNA FINISH THIS...
...AND MAYBE ONE MORE AFTER THAT.
PARDON ME, OFFICER...

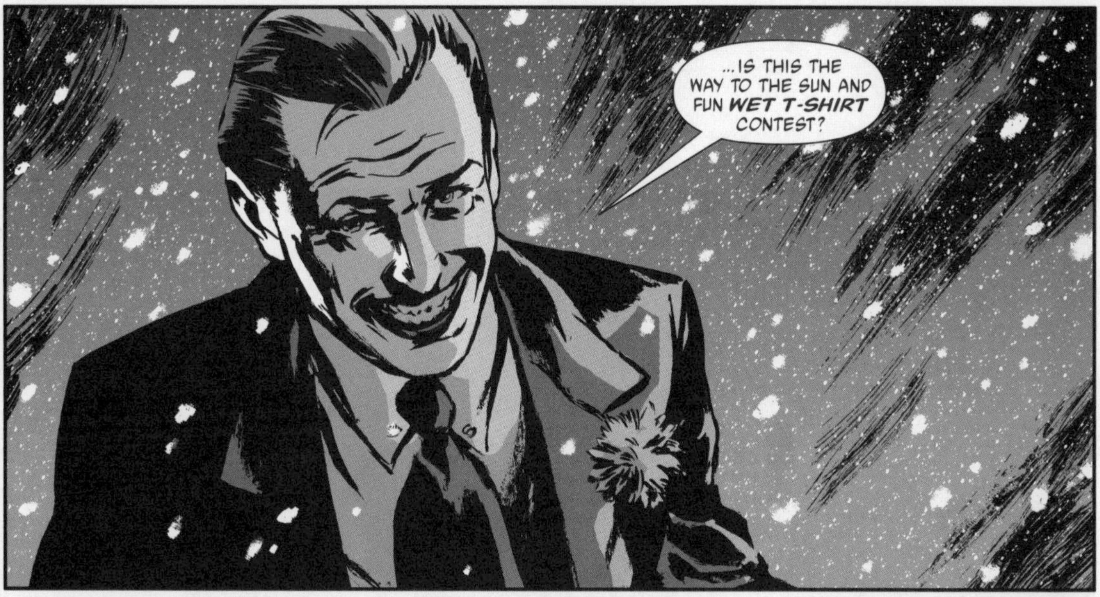
...IS THIS THE WAY TO THE SUN AND FUN WET T-SHIRT CONTEST?

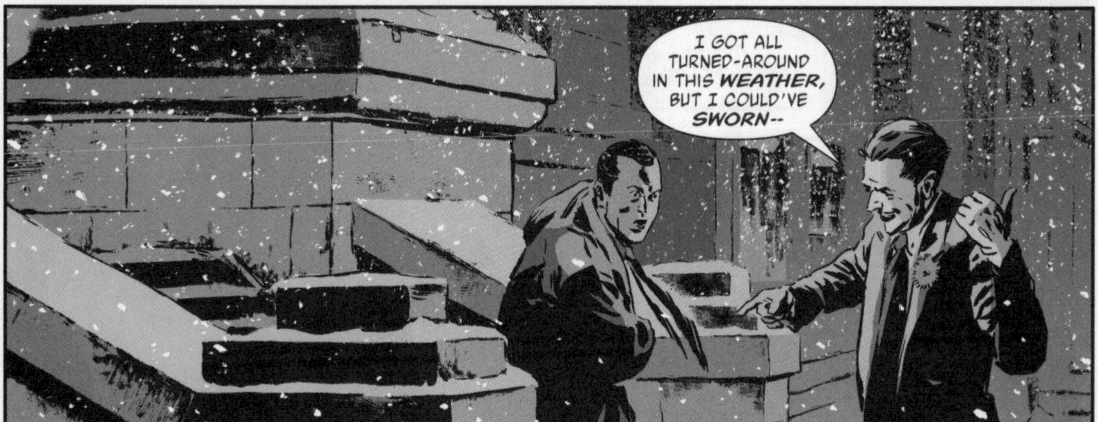
I GOT ALL TURNED-AROUND IN THIS WEATHER, BUT I COULD'VE SWORN--

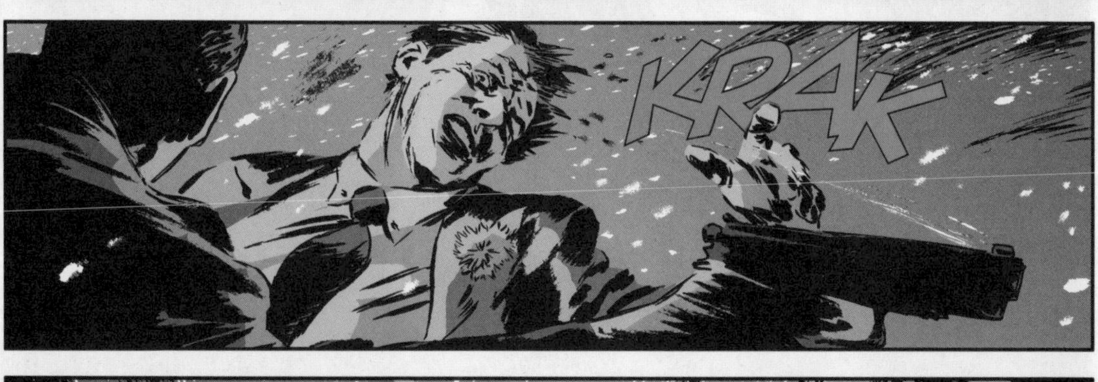
KRAK

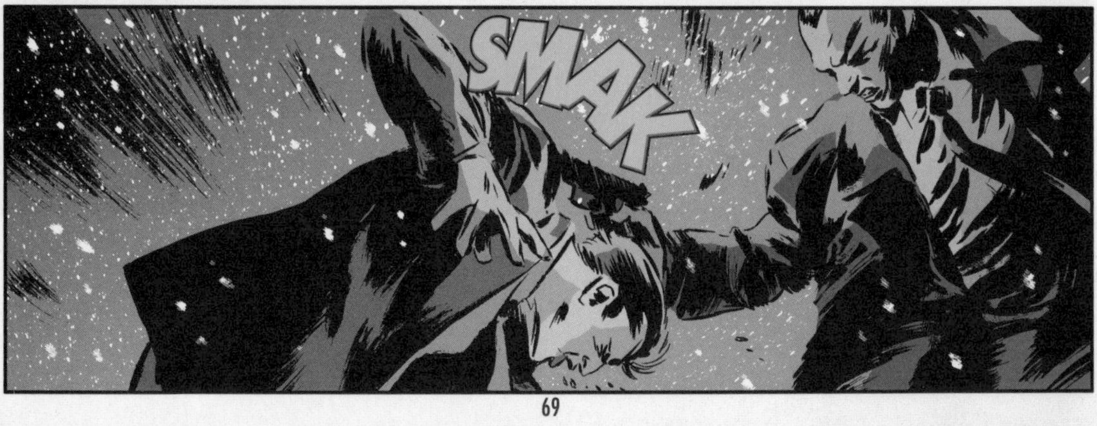
SMAK

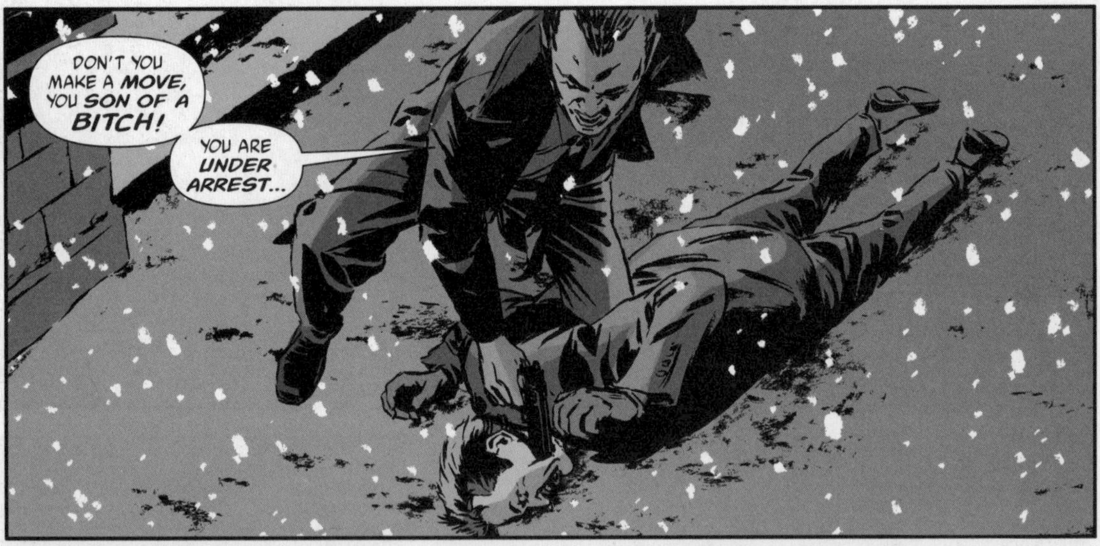
DON'T YOU MAKE A MOVE, YOU SON OF A BITCH!
YOU ARE UNDER ARREST...

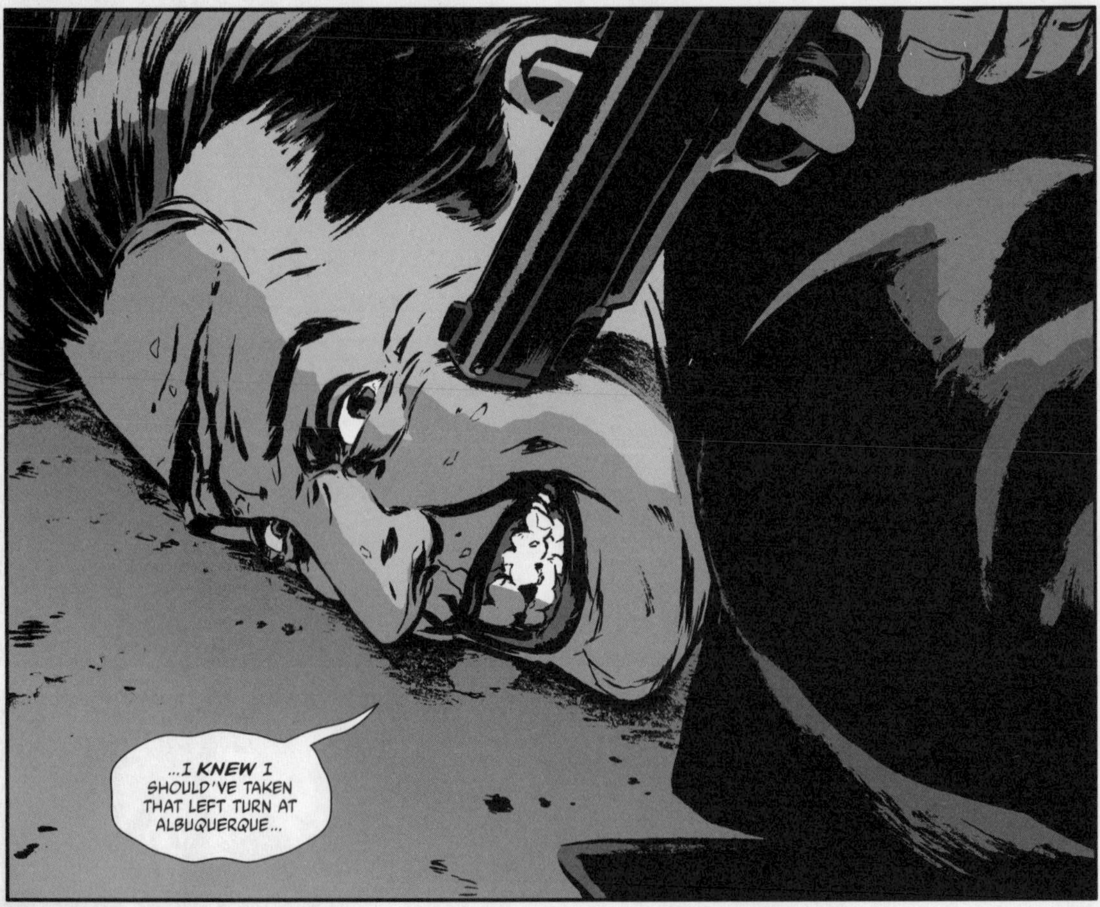
...I KNEW I SHOULD'VE TAKEN THAT LEFT TURN AT ALBUQUERQUE...

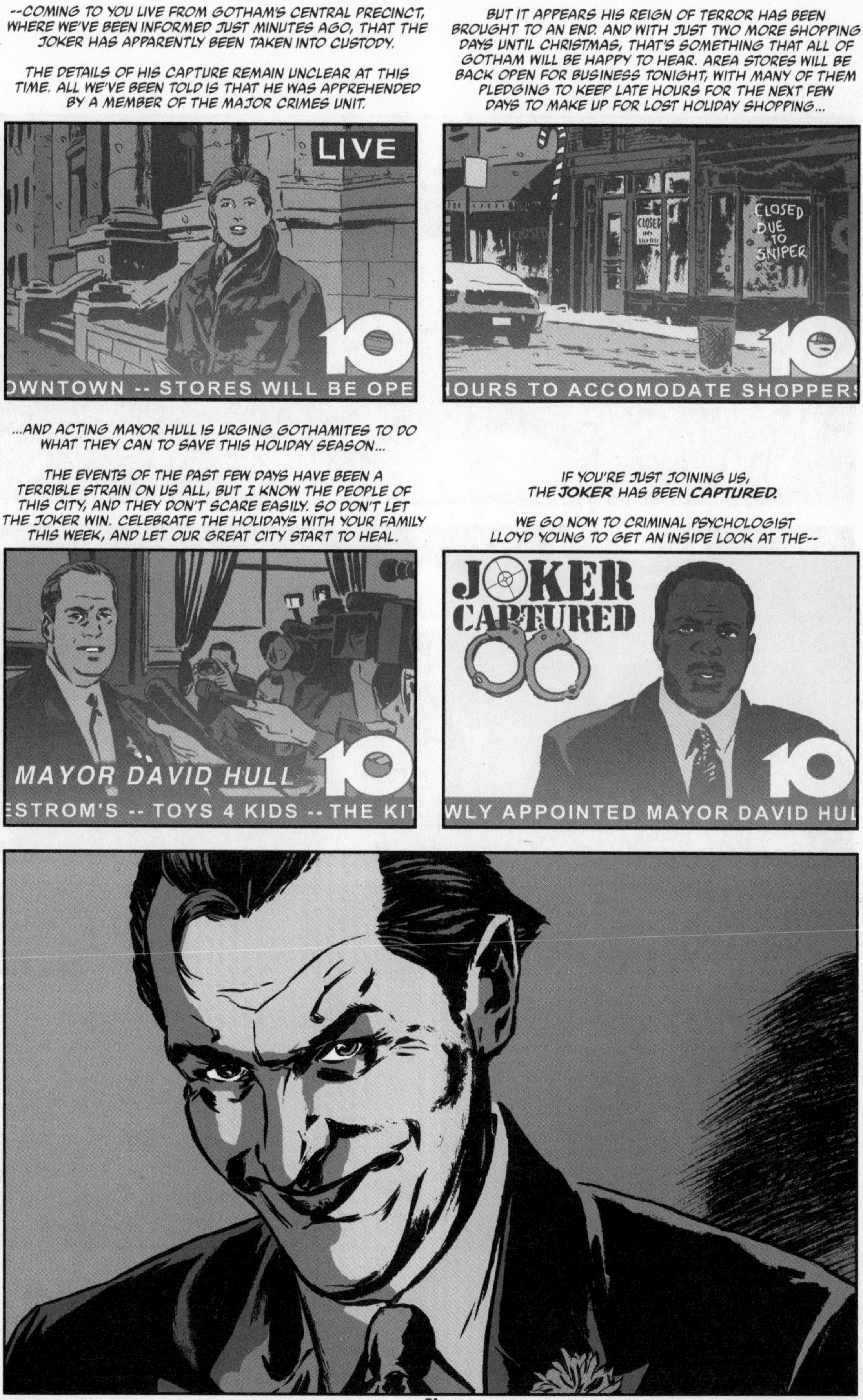
--COMING TO YOU LIVE FROM GOTHAM'S CENTRAL PRECINCT, WHERE WE'VE BEEN INFORMED JUST MINUTES AGO, THAT THE JOKER HAS APPARENTLY BEEN TAKEN INTO CUSTODY.
THE DETAILS OF HIS CAPTURE REMAIN UNCLEAR AT THIS TIME. ALL WE'VE BEEN TOLD IS THAT HE WAS APPREHENDED BY A MEMBER OF THE MAJOR CRIMES UNIT.
LIVE
10
OWNTOWN -- STORES WILL BE OPE
BUT IT APPEARS HIS REIGN OF TERROR HAS BEEN BROUGHT TO AN END. AND WITH JUST TWO MORE SHOPPING DAYS UNTIL CHRISTMAS, THAT'S SOMETHING THAT ALL OF GOTHAM WILL BE HAPPY TO HEAR. AREA STORES WILL BE BACK OPEN FOR BUSINESS TONIGHT, WITH MANY OF THEM PLEDGING TO KEEP LATE HOURS FOR THE NEXT FEW DAYS TO MAKE UP FOR LOST HOLIDAY SHOPPING...
CLOSED
CLOSED
CLOSED DUE TO SNIPER
10
IOURS TO ACCOMODATE SHOPPERS
...AND ACTING MAYOR HULL IS URGING GOTHAMITES TO DO WHAT THEY CAN TO SAVE THIS HOLIDAY SEASON...
THE EVENTS OF THE PAST FEW DAYS HAVE BEEN A TERRIBLE STRAIN ON US ALL, BUT I KNOW THE PEOPLE OF THIS CITY, AND THEY DON'T SCARE EASILY. SO DON'T LET THE JOKER WIN. CELEBRATE THE HOLIDAYS WITH YOUR FAMILY THIS WEEK, AND LET OUR GREAT CITY START TO HEAL.
MAYOR DAVID HULL
10
ESTROM'S -- TOYS 4 KIDS -- THE KIT
IF YOU'RE JUST JOINING US, THE JOKER HAS BEEN CAPTURED.
WE GO NOW TO CRIMINAL PSYCHOLOGIST LLOYD YOUNG TO GET AN INSIDE LOOK AT THE--
JOKER CAPTURED
10
WLY APPOINTED MAYOR DAVID HUL

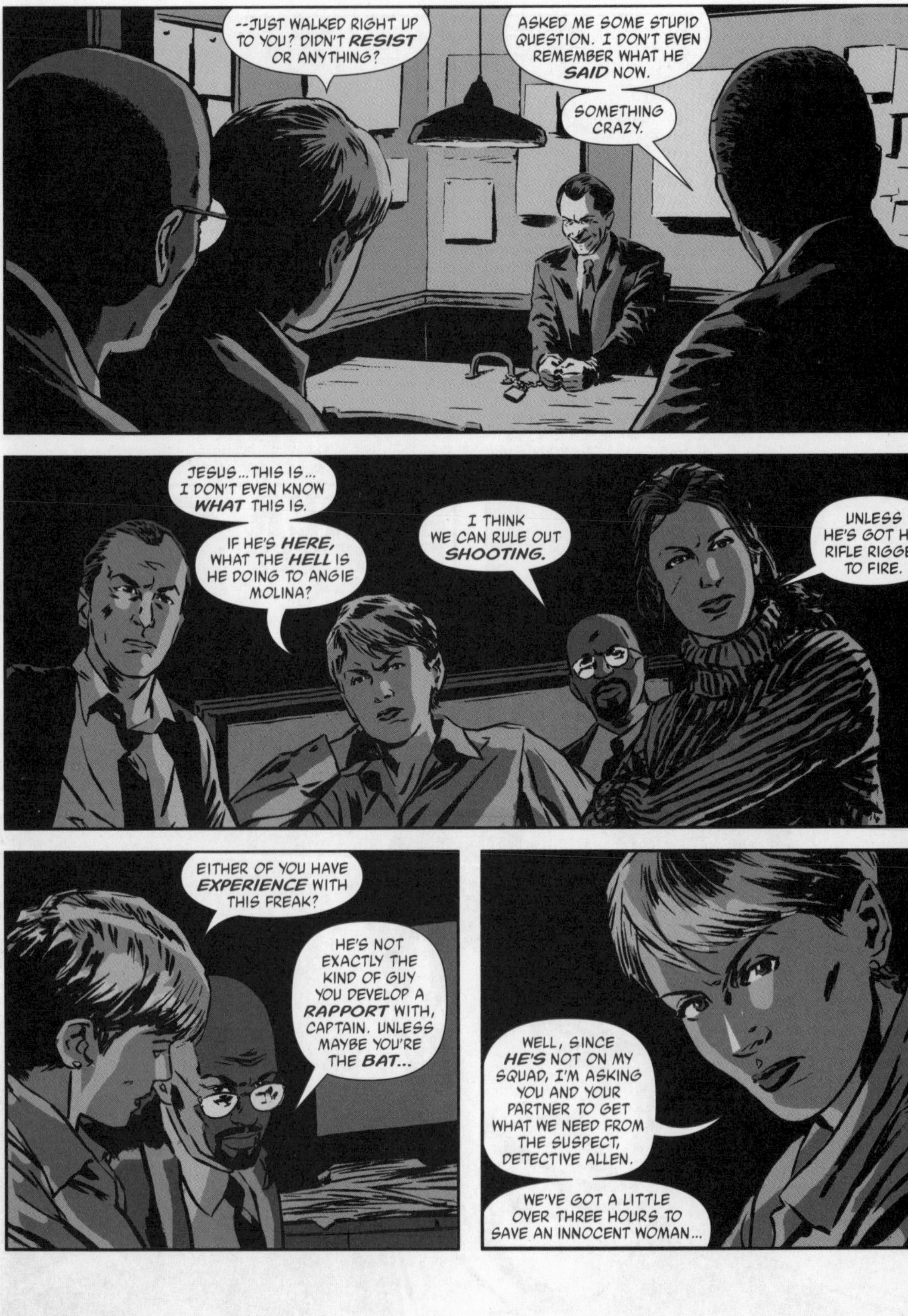
--JUST WALKED RIGHT UP TO YOU? DIDN'T RESIST OR ANYTHING?
ASKED ME SOME STUPID QUESTION. I DON'T EVEN REMEMBER WHAT HE SAID NOW.
SOMETHING CRAZY.
JESUS...THIS IS... I DON'T EVEN KNOW WHAT THIS IS.
IF HE'S HERE, WHAT THE HELL IS HE DOING TO ANGIE MOLINA?
I THINK WE CAN RULE OUT SHOOTING.
UNLESS HE'S GOT HIS RIFLE RIGGED TO FIRE.
EITHER OF YOU HAVE EXPERIENCE WITH THIS FREAK?
HE'S NOT EXACTLY THE KIND OF GUY YOU DEVELOP A RAPPORT WITH, CAPTAIN. UNLESS MAYBE YOU'RE THE BAT...
WELL, SINCE HE'S NOT ON MY SQUAD, I'M ASKING YOU AND YOUR PARTNER TO GET WHAT WE NEED FROM THE SUSPECT, DETECTIVE ALLEN.
WE'VE GOT A LITTLE OVER THREE HOURS TO SAVE AN INNOCENT WOMAN...

NORMALLY I'D OFFER YOU A DRINK OR SOMETHING, BUT IN THIS CASE, YOU KNOW, I THINK WE CAN JUST SKIP THE BULL$#%...

AN ICED TEA WOULD BE *FANTASTIC.* I DON'T KNOW ABOUT YOU, BUT I'VE ALWAYS FOUND POLICE BRUTALITY REALLY MAKES YOU THIRSTY.

WHO CAN SAY WHY?

YEAH, OUR HEARTS BLEED FOR YOUR SUFFERING. LET ME JUST GET THE FORMS FOR YOU TO FILE A COMPLAINT.

OOOH... YOU'RE FUNNY. I *LIKE* YOU.

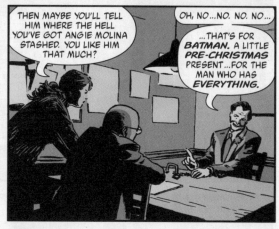

THEN MAYBE YOU'LL TELL HIM WHERE THE HELL YOU'VE GOT ANGIE MOLINA STASHED. YOU LIKE HIM THAT MUCH?

OH, NO...NO. NO. NO...

...THAT'S FOR *BATMAN.* A LITTLE *PRE-CHRISTMAS* PRESENT...FOR THE MAN WHO HAS *EVERYTHING.*

HOW 'BOUT THIS? YOU TELL *ME* WHERE SHE IS AND *I'LL* TELL HIM WHERE HE CAN PICK UP HIS PRESENT.

WOW, YOU'D DO THAT FOR *ME?* I THINK I'M GONNA CRY. MY *NEW* BEST FRIEND. I TOLD THEM I WAS DOWN WITH THE HOMEBOYS.

ALMOST MAKES ME SORRY I CAN'T HELP YOU, PAL O'MINE. BUT I NEVER SERVE A WINE BEFORE ITS *TIME.*

AFRAID YOU LOST ME. WE'RE TALKING ABOUT A WOMAN, RIGHT?

NOT A WOMAN, A *NEWSCASTER.* KEE-RYST, WHAT PLANET ARE *YOU* FROM? I MEAN, HELLOOO? DO YOU *OWN* A TV?

SO, OKAY, IT'S NOT ANGIE'S TIME YET? WHEN WILL SHE BE *READY,* THEN?

GEEZ. MISTER IMPATIENT...WHEN IS ANYTHING *EVER* READY? WHEN THE TIMER GOES *DING.*

OR, IN THIS CASE... BOOM.

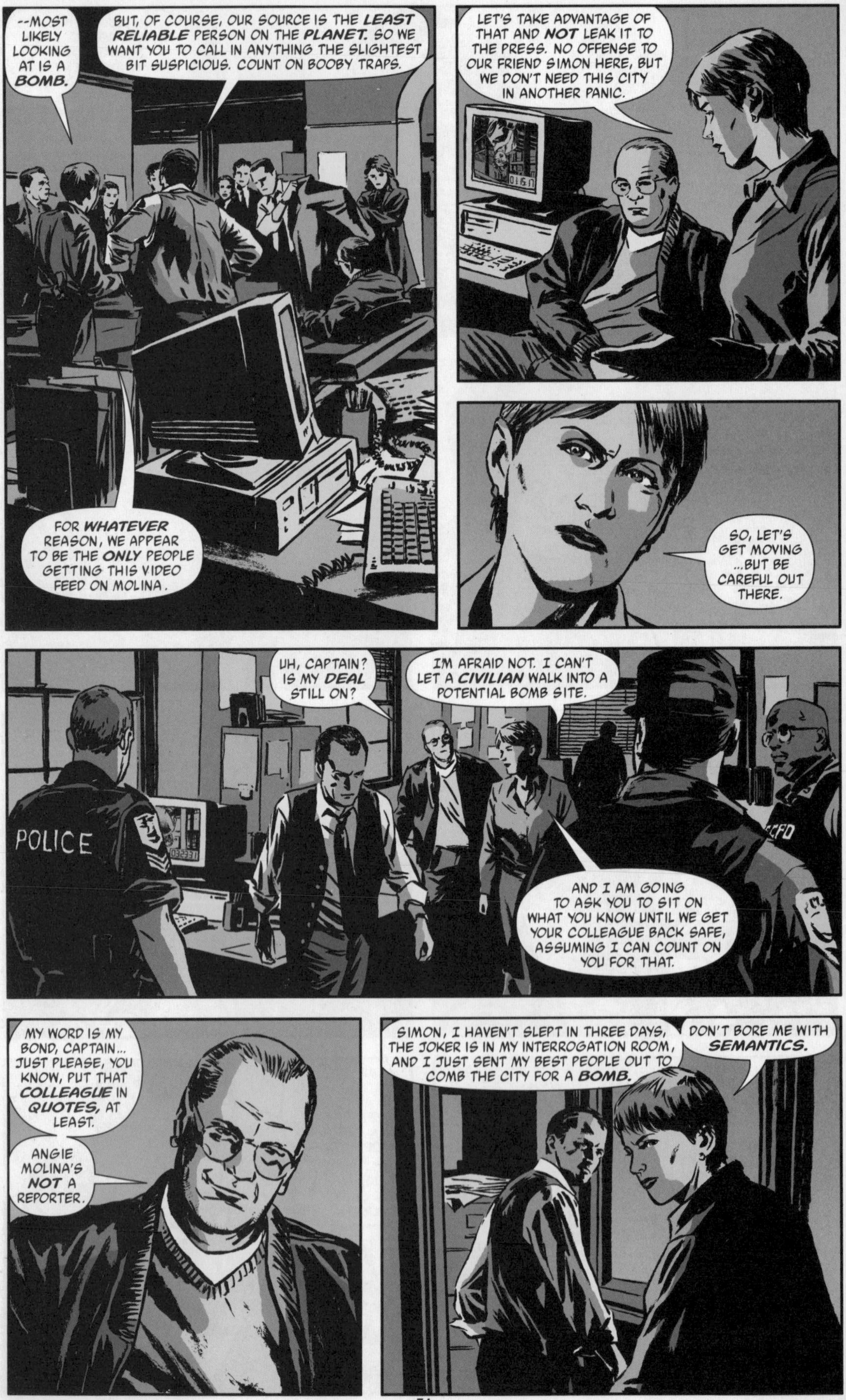
--MOST LIKELY LOOKING AT IS A BOMB.
BUT, OF COURSE, OUR SOURCE IS THE LEAST RELIABLE PERSON ON THE PLANET. SO WE WANT YOU TO CALL IN ANYTHING THE SLIGHTEST BIT SUSPICIOUS. COUNT ON BOOBY TRAPS.
FOR WHATEVER REASON, WE APPEAR TO BE THE ONLY PEOPLE GETTING THIS VIDEO FEED ON MOLINA.
LET'S TAKE ADVANTAGE OF THAT AND NOT LEAK IT TO THE PRESS. NO OFFENSE TO OUR FRIEND SIMON HERE, BUT WE DON'T NEED THIS CITY IN ANOTHER PANIC.
SO, LET'S GET MOVING ...BUT BE CAREFUL OUT THERE.
UH, CAPTAIN? IS MY DEAL STILL ON?
I'M AFRAID NOT. I CAN'T LET A CIVILIAN WALK INTO A POTENTIAL BOMB SITE.
AND I AM GOING TO ASK YOU TO SIT ON WHAT YOU KNOW UNTIL WE GET YOUR COLLEAGUE BACK SAFE, ASSUMING I CAN COUNT ON YOU FOR THAT.
POLICE
MY WORD IS MY BOND, CAPTAIN... JUST PLEASE, YOU KNOW, PUT THAT COLLEAGUE IN QUOTES, AT LEAST.
ANGIE MOLINA'S NOT A REPORTER.
SIMON, I HAVEN'T SLEPT IN THREE DAYS, THE JOKER IS IN MY INTERROGATION ROOM, AND I JUST SENT MY BEST PEOPLE OUT TO COMB THE CITY FOR A BOMB.
DON'T BORE ME WITH SEMANTICS.

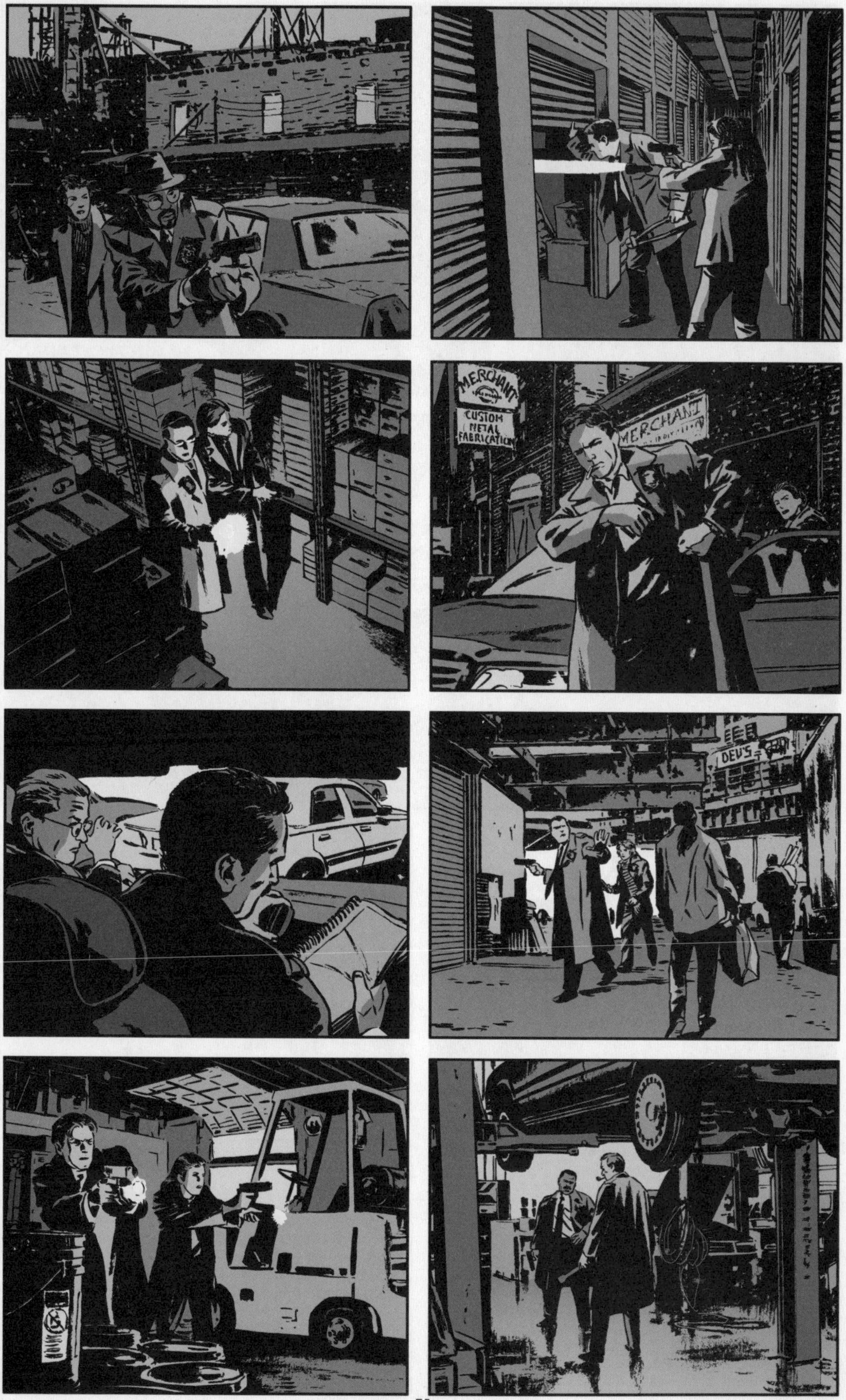
MERCHANT
CUSTOM METAL FABRICATION
MERCHANT
DEU'S

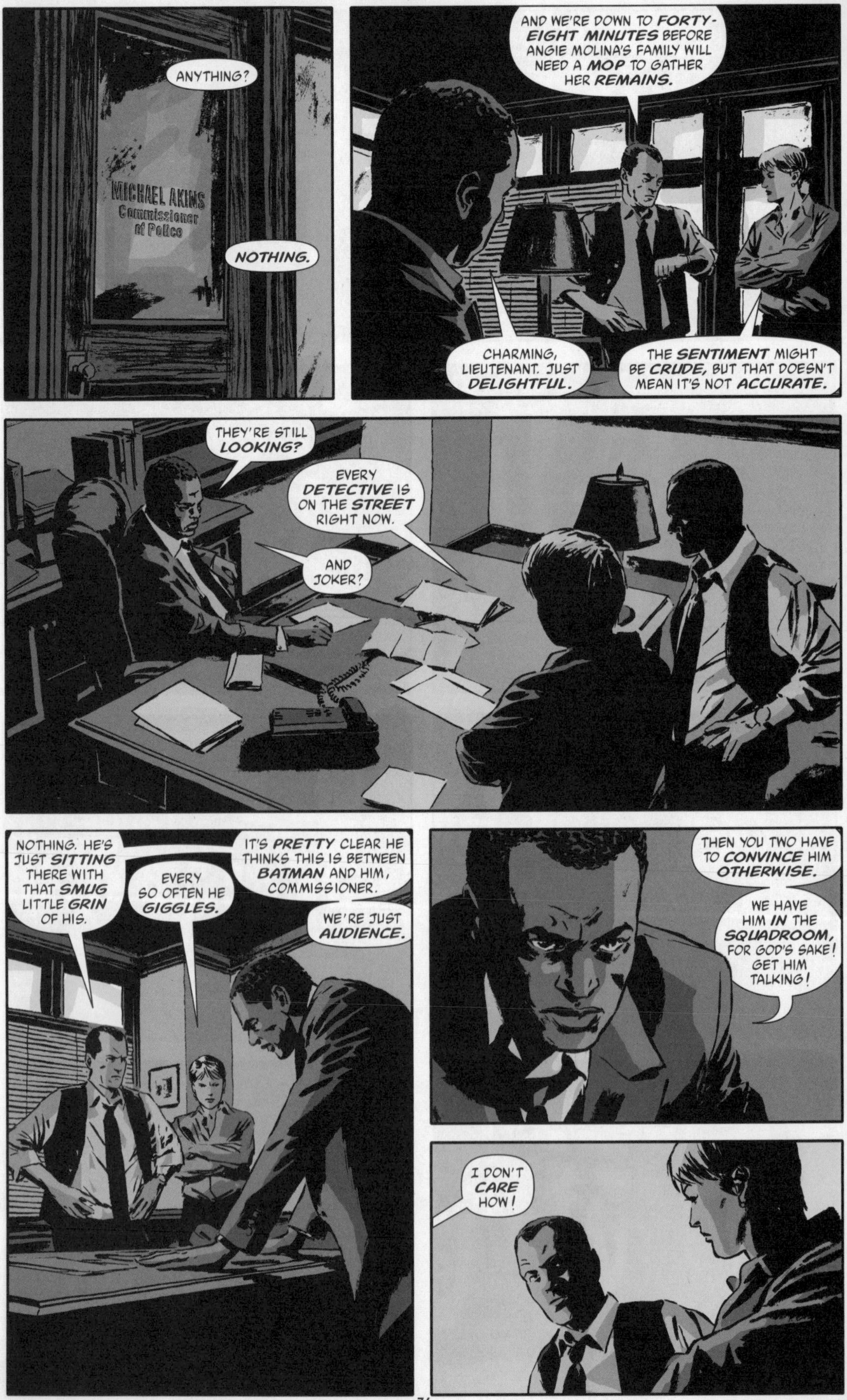
ANYTHING?
NOTHING.
MICHAEL AKINS
Commissioner
of Police
AND WE'RE DOWN TO FORTY-EIGHT MINUTES BEFORE ANGIE MOLINA'S FAMILY WILL NEED A MOP TO GATHER HER REMAINS.
CHARMING, LIEUTENANT. JUST DELIGHTFUL.
THE SENTIMENT MIGHT BE CRUDE, BUT THAT DOESN'T MEAN IT'S NOT ACCURATE.
THEY'RE STILL LOOKING?
EVERY DETECTIVE IS ON THE STREET RIGHT NOW.
AND JOKER?
NOTHING. HE'S JUST SITTING THERE WITH THAT SMUG LITTLE GRIN OF HIS.
EVERY SO OFTEN HE GIGGLES.
IT'S PRETTY CLEAR HE THINKS THIS IS BETWEEN BATMAN AND HIM, COMMISSIONER.
WE'RE JUST AUDIENCE.
THEN YOU TWO HAVE TO CONVINCE HIM OTHERWISE.
WE HAVE HIM IN THE SQUADROOM, FOR GOD'S SAKE! GET HIM TALKING!
I DON'T CARE HOW!

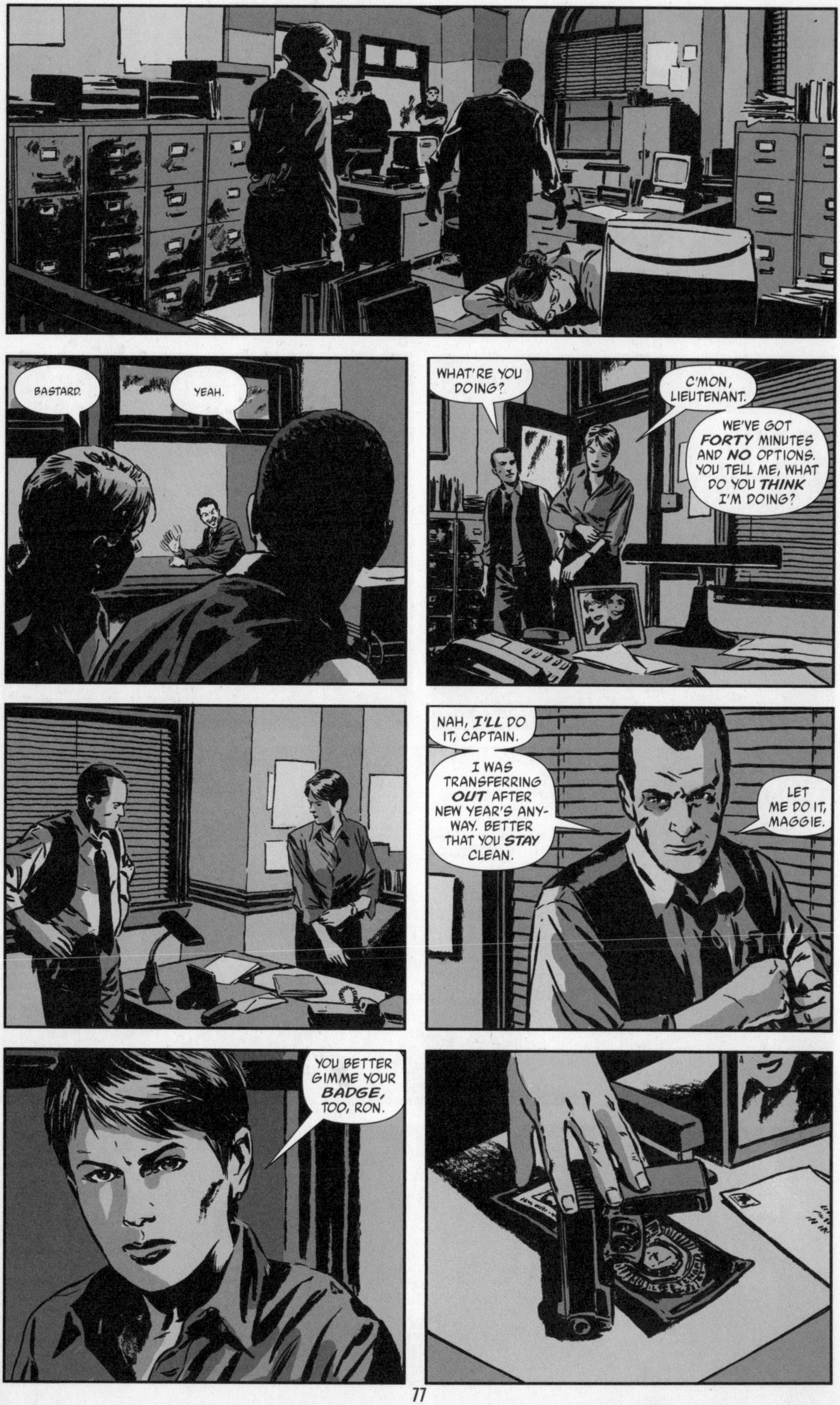
BASTARD.
YEAH.
WHAT'RE YOU DOING?
C'MON, LIEUTENANT.
WE'VE GOT FORTY MINUTES AND NO OPTIONS. YOU TELL ME, WHAT DO YOU THINK I'M DOING?
NAH, I'LL DO IT, CAPTAIN.
I WAS TRANSFERRING OUT AFTER NEW YEAR'S ANYWAY. BETTER THAT YOU STAY CLEAN.
LET ME DO IT, MAGGIE.
YOU BETTER GIMME YOUR BADGE, TOO, RON.

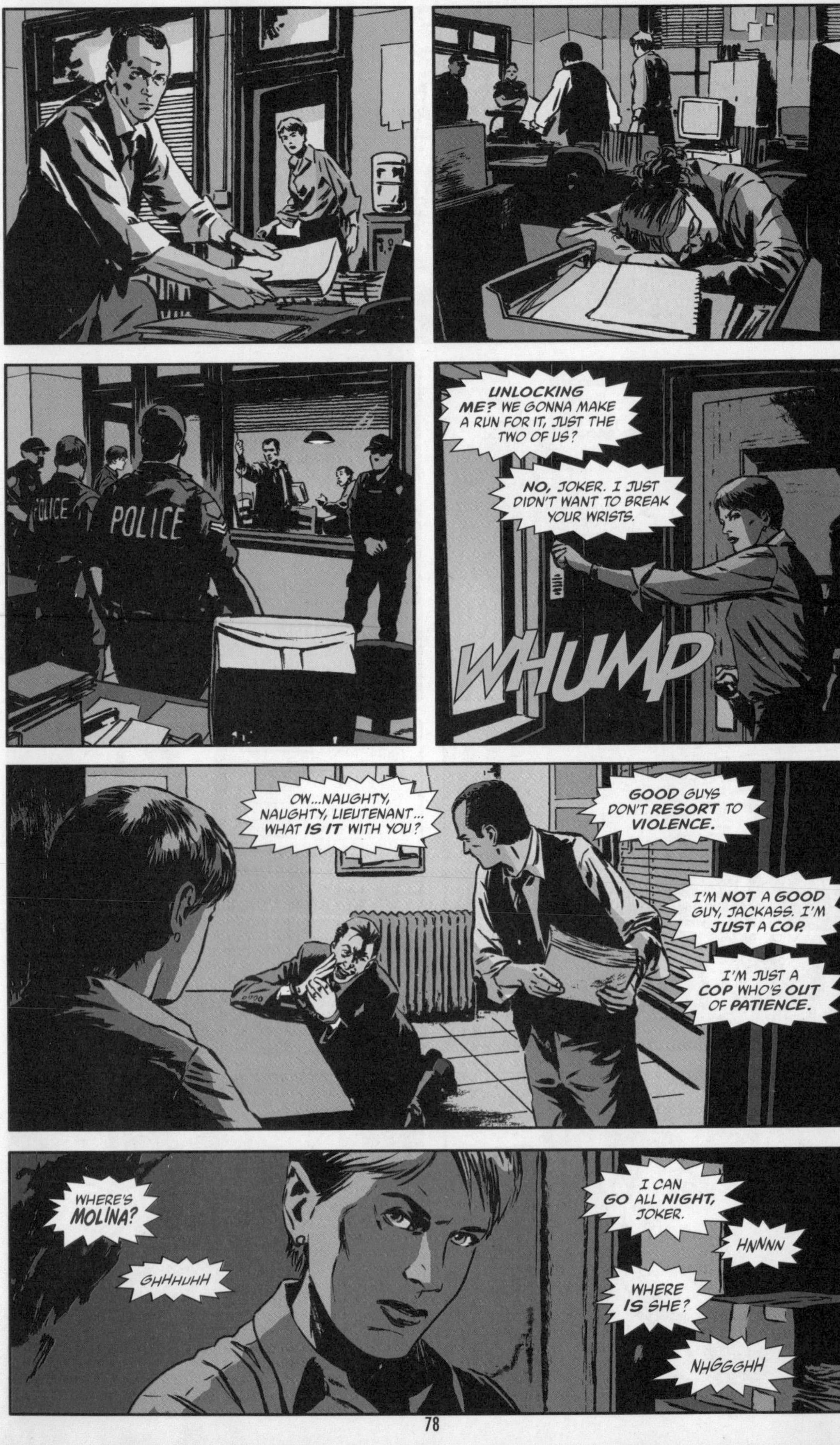

UNLOCKING ME? WE GONNA MAKE A RUN FOR IT, JUST THE TWO OF US?
NO, JOKER. I JUST DIDN'T WANT TO BREAK YOUR WRISTS.
WHUMP
OW...NAUGHTY, NAUGHTY, LIEUTENANT... WHAT IS IT WITH YOU?
GOOD GUYS DON'T RESORT TO VIOLENCE.
I'M NOT A GOOD GUY, JACKASS. I'M JUST A COP.
I'M JUST A COP WHO'S OUT OF PATIENCE.
WHERE'S MOLINA?
GHHHUHH
I CAN GO ALL NIGHT, JOKER.
HNNNN
WHERE IS SHE?
NHGGGHH

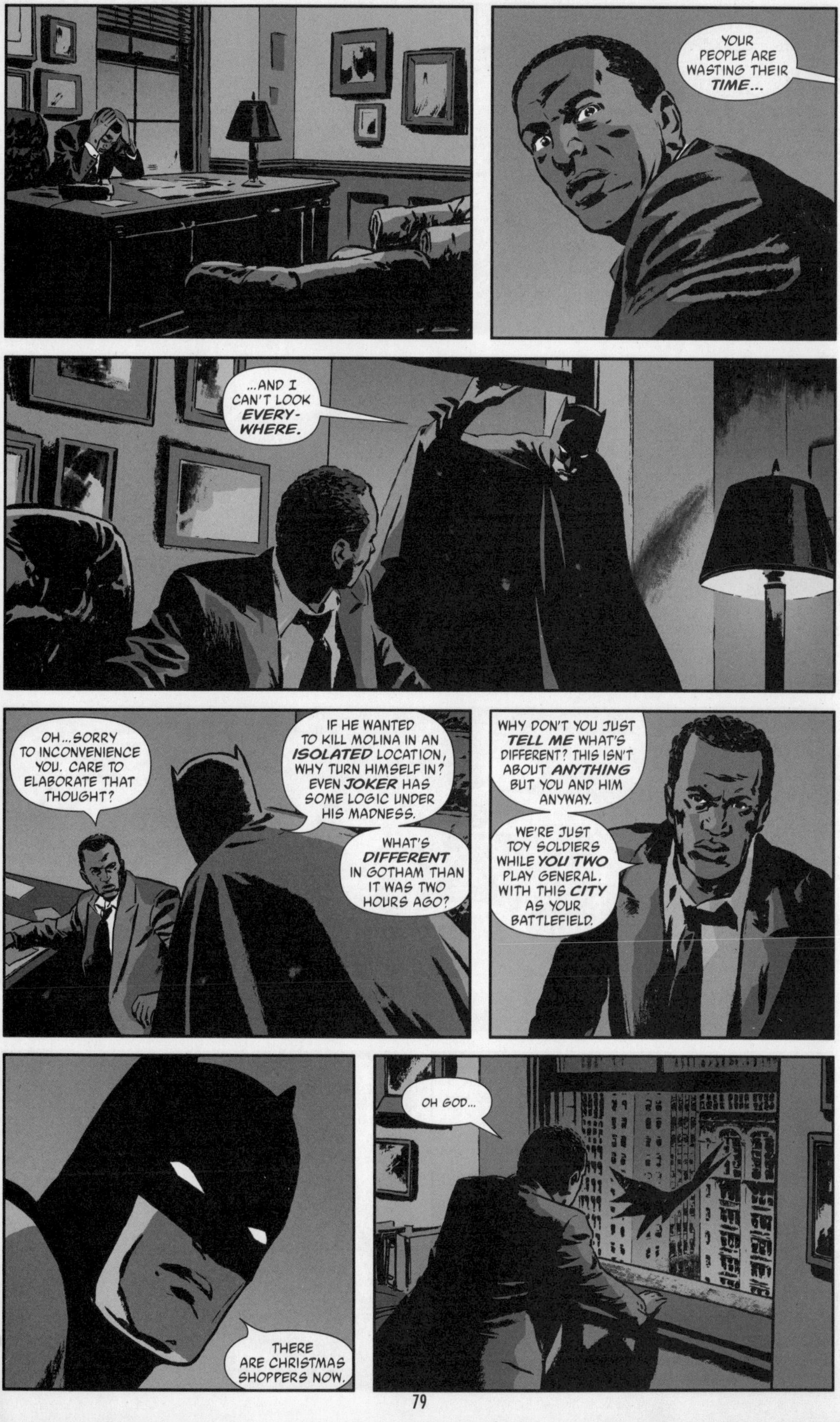
YOUR PEOPLE ARE WASTING THEIR TIME...
...AND I CAN'T LOOK EVERY-WHERE.
OH...SORRY TO INCONVENIENCE YOU. CARE TO ELABORATE THAT THOUGHT?
IF HE WANTED TO KILL MOLINA IN AN ISOLATED LOCATION, WHY TURN HIMSELF IN? EVEN JOKER HAS SOME LOGIC UNDER HIS MADNESS.
WHAT'S DIFFERENT IN GOTHAM THAN IT WAS TWO HOURS AGO?
WHY DON'T YOU JUST TELL ME WHAT'S DIFFERENT? THIS ISN'T ABOUT ANYTHING BUT YOU AND HIM ANYWAY.
WE'RE JUST TOY SOLDIERS WHILE YOU TWO PLAY GENERAL. WITH THIS CITY AS YOUR BATTLEFIELD.
THERE ARE CHRISTMAS SHOPPERS NOW.
OH GOD...

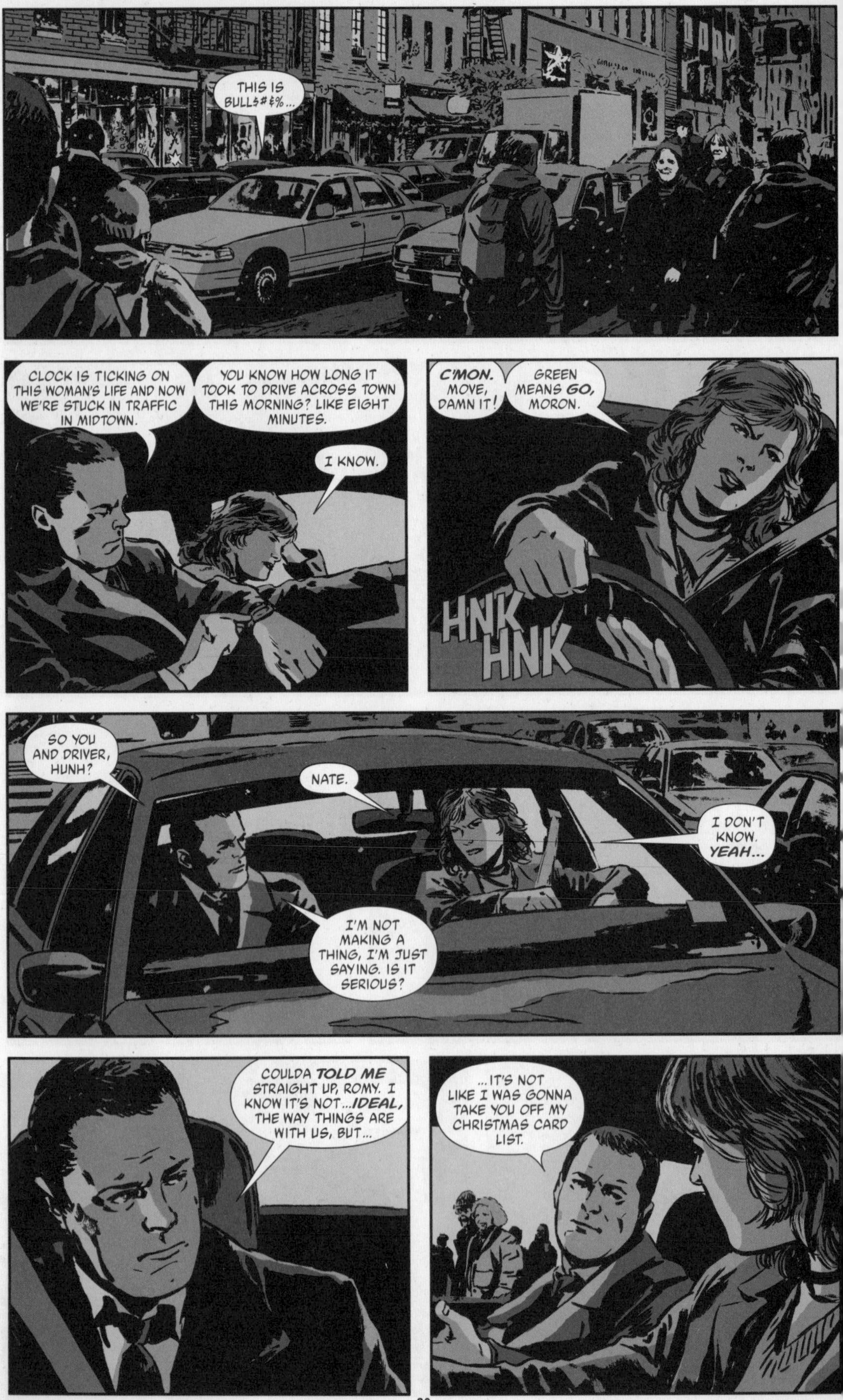
THIS IS BULL$#&%...
CLOCK IS TICKING ON THIS WOMAN'S LIFE AND NOW WE'RE STUCK IN TRAFFIC IN MIDTOWN.
YOU KNOW HOW LONG IT TOOK TO DRIVE ACROSS TOWN THIS MORNING? LIKE EIGHT MINUTES.
I KNOW.
C'MON. MOVE, DAMN IT!
GREEN MEANS GO, MORON.
HNK HNK
SO YOU AND DRIVER, HUNH?
NATE.
I DON'T KNOW. YEAH...
I'M NOT MAKING A THING, I'M JUST SAYING. IS IT SERIOUS?
COULDA TOLD ME STRAIGHT UP, ROMY. I KNOW IT'S NOT...IDEAL, THE WAY THINGS ARE WITH US, BUT...
...IT'S NOT LIKE I WAS GONNA TAKE YOU OFF MY CHRISTMAS CARD LIST.

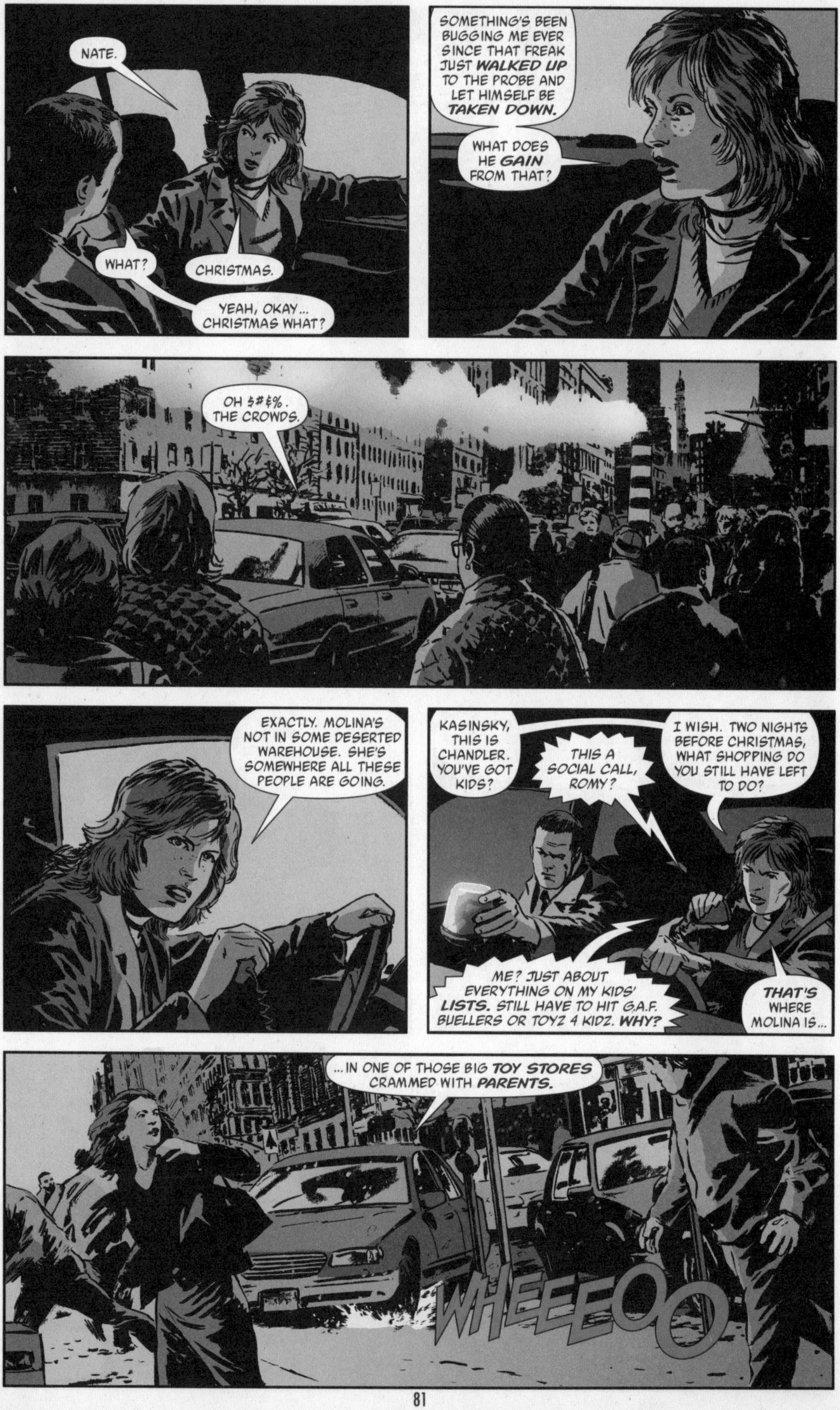
NATE.
WHAT?
CHRISTMAS.
YEAH, OKAY... CHRISTMAS WHAT?
SOMETHING'S BEEN BUGGING ME EVER SINCE THAT FREAK JUST WALKED UP TO THE PROBE AND LET HIMSELF BE TAKEN DOWN.
WHAT DOES HE GAIN FROM THAT?
OH $#&%. THE CROWDS.
EXACTLY. MOLINA'S NOT IN SOME DESERTED WAREHOUSE. SHE'S SOMEWHERE ALL THESE PEOPLE ARE GOING.
KASINSKY, THIS IS CHANDLER. YOU'VE GOT KIDS?
THIS A SOCIAL CALL, ROMY?
I WISH. TWO NIGHTS BEFORE CHRISTMAS, WHAT SHOPPING DO YOU STILL HAVE LEFT TO DO?
ME? JUST ABOUT EVERYTHING ON MY KIDS' LISTS. STILL HAVE TO HIT G.A.F. BUELLERS OR TOYZ 4 KIDZ. WHY?
THAT'S WHERE MOLINA IS...
...IN ONE OF THOSE BIG TOY STORES CRAMMED WITH PARENTS.
WHEEEOO

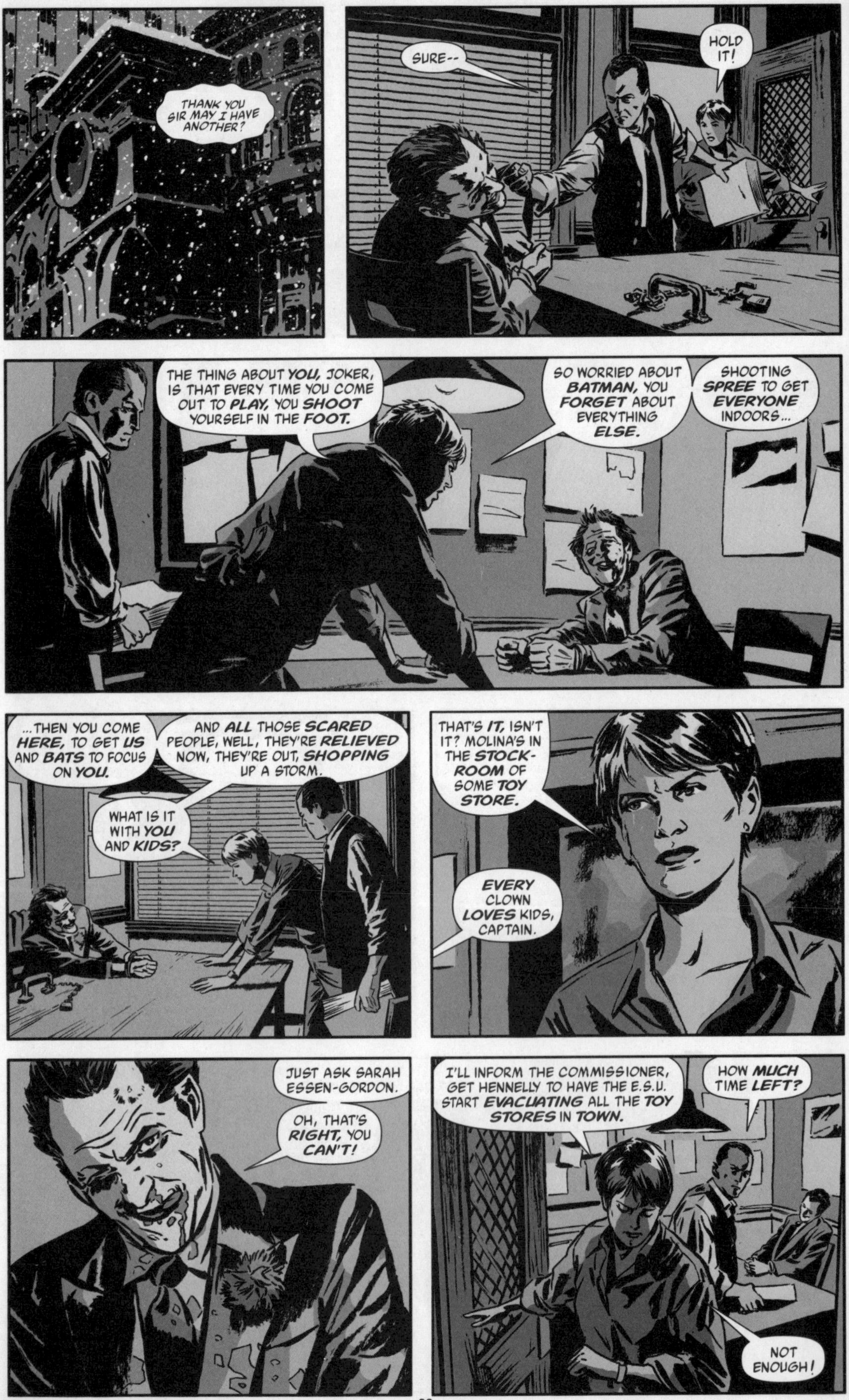
THANK YOU SIR MAY I HAVE ANOTHER?
SURE--
HOLD IT!
THE THING ABOUT YOU, JOKER, IS THAT EVERY TIME YOU COME OUT TO PLAY, YOU SHOOT YOURSELF IN THE FOOT.
SO WORRIED ABOUT BATMAN, YOU FORGET ABOUT EVERYTHING ELSE.
SHOOTING SPREE TO GET EVERYONE INDOORS...
...THEN YOU COME HERE, TO GET US AND BATS TO FOCUS ON YOU.
AND ALL THOSE SCARED PEOPLE, WELL, THEY'RE RELIEVED NOW, THEY'RE OUT, SHOPPING UP A STORM.
WHAT IS IT WITH YOU AND KIDS?
THAT'S IT, ISN'T IT? MOLINA'S IN THE STOCK-ROOM OF SOME TOY STORE.
EVERY CLOWN LOVES KIDS, CAPTAIN.
JUST ASK SARAH ESSEN-GORDON.
OH, THAT'S RIGHT, YOU CAN'T!
I'LL INFORM THE COMMISSIONER, GET HENNELLY TO HAVE THE E.S.U. START EVACUATING ALL THE TOY STORES IN TOWN.
HOW MUCH TIME LEFT?
NOT ENOUGH!

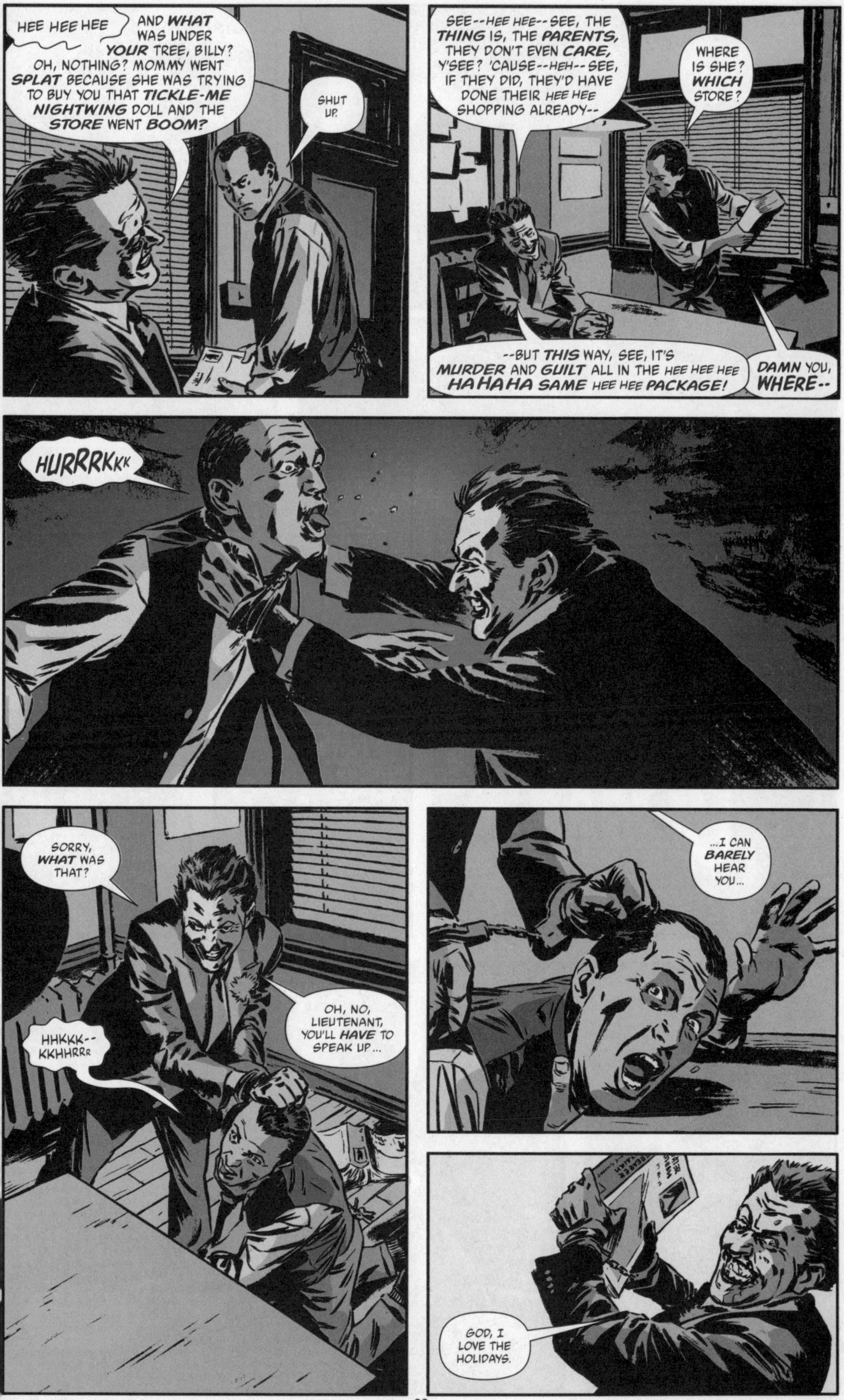
HEE HEE HEE
AND WHAT WAS UNDER YOUR TREE, BILLY? OH, NOTHING? MOMMY WENT SPLAT BECAUSE SHE WAS TRYING TO BUY YOU THAT TICKLE-ME NIGHTWING DOLL AND THE STORE WENT BOOM?
SHUT UP.
SEE--HEE HEE--SEE, THE THING IS, THE PARENTS, THEY DON'T EVEN CARE, Y'SEE? 'CAUSE--HEH--SEE, IF THEY DID, THEY'D HAVE DONE THEIR HEE HEE SHOPPING ALREADY--
WHERE IS SHE? WHICH STORE?
--BUT THIS WAY, SEE, IT'S MURDER AND GUILT ALL IN THE HEE HEE HEE HA HA HA SAME HEE HEE PACKAGE!
DAMN YOU, WHERE--
HURRRKKK
SORRY, WHAT WAS THAT?
OH, NO, LIEUTENANT, YOU'LL HAVE TO SPEAK UP...
HHKKK--KKHHRRR
...I CAN BARELY HEAR YOU...
GOD, I LOVE THE HOLIDAYS.

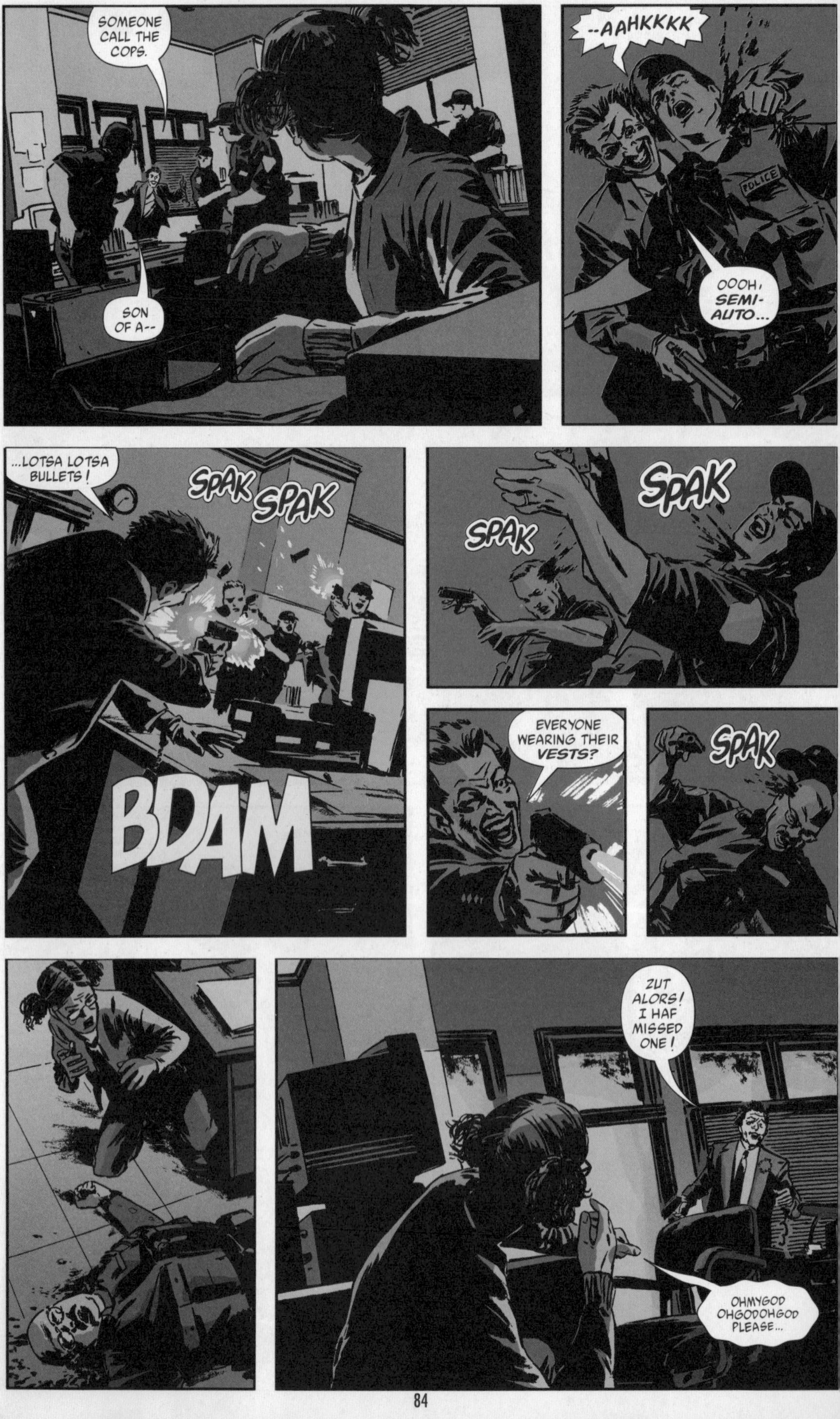
SOMEONE CALL THE COPS.
SON OF A--
--AAHKKKK
POLICE
OOOH, SEMI-AUTO...
...LOTSA LOTSA BULLETS!
SPAK SPAK
BDAM
SPAK
SPAK
EVERYONE WEARING THEIR VESTS?
SPAK
ZUT ALORS! I HAF MISSED ONE!
OHMYGOD OHGODOHGOD PLEASE...

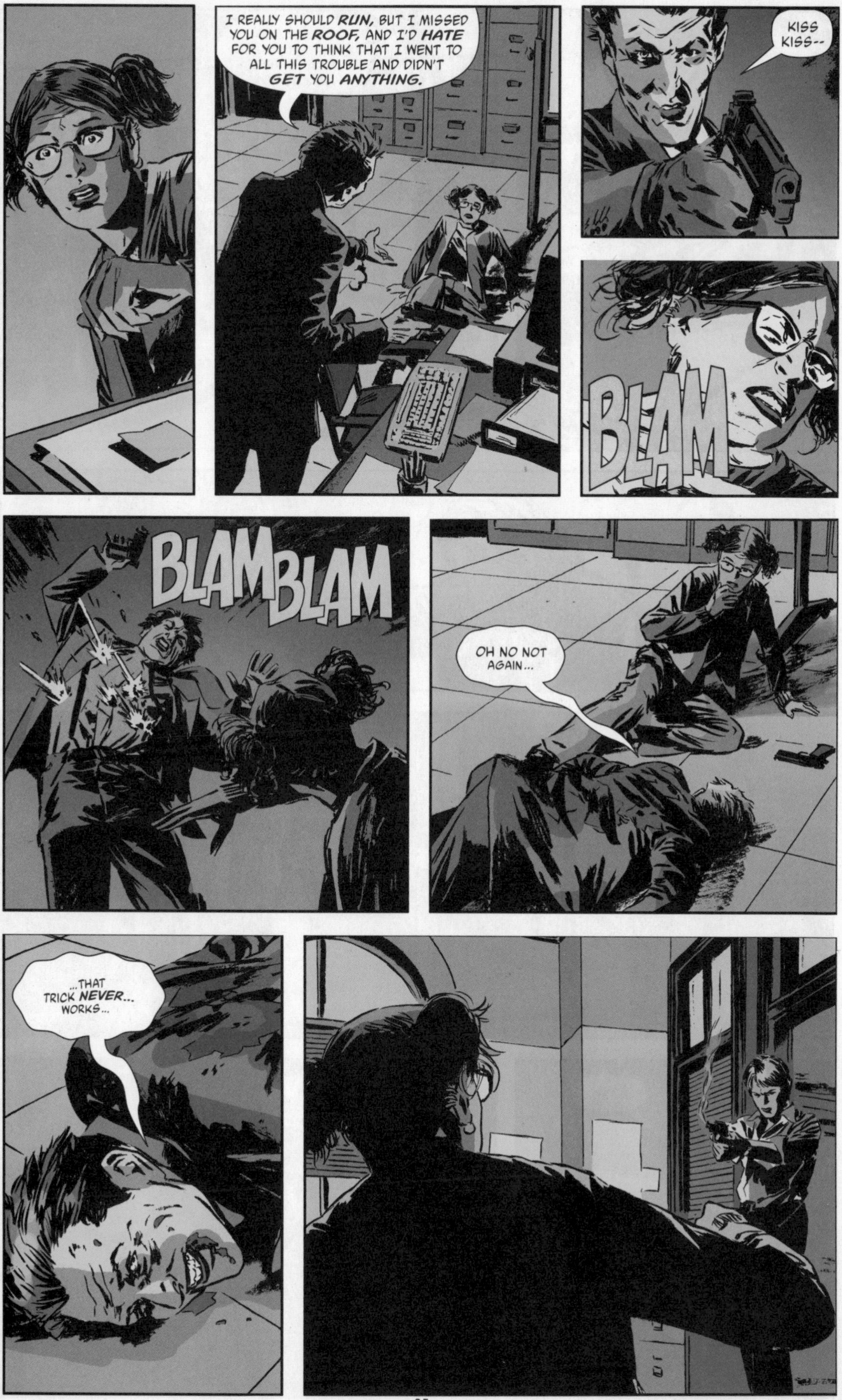
I REALLY SHOULD RUN, BUT I MISSED YOU ON THE ROOF, AND I'D HATE FOR YOU TO THINK THAT I WENT TO ALL THIS TROUBLE AND DIDN'T GET YOU ANYTHING.
KISS KISS--
BLAM
BLAMBLAM
OH NO NOT AGAIN...
...THAT TRICK NEVER... WORKS...

G.C.P.D. WHERE'S YOUR STOCK-ROOM?

WHAT? HEY, YOU CAN'T--

WHERE THE #$%*# IS YOUR GOD-DAMN STOCKROOM? NOW!

IT'S PAST ACTION FIGURES, ON THE FAR LEFT WALL. BUT YOU NEED A PASSCARD FOR THE DOOR--

I'LL GET THIS BACK TO YOU.

HEY!

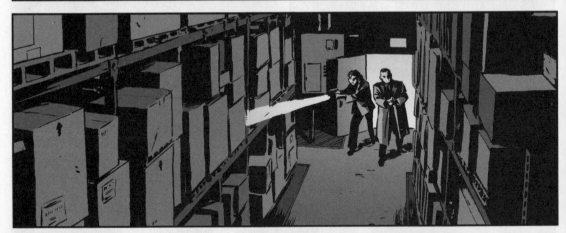

LISTEN...

--RUDOLPH WITH YOUR NOSE SO BRIGHT... ♪

THIS WAY!

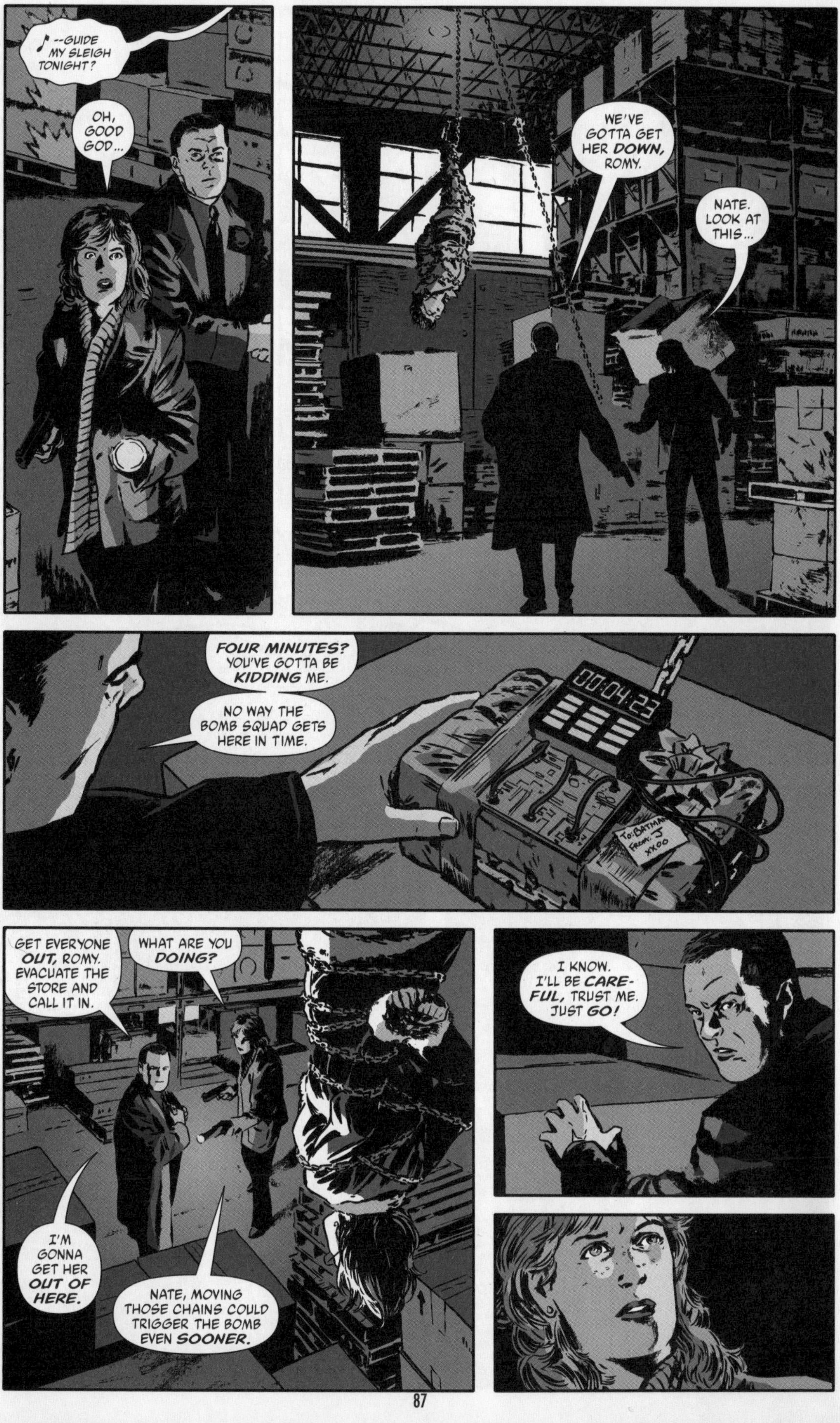
♪ --GUIDE MY SLEIGH TONIGHT?
OH, GOOD GOD...
WE'VE GOTTA GET HER DOWN, ROMY.
NATE. LOOK AT THIS...
FOUR MINUTES? YOU'VE GOTTA BE KIDDING ME.
NO WAY THE BOMB SQUAD GETS HERE IN TIME.
00:04:23
TO: BATMAN FROM: J XXOO
GET EVERYONE OUT, ROMY. EVACUATE THE STORE AND CALL IT IN.
WHAT ARE YOU DOING?
I'M GONNA GET HER OUT OF HERE.
NATE, MOVING THOSE CHAINS COULD TRIGGER THE BOMB EVEN SOONER.
I KNOW. I'LL BE CAREFUL, TRUST ME. JUST GO!

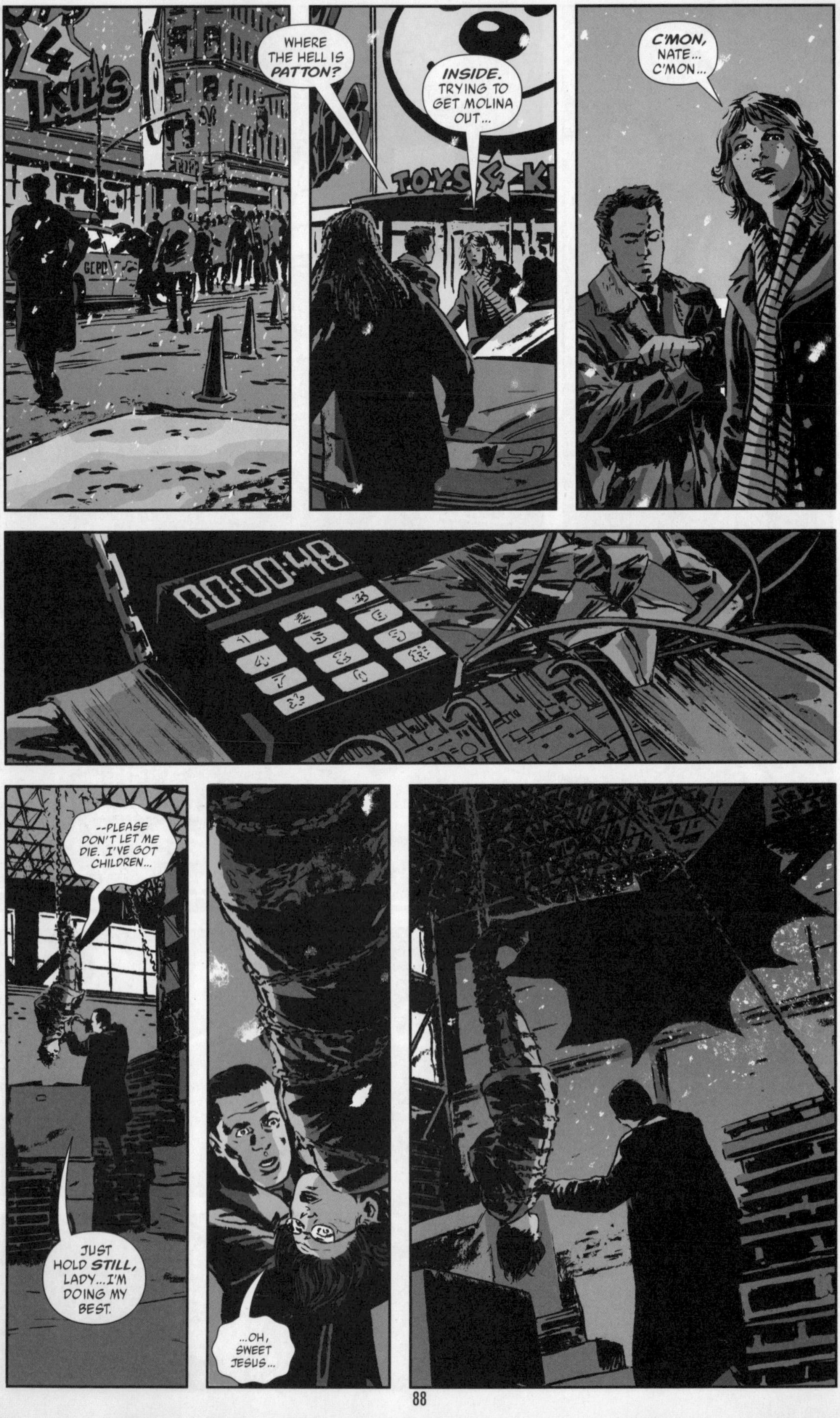
WHERE THE HELL IS PATTON?
INSIDE. TRYING TO GET MOLINA OUT...
C'MON, NATE... C'MON...
00:00:48
--PLEASE DON'T LET ME DIE. I'VE GOT CHILDREN...
JUST HOLD STILL, LADY...I'M DOING MY BEST.
...OH, SWEET JESUS...

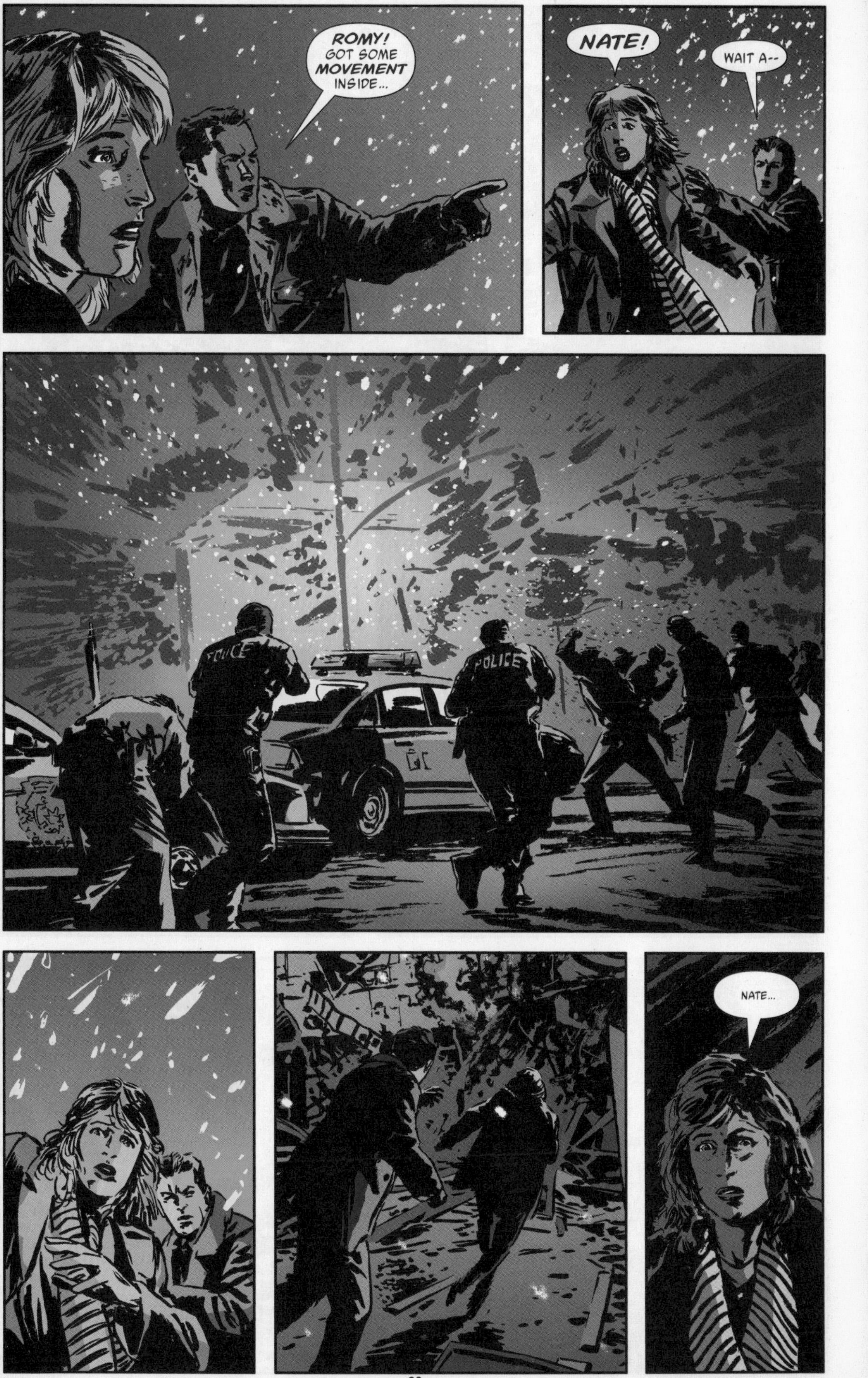
ROMY! GOT SOME MOVEMENT INSIDE...
NATE!
WAIT A--
NATE...

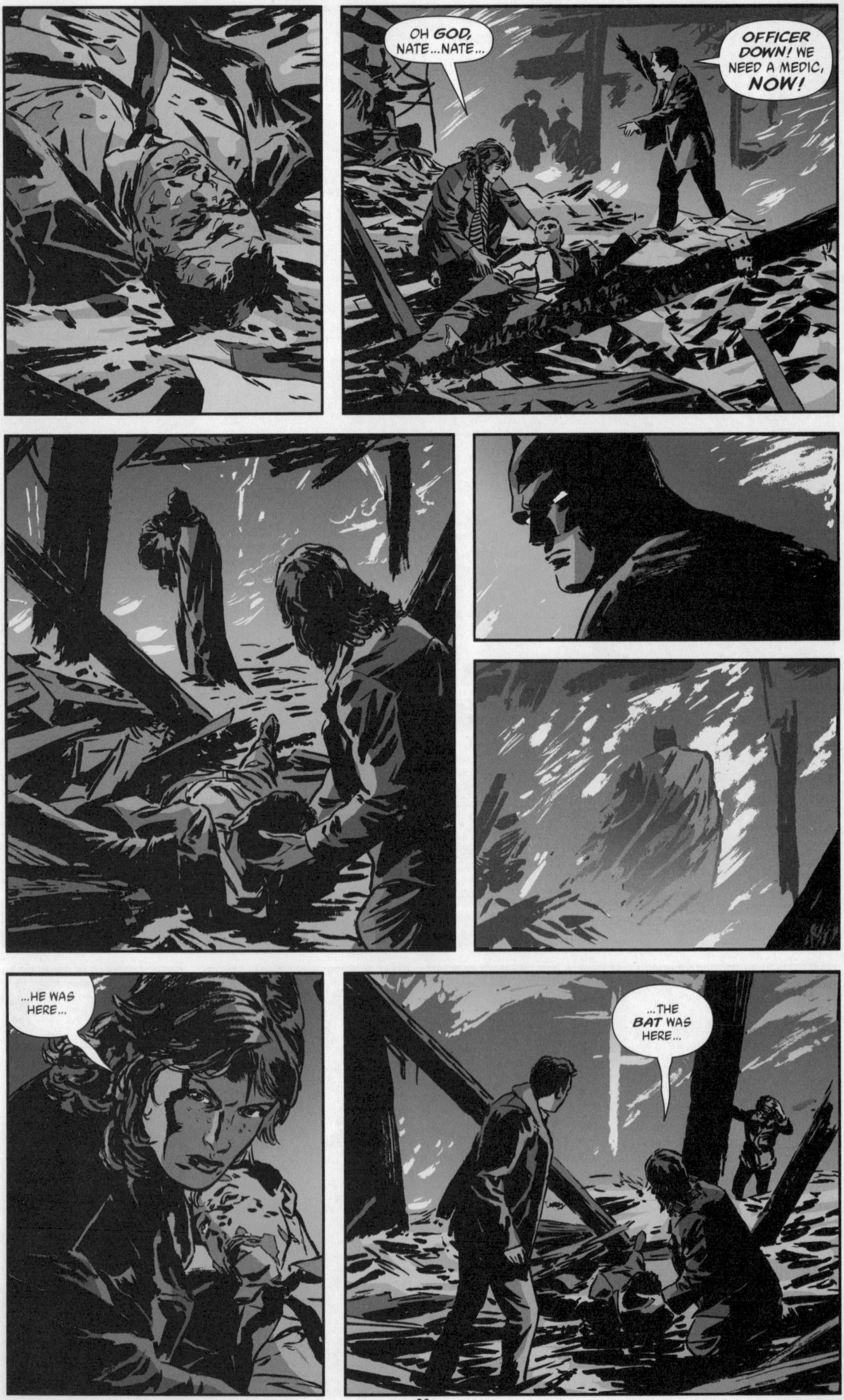

OH GOD, NATE...NATE...
OFFICER DOWN! WE NEED A MEDIC, NOW!
...HE WAS HERE...
...THE BAT WAS HERE...

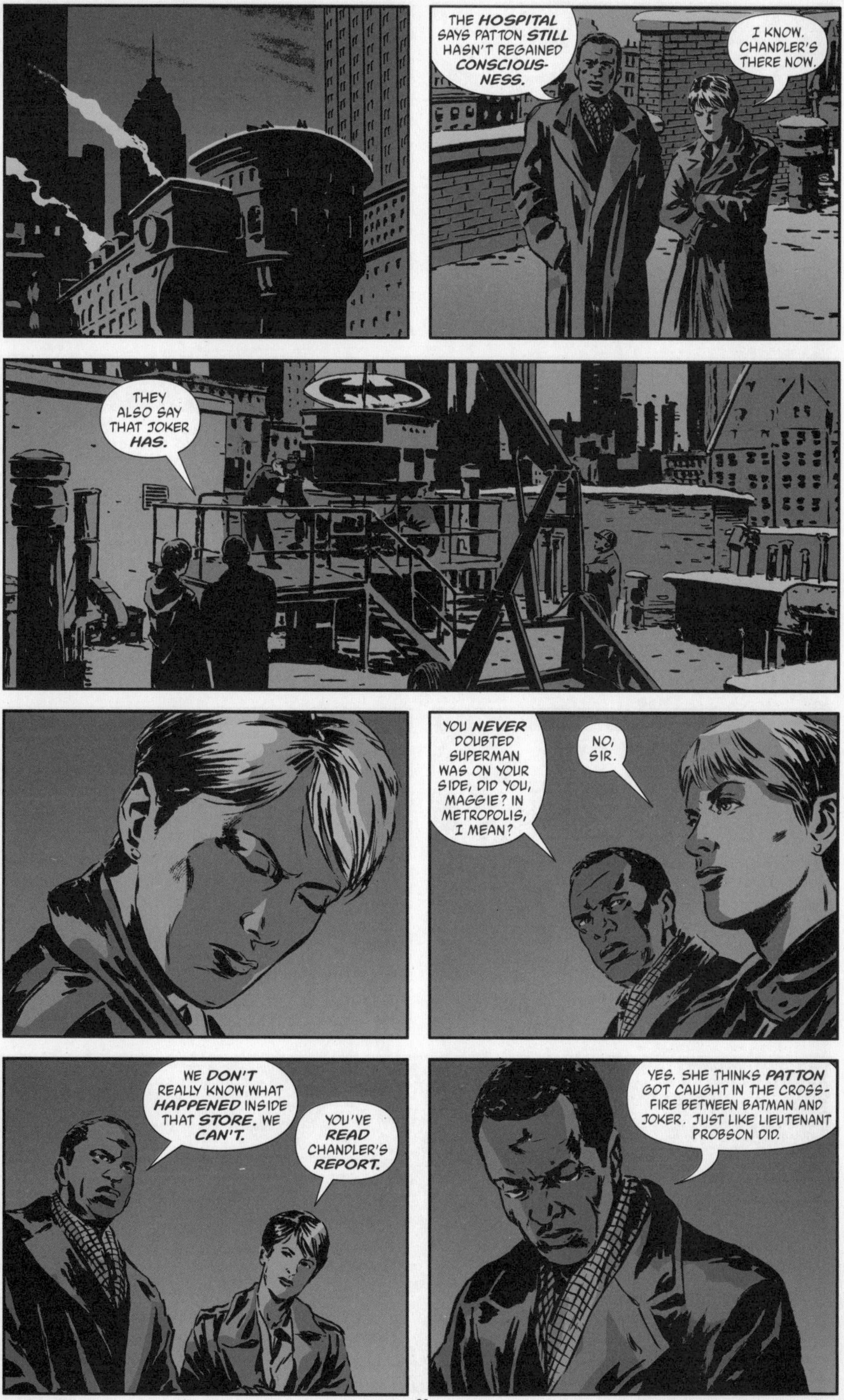
THE HOSPITAL SAYS PATTON STILL HASN'T REGAINED CONSCIOUSNESS.
I KNOW. CHANDLER'S THERE NOW.
THEY ALSO SAY THAT JOKER HAS.
YOU NEVER DOUBTED SUPERMAN WAS ON YOUR SIDE, DID YOU, MAGGIE? IN METROPOLIS, I MEAN?
NO, SIR.
WE DON'T REALLY KNOW WHAT HAPPENED INSIDE THAT STORE. WE CAN'T.
YOU'VE READ CHANDLER'S REPORT.
YES. SHE THINKS PATTON GOT CAUGHT IN THE CROSS-FIRE BETWEEN BATMAN AND JOKER. JUST LIKE LIEUTENANT PROBSON DID.

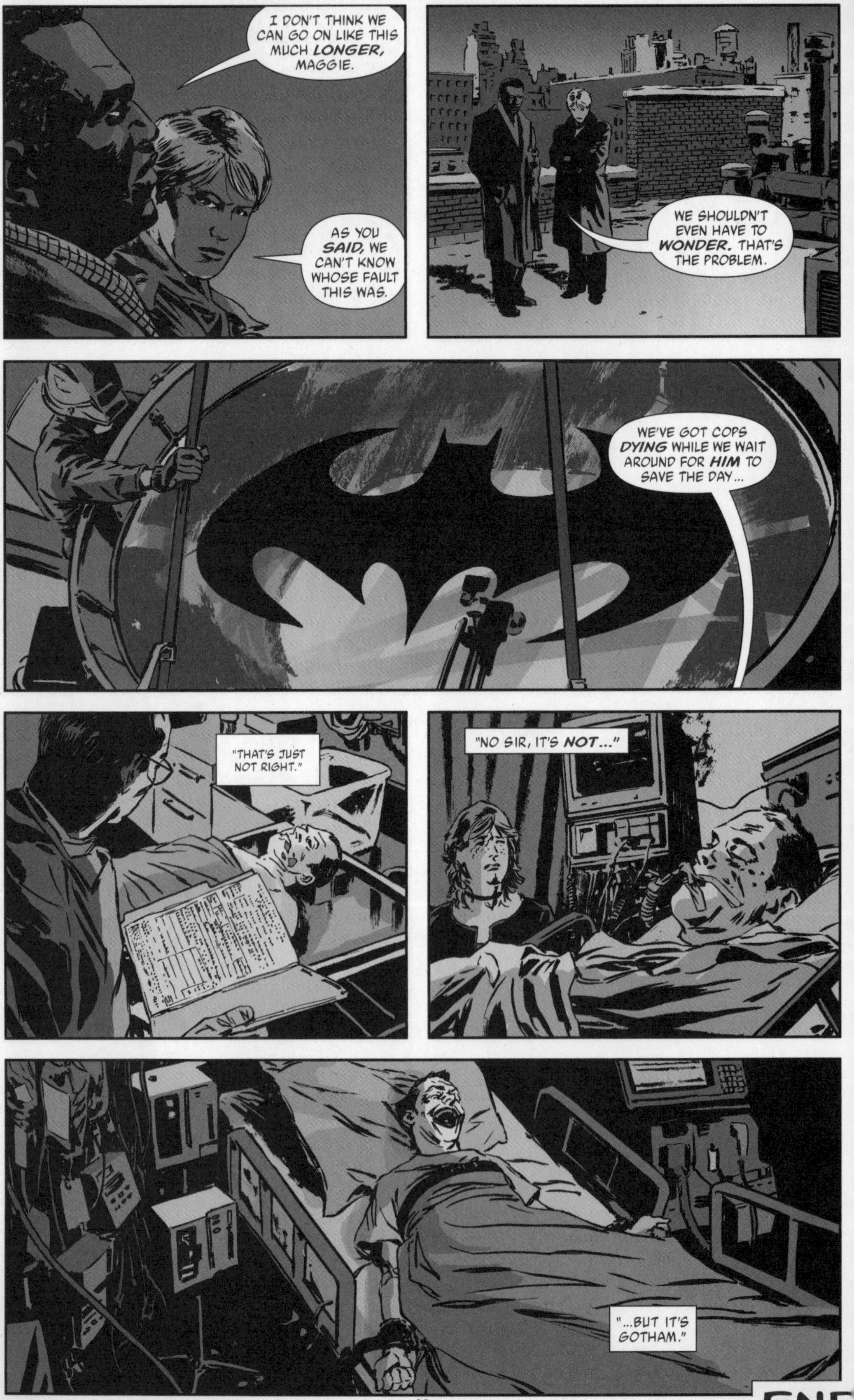
I DON'T THINK WE CAN GO ON LIKE THIS MUCH LONGER, MAGGIE.
AS YOU SAID, WE CAN'T KNOW WHOSE FAULT THIS WAS.
WE SHOULDN'T EVEN HAVE TO WONDER. THAT'S THE PROBLEM.
WE'VE GOT COPS DYING WHILE WE WAIT AROUND FOR HIM TO SAVE THE DAY...
"THAT'S JUST NOT RIGHT."
"NO SIR, IT'S NOT..."
"...BUT IT'S GOTHAM."
END

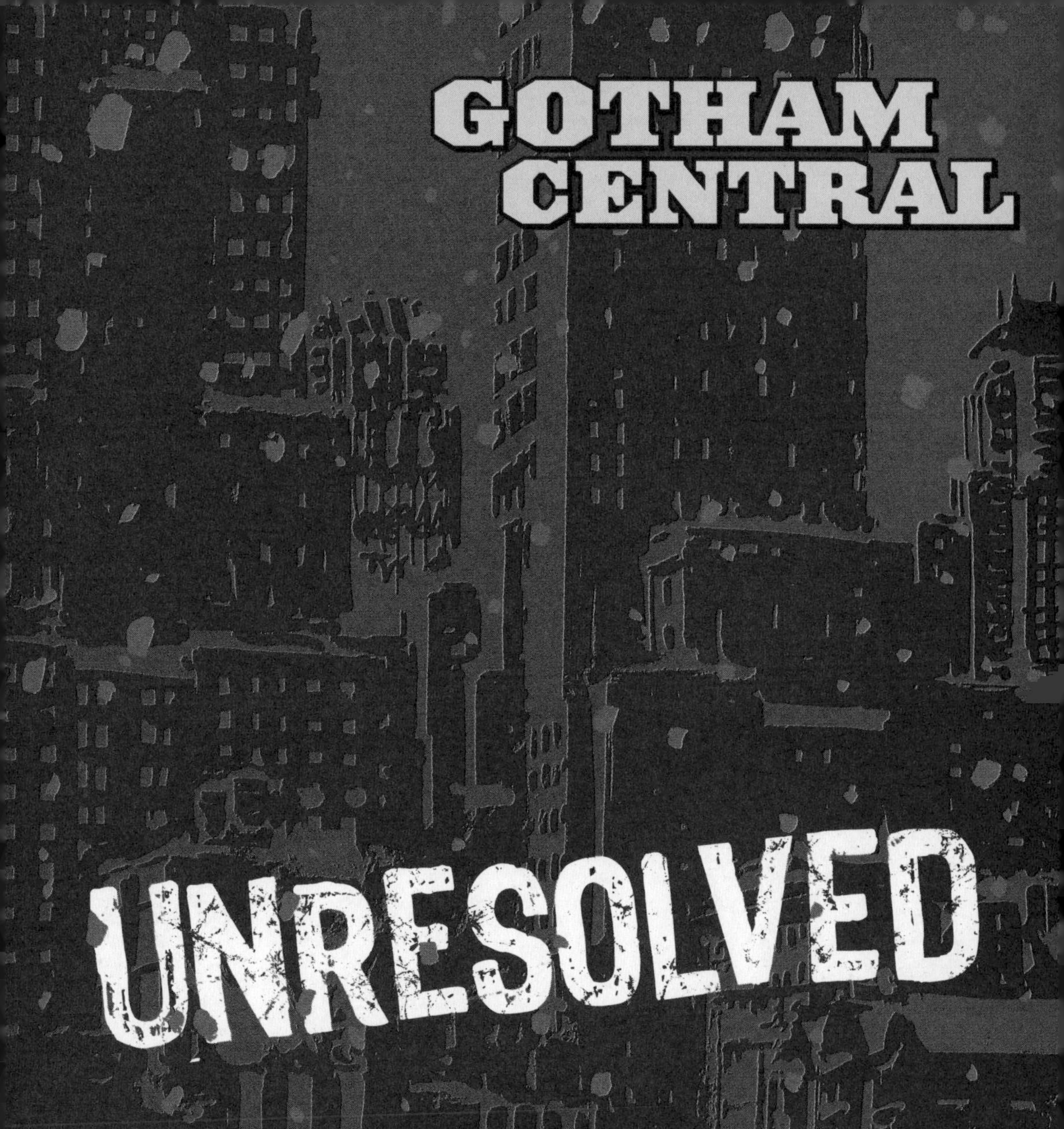

GOTHAM CENTRAL

UNRESOLVED

ED BRUBAKER
WRITER

MICHAEL LARK
& STEFANO GAUDIANO
ARTISTS

LEE LOUGHRIDGE COLORIST

CLEM ROBINS LETTERER

MICHAEL LARK ORIGINAL SERIES COVERS

unresolved

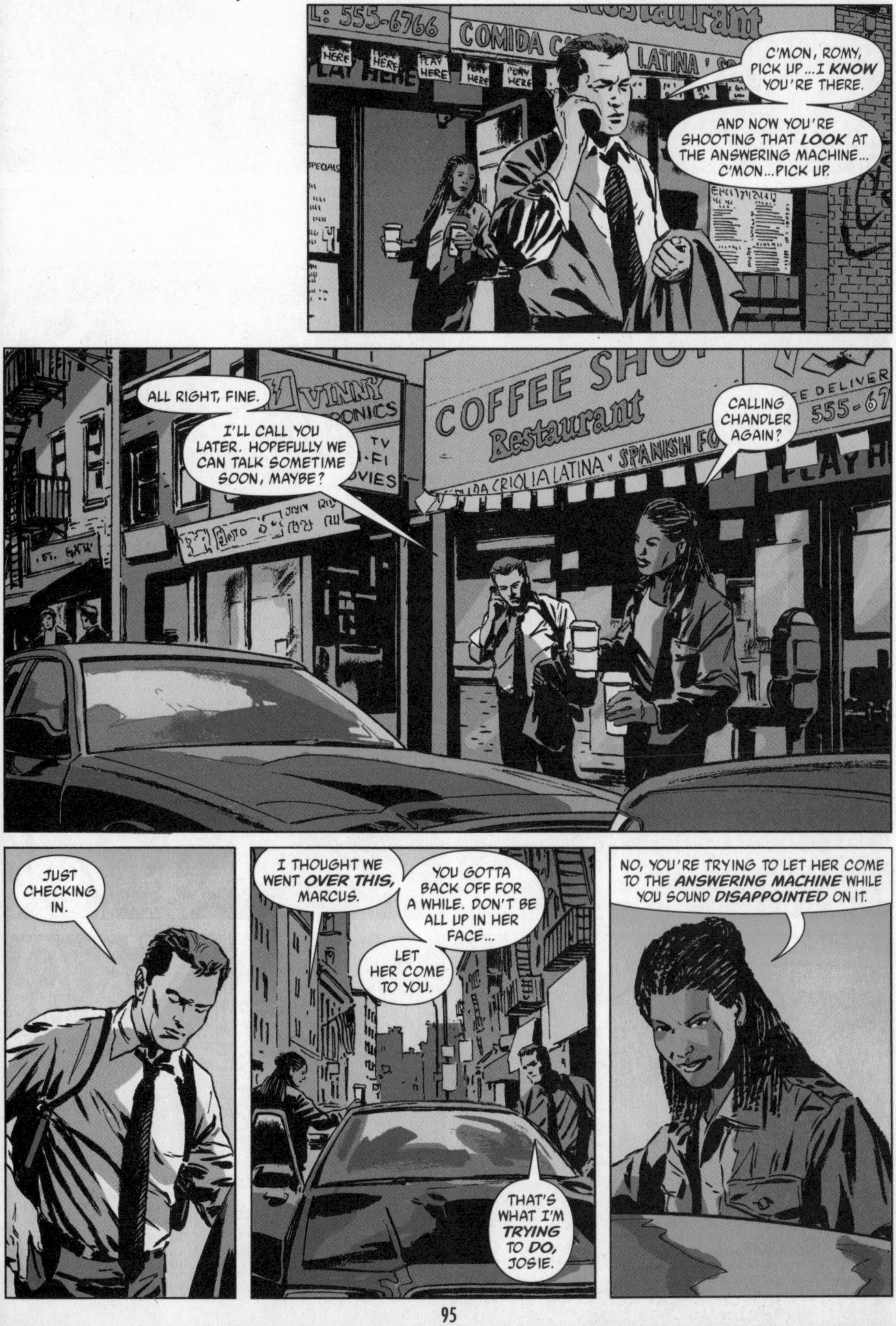

C'MON, ROMY, PICK UP... I KNOW YOU'RE THERE.
AND NOW YOU'RE SHOOTING THAT LOOK AT THE ANSWERING MACHINE... C'MON... PICK UP.
ALL RIGHT, FINE.
I'LL CALL YOU LATER. HOPEFULLY WE CAN TALK SOMETIME SOON, MAYBE?
CALLING CHANDLER AGAIN?
JUST CHECKING IN.
I THOUGHT WE WENT OVER THIS, MARCUS.
YOU GOTTA BACK OFF FOR A WHILE. DON'T BE ALL UP IN HER FACE...
LET HER COME TO YOU.
THAT'S WHAT I'M TRYING TO DO, JOSIE.
NO, YOU'RE TRYING TO LET HER COME TO THE ANSWERING MACHINE WHILE YOU SOUND DISAPPOINTED ON IT.

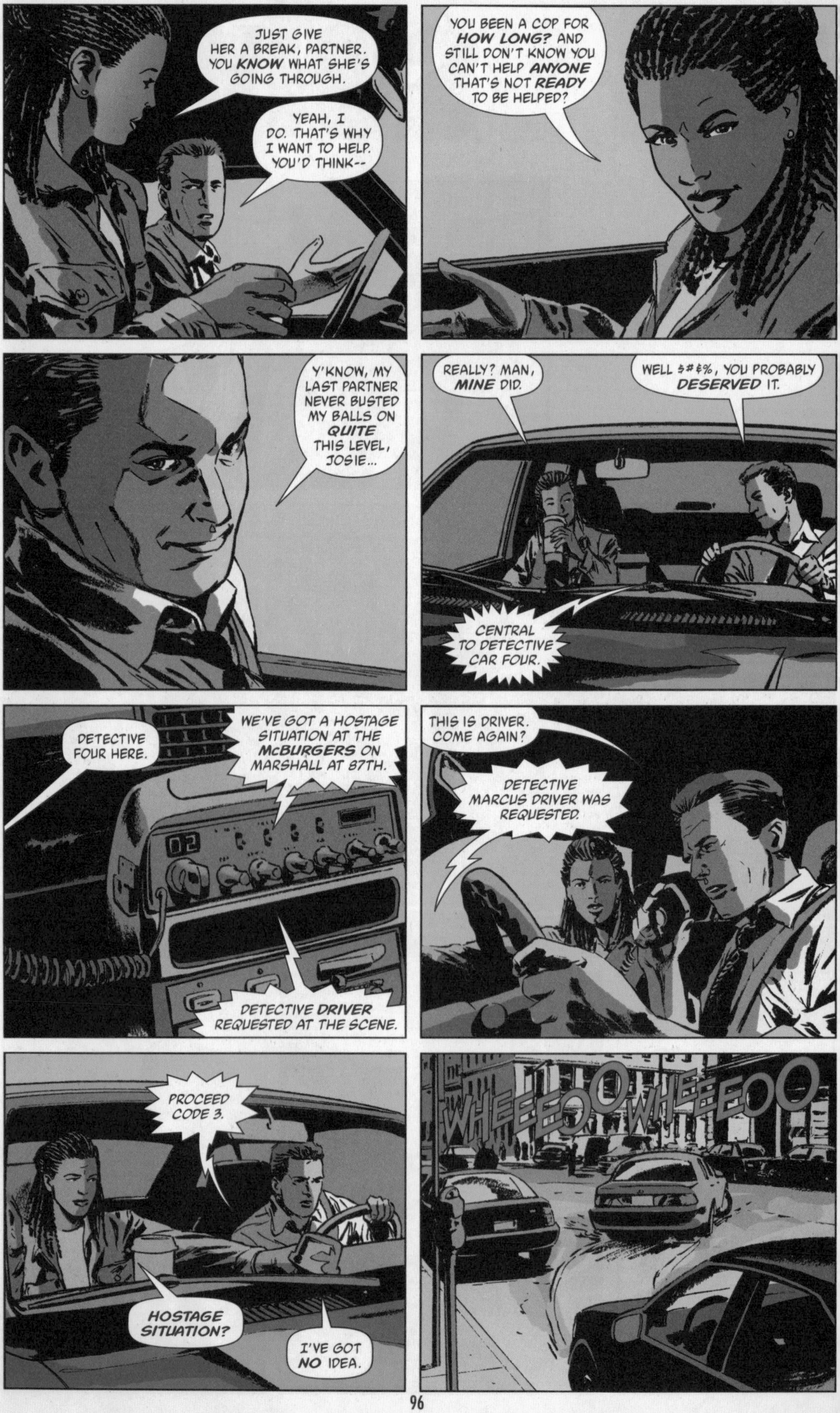

JUST GIVE HER A BREAK, PARTNER. YOU **KNOW** WHAT SHE'S GOING THROUGH.
YEAH, I DO. THAT'S WHY I WANT TO HELP. YOU'D THINK--
YOU BEEN A COP FOR **HOW LONG?** AND STILL DON'T KNOW YOU CAN'T HELP **ANYONE** THAT'S NOT **READY** TO BE HELPED?
Y'KNOW, MY LAST PARTNER NEVER BUSTED MY BALLS ON **QUITE** THIS LEVEL, JOSIE...
REALLY? MAN, **MINE** DID.
WELL $#&%, YOU PROBABLY **DESERVED** IT.
CENTRAL TO DETECTIVE CAR FOUR.
DETECTIVE FOUR HERE.
WE'VE GOT A HOSTAGE SITUATION AT THE **McBURGERS** ON MARSHALL AT 87TH.
DETECTIVE **DRIVER** REQUESTED AT THE SCENE.
THIS IS DRIVER. COME AGAIN?
DETECTIVE MARCUS DRIVER WAS REQUESTED.
PROCEED CODE 3.
HOSTAGE SITUATION?
I'VE GOT **NO** IDEA.
WHEEEOO WHEEEOO

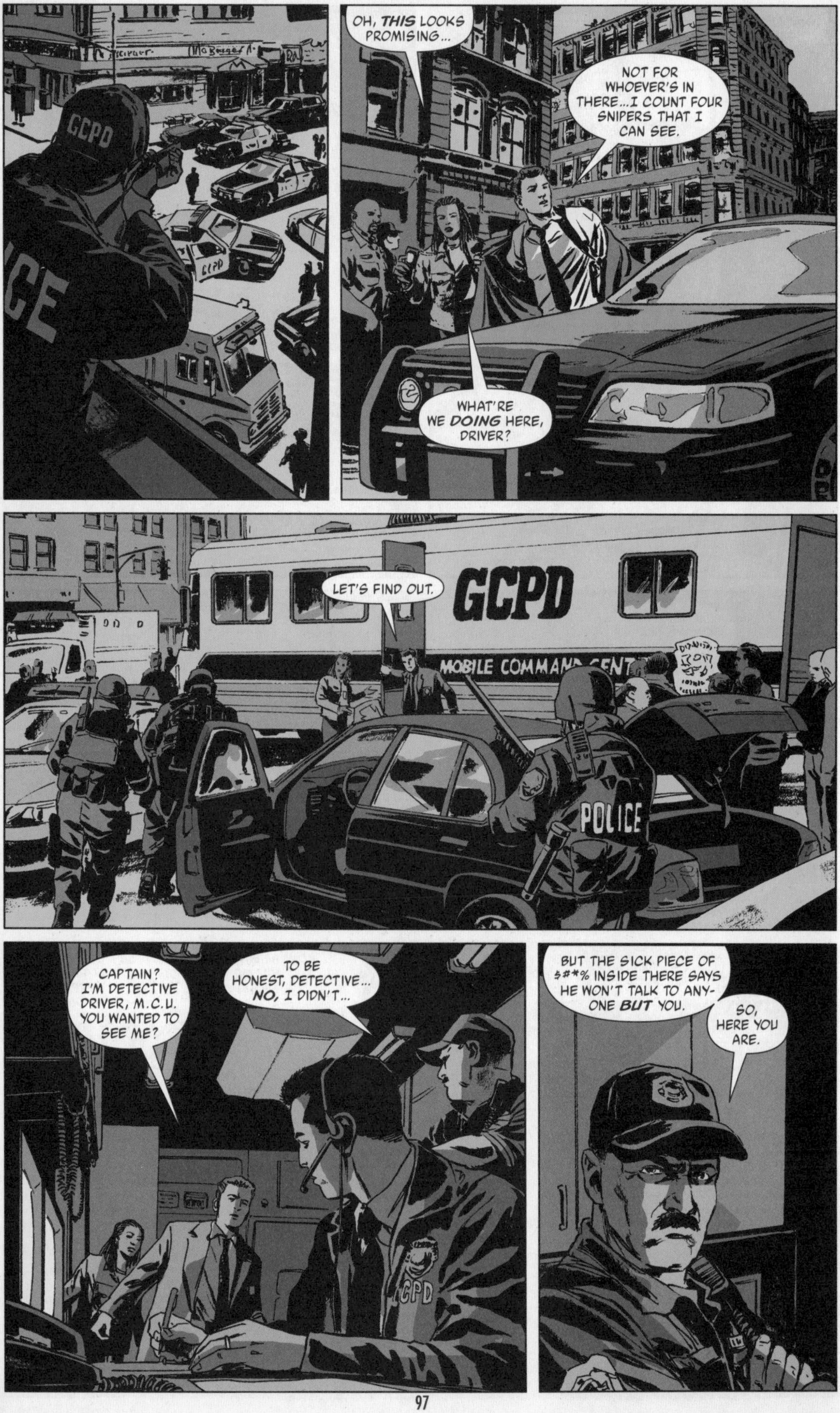
GCPD
POLICE
OH, THIS LOOKS PROMISING...
NOT FOR WHOEVER'S IN THERE...I COUNT FOUR SNIPERS THAT I CAN SEE.
WHAT'RE WE DOING HERE, DRIVER?
GCPD
LET'S FIND OUT.
POLICE
CAPTAIN? I'M DETECTIVE DRIVER, M.C.U. YOU WANTED TO SEE ME?
TO BE HONEST, DETECTIVE... NO, I DIDN'T...
BUT THE SICK PIECE OF $#*% INSIDE THERE SAYS HE WON'T TALK TO ANYONE BUT YOU.
SO, HERE YOU ARE.

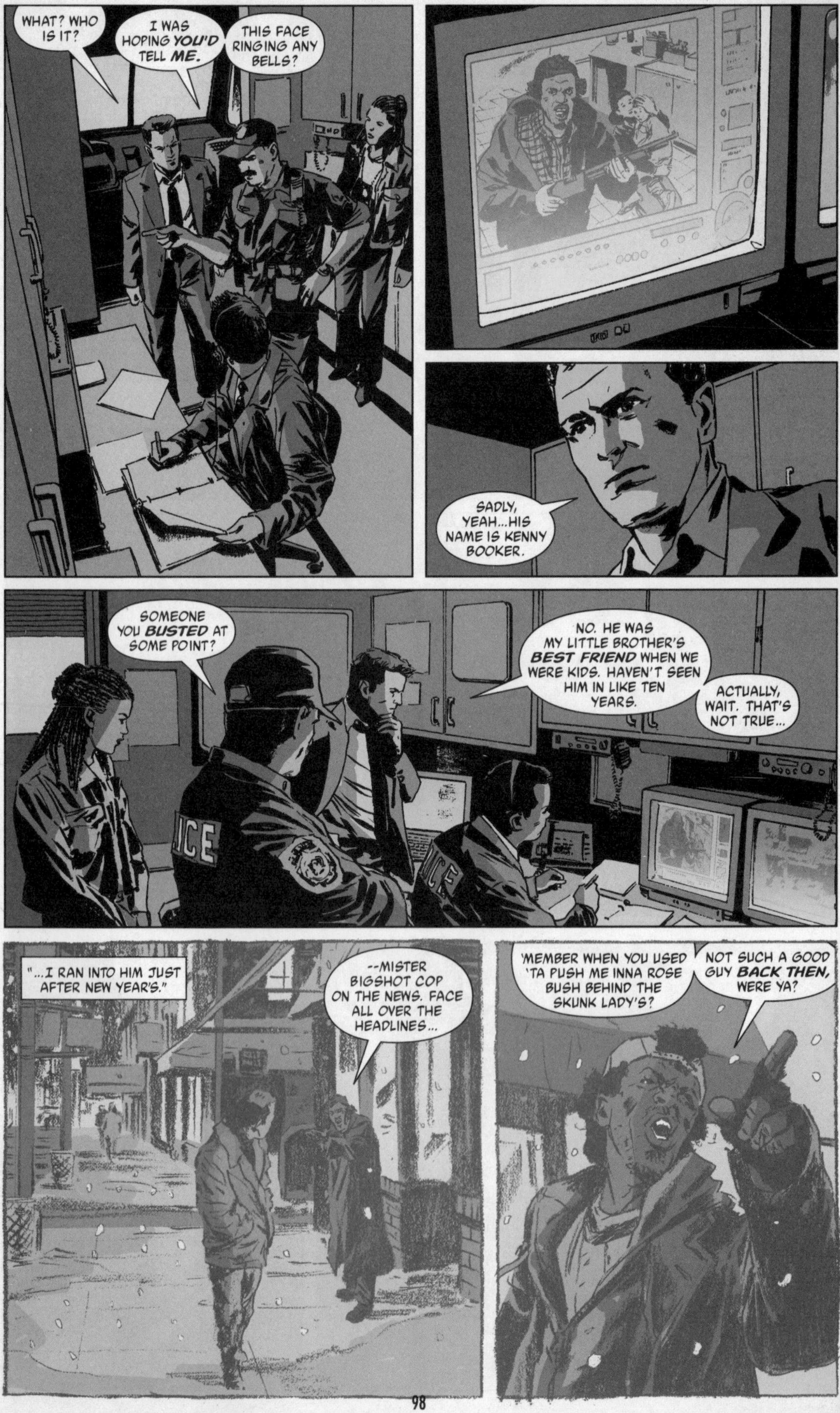
WHAT? WHO IS IT?
I WAS HOPING YOU'D TELL ME.
THIS FACE RINGING ANY BELLS?
SADLY, YEAH...HIS NAME IS KENNY BOOKER.
SOMEONE YOU BUSTED AT SOME POINT?
NO. HE WAS MY LITTLE BROTHER'S BEST FRIEND WHEN WE WERE KIDS. HAVEN'T SEEN HIM IN LIKE TEN YEARS.
ACTUALLY, WAIT. THAT'S NOT TRUE...
"...I RAN INTO HIM JUST AFTER NEW YEAR'S."
--MISTER BIGSHOT COP ON THE NEWS. FACE ALL OVER THE HEADLINES...
'MEMBER WHEN YOU USED 'TA PUSH ME INNA ROSE BUSH BEHIND THE SKUNK LADY'S?
NOT SUCH A GOOD GUY BACK THEN, WERE YA?

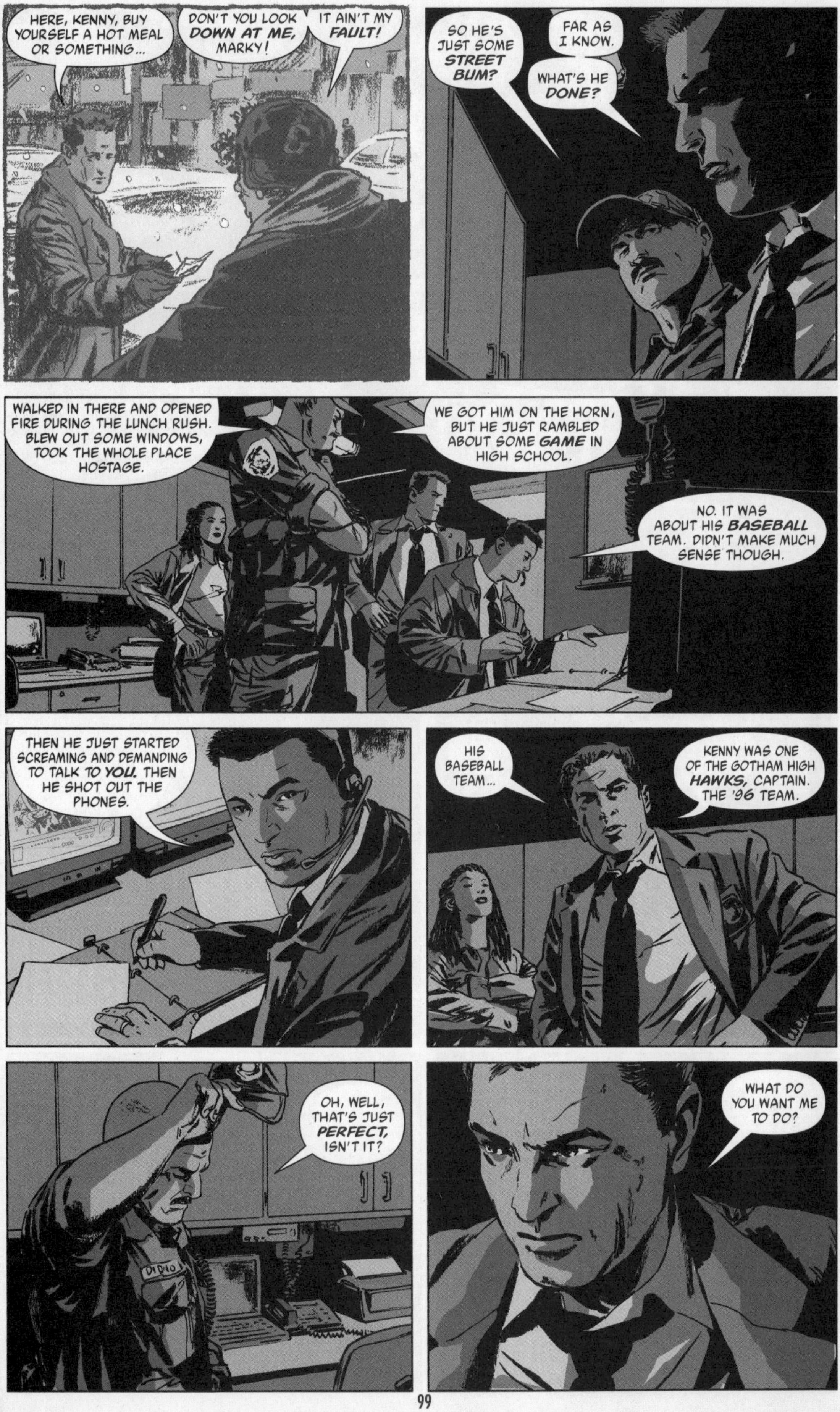
HERE, KENNY, BUY YOURSELF A HOT MEAL OR SOMETHING...
DON'T YOU LOOK DOWN AT ME, MARKY!
IT AIN'T MY FAULT!
SO HE'S JUST SOME STREET BUM?
FAR AS I KNOW.
WHAT'S HE DONE?
WALKED IN THERE AND OPENED FIRE DURING THE LUNCH RUSH. BLEW OUT SOME WINDOWS, TOOK THE WHOLE PLACE HOSTAGE.
WE GOT HIM ON THE HORN, BUT HE JUST RAMBLED ABOUT SOME GAME IN HIGH SCHOOL.
NO. IT WAS ABOUT HIS BASEBALL TEAM. DIDN'T MAKE MUCH SENSE THOUGH.
THEN HE JUST STARTED SCREAMING AND DEMANDING TO TALK TO YOU. THEN HE SHOT OUT THE PHONES.
HIS BASEBALL TEAM...
KENNY WAS ONE OF THE GOTHAM HIGH HAWKS, CAPTAIN. THE '96 TEAM.
OH, WELL, THAT'S JUST PERFECT, ISN'T IT?
WHAT DO YOU WANT ME TO DO?

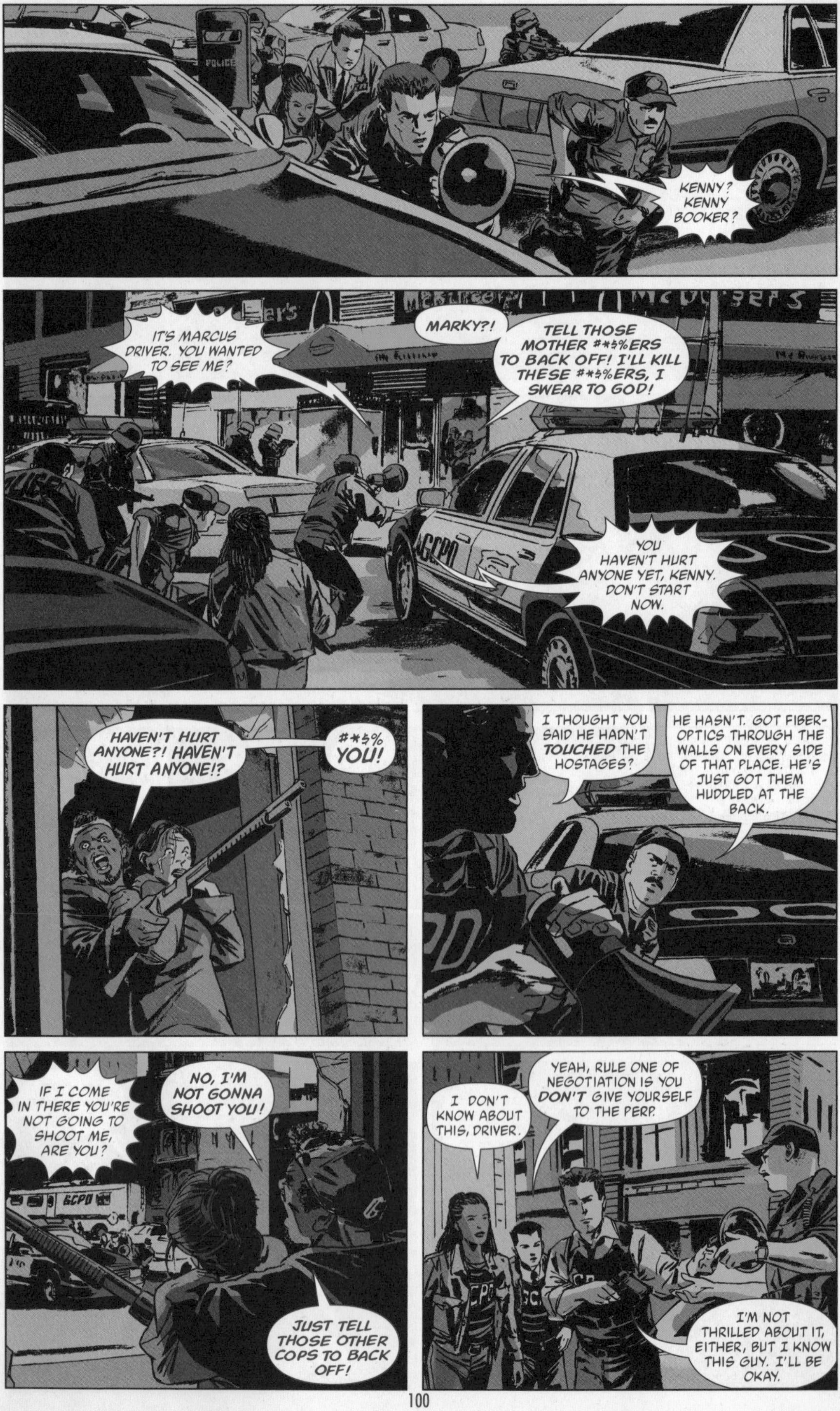
KENNY? KENNY BOOKER?
IT'S MARCUS DRIVER. YOU WANTED TO SEE ME?
MARKY?!
TELL THOSE MOTHER #*$%ERS TO BACK OFF! I'LL KILL THESE #*$%ERS, I SWEAR TO GOD!
YOU HAVEN'T HURT ANYONE YET, KENNY. DON'T START NOW.
HAVEN'T HURT ANYONE?! HAVEN'T HURT ANYONE!?
#*$% YOU!
I THOUGHT YOU SAID HE HADN'T TOUCHED THE HOSTAGES?
HE HASN'T. GOT FIBER-OPTICS THROUGH THE WALLS ON EVERY SIDE OF THAT PLACE. HE'S JUST GOT THEM HUDDLED AT THE BACK.
IF I COME IN THERE YOU'RE NOT GOING TO SHOOT ME, ARE YOU?
NO, I'M NOT GONNA SHOOT YOU!
JUST TELL THOSE OTHER COPS TO BACK OFF!
I DON'T KNOW ABOUT THIS, DRIVER.
YEAH, RULE ONE OF NEGOTIATION IS YOU DON'T GIVE YOURSELF TO THE PERP.
I'M NOT THRILLED ABOUT IT, EITHER, BUT I KNOW THIS GUY. I'LL BE OKAY.

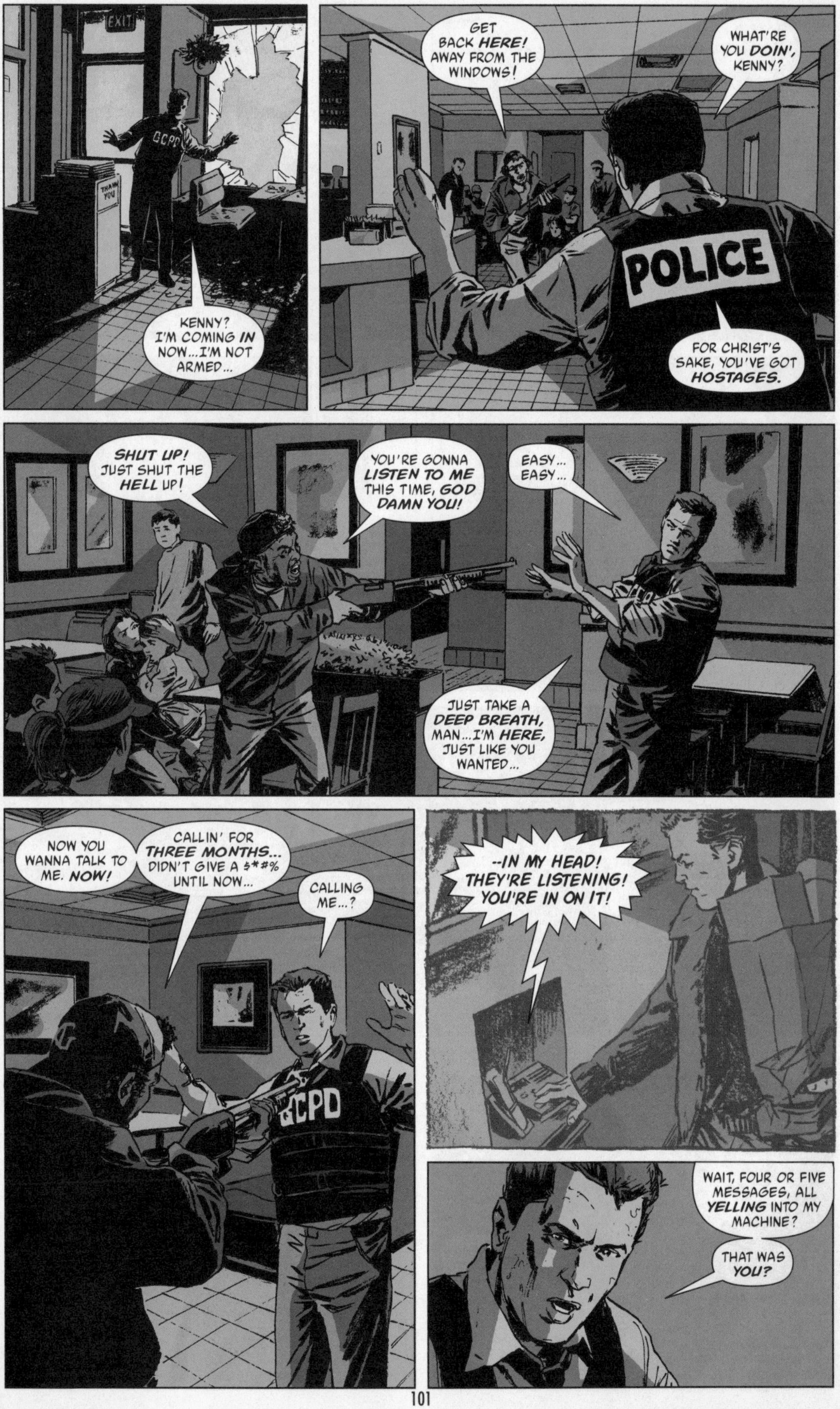
KENNY? I'M COMING IN NOW...I'M NOT ARMED...
GET BACK HERE! AWAY FROM THE WINDOWS!
WHAT'RE YOU DOIN', KENNY?
POLICE
FOR CHRIST'S SAKE, YOU'VE GOT HOSTAGES.
SHUT UP! JUST SHUT THE HELL UP!
YOU'RE GONNA LISTEN TO ME THIS TIME, GOD DAMN YOU!
EASY... EASY...
JUST TAKE A DEEP BREATH, MAN...I'M HERE, JUST LIKE YOU WANTED...
NOW YOU WANNA TALK TO ME. NOW!
CALLIN' FOR THREE MONTHS... DIDN'T GIVE A $*#% UNTIL NOW...
CALLING ME...?
GCPD
--IN MY HEAD! THEY'RE LISTENING! YOU'RE IN ON IT!
WAIT, FOUR OR FIVE MESSAGES, ALL YELLING INTO MY MACHINE?
THAT WAS YOU?

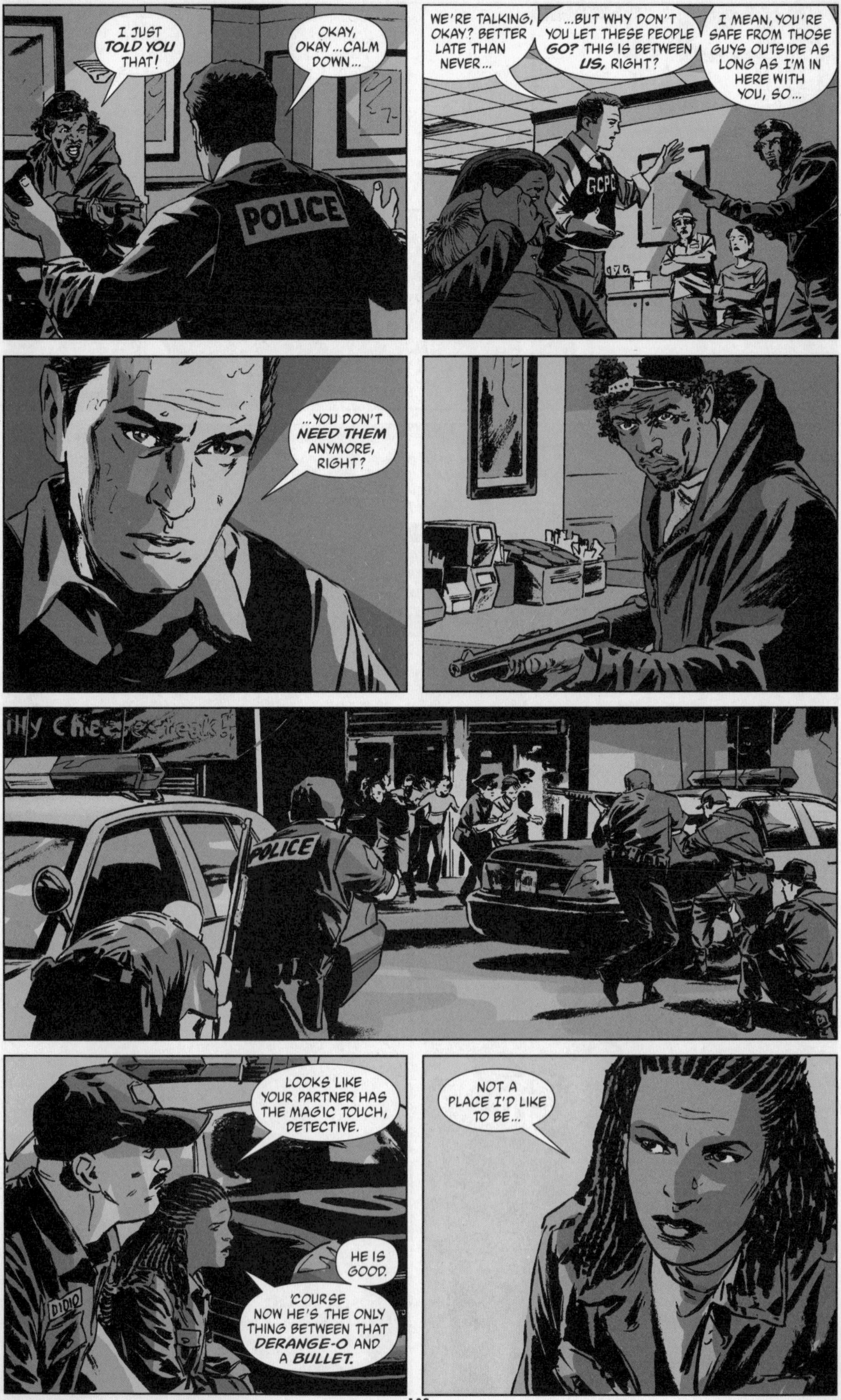
I JUST TOLD YOU THAT!
OKAY, OKAY...CALM DOWN...
POLICE
WE'RE TALKING, OKAY? BETTER LATE THAN NEVER...
...BUT WHY DON'T YOU LET THESE PEOPLE GO? THIS IS BETWEEN US, RIGHT?
I MEAN, YOU'RE SAFE FROM THOSE GUYS OUTSIDE AS LONG AS I'M IN HERE WITH YOU, SO...
GCPD
...YOU DON'T NEED THEM ANYMORE, RIGHT?
POLICE
LOOKS LIKE YOUR PARTNER HAS THE MAGIC TOUCH, DETECTIVE.
HE IS GOOD.
'COURSE NOW HE'S THE ONLY THING BETWEEN THAT DERANGE-O AND A BULLET.
DIDIO
NOT A PLACE I'D LIKE TO BE...

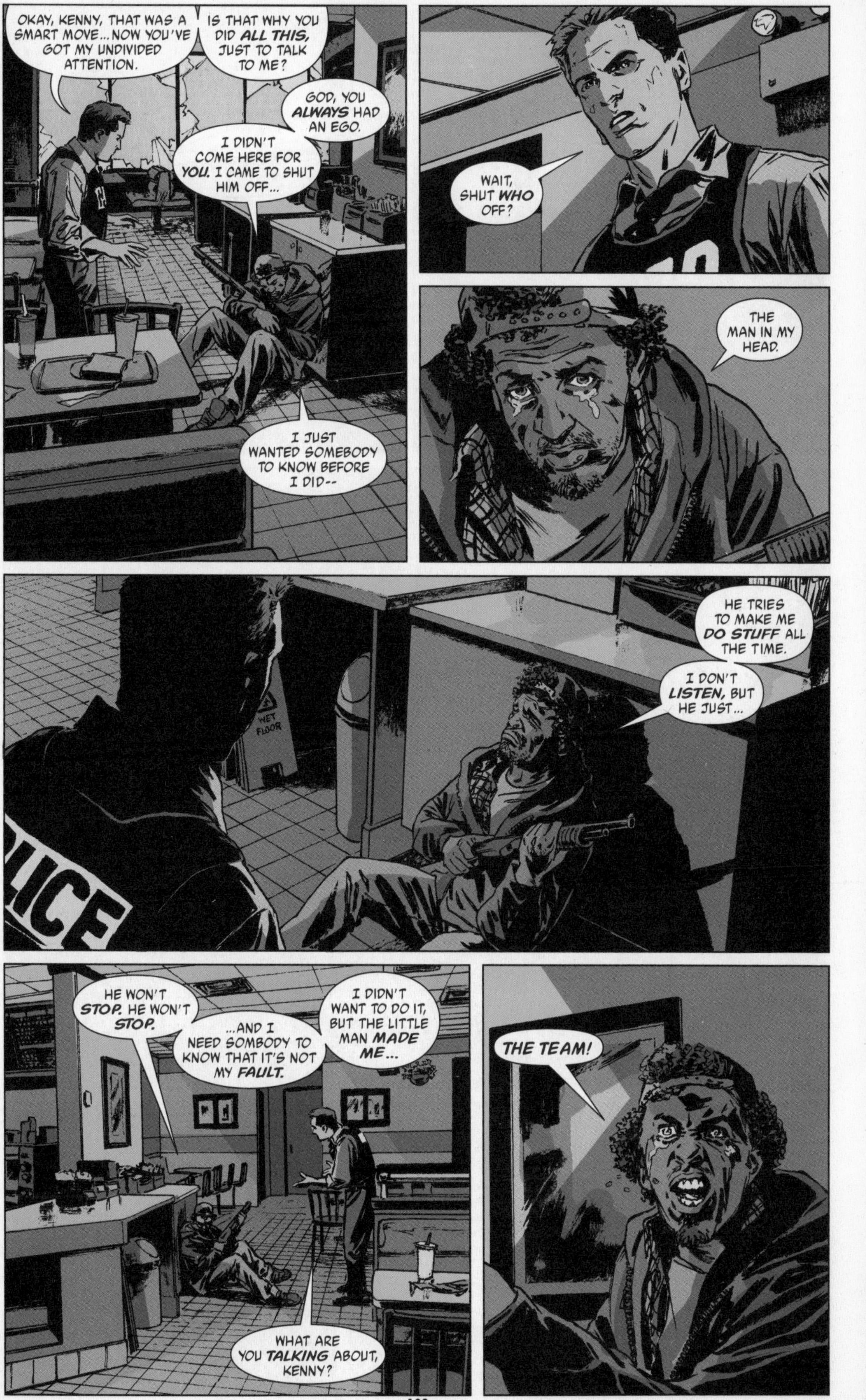

OKAY, KENNY, THAT WAS A SMART MOVE...NOW YOU'VE GOT MY UNDIVIDED ATTENTION.
IS THAT WHY YOU DID ALL THIS, JUST TO TALK TO ME?
GOD, YOU ALWAYS HAD AN EGO.
I DIDN'T COME HERE FOR YOU. I CAME TO SHUT HIM OFF...
I JUST WANTED SOMEBODY TO KNOW BEFORE I DID--
WAIT, SHUT WHO OFF?
THE MAN IN MY HEAD.
HE TRIES TO MAKE ME DO STUFF ALL THE TIME.
I DON'T LISTEN, BUT HE JUST...
WET FLOOR
HE WON'T STOP. HE WON'T STOP.
...AND I NEED SOMBODY TO KNOW THAT IT'S NOT MY FAULT.
I DIDN'T WANT TO DO IT, BUT THE LITTLE MAN MADE ME...
WHAT ARE YOU TALKING ABOUT, KENNY?
THE TEAM!

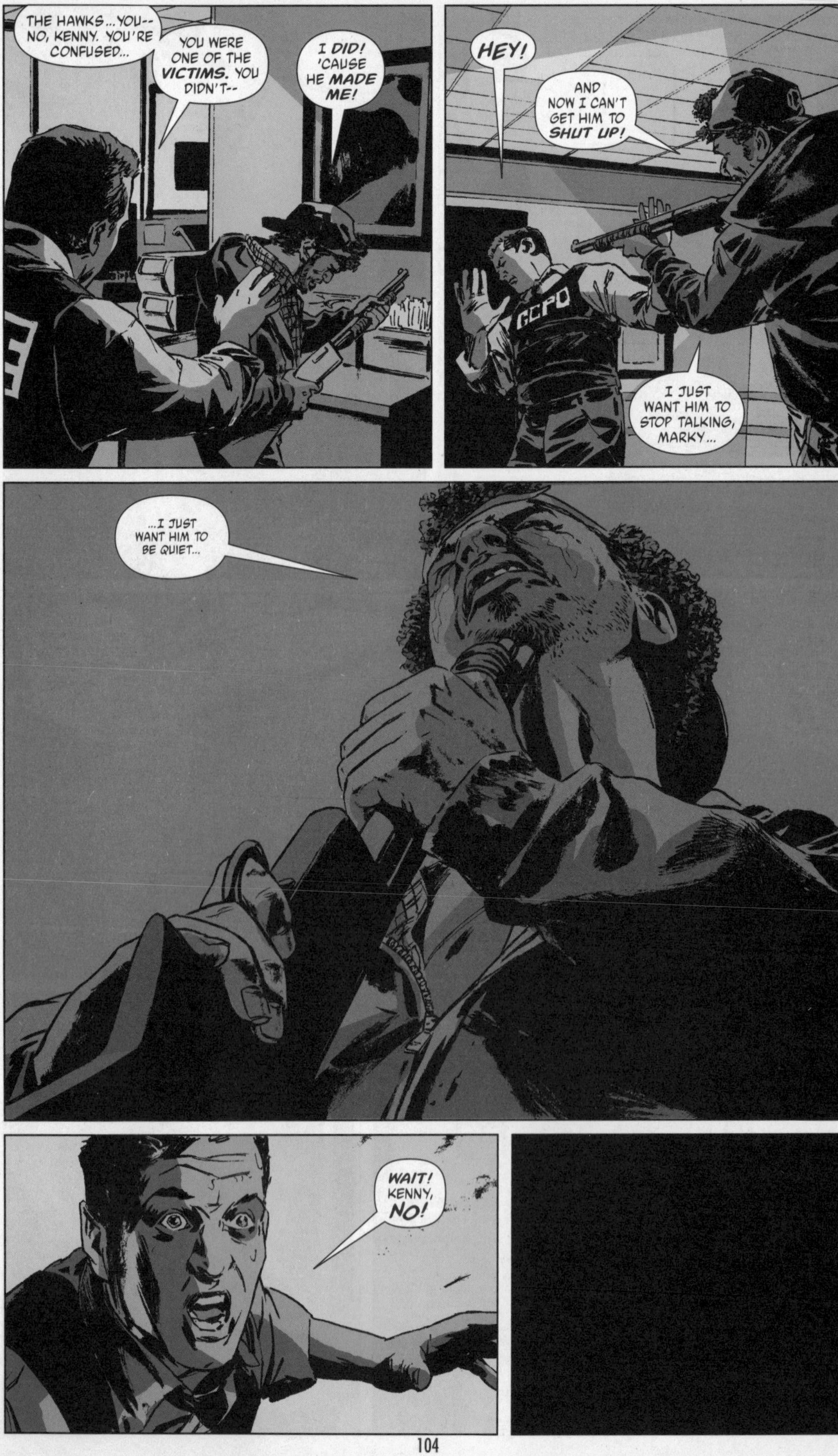
THE HAWKS... YOU--
NO, KENNY. YOU'RE CONFUSED...
YOU WERE ONE OF THE VICTIMS. YOU DIDN'T--
I DID! 'CAUSE HE MADE ME!
HEY!
AND NOW I CAN'T GET HIM TO SHUT UP!
I JUST WANT HIM TO STOP TALKING, MARKY...
...I JUST WANT HIM TO BE QUIET...
WAIT! KENNY, NO!
GCPD

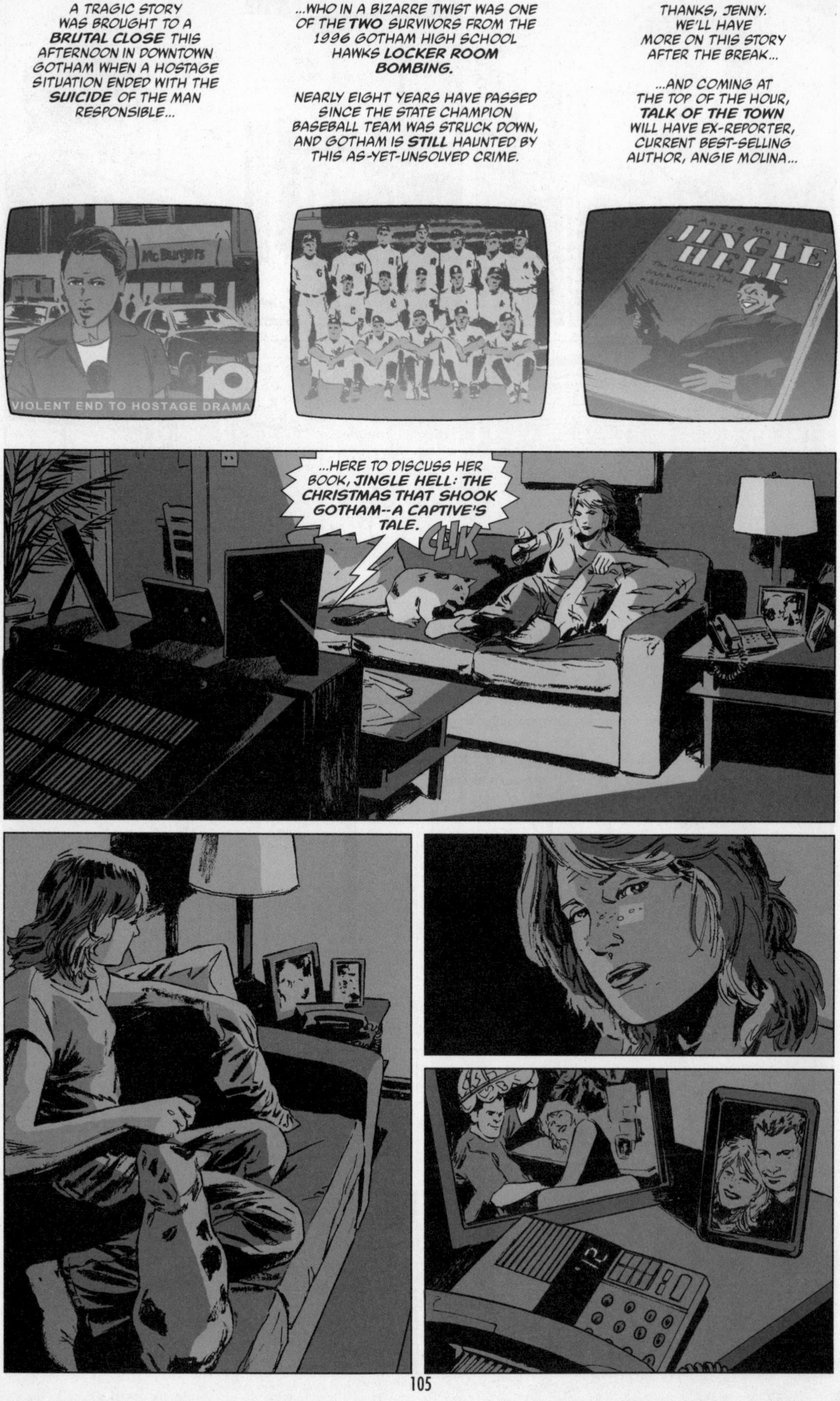
A TRAGIC STORY WAS BROUGHT TO A BRUTAL CLOSE THIS AFTERNOON IN DOWNTOWN GOTHAM WHEN A HOSTAGE SITUATION ENDED WITH THE SUICIDE OF THE MAN RESPONSIBLE...
McBurgers
10
VIOLENT END TO HOSTAGE DRAMA
...WHO IN A BIZARRE TWIST WAS ONE OF THE TWO SURVIVORS FROM THE 1996 GOTHAM HIGH SCHOOL HAWKS LOCKER ROOM BOMBING.
NEARLY EIGHT YEARS HAVE PASSED SINCE THE STATE CHAMPION BASEBALL TEAM WAS STRUCK DOWN, AND GOTHAM IS STILL HAUNTED BY THIS AS-YET-UNSOLVED CRIME.
THANKS, JENNY. WE'LL HAVE MORE ON THIS STORY AFTER THE BREAK...
...AND COMING AT THE TOP OF THE HOUR, TALK OF THE TOWN WILL HAVE EX-REPORTER, CURRENT BEST-SELLING AUTHOR, ANGIE MOLINA...
Angie Molina
JINGLE HELL
...HERE TO DISCUSS HER BOOK, JINGLE HELL: THE CHRISTMAS THAT SHOOK GOTHAM--A CAPTIVE'S TALE.
CLIK

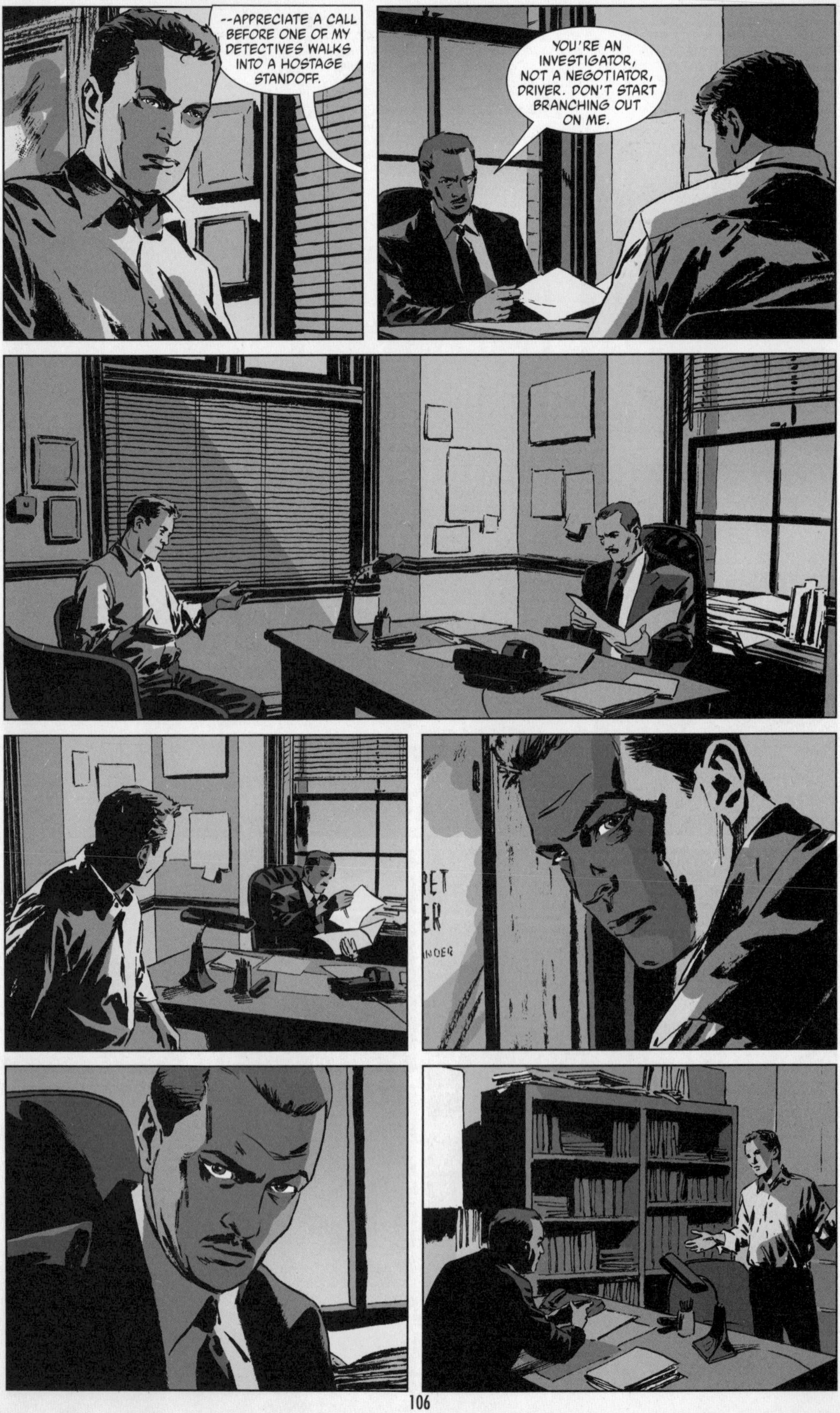
--APPRECIATE A CALL BEFORE ONE OF MY DETECTIVES WALKS INTO A HOSTAGE STANDOFF.
YOU'RE AN INVESTIGATOR, NOT A NEGOTIATOR, DRIVER. DON'T START BRANCHING OUT ON ME.

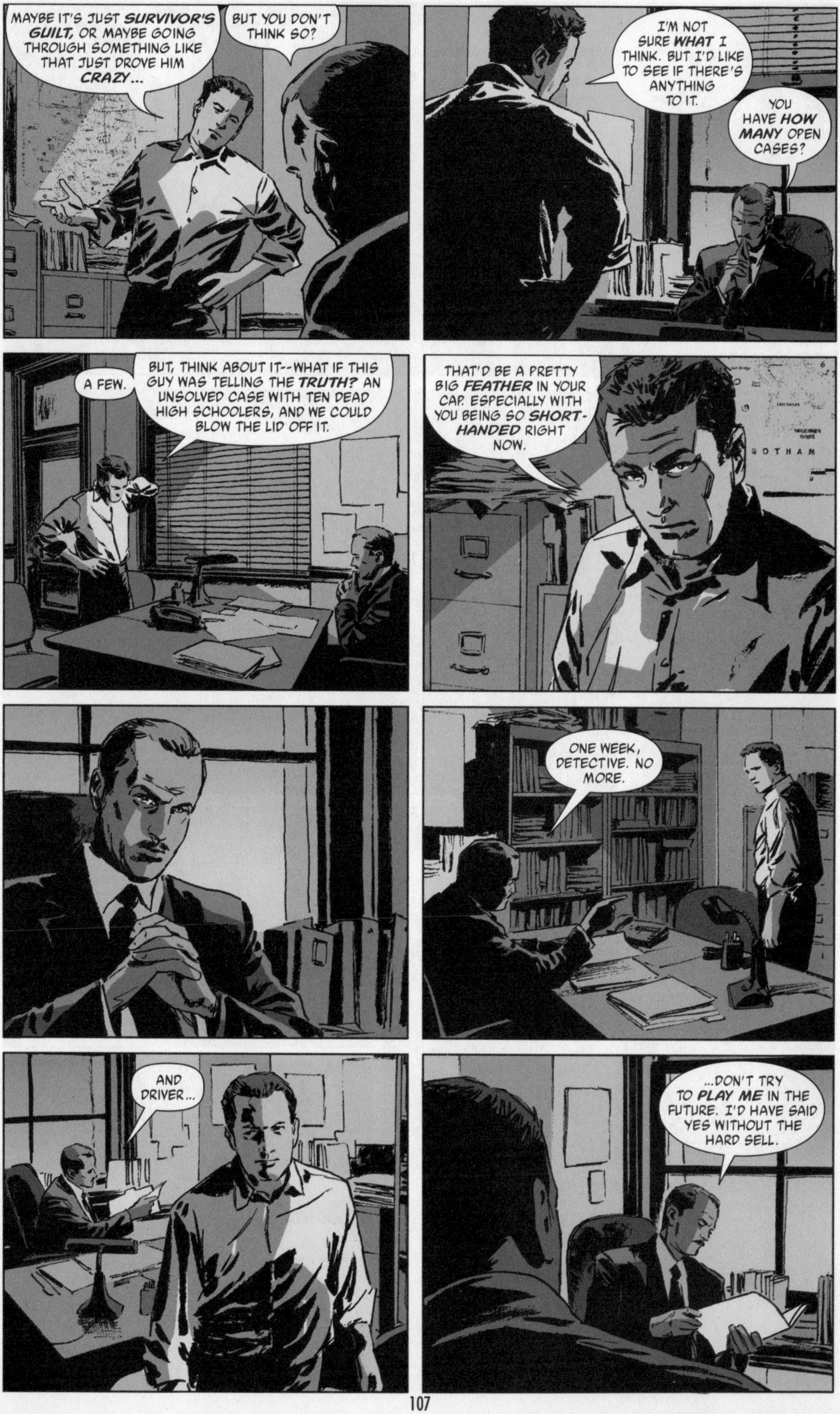
MAYBE IT'S JUST **SURVIVOR'S GUILT,** OR MAYBE GOING THROUGH SOMETHING LIKE THAT JUST DROVE HIM **CRAZY...**
BUT YOU DON'T THINK SO?
I'M NOT SURE **WHAT** I THINK. BUT I'D LIKE TO SEE IF THERE'S ANYTHING TO IT.
YOU HAVE **HOW MANY** OPEN CASES?
A FEW.
BUT, THINK ABOUT IT--WHAT IF THIS GUY WAS TELLING THE **TRUTH?** AN UNSOLVED CASE WITH TEN DEAD HIGH SCHOOLERS, AND WE COULD BLOW THE LID OFF IT.
THAT'D BE A PRETTY BIG **FEATHER** IN YOUR CAP. ESPECIALLY WITH YOU BEING SO **SHORT-HANDED** RIGHT NOW.
GOTHAM
ONE WEEK, DETECTIVE. NO MORE.
AND DRIVER...
...DON'T TRY TO **PLAY ME** IN THE FUTURE. I'D HAVE SAID YES WITHOUT THE HARD SELL.

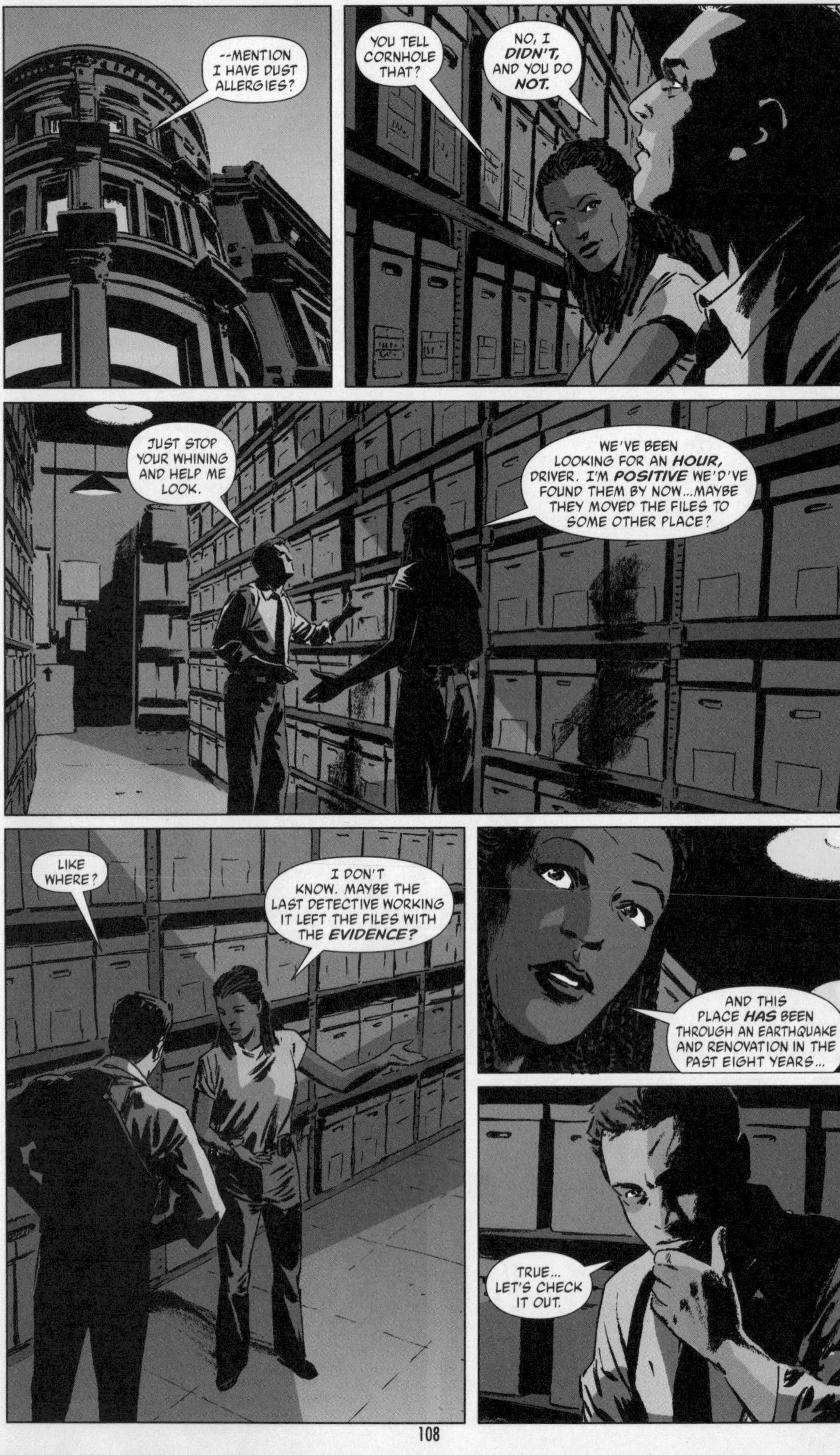

--MENTION I HAVE DUST ALLERGIES?
YOU TELL CORNHOLE THAT?
NO, I *DIDN'T,* AND YOU DO *NOT.*
JUST STOP YOUR WHINING AND HELP ME LOOK.
WE'VE BEEN LOOKING FOR AN *HOUR,* DRIVER. I'M *POSITIVE* WE'D'VE FOUND THEM BY NOW...MAYBE THEY MOVED THE FILES TO SOME OTHER PLACE?
LIKE WHERE?
I DON'T KNOW. MAYBE THE LAST DETECTIVE WORKING IT LEFT THE FILES WITH THE *EVIDENCE?*
AND THIS PLACE *HAS* BEEN THROUGH AN EARTHQUAKE AND RENOVATION IN THE PAST EIGHT YEARS...
TRUE... LET'S CHECK IT OUT.

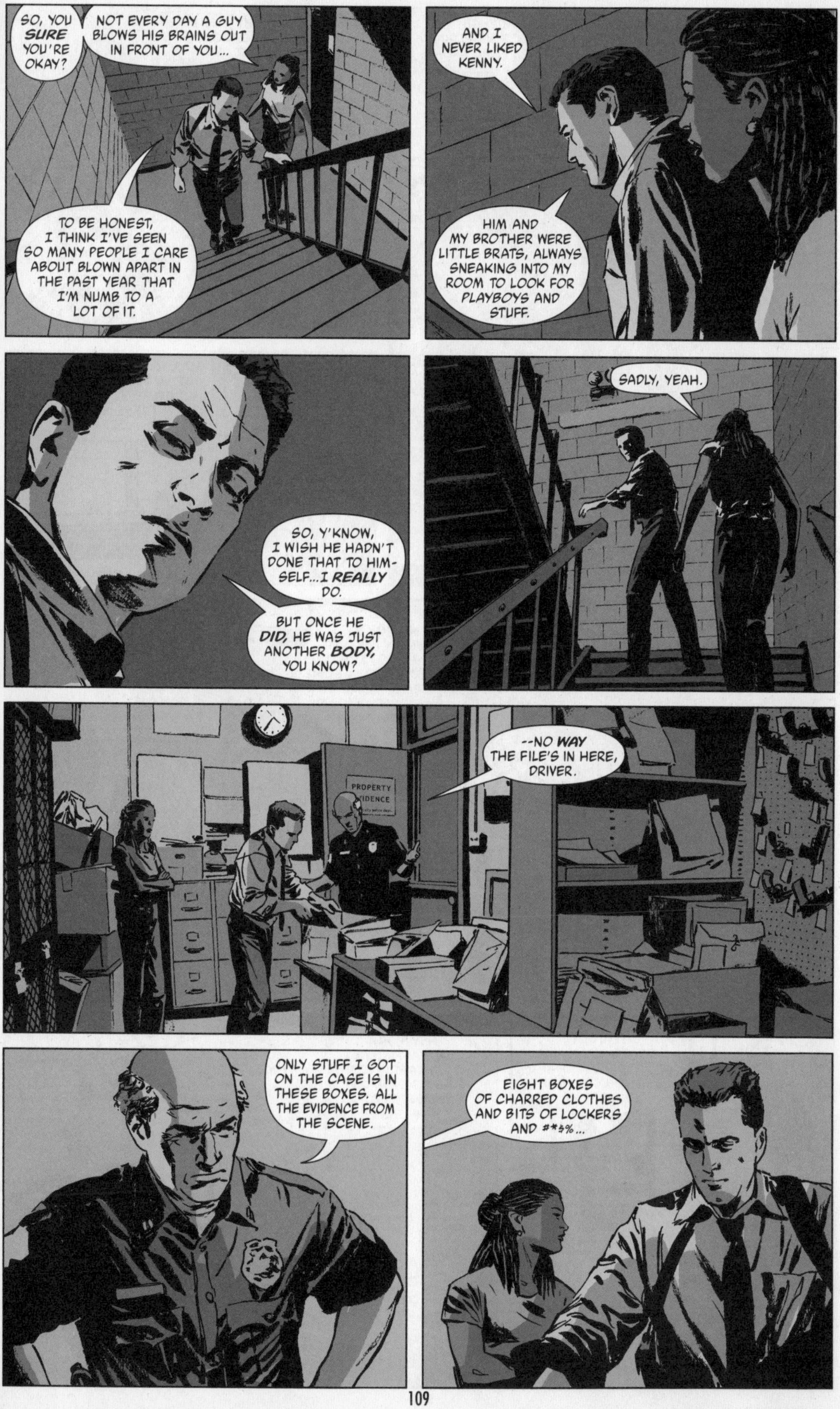
SO, YOU SURE YOU'RE OKAY?
NOT EVERY DAY A GUY BLOWS HIS BRAINS OUT IN FRONT OF YOU...
TO BE HONEST, I THINK I'VE SEEN SO MANY PEOPLE I CARE ABOUT BLOWN APART IN THE PAST YEAR THAT I'M NUMB TO A LOT OF IT.
AND I NEVER LIKED KENNY.
HIM AND MY BROTHER WERE LITTLE BRATS, ALWAYS SNEAKING INTO MY ROOM TO LOOK FOR PLAYBOYS AND STUFF.
SO, Y'KNOW, I WISH HE HADN'T DONE THAT TO HIM-SELF...I REALLY DO.
BUT ONCE HE DID, HE WAS JUST ANOTHER BODY, YOU KNOW?
SADLY, YEAH.
PROPERTY EVIDENCE
--NO WAY THE FILE'S IN HERE, DRIVER.
ONLY STUFF I GOT ON THE CASE IS IN THESE BOXES. ALL THE EVIDENCE FROM THE SCENE.
EIGHT BOXES OF CHARRED CLOTHES AND BITS OF LOCKERS AND #*$%...

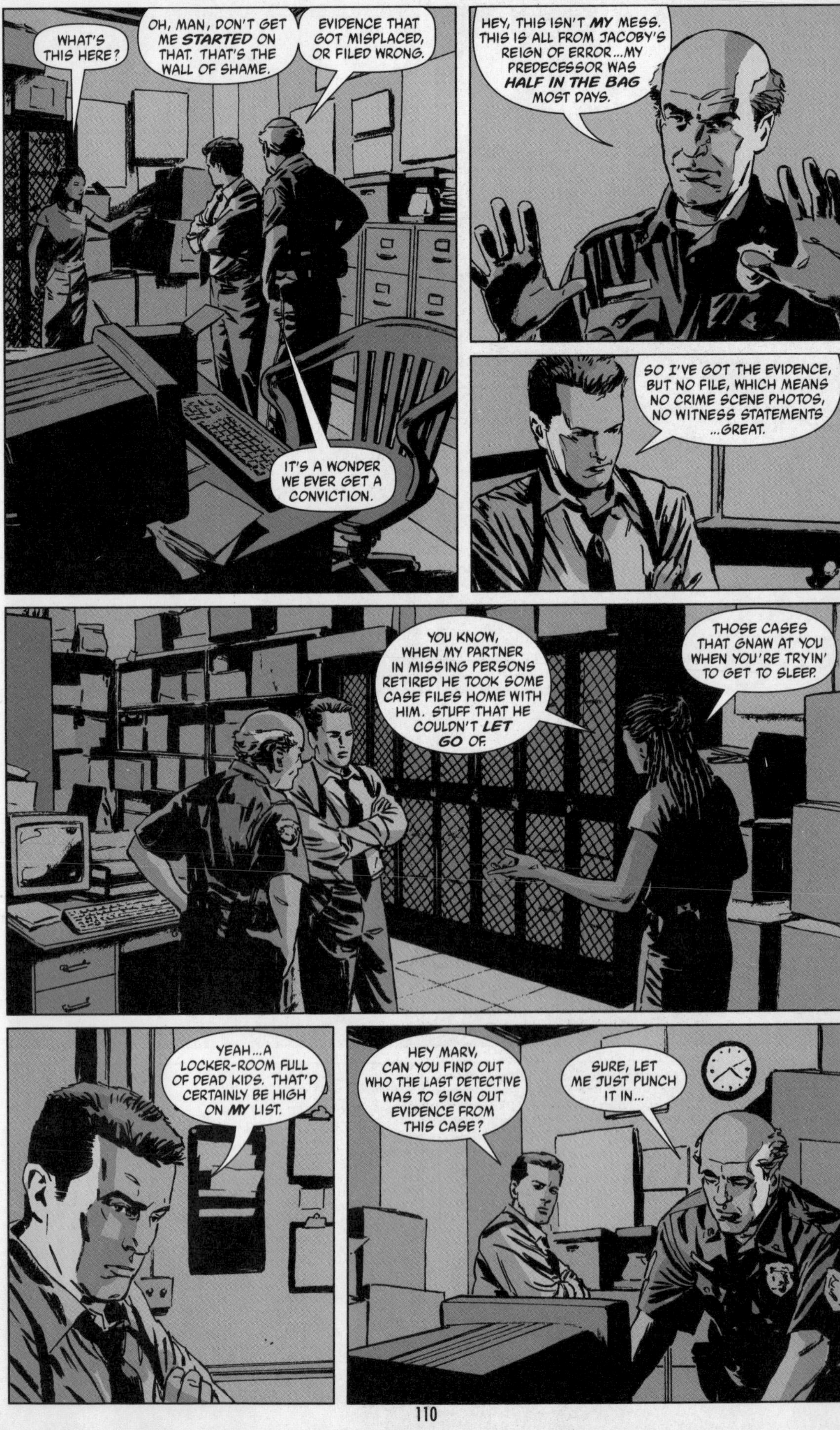

WHAT'S THIS HERE?
OH, MAN, DON'T GET ME STARTED ON THAT. THAT'S THE WALL OF SHAME.
EVIDENCE THAT GOT MISPLACED, OR FILED WRONG.
IT'S A WONDER WE EVER GET A CONVICTION.
HEY, THIS ISN'T MY MESS. THIS IS ALL FROM JACOBY'S REIGN OF ERROR...MY PREDECESSOR WAS HALF IN THE BAG MOST DAYS.
SO I'VE GOT THE EVIDENCE, BUT NO FILE, WHICH MEANS NO CRIME SCENE PHOTOS, NO WITNESS STATEMENTS ...GREAT.
YOU KNOW, WHEN MY PARTNER IN MISSING PERSONS RETIRED HE TOOK SOME CASE FILES HOME WITH HIM. STUFF THAT HE COULDN'T LET GO OF.
THOSE CASES THAT GNAW AT YOU WHEN YOU'RE TRYIN' TO GET TO SLEEP.
YEAH...A LOCKER-ROOM FULL OF DEAD KIDS. THAT'D CERTAINLY BE HIGH ON MY LIST.
HEY MARY, CAN YOU FIND OUT WHO THE LAST DETECTIVE WAS TO SIGN OUT EVIDENCE FROM THIS CASE?
SURE, LET ME JUST PUNCH IT IN...

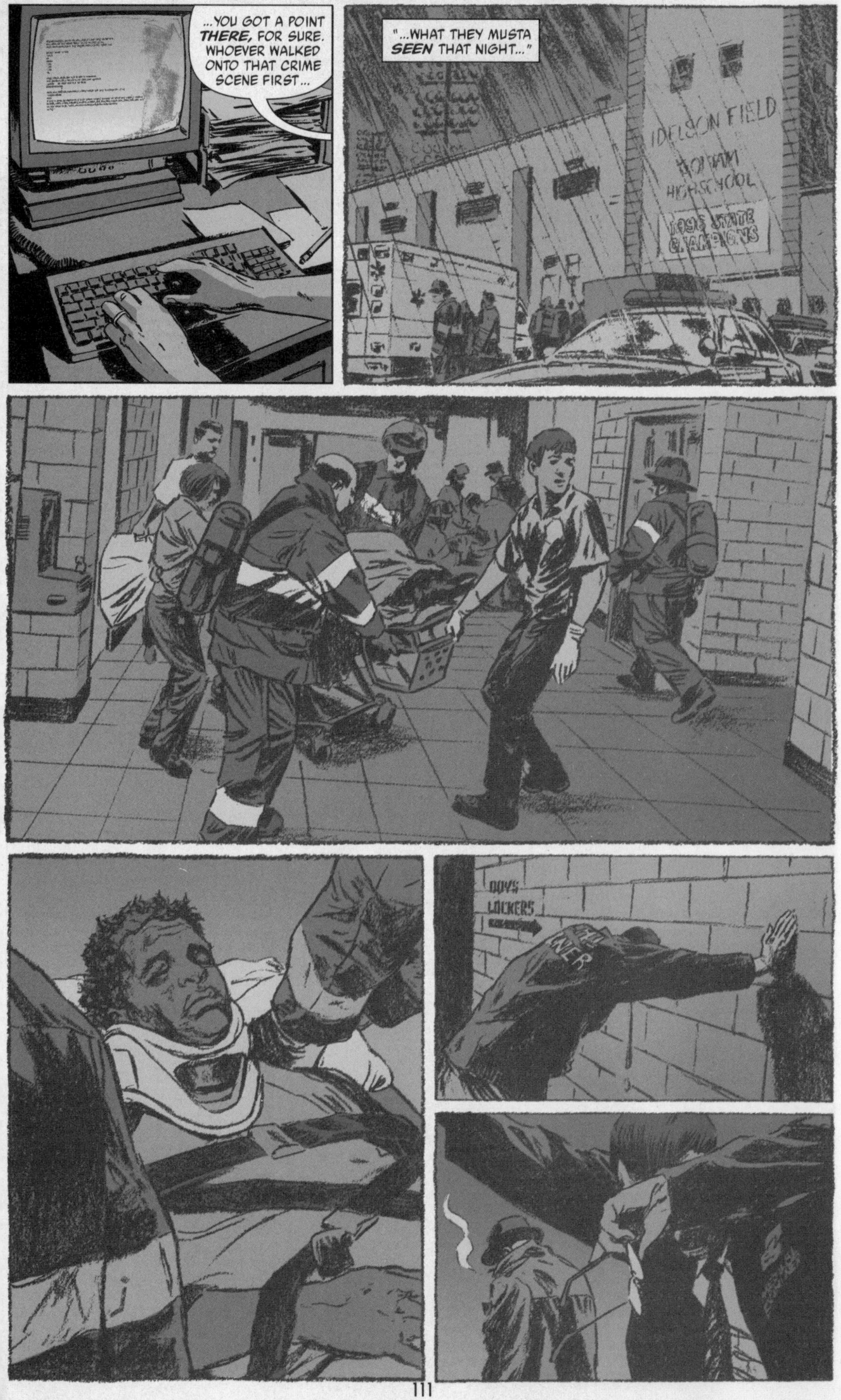
...YOU GOT A POINT *THERE,* FOR SURE. WHOEVER WALKED ONTO THAT CRIME SCENE FIRST...
"...WHAT THEY MUSTA *SEEN* THAT NIGHT..."
IDELSON FIELD
HIGHSCHOOL
BOYS LOCKERS

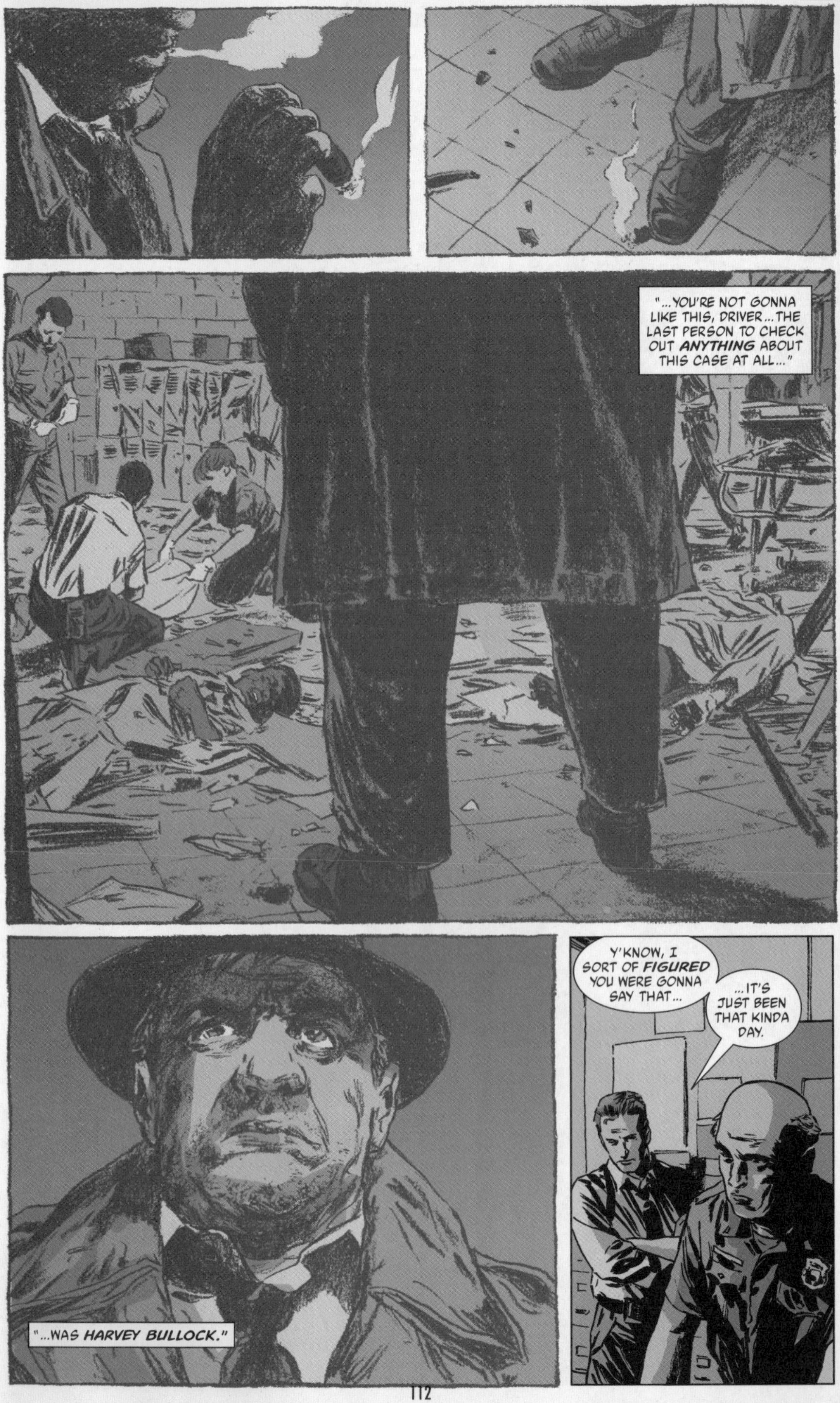
"...YOU'RE NOT GONNA LIKE THIS, DRIVER...THE LAST PERSON TO CHECK OUT ANYTHING ABOUT THIS CASE AT ALL..."
"...WAS HARVEY BULLOCK."
Y'KNOW, I SORT OF FIGURED YOU WERE GONNA SAY THAT...
...IT'S JUST BEEN THAT KINDA DAY.

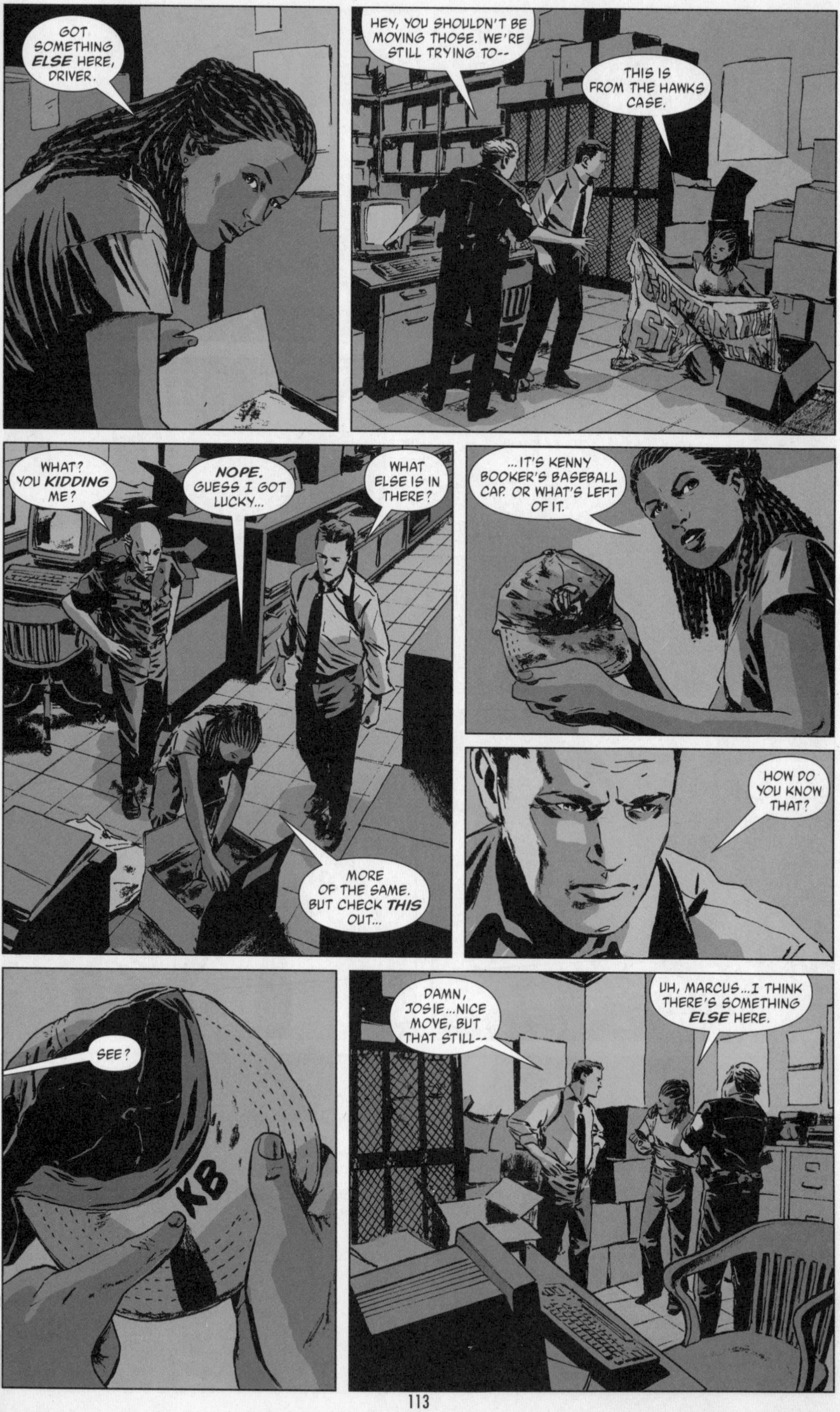
GOT SOMETHING ELSE HERE, DRIVER.
HEY, YOU SHOULDN'T BE MOVING THOSE. WE'RE STILL TRYING TO--
THIS IS FROM THE HAWKS CASE.
WHAT? YOU KIDDING ME?
NOPE. GUESS I GOT LUCKY...
WHAT ELSE IS IN THERE?
MORE OF THE SAME. BUT CHECK THIS OUT...
...IT'S KENNY BOOKER'S BASEBALL CAP. OR WHAT'S LEFT OF IT.
HOW DO YOU KNOW THAT?
SEE?
KB
DAMN, JOSIE...NICE MOVE, BUT THAT STILL--
UH, MARCUS...I THINK THERE'S SOMETHING ELSE HERE.

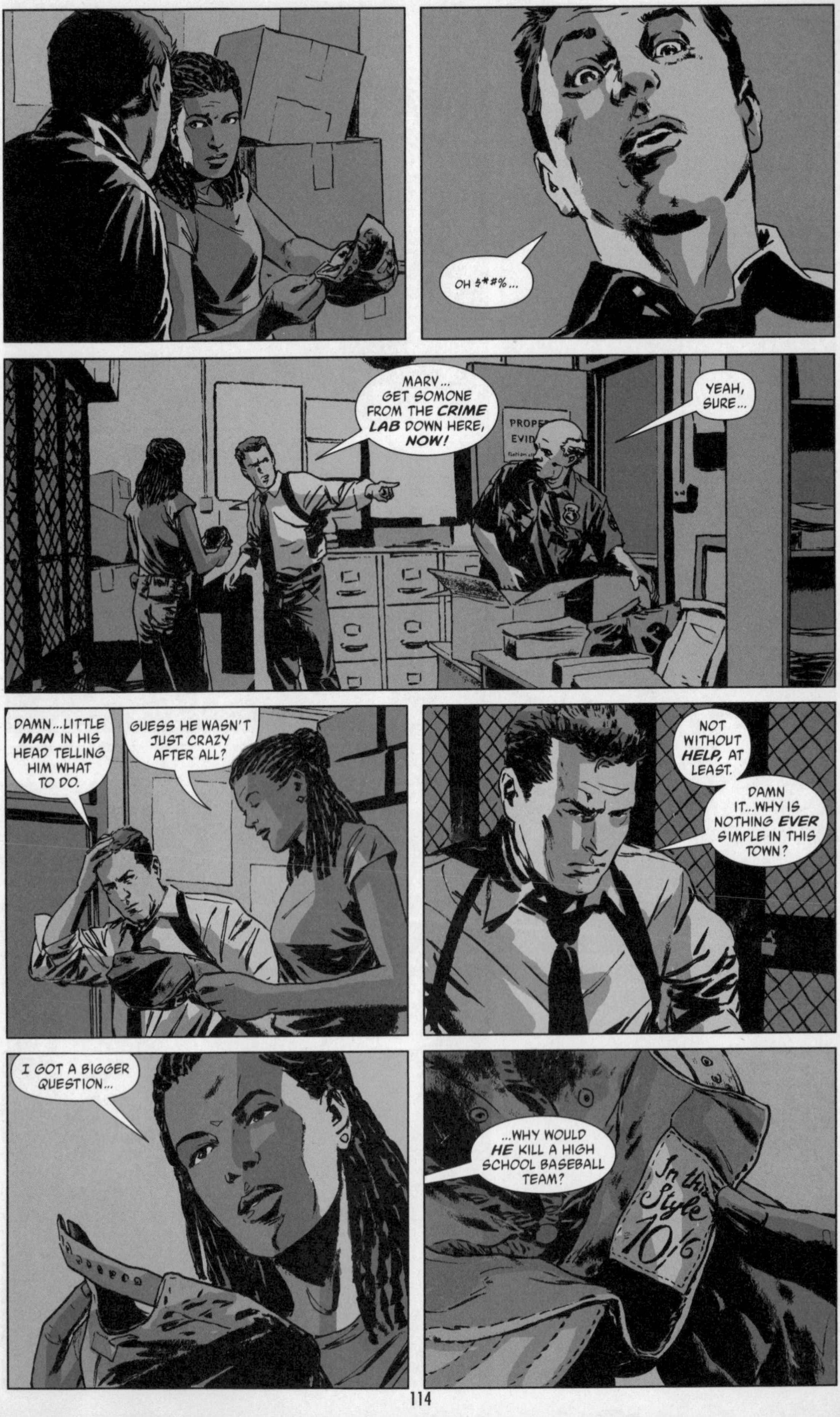
OH $*#%...
MARV... GET SOMONE FROM THE CRIME LAB DOWN HERE, NOW!
YEAH, SURE...
DAMN...LITTLE MAN IN HIS HEAD TELLING HIM WHAT TO DO.
GUESS HE WASN'T JUST CRAZY AFTER ALL?
NOT WITHOUT HELP, AT LEAST.
DAMN IT...WHY IS NOTHING EVER SIMPLE IN THIS TOWN?
I GOT A BIGGER QUESTION...
...WHY WOULD HE KILL A HIGH SCHOOL BASEBALL TEAM?
In the Style 10 1/6

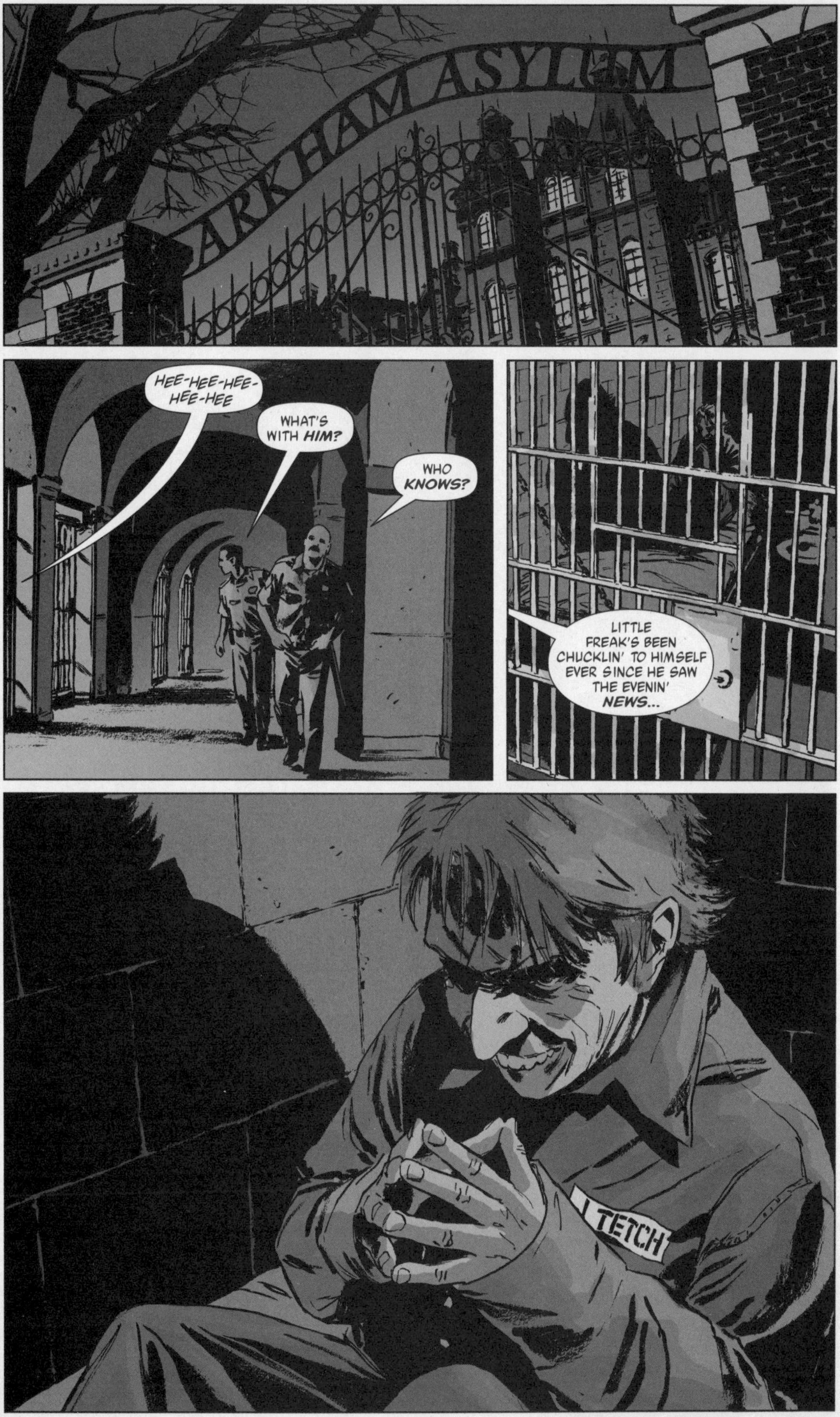

ARKHAM ASYLUM
HEE-HEE-HEE-HEE-HEE
WHAT'S WITH *HIM?*
WHO *KNOWS?*
LITTLE FREAK'S BEEN CHUCKLIN' TO HIMSELF EVER SINCE HE SAW THE EVENIN' *NEWS...*
TETCH

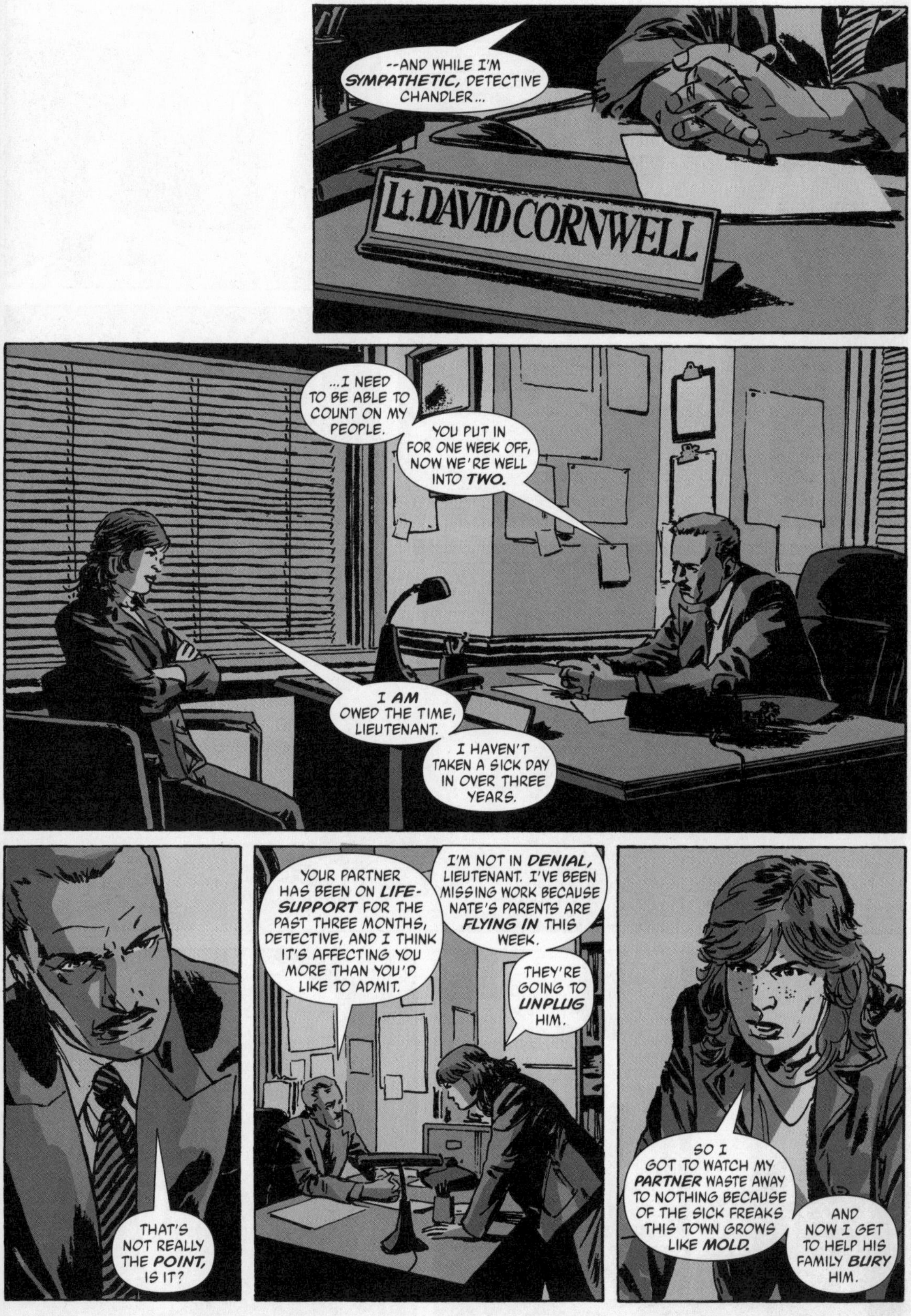
--AND WHILE I'M SYMPATHETIC, DETECTIVE CHANDLER...
Lt. DAVID CORNWELL
...I NEED TO BE ABLE TO COUNT ON MY PEOPLE.
YOU PUT IN FOR ONE WEEK OFF, NOW WE'RE WELL INTO TWO.
I AM OWED THE TIME, LIEUTENANT.
I HAVEN'T TAKEN A SICK DAY IN OVER THREE YEARS.
THAT'S NOT REALLY THE POINT, IS IT?
YOUR PARTNER HAS BEEN ON LIFE-SUPPORT FOR THE PAST THREE MONTHS, DETECTIVE, AND I THINK IT'S AFFECTING YOU MORE THAN YOU'D LIKE TO ADMIT.
I'M NOT IN DENIAL, LIEUTENANT. I'VE BEEN MISSING WORK BECAUSE NATE'S PARENTS ARE FLYING IN THIS WEEK.
THEY'RE GOING TO UNPLUG HIM.
SO I GOT TO WATCH MY PARTNER WASTE AWAY TO NOTHING BECAUSE OF THE SICK FREAKS THIS TOWN GROWS LIKE MOLD.
AND NOW I GET TO HELP HIS FAMILY BURY HIM.

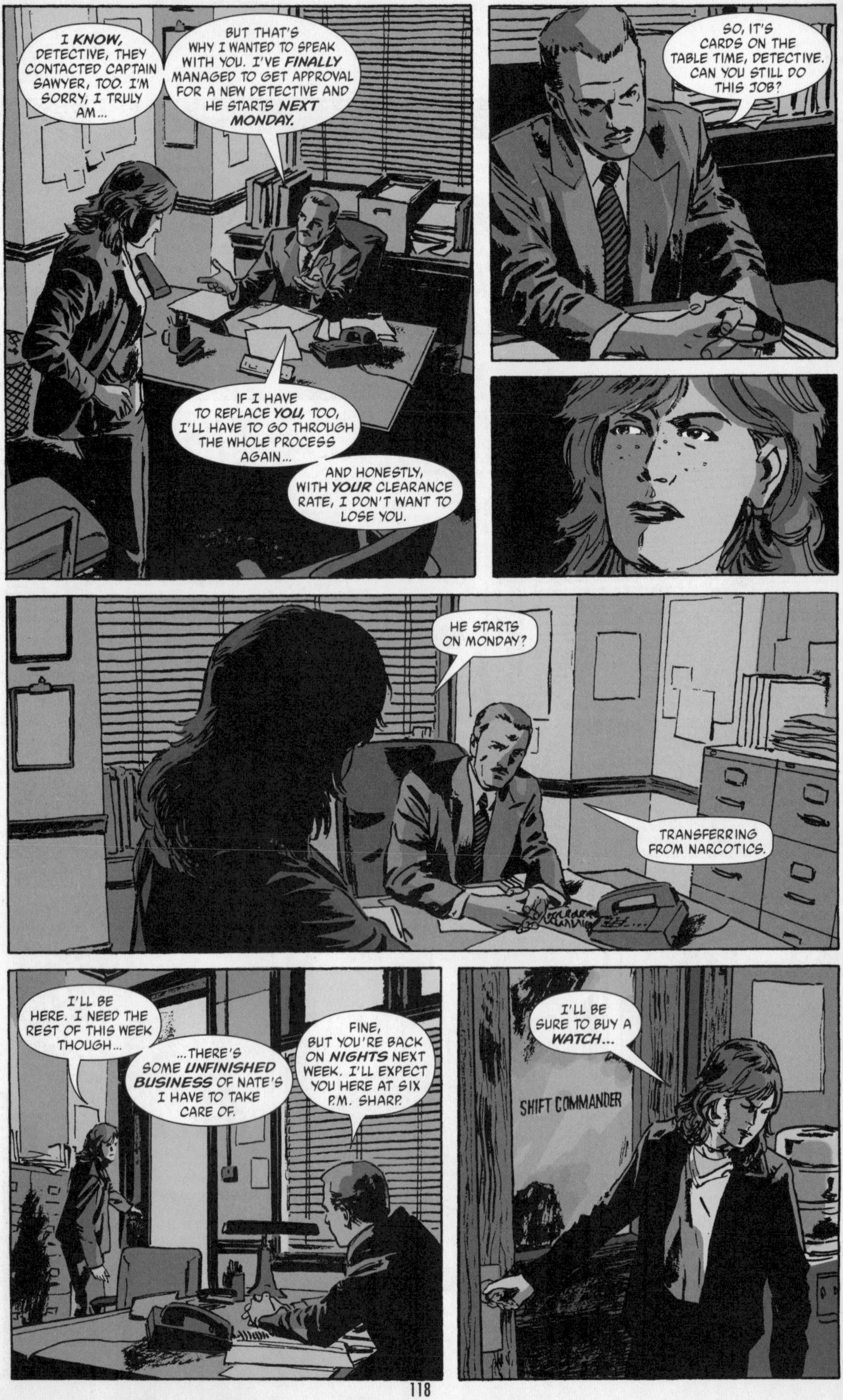
I KNOW, DETECTIVE, THEY CONTACTED CAPTAIN SAWYER, TOO. I'M SORRY, I TRULY AM...
BUT THAT'S WHY I WANTED TO SPEAK WITH YOU. I'VE FINALLY MANAGED TO GET APPROVAL FOR A NEW DETECTIVE AND HE STARTS NEXT MONDAY.
IF I HAVE TO REPLACE YOU, TOO, I'LL HAVE TO GO THROUGH THE WHOLE PROCESS AGAIN...
AND HONESTLY, WITH YOUR CLEARANCE RATE, I DON'T WANT TO LOSE YOU.
SO, IT'S CARDS ON THE TABLE TIME, DETECTIVE. CAN YOU STILL DO THIS JOB?
HE STARTS ON MONDAY?
TRANSFERRING FROM NARCOTICS.
I'LL BE HERE. I NEED THE REST OF THIS WEEK THOUGH...
...THERE'S SOME UNFINISHED BUSINESS OF NATE'S I HAVE TO TAKE CARE OF.
FINE, BUT YOU'RE BACK ON NIGHTS NEXT WEEK. I'LL EXPECT YOU HERE AT SIX P.M. SHARP.
I'LL BE SURE TO BUY A WATCH...
SHIFT COMMANDER

HEY, ROMY, HOW YOU *DOIN'* GIRL?

HEY, SARGE...

...YOU SEE MOLINA'S *BOOK?*

NOT REALLY... COULDN'T GET PAST THE DEDICATION.

LUCKY *YOU.*

YOU GONNA BE OKAY?

YEAH, JUST, YOU KNOW...

MEETING WITH CORNHOLE. ACTUALLY MAKES ME MISS *PROBSON.*

YOU'RE NOT ALONE THERE. HOLD ON A SEC...

M.C.U., SERGEANT DAVIES.

OH, HEY, DRIVER...YEAH, *THAT'S* THE PLACE...

...NO, THE ONE ON *FINGER,* NOT CUTTLER.

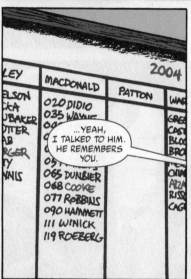

2004

LEY | MACDONALD | PATTON | WAR

ELSON | 020 DIDIO | | GREE
CKA | 035 WAYNE | | CAS
UBAKER | 00 | | BLOO
TTER | | | BRO
B |
RGER |
TY | 057 | |
NNIS | 065 DUNBIER | | CHU
| 068 COOKE | | AZA
| 077 ROBBINS | | RISS
| 090 HAMMETT | | CAG
| 111 WINICK |
| 119 ROEBERG |

...YEAH, I TALKED TO HIM. HE REMEMBERS YOU.

ANYWAY, I *VOUCHED* JUST IN CASE...UH HUNH...

NO...NO, I WOULDN'T SAY RETIREMENT HAS MELLOWED HIM OUT ANY.

...YEAH, WELL, GOOD LUCK.

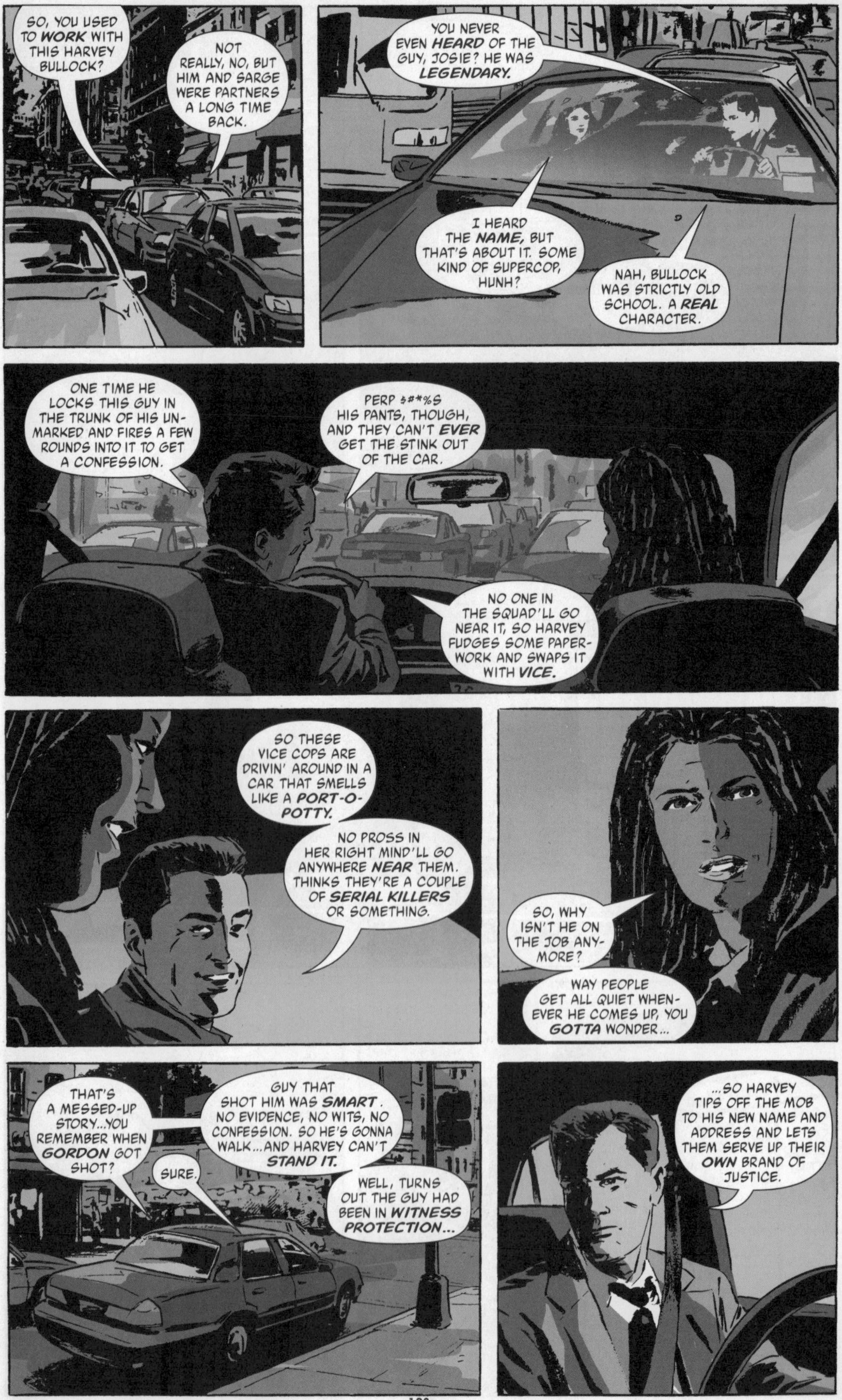
SO, YOU USED TO WORK WITH THIS HARVEY BULLOCK?
NOT REALLY, NO, BUT HIM AND SARGE WERE PARTNERS A LONG TIME BACK.
YOU NEVER EVEN HEARD OF THE GUY, JOSIE? HE WAS LEGENDARY.
I HEARD THE NAME, BUT THAT'S ABOUT IT. SOME KIND OF SUPERCOP, HUNH?
NAH, BULLOCK WAS STRICTLY OLD SCHOOL. A REAL CHARACTER.
ONE TIME HE LOCKS THIS GUY IN THE TRUNK OF HIS UNMARKED AND FIRES A FEW ROUNDS INTO IT TO GET A CONFESSION.
PERP $#*%S HIS PANTS, THOUGH, AND THEY CAN'T EVER GET THE STINK OUT OF THE CAR.
NO ONE IN THE SQUAD'LL GO NEAR IT, SO HARVEY FUDGES SOME PAPERWORK AND SWAPS IT WITH VICE.
SO THESE VICE COPS ARE DRIVIN' AROUND IN A CAR THAT SMELLS LIKE A PORT-O-POTTY.
NO PROSS IN HER RIGHT MIND'LL GO ANYWHERE NEAR THEM. THINKS THEY'RE A COUPLE OF SERIAL KILLERS OR SOMETHING.
SO, WHY ISN'T HE ON THE JOB ANYMORE?
WAY PEOPLE GET ALL QUIET WHENEVER HE COMES UP, YOU GOTTA WONDER...
THAT'S A MESSED-UP STORY...YOU REMEMBER WHEN GORDON GOT SHOT?
SURE.
GUY THAT SHOT HIM WAS SMART. NO EVIDENCE, NO WITS, NO CONFESSION. SO HE'S GONNA WALK...AND HARVEY CAN'T STAND IT.
WELL, TURNS OUT THE GUY HAD BEEN IN WITNESS PROTECTION...
...SO HARVEY TIPS OFF THE MOB TO HIS NEW NAME AND ADDRESS AND LETS THEM SERVE UP THEIR OWN BRAND OF JUSTICE.

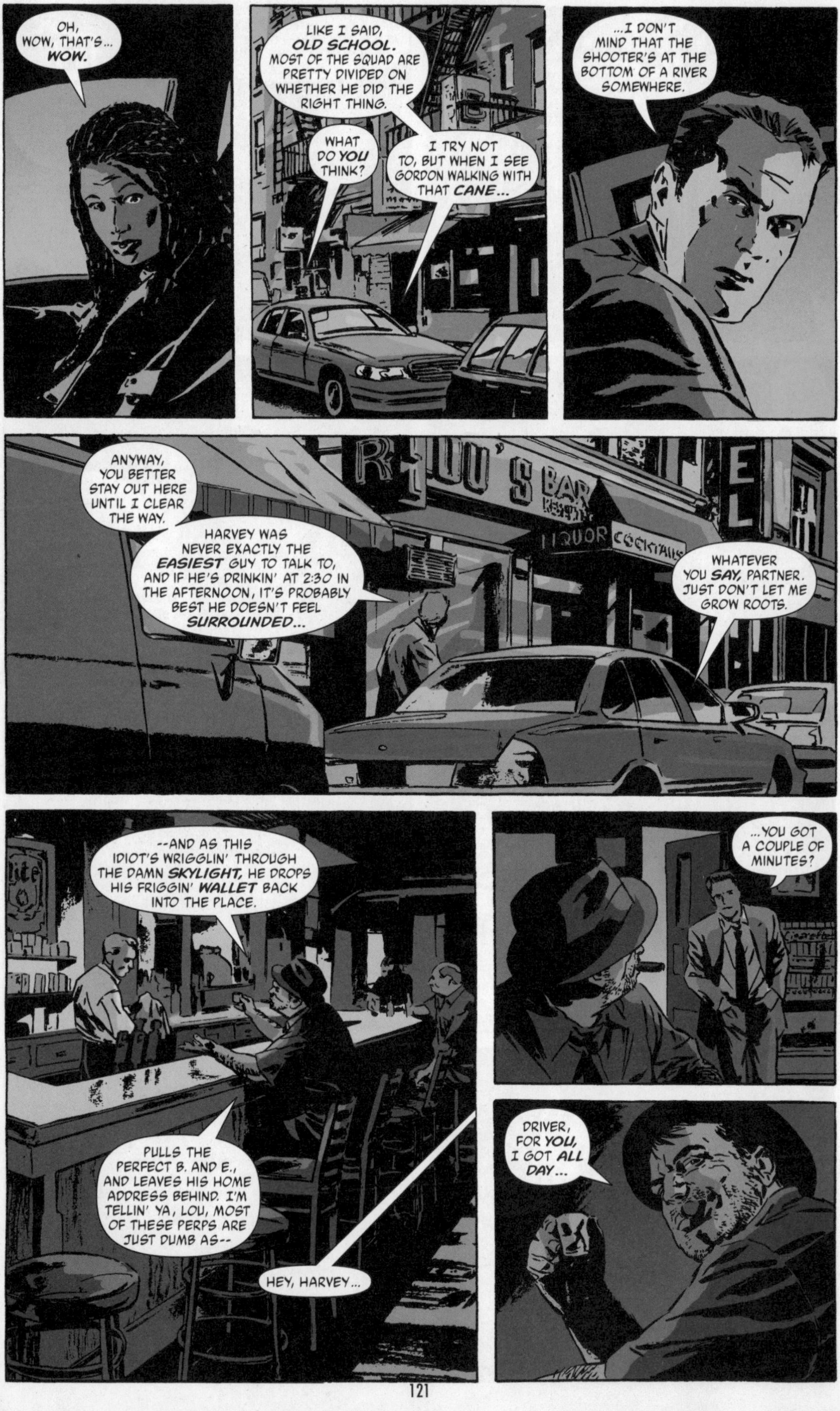

OH, WOW, THAT'S... WOW.
LIKE I SAID, OLD SCHOOL. MOST OF THE SQUAD ARE PRETTY DIVIDED ON WHETHER HE DID THE RIGHT THING.
WHAT DO YOU THINK?
I TRY NOT TO, BUT WHEN I SEE GORDON WALKING WITH THAT CANE...
...I DON'T MIND THAT THE SHOOTER'S AT THE BOTTOM OF A RIVER SOMEWHERE.
ANYWAY, YOU BETTER STAY OUT HERE UNTIL I CLEAR THE WAY.
HARVEY WAS NEVER EXACTLY THE EASIEST GUY TO TALK TO, AND IF HE'S DRINKIN' AT 2:30 IN THE AFTERNOON, IT'S PROBABLY BEST HE DOESN'T FEEL SURROUNDED...
WHATEVER YOU SAY, PARTNER. JUST DON'T LET ME GROW ROOTS.
LIQUOR
COCKTAILS
--AND AS THIS IDIOT'S WRIGGLIN' THROUGH THE DAMN SKYLIGHT, HE DROPS HIS FRIGGIN' WALLET BACK INTO THE PLACE.
PULLS THE PERFECT B. AND E., AND LEAVES HIS HOME ADDRESS BEHIND. I'M TELLIN' YA, LOU, MOST OF THESE PERPS ARE JUST DUMB AS--
HEY, HARVEY...
...YOU GOT A COUPLE OF MINUTES?
DRIVER, FOR YOU, I GOT ALL DAY...

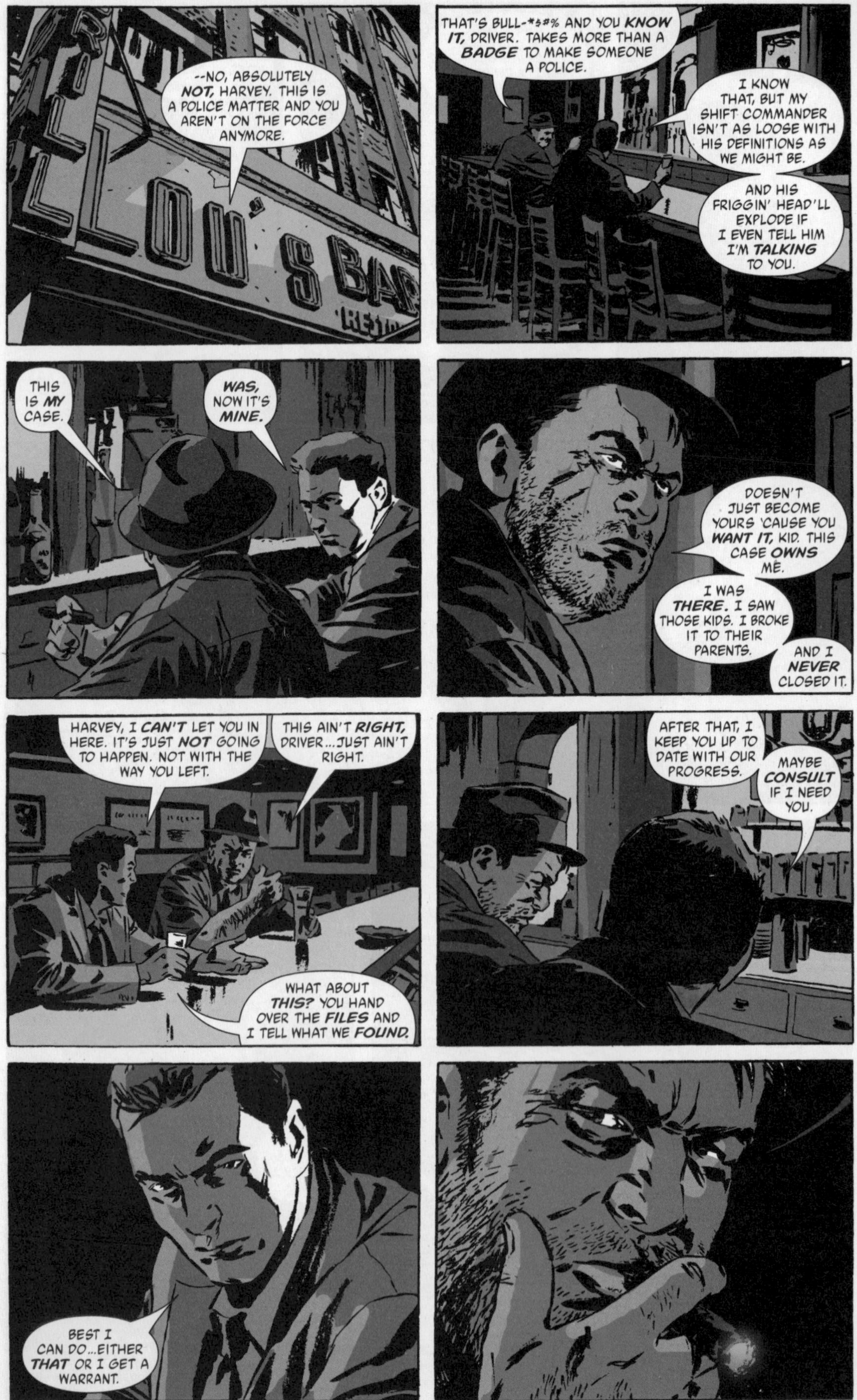
--NO, ABSOLUTELY NOT, HARVEY. THIS IS A POLICE MATTER AND YOU AREN'T ON THE FORCE ANYMORE.
THAT'S BULL-*$#% AND YOU KNOW IT, DRIVER. TAKES MORE THAN A BADGE TO MAKE SOMEONE A POLICE.
I KNOW THAT, BUT MY SHIFT COMMANDER ISN'T AS LOOSE WITH HIS DEFINITIONS AS WE MIGHT BE.
AND HIS FRIGGIN' HEAD'LL EXPLODE IF I EVEN TELL HIM I'M TALKING TO YOU.
THIS IS MY CASE.
WAS, NOW IT'S MINE.
DOESN'T JUST BECOME YOURS 'CAUSE YOU WANT IT, KID. THIS CASE OWNS ME.
I WAS THERE. I SAW THOSE KIDS. I BROKE IT TO THEIR PARENTS.
AND I NEVER CLOSED IT.
HARVEY, I CAN'T LET YOU IN HERE. IT'S JUST NOT GOING TO HAPPEN. NOT WITH THE WAY YOU LEFT.
THIS AIN'T RIGHT, DRIVER... JUST AIN'T RIGHT.
WHAT ABOUT THIS? YOU HAND OVER THE FILES AND I TELL WHAT WE FOUND.
AFTER THAT, I KEEP YOU UP TO DATE WITH OUR PROGRESS.
MAYBE CONSULT IF I NEED YOU.
BEST I CAN DO... EITHER THAT OR I GET A WARRANT.

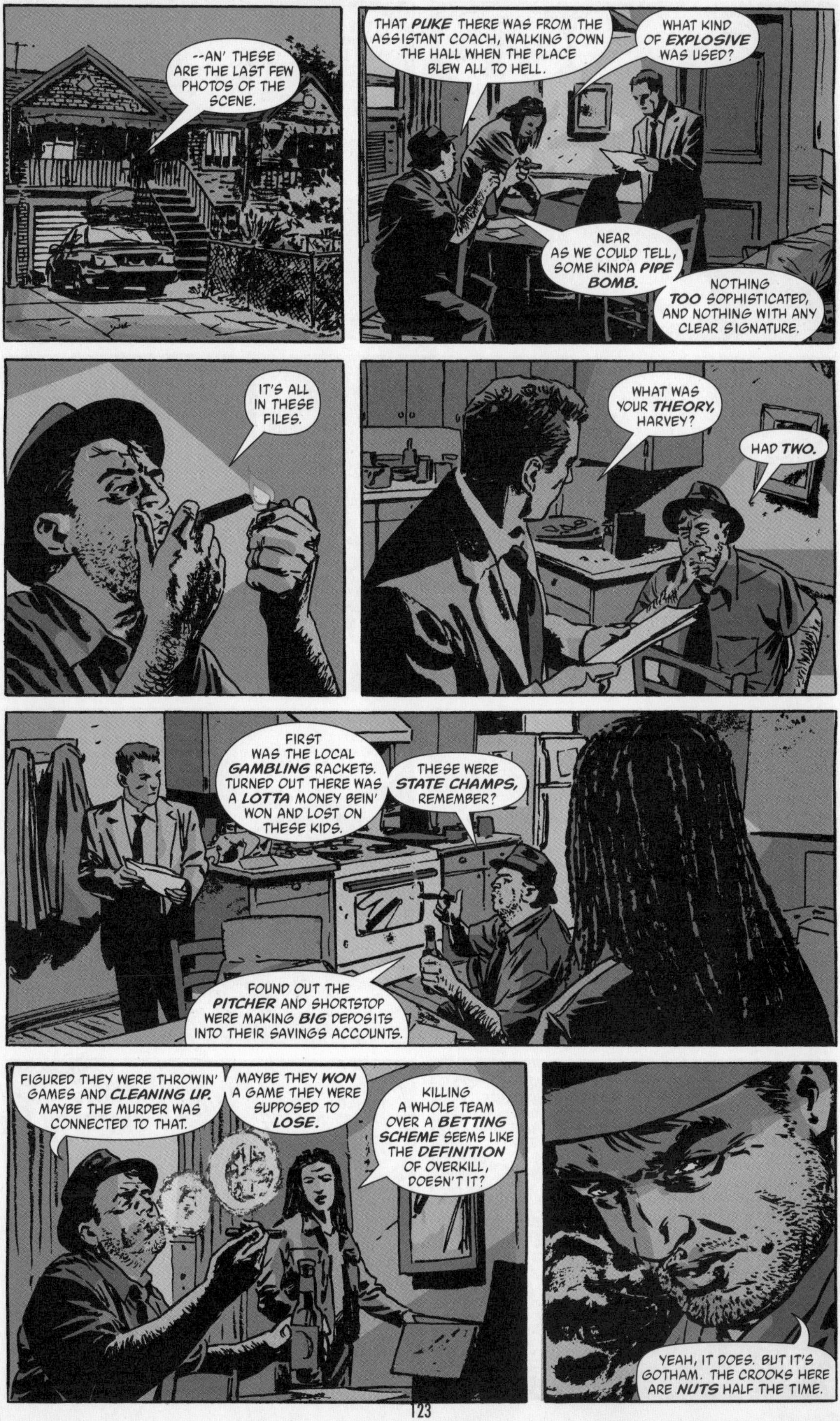
--AN' THESE ARE THE LAST FEW PHOTOS OF THE SCENE.
THAT PUKE THERE WAS FROM THE ASSISTANT COACH, WALKING DOWN THE HALL WHEN THE PLACE BLEW ALL TO HELL.
WHAT KIND OF EXPLOSIVE WAS USED?
NEAR AS WE COULD TELL, SOME KINDA PIPE BOMB.
NOTHING TOO SOPHISTICATED, AND NOTHING WITH ANY CLEAR SIGNATURE.
IT'S ALL IN THESE FILES.
WHAT WAS YOUR THEORY, HARVEY?
HAD TWO.
FIRST WAS THE LOCAL GAMBLING RACKETS. TURNED OUT THERE WAS A LOTTA MONEY BEIN' WON AND LOST ON THESE KIDS.
THESE WERE STATE CHAMPS, REMEMBER?
FOUND OUT THE PITCHER AND SHORTSTOP WERE MAKING BIG DEPOSITS INTO THEIR SAVINGS ACCOUNTS.
FIGURED THEY WERE THROWIN' GAMES AND CLEANING UP. MAYBE THE MURDER WAS CONNECTED TO THAT.
MAYBE THEY WON A GAME THEY WERE SUPPOSED TO LOSE.
KILLING A WHOLE TEAM OVER A BETTING SCHEME SEEMS LIKE THE DEFINITION OF OVERKILL, DOESN'T IT?
YEAH, IT DOES. BUT IT'S GOTHAM. THE CROOKS HERE ARE NUTS HALF THE TIME.

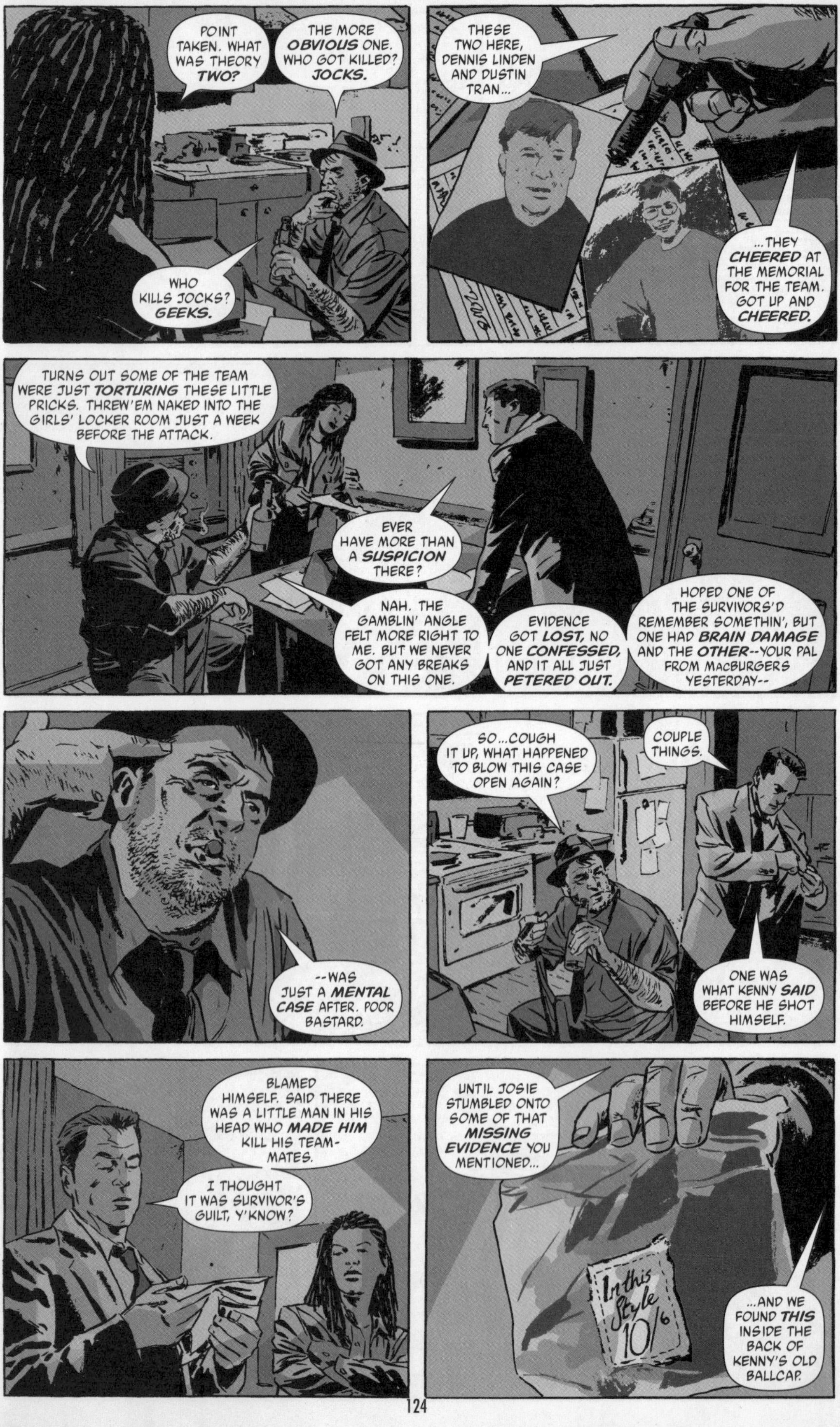
POINT TAKEN. WHAT WAS THEORY TWO?
THE MORE OBVIOUS ONE. WHO GOT KILLED? JOCKS.
WHO KILLS JOCKS? GEEKS.
THESE TWO HERE, DENNIS LINDEN AND DUSTIN TRAN...
...THEY CHEERED AT THE MEMORIAL FOR THE TEAM. GOT UP AND CHEERED.
TURNS OUT SOME OF THE TEAM WERE JUST TORTURING THESE LITTLE PRICKS. THREW'EM NAKED INTO THE GIRLS' LOCKER ROOM JUST A WEEK BEFORE THE ATTACK.
EVER HAVE MORE THAN A SUSPICION THERE?
NAH. THE GAMBLIN' ANGLE FELT MORE RIGHT TO ME. BUT WE NEVER GOT ANY BREAKS ON THIS ONE.
EVIDENCE GOT LOST, NO ONE CONFESSED, AND IT ALL JUST PETERED OUT.
HOPED ONE OF THE SURVIVORS'D REMEMBER SOMETHIN', BUT ONE HAD BRAIN DAMAGE AND THE OTHER--YOUR PAL FROM MACBURGERS YESTERDAY--
--WAS JUST A MENTAL CASE AFTER. POOR BASTARD.
SO...COUGH IT UP, WHAT HAPPENED TO BLOW THIS CASE OPEN AGAIN?
COUPLE THINGS.
ONE WAS WHAT KENNY SAID BEFORE HE SHOT HIMSELF.
BLAMED HIMSELF. SAID THERE WAS A LITTLE MAN IN HIS HEAD WHO MADE HIM KILL HIS TEAM-MATES.
I THOUGHT IT WAS SURVIVOR'S GUILT, Y'KNOW?
UNTIL JOSIE STUMBLED ONTO SOME OF THAT MISSING EVIDENCE YOU MENTIONED...
In this Style 10/6
...AND WE FOUND THIS INSIDE THE BACK OF KENNY'S OLD BALLCAP.

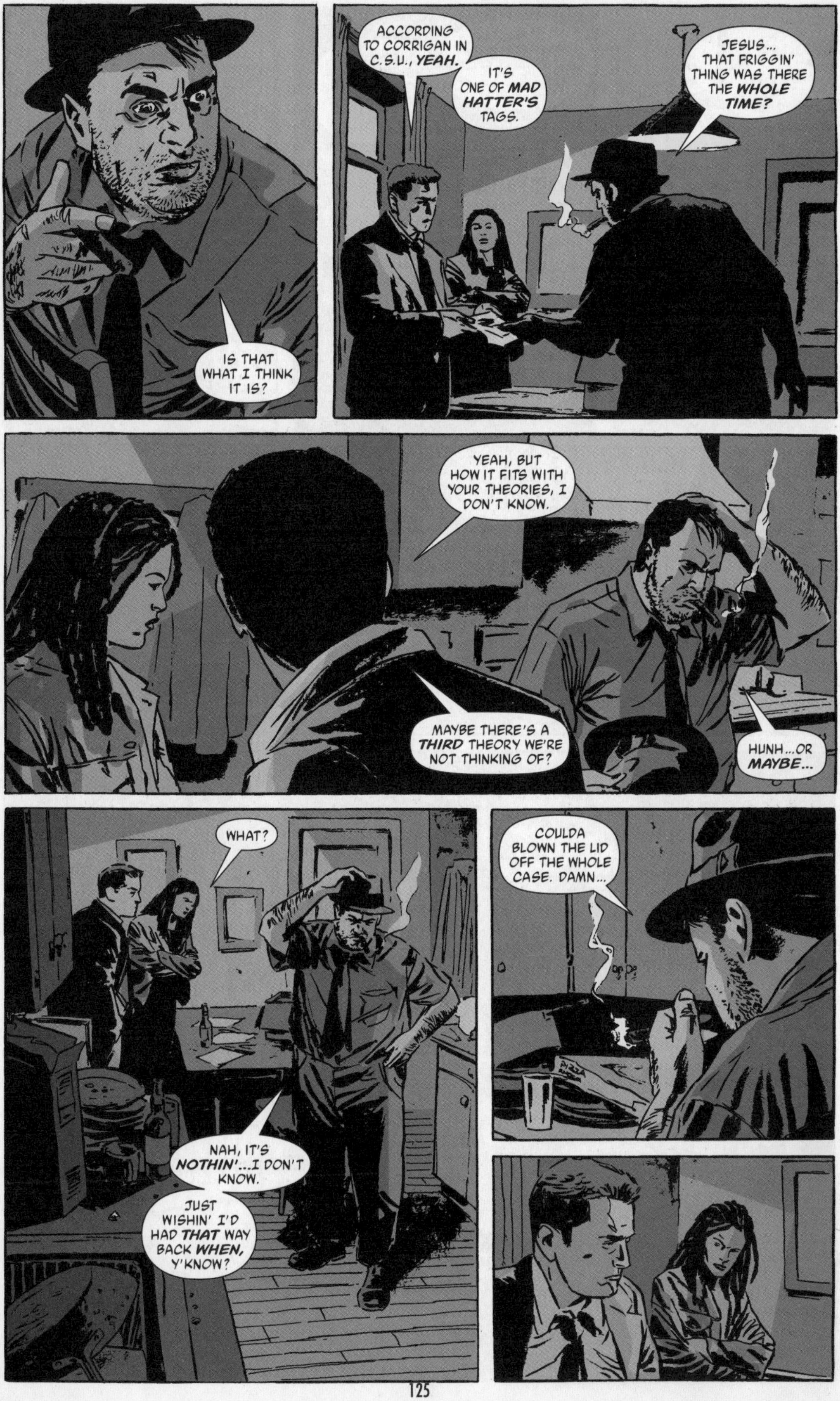

IS THAT WHAT I THINK IT IS?
ACCORDING TO CORRIGAN IN C.S.U., **YEAH.**
IT'S ONE OF **MAD HATTER'S** TAGS.
JESUS... THAT FRIGGIN' THING WAS THERE THE **WHOLE TIME?**
YEAH, BUT HOW IT FITS WITH YOUR THEORIES, I DON'T KNOW.
MAYBE THERE'S A **THIRD** THEORY WE'RE NOT THINKING OF?
HUNH...OR **MAYBE...**
WHAT?
NAH, IT'S **NOTHIN'**...I DON'T KNOW.
JUST WISHIN' I'D HAD **THAT** WAY BACK **WHEN,** Y'KNOW?
COULDA BLOWN THE LID OFF THE WHOLE CASE. DAMN...

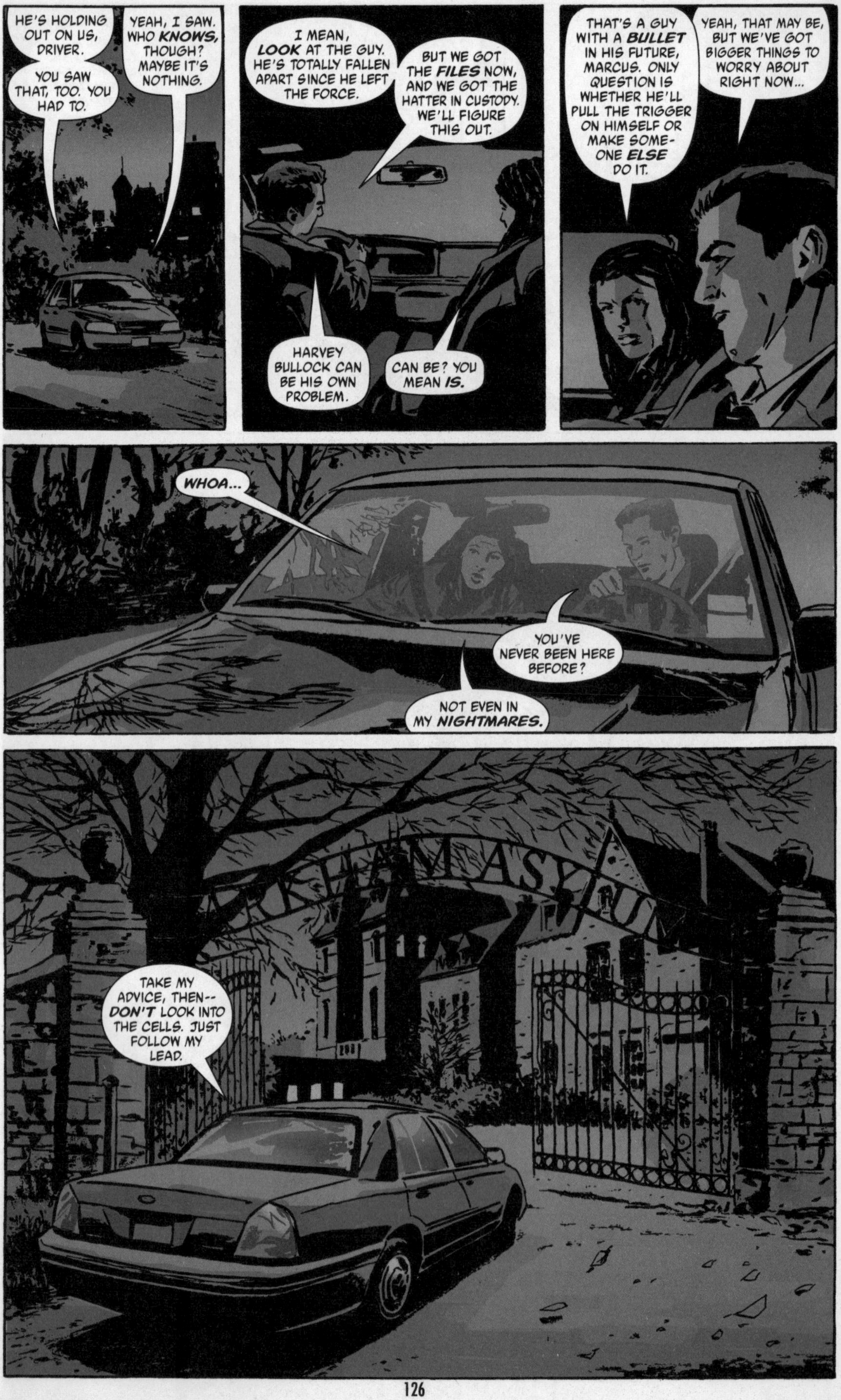
HE'S HOLDING OUT ON US, DRIVER.
YEAH, I SAW. WHO KNOWS, THOUGH? MAYBE IT'S NOTHING.
YOU SAW THAT, TOO. YOU HAD TO.
I MEAN, LOOK AT THE GUY. HE'S TOTALLY FALLEN APART SINCE HE LEFT THE FORCE.
BUT WE GOT THE FILES NOW, AND WE GOT THE HATTER IN CUSTODY. WE'LL FIGURE THIS OUT.
HARVEY BULLOCK CAN BE HIS OWN PROBLEM.
CAN BE? YOU MEAN IS.
THAT'S A GUY WITH A BULLET IN HIS FUTURE, MARCUS. ONLY QUESTION IS WHETHER HE'LL PULL THE TRIGGER ON HIMSELF OR MAKE SOME-ONE ELSE DO IT.
YEAH, THAT MAY BE, BUT WE'VE GOT BIGGER THINGS TO WORRY ABOUT RIGHT NOW...
WHOA...
YOU'VE NEVER BEEN HERE BEFORE?
NOT EVEN IN MY NIGHTMARES.
TAKE MY ADVICE, THEN-- DON'T LOOK INTO THE CELLS. JUST FOLLOW MY LEAD.

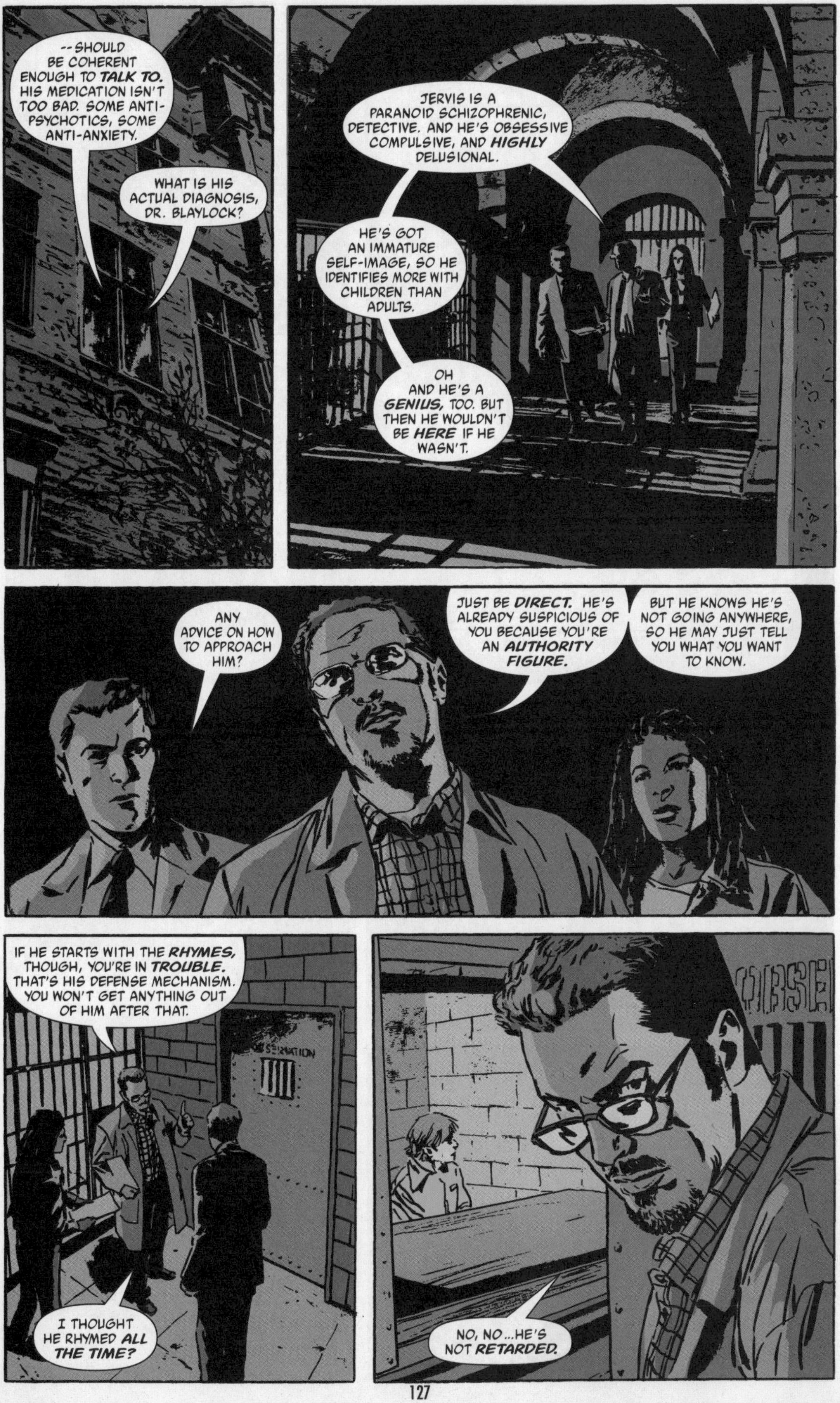
--SHOULD BE COHERENT ENOUGH TO TALK TO. HIS MEDICATION ISN'T TOO BAD. SOME ANTI-PSYCHOTICS, SOME ANTI-ANXIETY.
WHAT IS HIS ACTUAL DIAGNOSIS, DR. BLAYLOCK?
JERVIS IS A PARANOID SCHIZOPHRENIC, DETECTIVE. AND HE'S OBSESSIVE COMPULSIVE, AND HIGHLY DELUSIONAL.
HE'S GOT AN IMMATURE SELF-IMAGE, SO HE IDENTIFIES MORE WITH CHILDREN THAN ADULTS.
OH AND HE'S A GENIUS, TOO. BUT THEN HE WOULDN'T BE HERE IF HE WASN'T.
ANY ADVICE ON HOW TO APPROACH HIM?
JUST BE DIRECT. HE'S ALREADY SUSPICIOUS OF YOU BECAUSE YOU'RE AN AUTHORITY FIGURE.
BUT HE KNOWS HE'S NOT GOING ANYWHERE, SO HE MAY JUST TELL YOU WHAT YOU WANT TO KNOW.
IF HE STARTS WITH THE RHYMES, THOUGH, YOU'RE IN TROUBLE. THAT'S HIS DEFENSE MECHANISM. YOU WON'T GET ANYTHING OUT OF HIM AFTER THAT.
I THOUGHT HE RHYMED ALL THE TIME?
NO, NO...HE'S NOT RETARDED.

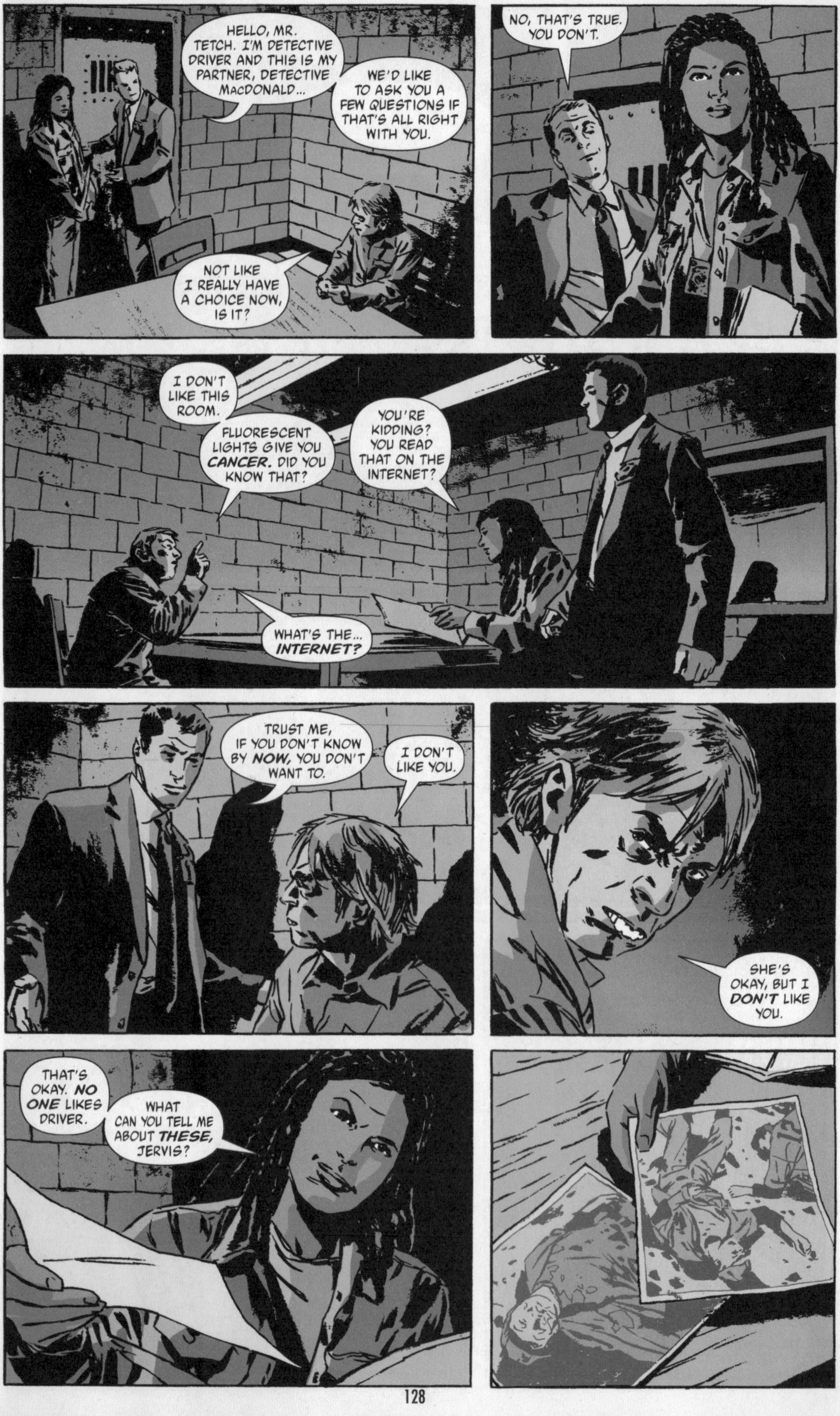
HELLO, MR. TETCH. I'M DETECTIVE DRIVER AND THIS IS MY PARTNER, DETECTIVE MacDONALD...
WE'D LIKE TO ASK YOU A FEW QUESTIONS IF THAT'S ALL RIGHT WITH YOU.
NOT LIKE I REALLY HAVE A CHOICE NOW, IS IT?
NO, THAT'S TRUE. YOU DON'T.
I DON'T LIKE THIS ROOM.
FLUORESCENT LIGHTS GIVE YOU **CANCER.** DID YOU KNOW THAT?
YOU'RE KIDDING? YOU READ THAT ON THE INTERNET?
WHAT'S THE... ***INTERNET?***
TRUST ME, IF YOU DON'T KNOW BY ***NOW,*** YOU DON'T WANT TO.
I DON'T LIKE YOU.
SHE'S OKAY, BUT I ***DON'T*** LIKE YOU.
THAT'S OKAY. ***NO ONE*** LIKES DRIVER.
WHAT CAN YOU TELL ME ABOUT ***THESE,*** JERVIS?

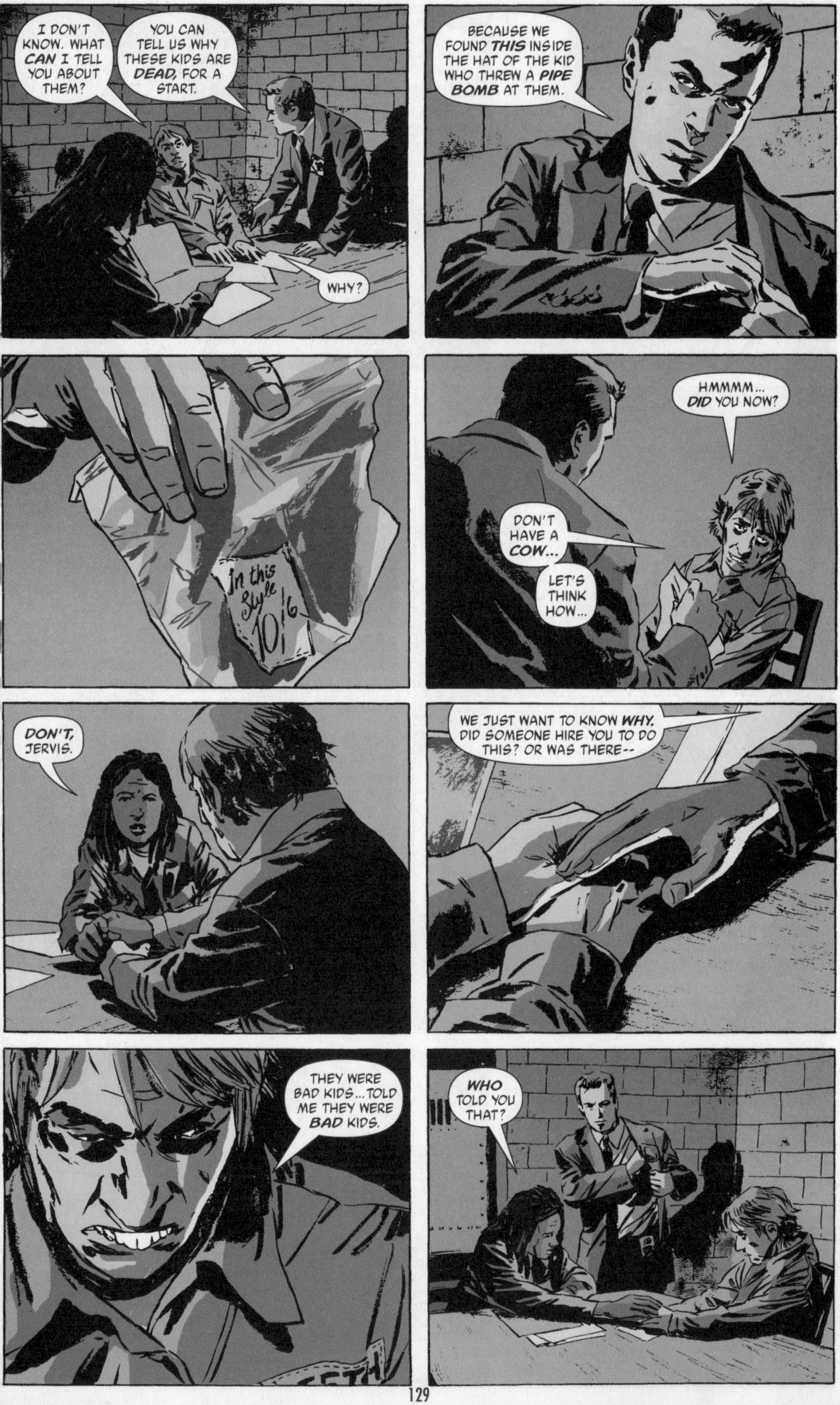

I DON'T KNOW. WHAT CAN I TELL YOU ABOUT THEM?
YOU CAN TELL US WHY THESE KIDS ARE DEAD, FOR A START.
WHY?
BECAUSE WE FOUND THIS INSIDE THE HAT OF THE KID WHO THREW A PIPE BOMB AT THEM.
In this Style 10/6
HMMMM... DID YOU NOW?
DON'T HAVE A COW...
LET'S THINK HOW...
DON'T, JERVIS.
WE JUST WANT TO KNOW WHY. DID SOMEONE HIRE YOU TO DO THIS? OR WAS THERE--
THEY WERE BAD KIDS... TOLD ME THEY WERE BAD KIDS.
WHO TOLD YOU THAT?

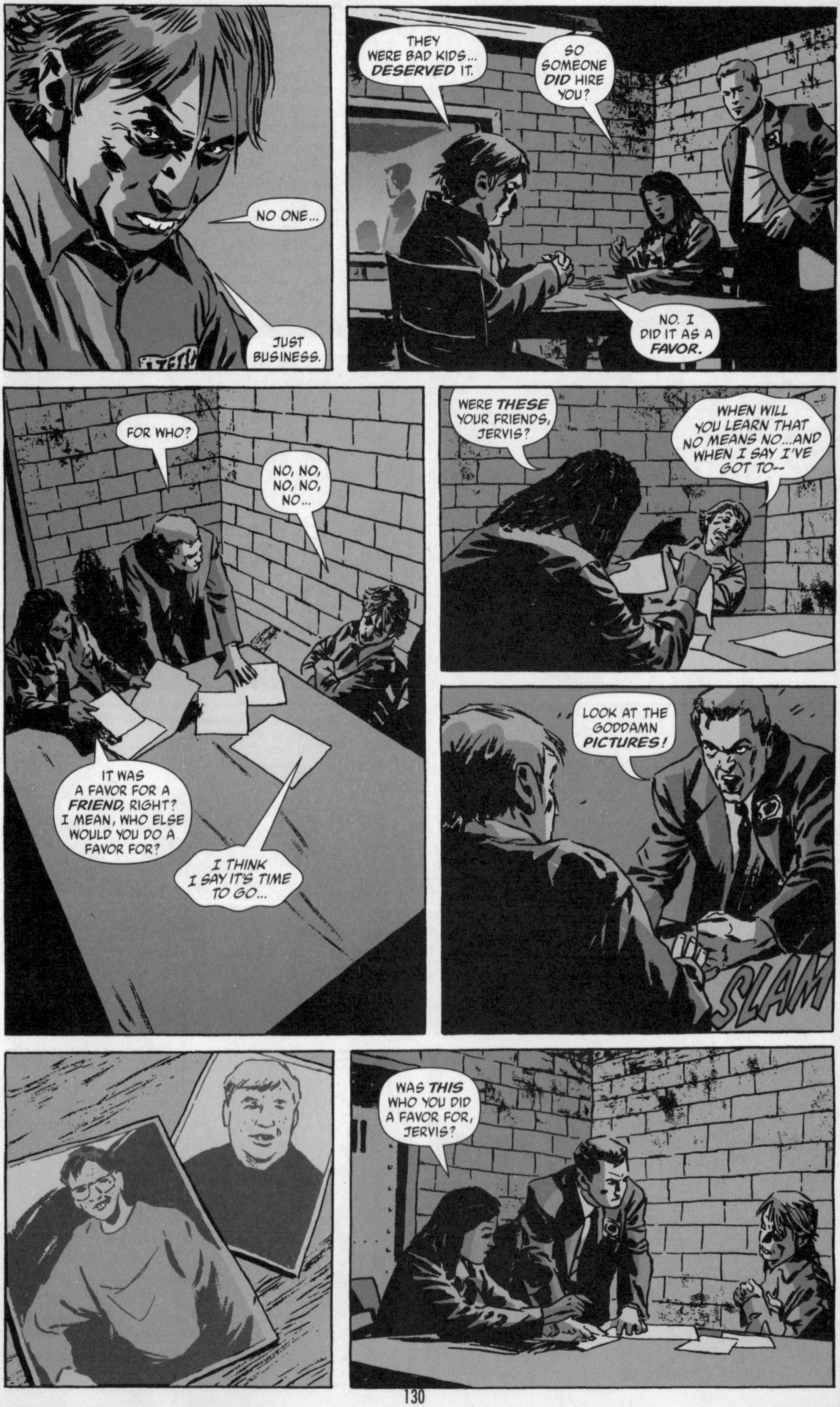

NO ONE...
JUST BUSINESS.
THEY WERE BAD KIDS... DESERVED IT.
SO SOMEONE DID HIRE YOU?
NO. I DID IT AS A FAVOR.
FOR WHO?
NO, NO, NO, NO, NO...
IT WAS A FAVOR FOR A FRIEND, RIGHT? I MEAN, WHO ELSE WOULD YOU DO A FAVOR FOR?
I THINK I SAY IT'S TIME TO GO...
WERE THESE YOUR FRIENDS, JERVIS?
WHEN WILL YOU LEARN THAT NO MEANS NO...AND WHEN I SAY I'VE GOT TO--
LOOK AT THE GODDAMN PICTURES!
SLAM
WAS THIS WHO YOU DID A FAVOR FOR, JERVIS?

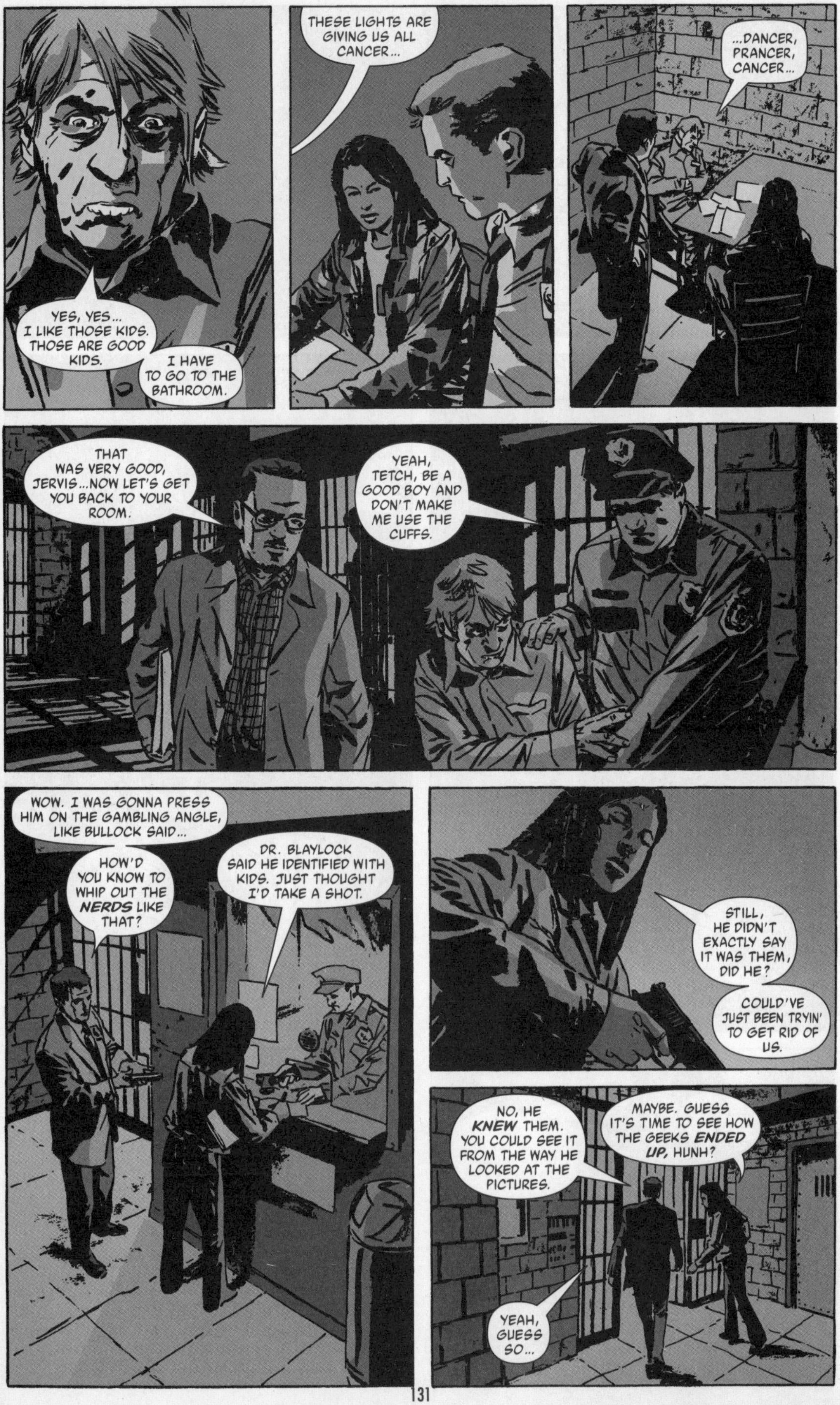
YES, YES... I LIKE THOSE KIDS. THOSE ARE GOOD KIDS.
I HAVE TO GO TO THE BATHROOM.
THESE LIGHTS ARE GIVING US ALL CANCER...
...DANCER, PRANCER, CANCER...
THAT WAS VERY GOOD, JERVIS...NOW LET'S GET YOU BACK TO YOUR ROOM.
YEAH, TETCH, BE A GOOD BOY AND DON'T MAKE ME USE THE CUFFS.
WOW. I WAS GONNA PRESS HIM ON THE GAMBLING ANGLE, LIKE BULLOCK SAID...
HOW'D YOU KNOW TO WHIP OUT THE NERDS LIKE THAT?
DR. BLAYLOCK SAID HE IDENTIFIED WITH KIDS. JUST THOUGHT I'D TAKE A SHOT.
STILL, HE DIDN'T EXACTLY SAY IT WAS THEM, DID HE?
COULD'VE JUST BEEN TRYIN' TO GET RID OF US.
NO, HE KNEW THEM. YOU COULD SEE IT FROM THE WAY HE LOOKED AT THE PICTURES.
MAYBE. GUESS IT'S TIME TO SEE HOW THE GEEKS ENDED UP, HUNH?
YEAH, GUESS SO...

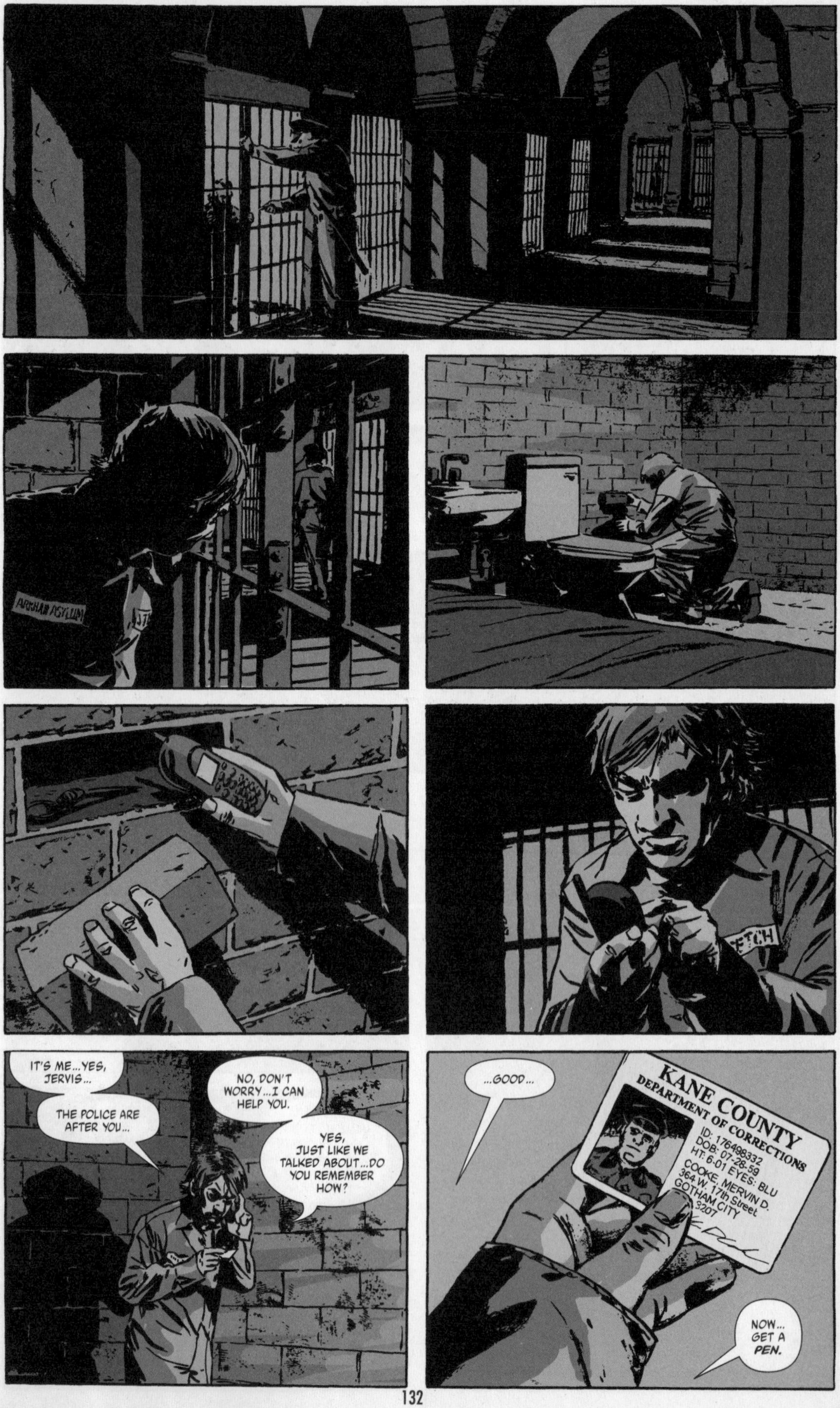
ARKHAM ASYLUM
FETCH
IT'S ME...YES, JERVIS...
THE POLICE ARE AFTER YOU...
NO, DON'T WORRY...I CAN HELP YOU.
YES, JUST LIKE WE TALKED ABOUT...DO YOU REMEMBER HOW?
...GOOD...
KANE COUNTY
DEPARTMENT OF CORRECTIONS
ID: 176498332
DOB: 07-28-59
HT: 6-01 EYES: BLU
COOKE, MERVIN D.
364 W. 17th Street
GOTHAM CITY
3207
NOW... GET A *PEN.*

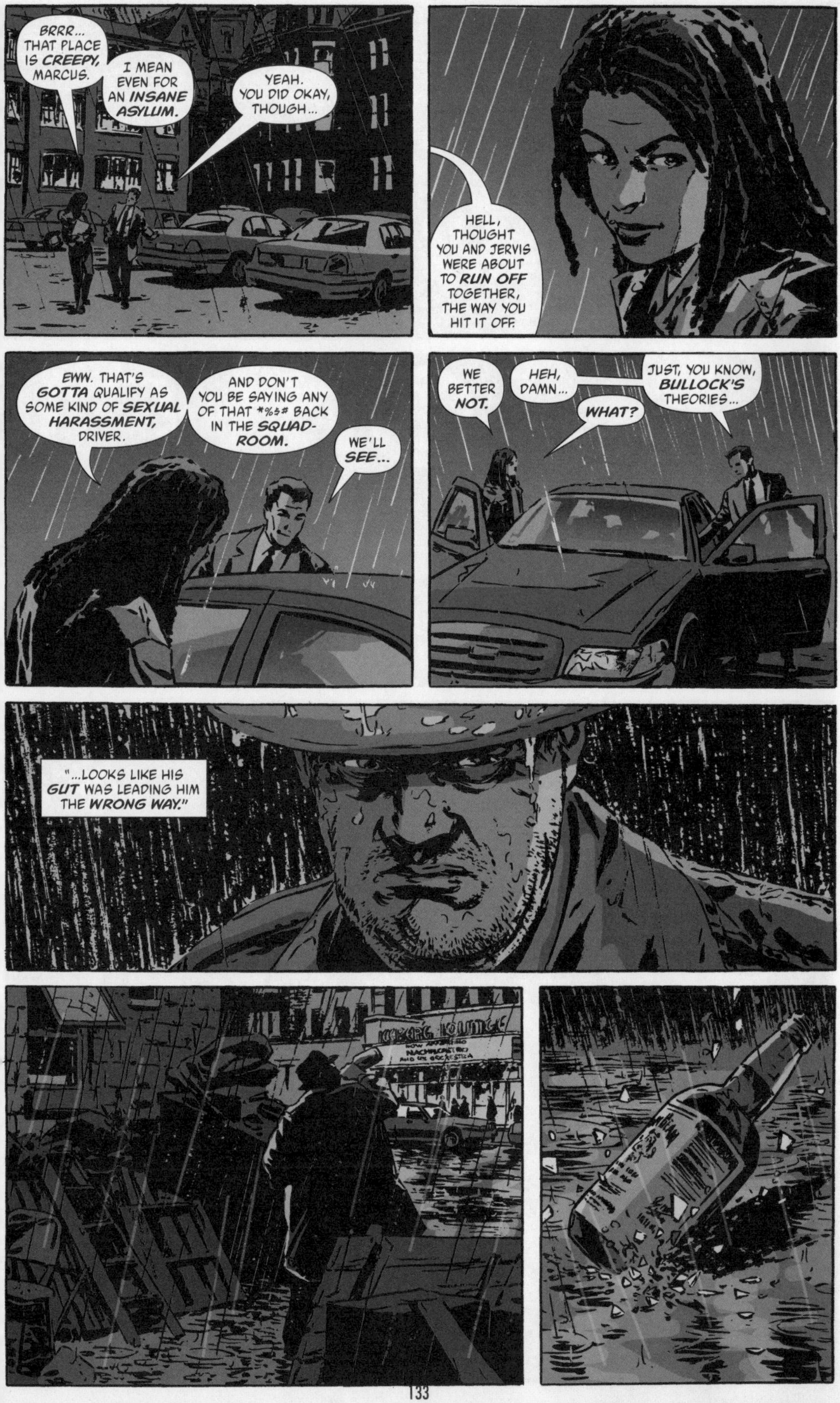
BRRR... THAT PLACE IS CREEPY, MARCUS.
I MEAN EVEN FOR AN INSANE ASYLUM.
YEAH. YOU DID OKAY, THOUGH...
HELL, THOUGHT YOU AND JERVIS WERE ABOUT TO RUN OFF TOGETHER, THE WAY YOU HIT IT OFF.
EWW. THAT'S GOTTA QUALIFY AS SOME KIND OF SEXUAL HARASSMENT, DRIVER.
AND DON'T YOU BE SAYING ANY OF THAT *%$# BACK IN THE SQUAD-ROOM.
WE'LL SEE...
WE BETTER NOT.
HEH, DAMN...
JUST, YOU KNOW, BULLOCK'S THEORIES...
WHAT?
"...LOOKS LIKE HIS GUT WAS LEADING HIM THE WRONG WAY."

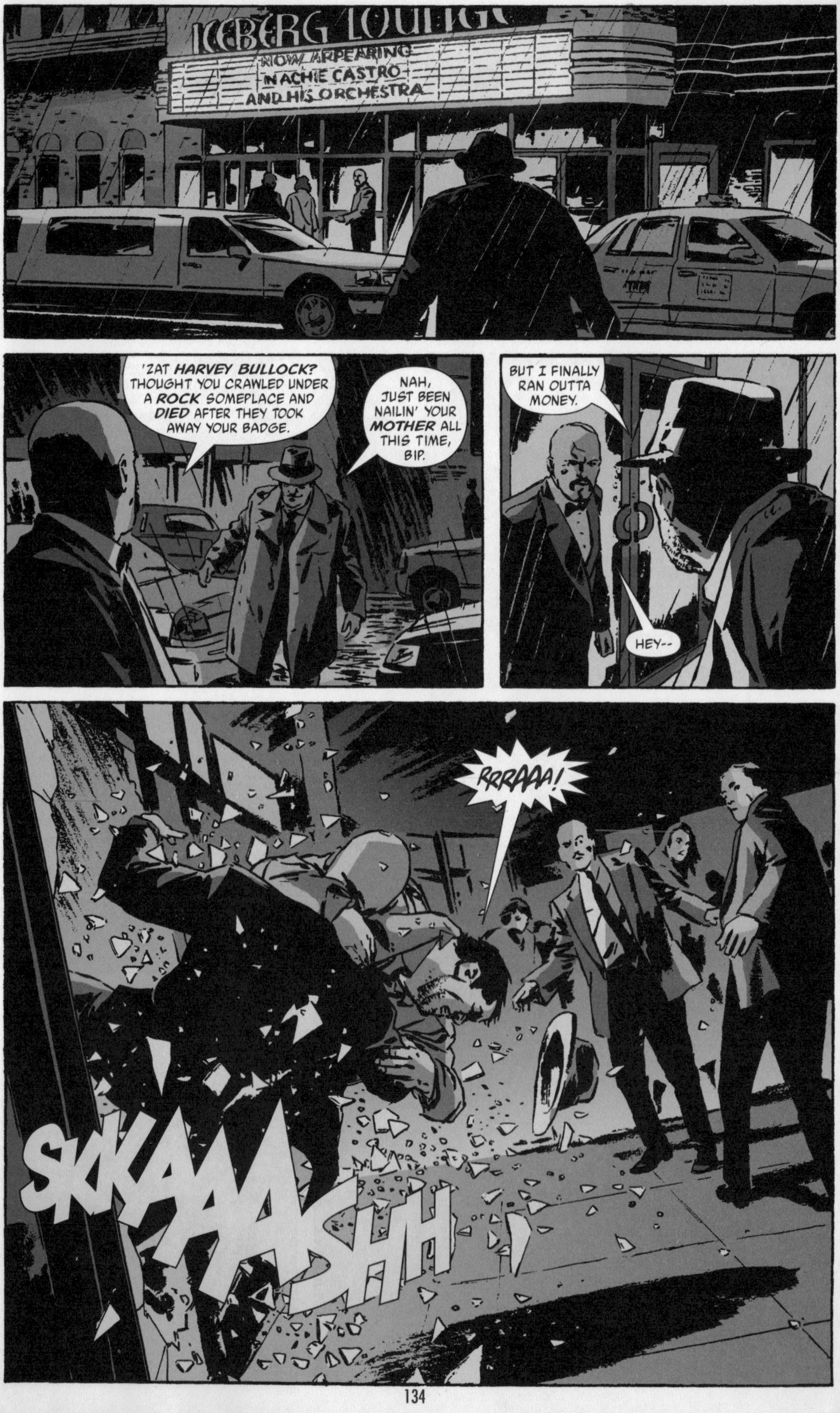
ICEBERG LOUNGE
NOW APPEARING
NACHIE CASTRO
AND HIS ORCHESTRA
'ZAT HARVEY BULLOCK? THOUGHT YOU CRAWLED UNDER A ROCK SOMEPLACE AND DIED AFTER THEY TOOK AWAY YOUR BADGE.
NAH, JUST BEEN NAILIN' YOUR MOTHER ALL THIS TIME, BIP.
BUT I FINALLY RAN OUTTA MONEY.
HEY--
RRRAAA!
SKKAAASHH

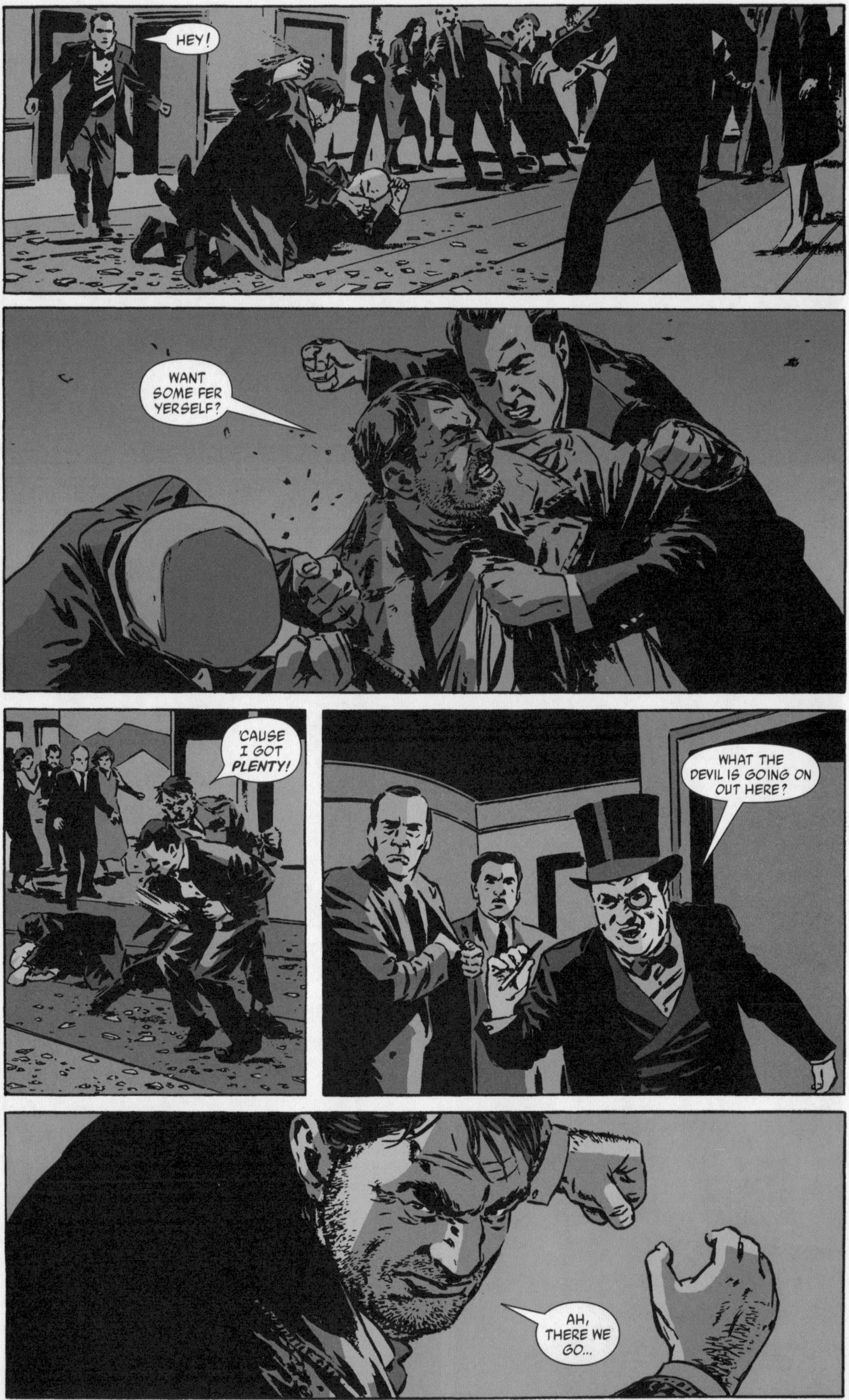
HEY!
WANT SOME FER YERSELF?
'CAUSE I GOT PLENTY!
WHAT THE DEVIL IS GOING ON OUT HERE?
AH, THERE WE GO...

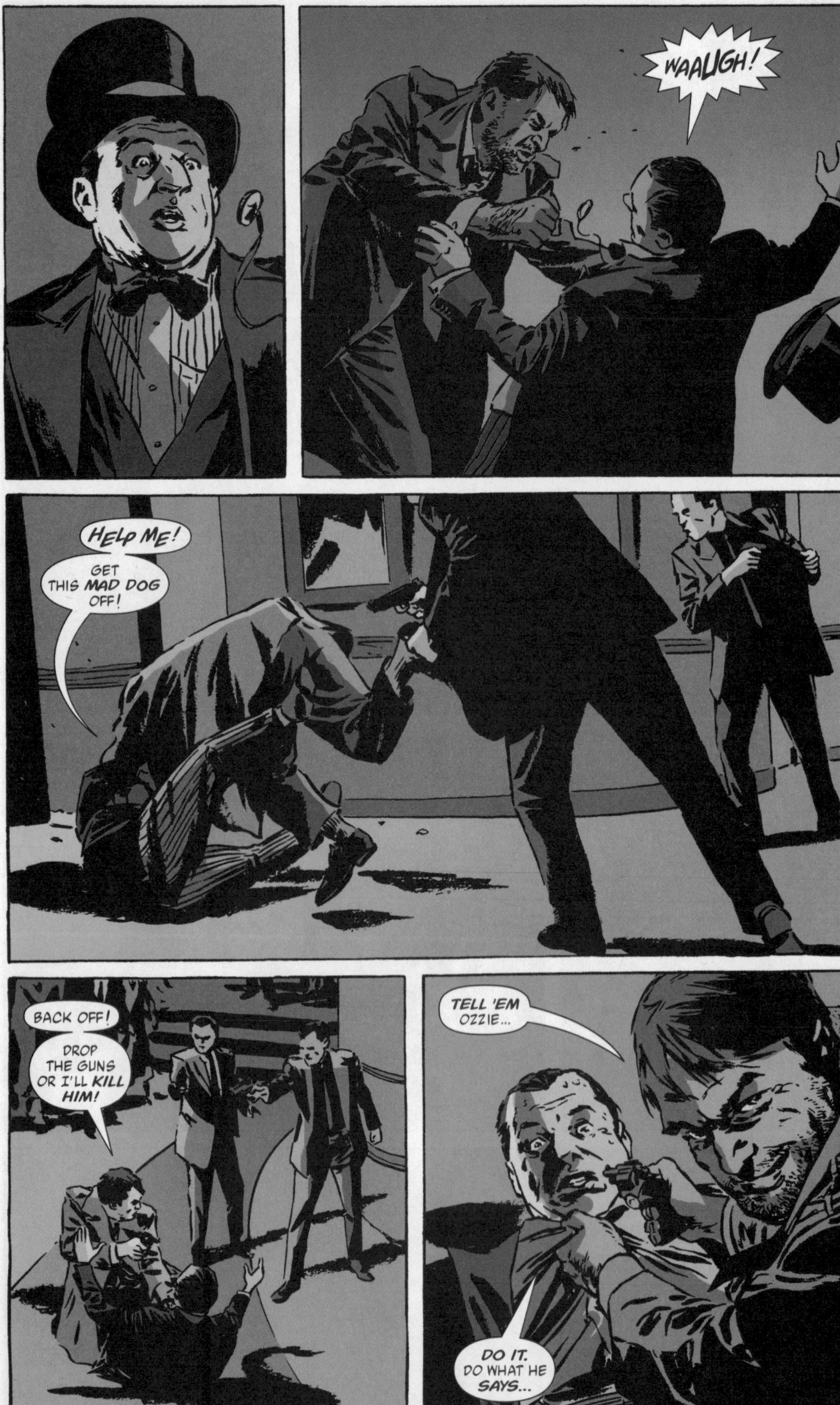
WAAUGH!
HELP ME!
GET THIS MAD DOG OFF!
BACK OFF!
DROP THE GUNS OR I'LL KILL HIM!
TELL 'EM OZZIE...
DO IT. DO WHAT HE SAYS...

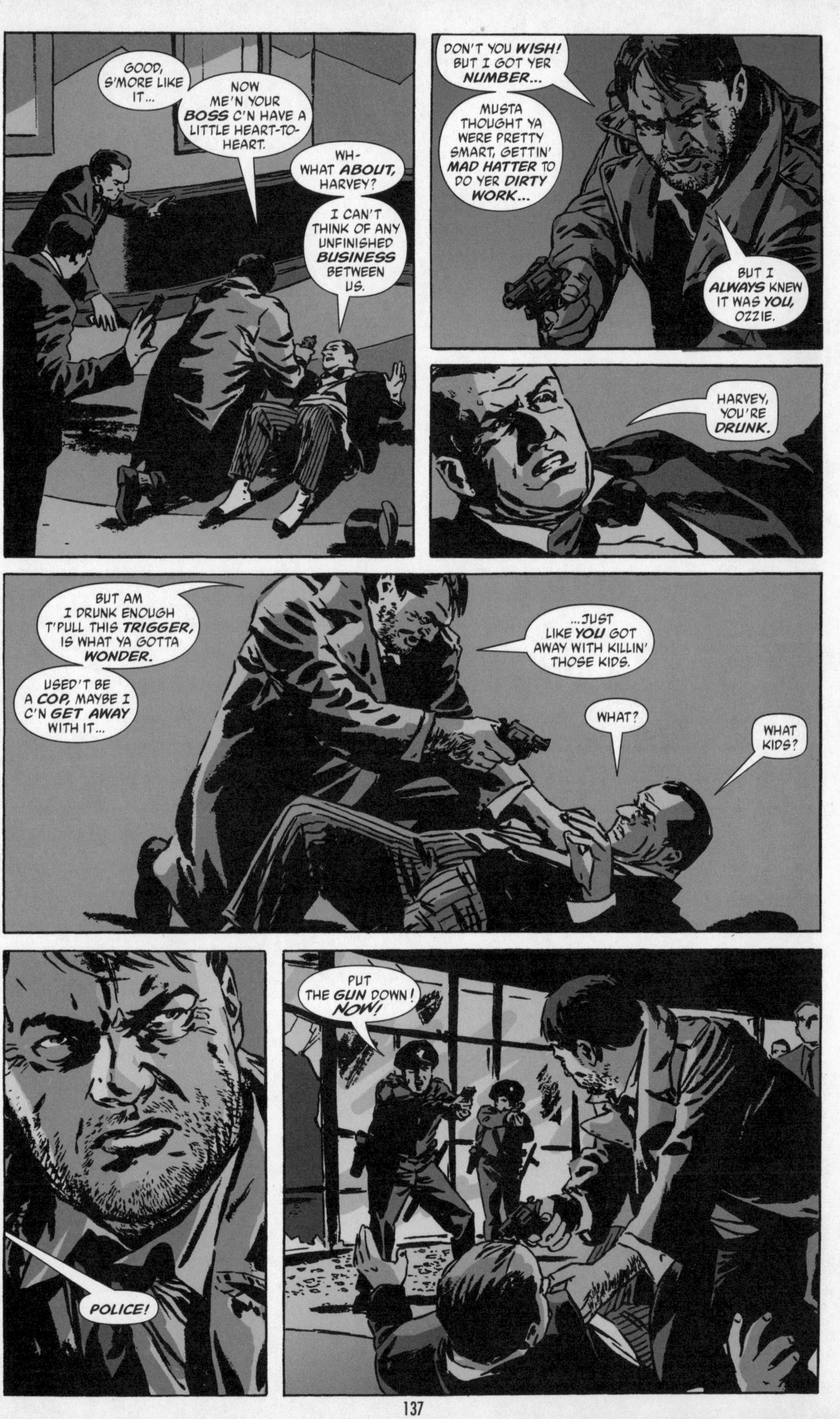
GOOD, S'MORE LIKE IT...
NOW ME'N YOUR BOSS C'N HAVE A LITTLE HEART-TO-HEART.
WH- WHAT ABOUT, HARVEY?
I CAN'T THINK OF ANY UNFINISHED BUSINESS BETWEEN US.
DON'T YOU WISH! BUT I GOT YER NUMBER...
MUSTA THOUGHT YA WERE PRETTY SMART, GETTIN' MAD HATTER TO DO YER DIRTY WORK...
BUT I ALWAYS KNEW IT WAS YOU, OZZIE.
HARVEY, YOU'RE DRUNK.
BUT AM I DRUNK ENOUGH T'PULL THIS TRIGGER, IS WHAT YA GOTTA WONDER.
USED'T BE A COP, MAYBE I C'N GET AWAY WITH IT...
...JUST LIKE YOU GOT AWAY WITH KILLIN' THOSE KIDS.
WHAT?
WHAT KIDS?
POLICE!
PUT THE GUN DOWN! NOW!

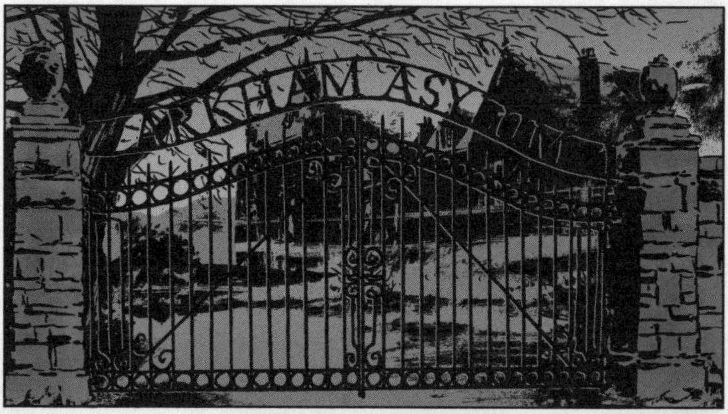

ARKHAM ASY

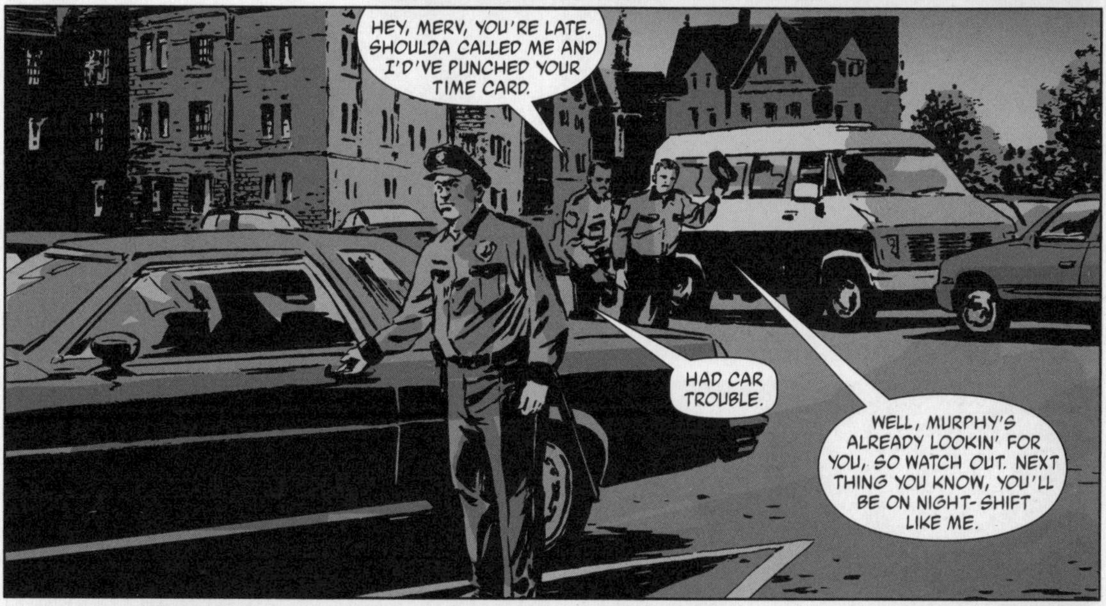

HEY, MERV, YOU'RE LATE. SHOULDA CALLED ME AND I'D'VE PUNCHED YOUR TIME CARD.
HAD CAR TROUBLE.
WELL, MURPHY'S ALREADY LOOKIN' FOR YOU, SO WATCH OUT. NEXT THING YOU KNOW, YOU'LL BE ON NIGHT-SHIFT LIKE ME.

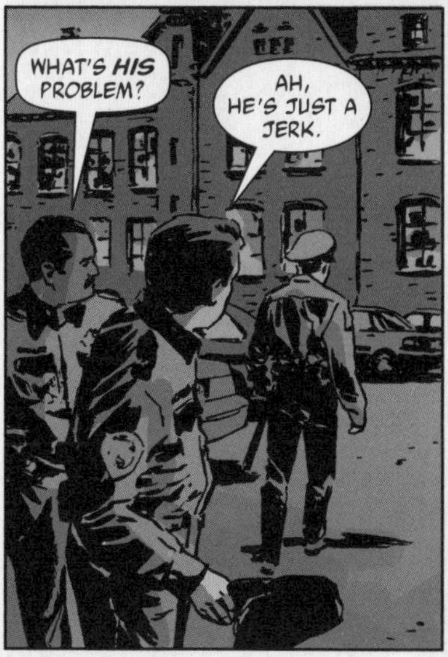

WHAT'S **HIS** PROBLEM?
AH, HE'S JUST A JERK.

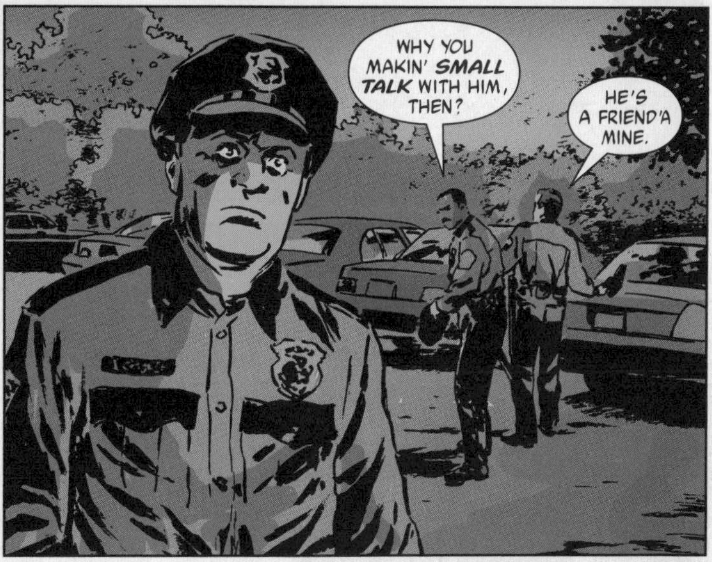

WHY YOU MAKIN' **SMALL TALK** WITH HIM, THEN?
HE'S A FRIEND'A MINE.

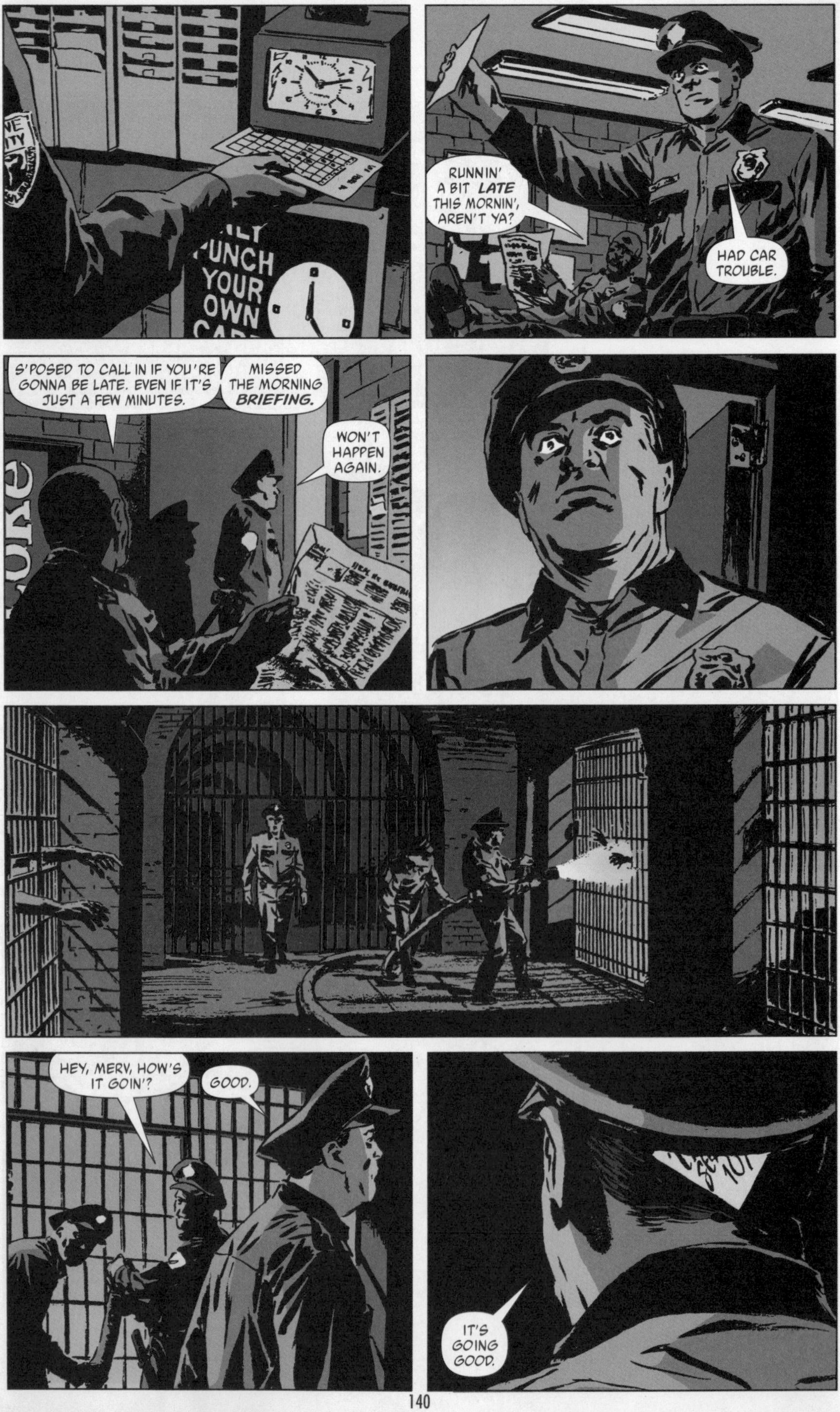
PUNCH YOUR OWN
RUNNIN' A BIT LATE THIS MORNIN', AREN'T YA?
HAD CAR TROUBLE.
S'POSED TO CALL IN IF YOU'RE GONNA BE LATE. EVEN IF IT'S JUST A FEW MINUTES.
MISSED THE MORNING BRIEFING.
WON'T HAPPEN AGAIN.
HEY, MERV, HOW'S IT GOIN'?
GOOD.
IT'S GOING GOOD.

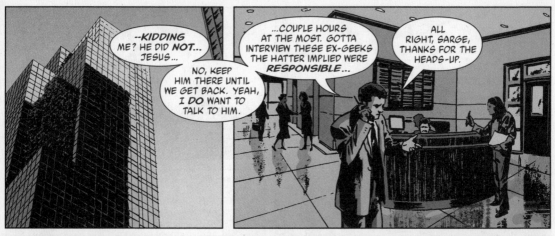

--KIDDING ME? HE DID *NOT*... JESUS...

NO, KEEP HIM THERE UNTIL WE GET BACK. YEAH, *I* *DO* WANT TO TALK TO HIM.

...COUPLE HOURS AT THE MOST. GOTTA INTERVIEW THESE EX-GEEKS THE HATTER IMPLIED WERE *RESPONSIBLE*...

ALL RIGHT, SARGE, THANKS FOR THE HEADS-UP.

YOU'RE NOT GOING TO BELIEVE *THIS*, JOSIE.

WHAT?

FRIGGING *BULLOCK* TOOK A RUN AT THE *PENGUIN* LAST NIGHT RIGHT IN THE ICEBERG LOUNGE.

WHAT? *WHY?*

I DON'T KNOW. HE WAS DRUNK. THEY GOT HIM IN A *HOLDING CELL* BACK AT CENTRAL.

I *TOLD YOU* THAT SON OF A BITCH WAS HOLDING OUT ON US, DRIVER.

I KNOW.

SO, WHAT'S THE DEAL? ARE BOTH OF THEM HERE?

YEAH, THEY'RE ON THE TOP FLOOR. CYBER-SOFT ENTERPRISES.

ANOTHER CASE OF THE GEEKS *WINNING* IN THE END, HUNH?

WELL, UNLESS WE ARREST THEM FOR *MASS MURDER.*

THERE *IS* THAT...

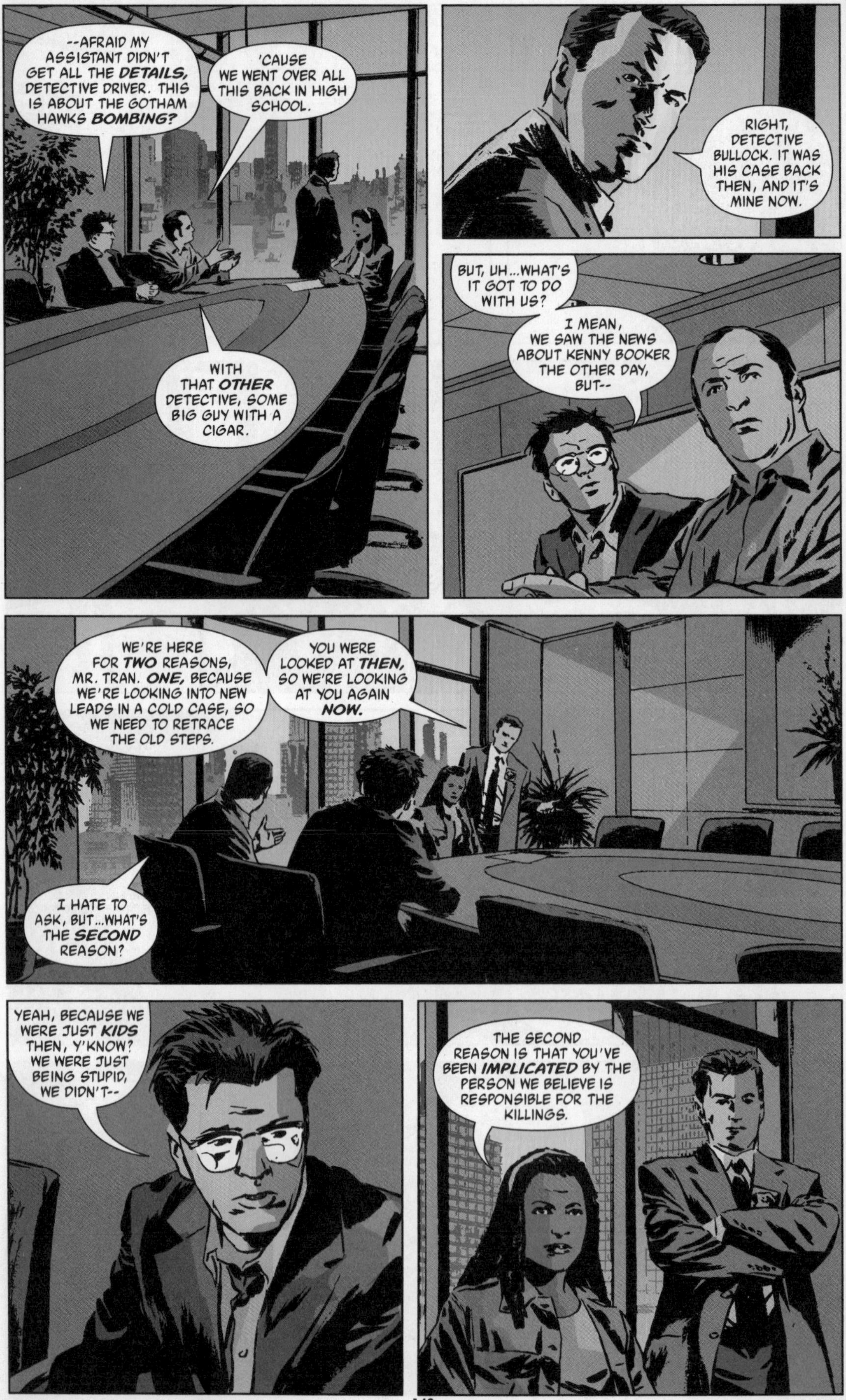
--AFRAID MY ASSISTANT DIDN'T GET ALL THE DETAILS, DETECTIVE DRIVER. THIS IS ABOUT THE GOTHAM HAWKS BOMBING?
'CAUSE WE WENT OVER ALL THIS BACK IN HIGH SCHOOL.
WITH THAT OTHER DETECTIVE, SOME BIG GUY WITH A CIGAR.
RIGHT, DETECTIVE BULLOCK. IT WAS HIS CASE BACK THEN, AND IT'S MINE NOW.
BUT, UH...WHAT'S IT GOT TO DO WITH US?
I MEAN, WE SAW THE NEWS ABOUT KENNY BOOKER THE OTHER DAY, BUT--
WE'RE HERE FOR TWO REASONS, MR. TRAN. ONE, BECAUSE WE'RE LOOKING INTO NEW LEADS IN A COLD CASE, SO WE NEED TO RETRACE THE OLD STEPS.
YOU WERE LOOKED AT THEN, SO WE'RE LOOKING AT YOU AGAIN NOW.
I HATE TO ASK, BUT...WHAT'S THE SECOND REASON?
YEAH, BECAUSE WE WERE JUST KIDS THEN, Y'KNOW? WE WERE JUST BEING STUPID, WE DIDN'T--
THE SECOND REASON IS THAT YOU'VE BEEN IMPLICATED BY THE PERSON WE BELIEVE IS RESPONSIBLE FOR THE KILLINGS.

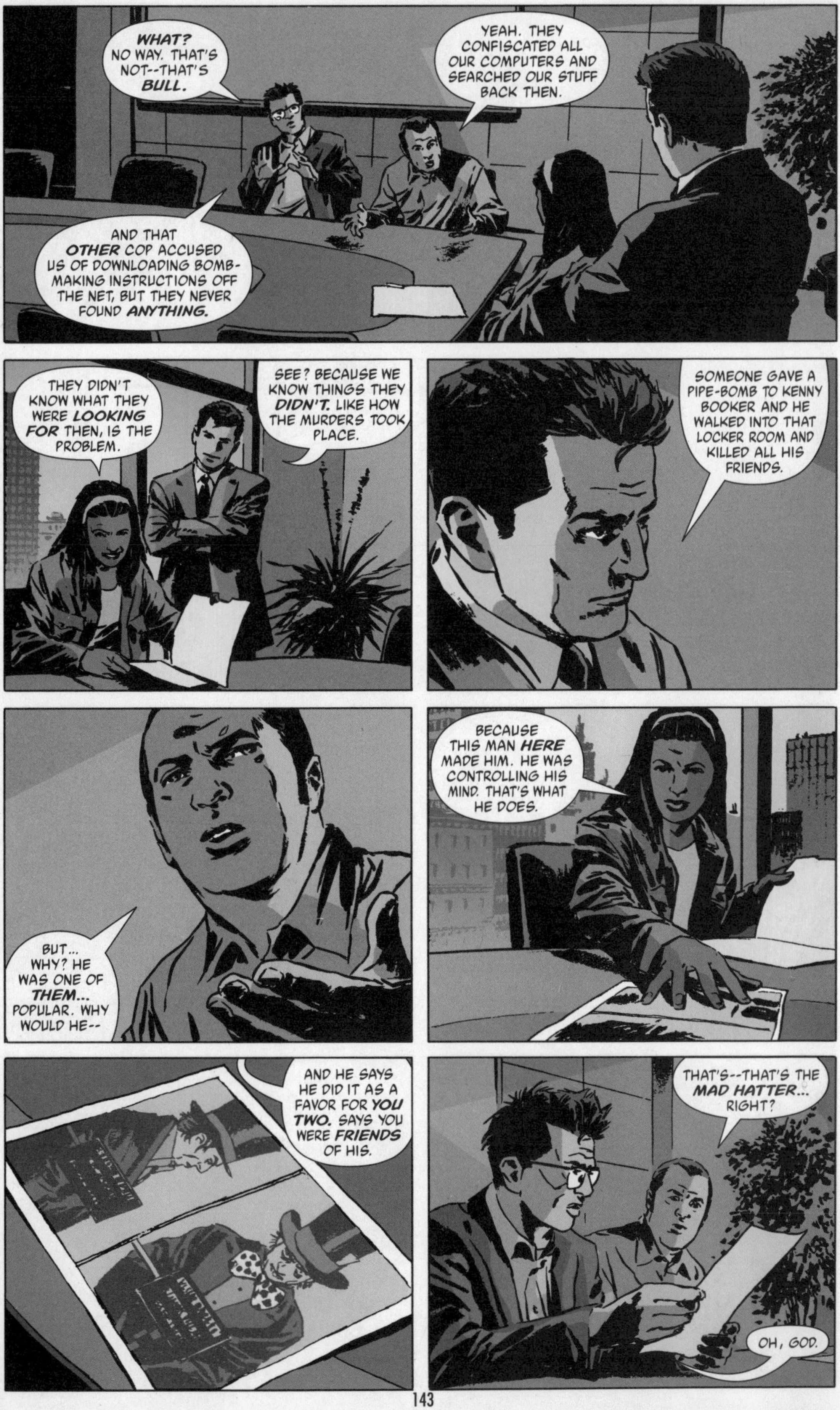
WHAT? NO WAY. THAT'S NOT--THAT'S BULL.
YEAH. THEY CONFISCATED ALL OUR COMPUTERS AND SEARCHED OUR STUFF BACK THEN.
AND THAT OTHER COP ACCUSED US OF DOWNLOADING BOMB-MAKING INSTRUCTIONS OFF THE NET, BUT THEY NEVER FOUND ANYTHING.
THEY DIDN'T KNOW WHAT THEY WERE LOOKING FOR THEN, IS THE PROBLEM.
SEE? BECAUSE WE KNOW THINGS THEY DIDN'T. LIKE HOW THE MURDERS TOOK PLACE.
SOMEONE GAVE A PIPE-BOMB TO KENNY BOOKER AND HE WALKED INTO THAT LOCKER ROOM AND KILLED ALL HIS FRIENDS.
BUT... WHY? HE WAS ONE OF THEM... POPULAR. WHY WOULD HE--
BECAUSE THIS MAN HERE MADE HIM. HE WAS CONTROLLING HIS MIND. THAT'S WHAT HE DOES.
AND HE SAYS HE DID IT AS A FAVOR FOR YOU TWO. SAYS YOU WERE FRIENDS OF HIS.
THAT'S--THAT'S THE MAD HATTER... RIGHT?
OH, GOD.

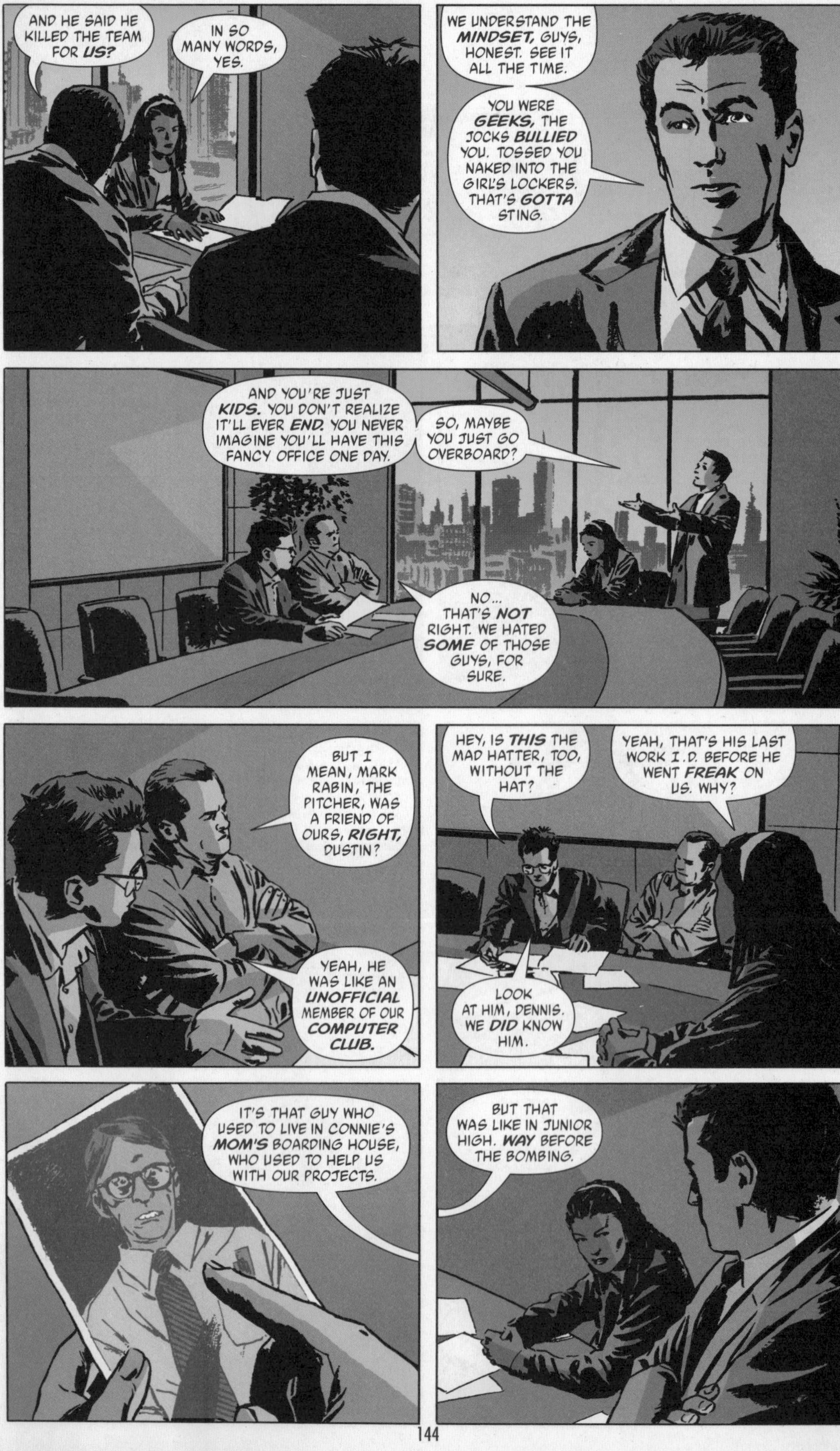
AND HE SAID HE KILLED THE TEAM FOR US?
IN SO MANY WORDS, YES.
WE UNDERSTAND THE MINDSET, GUYS, HONEST. SEE IT ALL THE TIME.
YOU WERE GEEKS, THE JOCKS BULLIED YOU. TOSSED YOU NAKED INTO THE GIRL'S LOCKERS. THAT'S GOTTA STING.
AND YOU'RE JUST KIDS. YOU DON'T REALIZE IT'LL EVER END. YOU NEVER IMAGINE YOU'LL HAVE THIS FANCY OFFICE ONE DAY.
SO, MAYBE YOU JUST GO OVERBOARD?
NO... THAT'S NOT RIGHT. WE HATED SOME OF THOSE GUYS, FOR SURE.
BUT I MEAN, MARK RABIN, THE PITCHER, WAS A FRIEND OF OURS, RIGHT, DUSTIN?
YEAH, HE WAS LIKE AN UNOFFICIAL MEMBER OF OUR COMPUTER CLUB.
HEY, IS THIS THE MAD HATTER, TOO, WITHOUT THE HAT?
YEAH, THAT'S HIS LAST WORK I.D. BEFORE HE WENT FREAK ON US. WHY?
LOOK AT HIM, DENNIS. WE DID KNOW HIM.
IT'S THAT GUY WHO USED TO LIVE IN CONNIE'S MOM'S BOARDING HOUSE, WHO USED TO HELP US WITH OUR PROJECTS.
BUT THAT WAS LIKE IN JUNIOR HIGH. WAY BEFORE THE BOMBING.

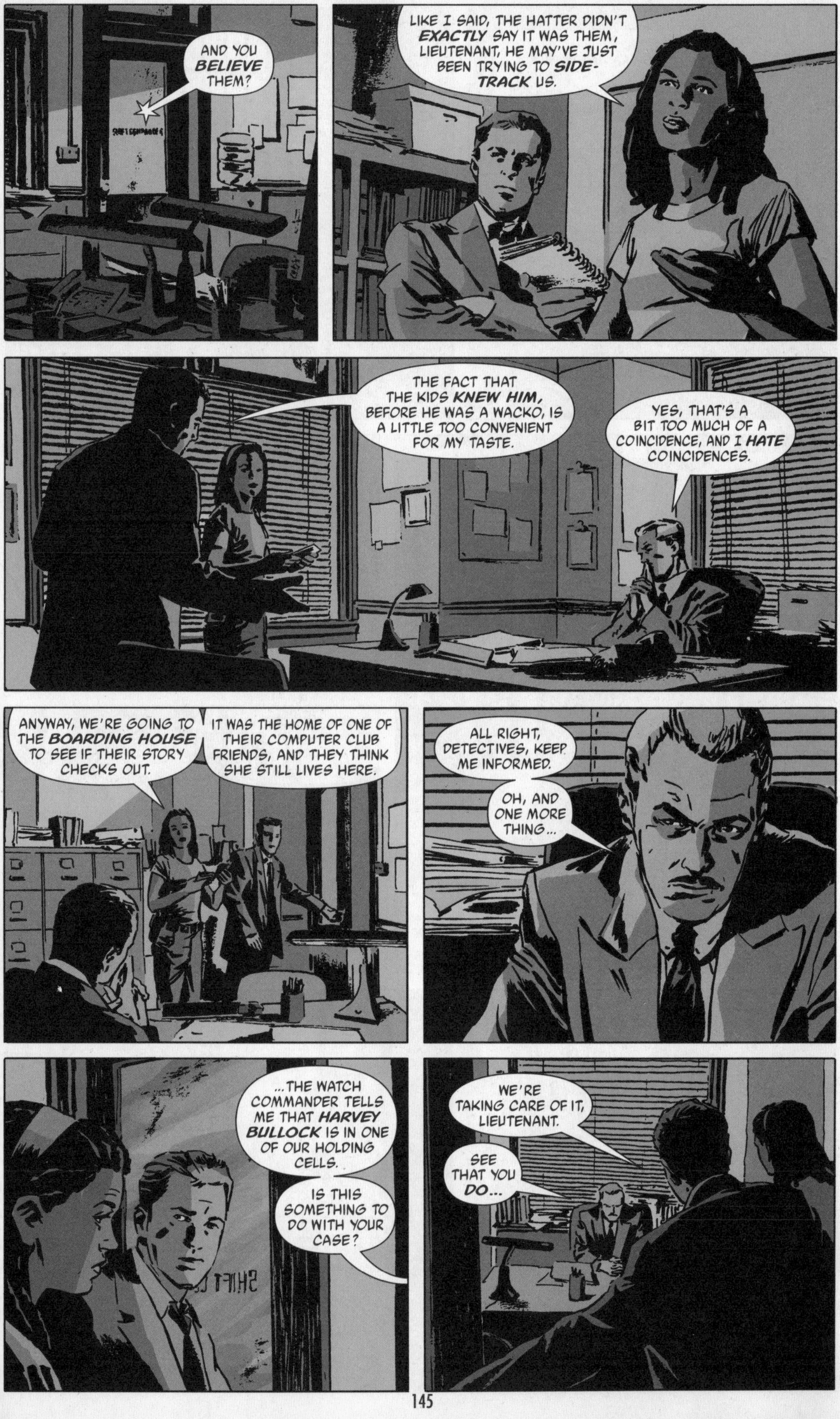
AND YOU BELIEVE THEM?
LIKE I SAID, THE HATTER DIDN'T EXACTLY SAY IT WAS THEM, LIEUTENANT, HE MAY'VE JUST BEEN TRYING TO SIDE-TRACK US.
THE FACT THAT THE KIDS KNEW HIM, BEFORE HE WAS A WACKO, IS A LITTLE TOO CONVENIENT FOR MY TASTE.
YES, THAT'S A BIT TOO MUCH OF A COINCIDENCE, AND I HATE COINCIDENCES.
ANYWAY, WE'RE GOING TO THE BOARDING HOUSE TO SEE IF THEIR STORY CHECKS OUT.
IT WAS THE HOME OF ONE OF THEIR COMPUTER CLUB FRIENDS, AND THEY THINK SHE STILL LIVES HERE.
ALL RIGHT, DETECTIVES, KEEP ME INFORMED.
OH, AND ONE MORE THING...
...THE WATCH COMMANDER TELLS ME THAT HARVEY BULLOCK IS IN ONE OF OUR HOLDING CELLS.
IS THIS SOMETHING TO DO WITH YOUR CASE?
WE'RE TAKING CARE OF IT, LIEUTENANT.
SEE THAT YOU DO...

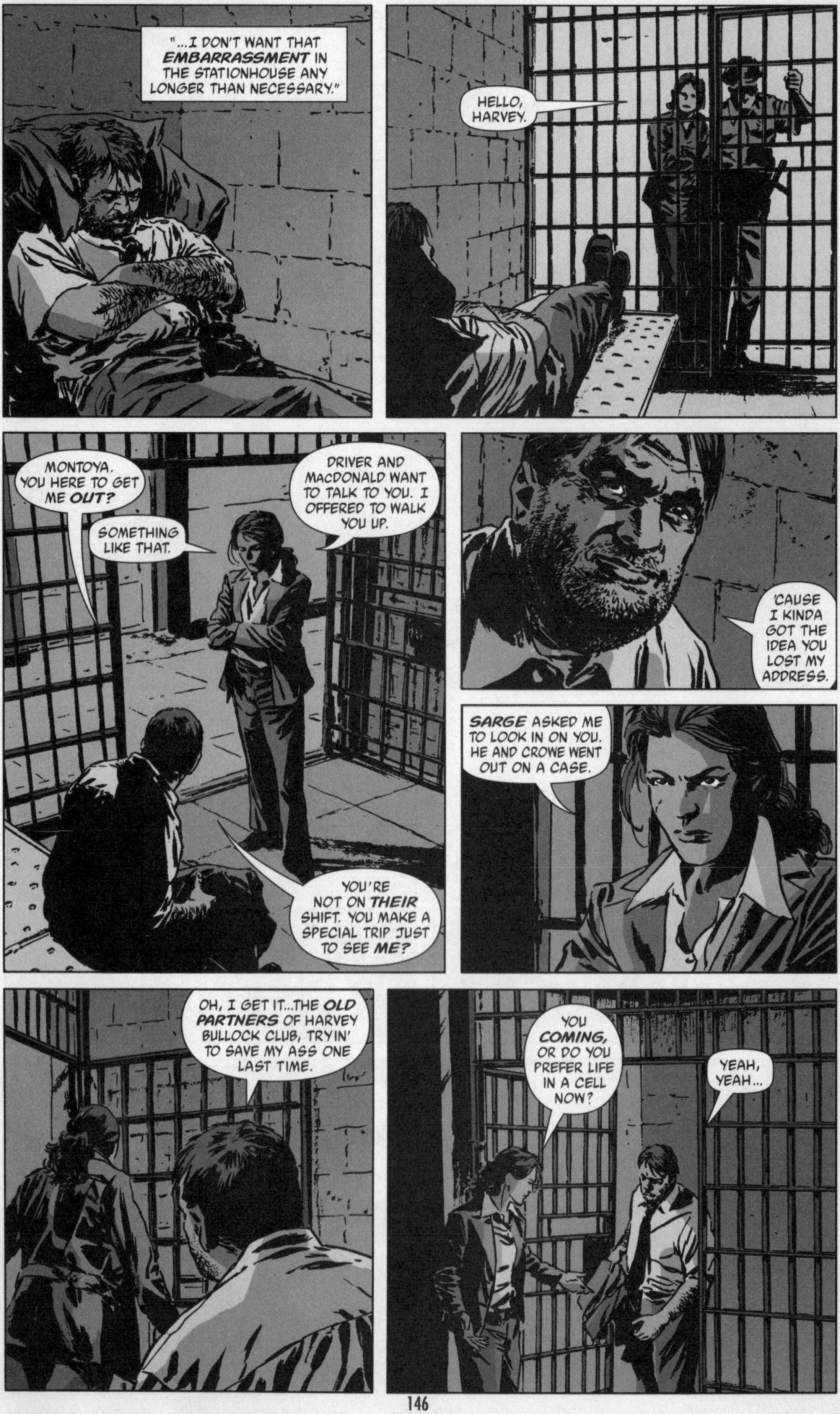
"...I DON'T WANT THAT EMBARRASSMENT IN THE STATIONHOUSE ANY LONGER THAN NECESSARY."
HELLO, HARVEY.
MONTOYA. YOU HERE TO GET ME OUT?
SOMETHING LIKE THAT.
DRIVER AND MACDONALD WANT TO TALK TO YOU. I OFFERED TO WALK YOU UP.
YOU'RE NOT ON THEIR SHIFT. YOU MAKE A SPECIAL TRIP JUST TO SEE ME?
'CAUSE I KINDA GOT THE IDEA YOU LOST MY ADDRESS.
SARGE ASKED ME TO LOOK IN ON YOU. HE AND CROWE WENT OUT ON A CASE.
OH, I GET IT...THE OLD PARTNERS OF HARVEY BULLOCK CLUB, TRYIN' TO SAVE MY ASS ONE LAST TIME.
YOU COMING, OR DO YOU PREFER LIFE IN A CELL NOW?
YEAH, YEAH...

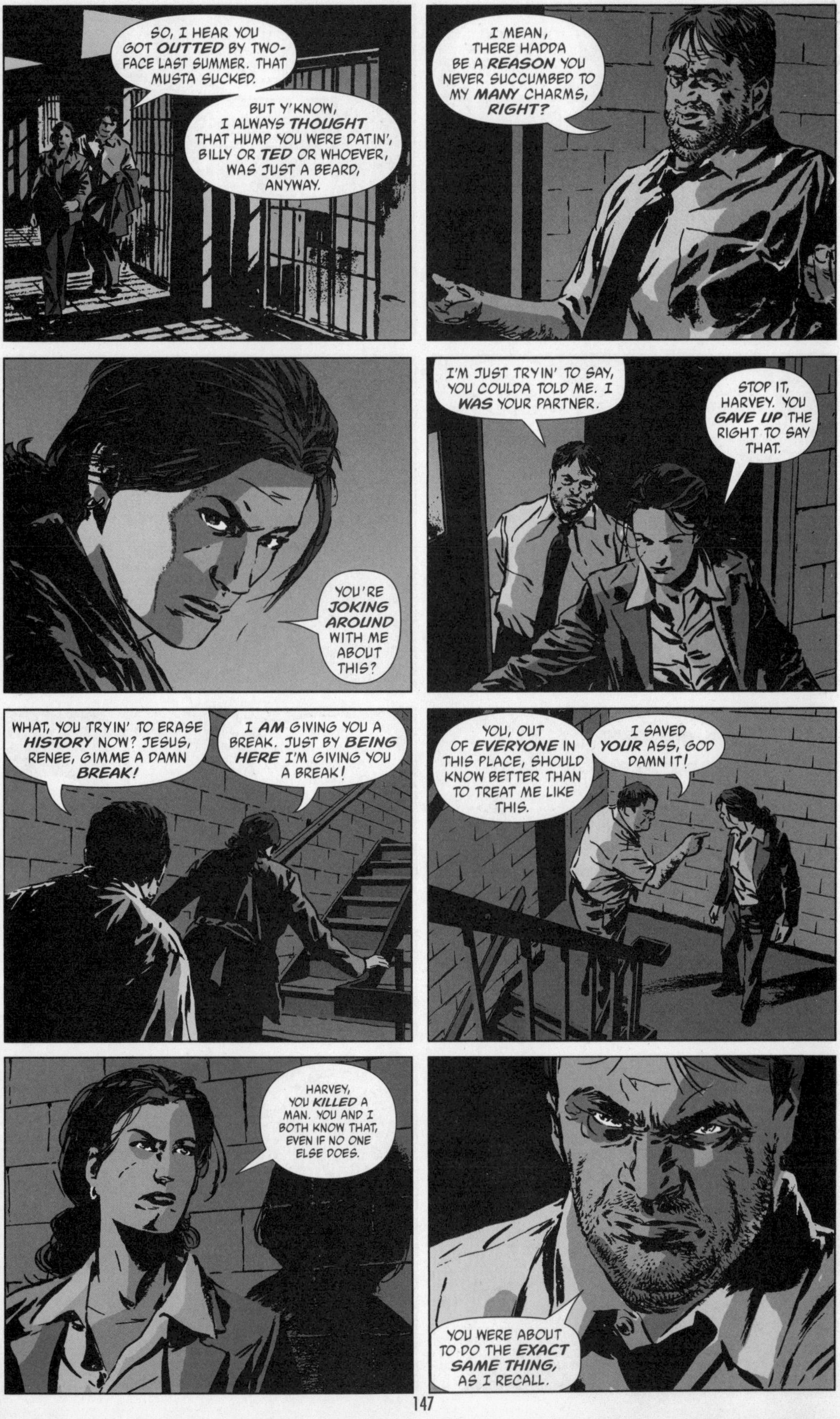
SO, I HEAR YOU GOT OUTTED BY TWO-FACE LAST SUMMER. THAT MUSTA SUCKED.
BUT Y'KNOW, I ALWAYS THOUGHT THAT HUMP YOU WERE DATIN', BILLY OR TED OR WHOEVER, WAS JUST A BEARD, ANYWAY.
I MEAN, THERE HADDA BE A REASON YOU NEVER SUCCUMBED TO MY MANY CHARMS, RIGHT?
YOU'RE JOKING AROUND WITH ME ABOUT THIS?
I'M JUST TRYIN' TO SAY, YOU COULDA TOLD ME. I WAS YOUR PARTNER.
STOP IT, HARVEY. YOU GAVE UP THE RIGHT TO SAY THAT.
WHAT, YOU TRYIN' TO ERASE HISTORY NOW? JESUS, RENEE, GIMME A DAMN BREAK!
I AM GIVING YOU A BREAK. JUST BY BEING HERE I'M GIVING YOU A BREAK!
YOU, OUT OF EVERYONE IN THIS PLACE, SHOULD KNOW BETTER THAN TO TREAT ME LIKE THIS.
I SAVED YOUR ASS, GOD DAMN IT!
HARVEY, YOU KILLED A MAN. YOU AND I BOTH KNOW THAT, EVEN IF NO ONE ELSE DOES.
YOU WERE ABOUT TO DO THE EXACT SAME THING, AS I RECALL.

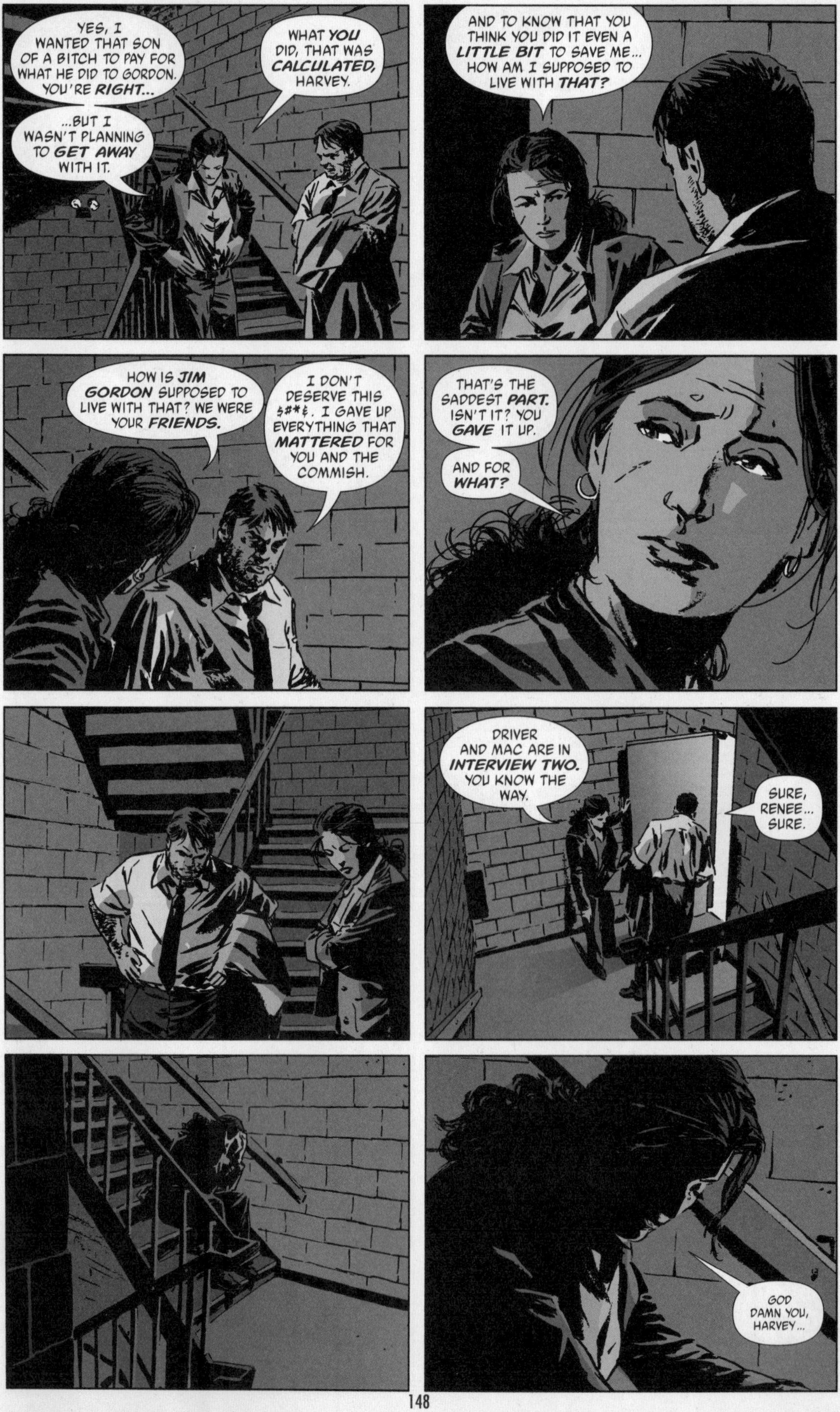
YES, I WANTED THAT SON OF A BITCH TO PAY FOR WHAT HE DID TO GORDON. YOU'RE RIGHT...
...BUT I WASN'T PLANNING TO GET AWAY WITH IT.
WHAT YOU DID, THAT WAS CALCULATED, HARVEY.
AND TO KNOW THAT YOU THINK YOU DID IT EVEN A LITTLE BIT TO SAVE ME... HOW AM I SUPPOSED TO LIVE WITH THAT?
HOW IS JIM GORDON SUPPOSED TO LIVE WITH THAT? WE WERE YOUR FRIENDS.
I DON'T DESERVE THIS $#*&. I GAVE UP EVERYTHING THAT MATTERED FOR YOU AND THE COMMISH.
THAT'S THE SADDEST PART. ISN'T IT? YOU GAVE IT UP.
AND FOR WHAT?
DRIVER AND MAC ARE IN INTERVIEW TWO. YOU KNOW THE WAY.
SURE, RENEE... SURE.
GOD DAMN YOU, HARVEY...

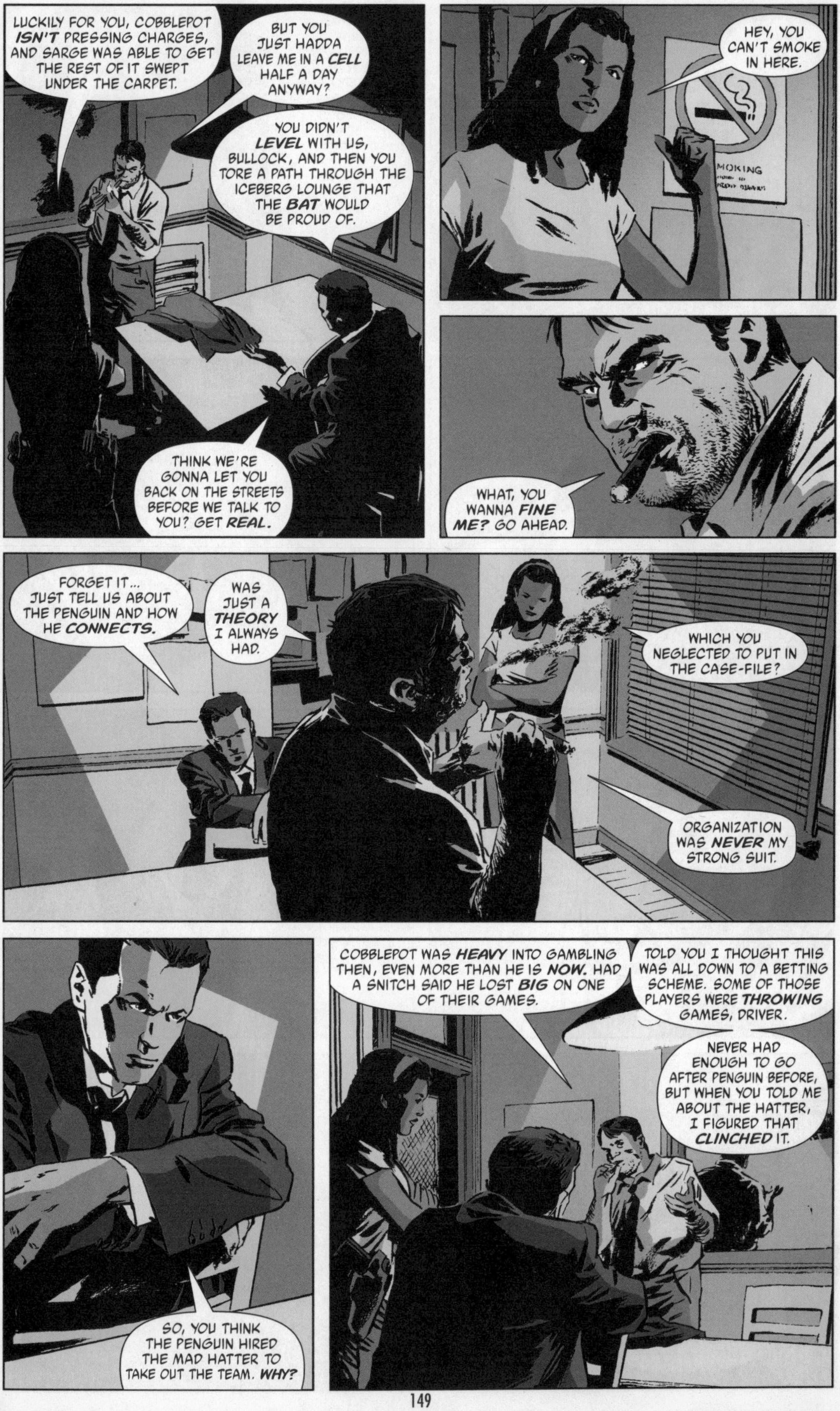
LUCKILY FOR YOU, COBBLEPOT ISN'T PRESSING CHARGES, AND SARGE WAS ABLE TO GET THE REST OF IT SWEPT UNDER THE CARPET.
BUT YOU JUST HADDA LEAVE ME IN A CELL HALF A DAY ANYWAY?
YOU DIDN'T LEVEL WITH US, BULLOCK, AND THEN YOU TORE A PATH THROUGH THE ICEBERG LOUNGE THAT THE BAT WOULD BE PROUD OF.
THINK WE'RE GONNA LET YOU BACK ON THE STREETS BEFORE WE TALK TO YOU? GET REAL.
HEY, YOU CAN'T SMOKE IN HERE.
WHAT, YOU WANNA FINE ME? GO AHEAD.
FORGET IT... JUST TELL US ABOUT THE PENGUIN AND HOW HE CONNECTS.
WAS JUST A THEORY I ALWAYS HAD.
WHICH YOU NEGLECTED TO PUT IN THE CASE-FILE?
ORGANIZATION WAS NEVER MY STRONG SUIT.
SO, YOU THINK THE PENGUIN HIRED THE MAD HATTER TO TAKE OUT THE TEAM. WHY?
COBBLEPOT WAS HEAVY INTO GAMBLING THEN, EVEN MORE THAN HE IS NOW. HAD A SNITCH SAID HE LOST BIG ON ONE OF THEIR GAMES.
TOLD YOU I THOUGHT THIS WAS ALL DOWN TO A BETTING SCHEME. SOME OF THOSE PLAYERS WERE THROWING GAMES, DRIVER.
NEVER HAD ENOUGH TO GO AFTER PENGUIN BEFORE, BUT WHEN YOU TOLD ME ABOUT THE HATTER, I FIGURED THAT CLINCHED IT.

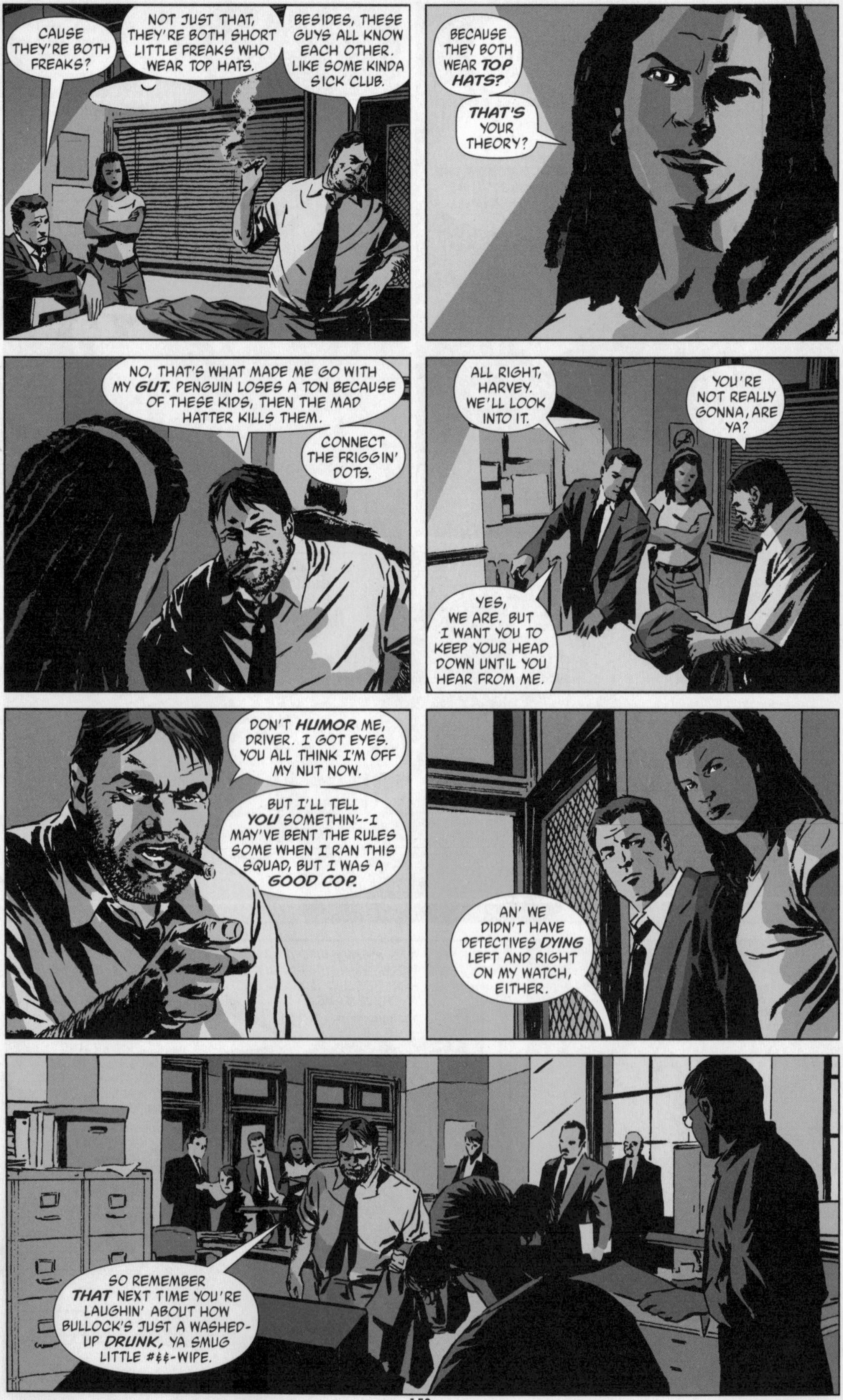
CAUSE THEY'RE BOTH FREAKS?
NOT JUST THAT, THEY'RE BOTH SHORT LITTLE FREAKS WHO WEAR TOP HATS.
BESIDES, THESE GUYS ALL KNOW EACH OTHER. LIKE SOME KINDA SICK CLUB.
BECAUSE THEY BOTH WEAR TOP HATS?
THAT'S YOUR THEORY?
NO, THAT'S WHAT MADE ME GO WITH MY GUT. PENGUIN LOSES A TON BECAUSE OF THESE KIDS, THEN THE MAD HATTER KILLS THEM.
CONNECT THE FRIGGIN' DOTS.
ALL RIGHT, HARVEY. WE'LL LOOK INTO IT.
YOU'RE NOT REALLY GONNA, ARE YA?
YES, WE ARE. BUT I WANT YOU TO KEEP YOUR HEAD DOWN UNTIL YOU HEAR FROM ME.
DON'T HUMOR ME, DRIVER. I GOT EYES. YOU ALL THINK I'M OFF MY NUT NOW.
BUT I'LL TELL YOU SOMETHIN'--I MAY'VE BENT THE RULES SOME WHEN I RAN THIS SQUAD, BUT I WAS A GOOD COP.
AN' WE DIDN'T HAVE DETECTIVES DYING LEFT AND RIGHT ON MY WATCH, EITHER.
SO REMEMBER THAT NEXT TIME YOU'RE LAUGHIN' ABOUT HOW BULLOCK'S JUST A WASHED-UP DRUNK, YA SMUG LITTLE #$$-WIPE.

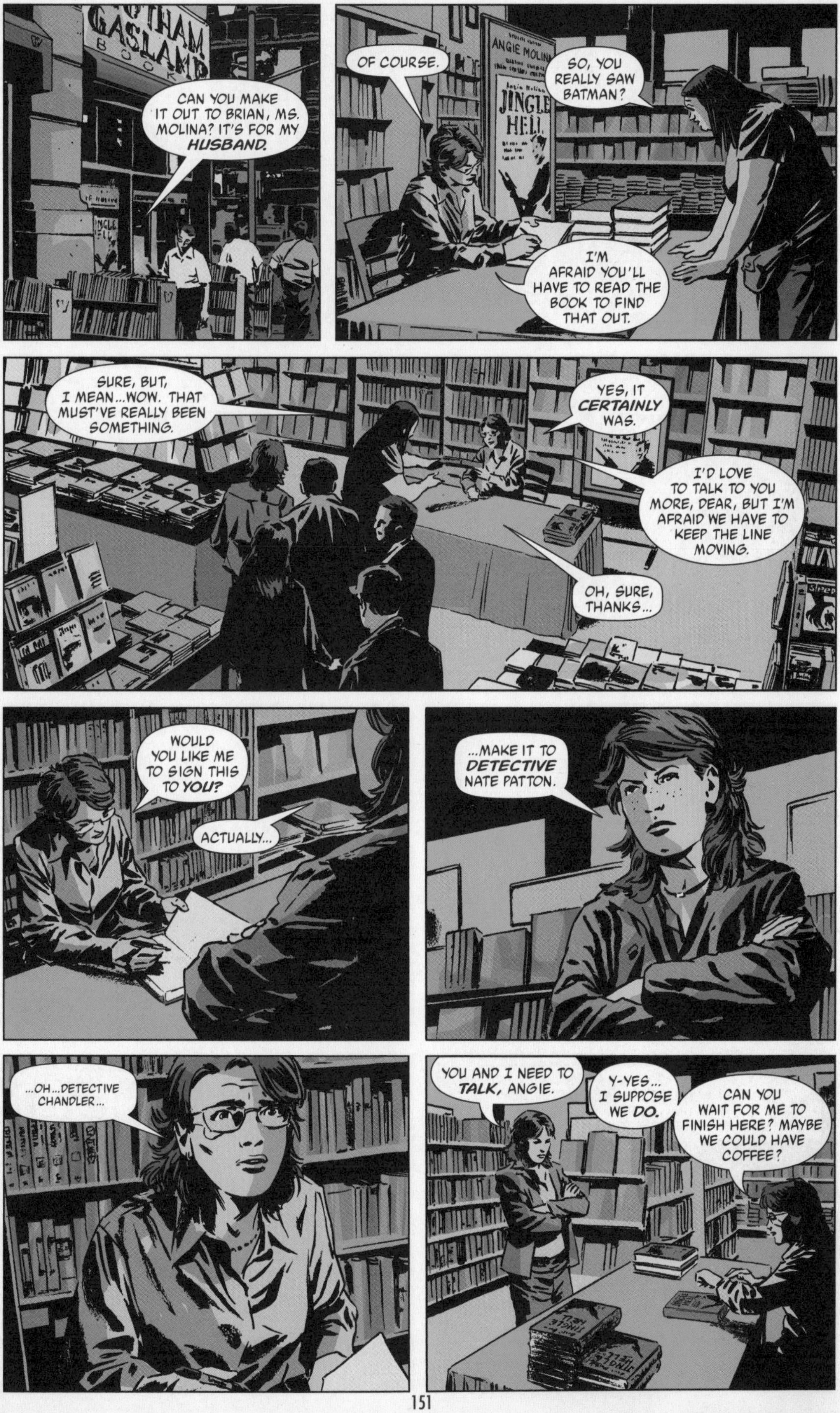
CAN YOU MAKE IT OUT TO BRIAN, MS. MOLINA? IT'S FOR MY *HUSBAND.*
OF COURSE.
ANGIE MOLINA
JINGLE HELL
SO, YOU REALLY SAW BATMAN?
I'M AFRAID YOU'LL HAVE TO READ THE BOOK TO FIND THAT OUT.
SURE, BUT, I MEAN...WOW. THAT MUST'VE REALLY BEEN SOMETHING.
YES, IT *CERTAINLY* WAS.
I'D LOVE TO TALK TO YOU MORE, DEAR, BUT I'M AFRAID WE HAVE TO KEEP THE LINE MOVING.
OH, SURE, THANKS...
WOULD YOU LIKE ME TO SIGN THIS TO *YOU?*
ACTUALLY...
...MAKE IT TO *DETECTIVE* NATE PATTON.
...OH...DETECTIVE CHANDLER...
YOU AND I NEED TO *TALK,* ANGIE.
Y-YES... I SUPPOSE WE *DO.*
CAN YOU WAIT FOR ME TO FINISH HERE? MAYBE WE COULD HAVE COFFEE?

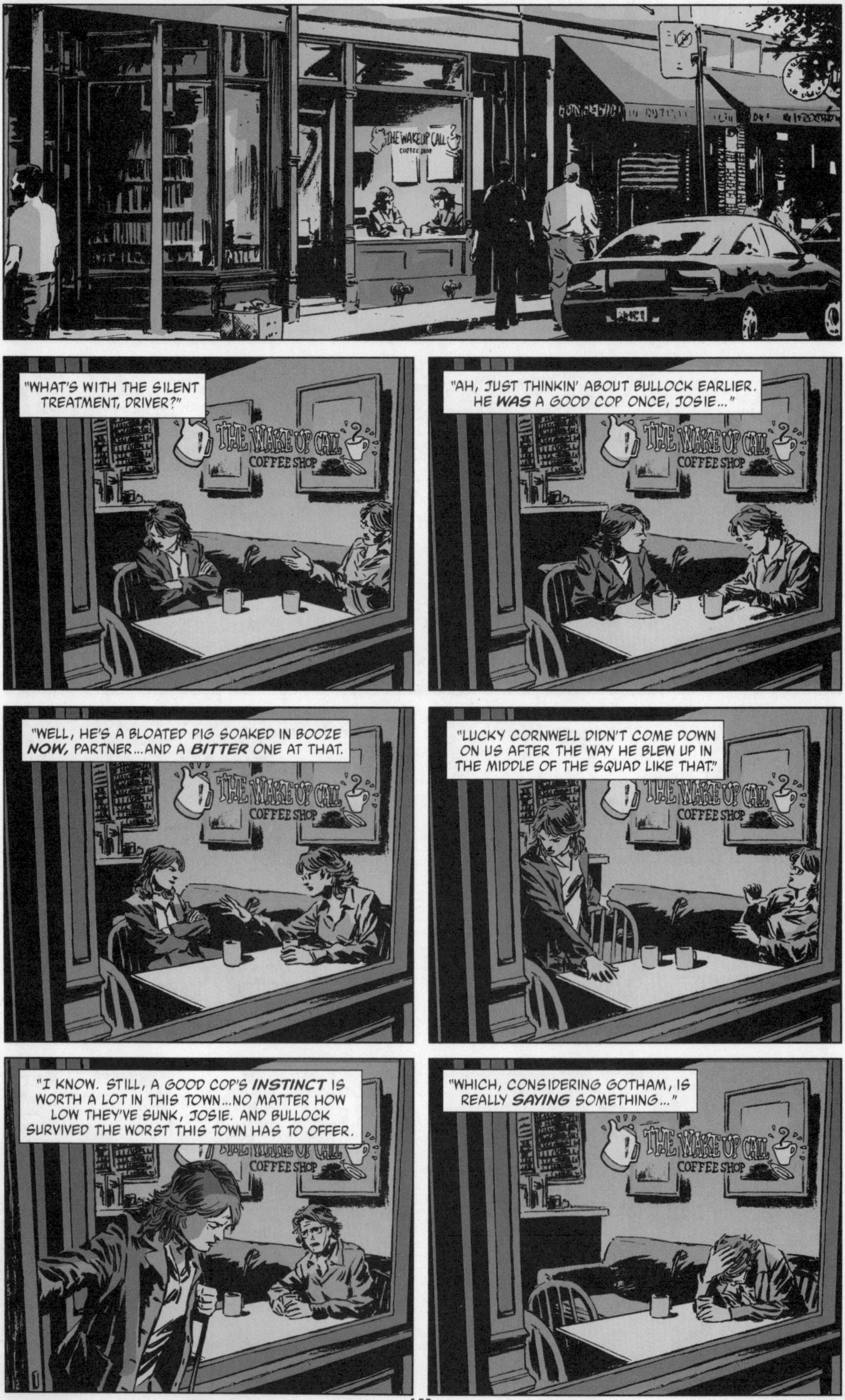
THE WAKE UP CALL
COFFEE SHOP
"WHAT'S WITH THE SILENT TREATMENT, DRIVER?"
"AH, JUST THINKIN' ABOUT BULLOCK EARLIER. HE **WAS** A GOOD COP ONCE, JOSIE..."
"WELL, HE'S A BLOATED PIG SOAKED IN BOOZE **NOW,** PARTNER...AND A **BITTER** ONE AT THAT.
"LUCKY CORNWELL DIDN'T COME DOWN ON US AFTER THE WAY HE BLEW UP IN THE MIDDLE OF THE SQUAD LIKE THAT."
"I KNOW. STILL, A GOOD COP'S **INSTINCT** IS WORTH A LOT IN THIS TOWN...NO MATTER HOW LOW THEY'VE SUNK, JOSIE. AND BULLOCK SURVIVED THE WORST THIS TOWN HAS TO OFFER.
"WHICH, CONSIDERING GOTHAM, IS REALLY **SAYING** SOMETHING..."

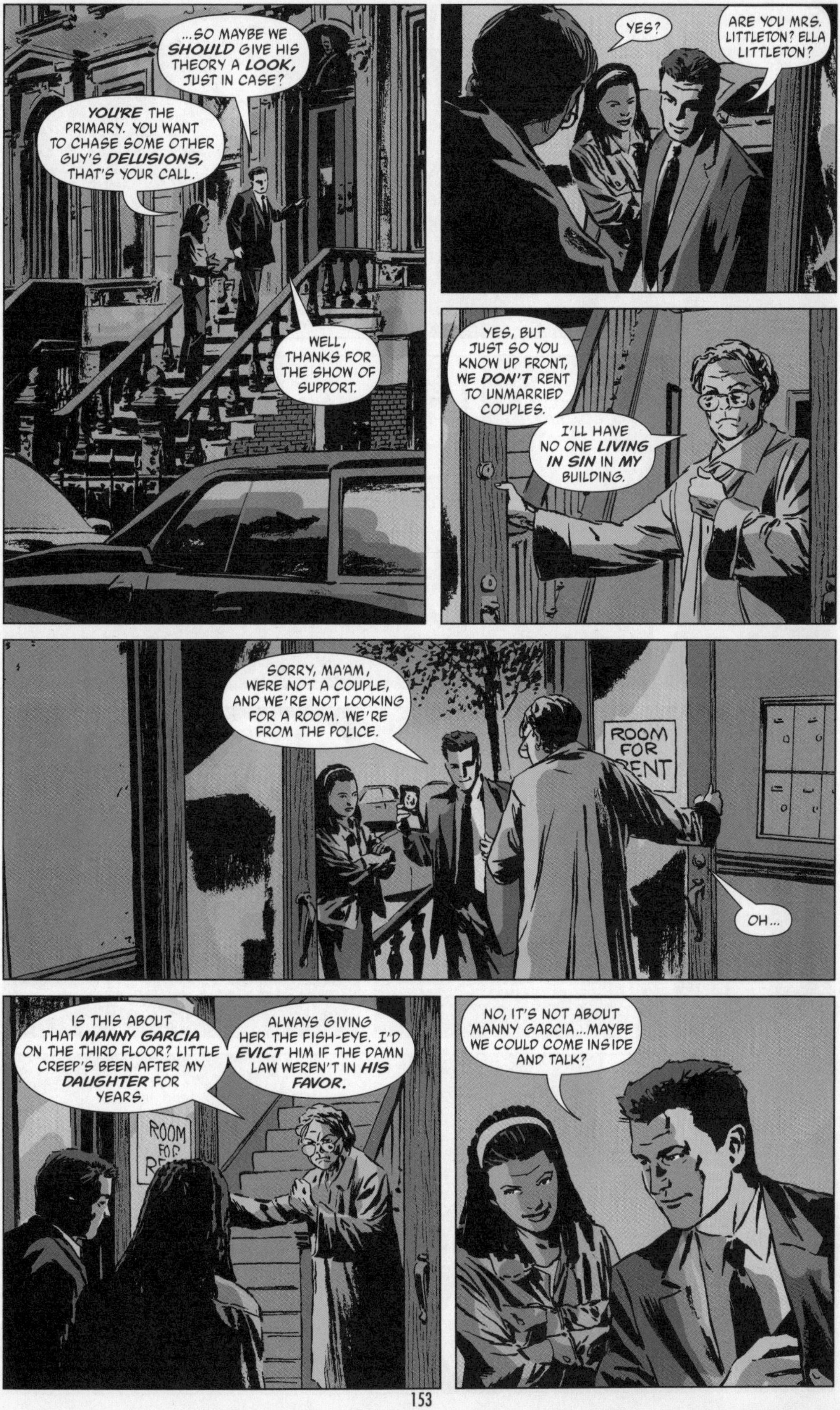

...SO MAYBE WE SHOULD GIVE HIS THEORY A LOOK, JUST IN CASE?
YOU'RE THE PRIMARY. YOU WANT TO CHASE SOME OTHER GUY'S DELUSIONS, THAT'S YOUR CALL.
WELL, THANKS FOR THE SHOW OF SUPPORT.
YES?
ARE YOU MRS. LITTLETON? ELLA LITTLETON?
YES, BUT JUST SO YOU KNOW UP FRONT, WE DON'T RENT TO UNMARRIED COUPLES.
I'LL HAVE NO ONE LIVING IN SIN IN MY BUILDING.
SORRY, MA'AM, WERE NOT A COUPLE, AND WE'RE NOT LOOKING FOR A ROOM. WE'RE FROM THE POLICE.
ROOM FOR RENT
OH...
IS THIS ABOUT THAT MANNY GARCIA ON THE THIRD FLOOR? LITTLE CREEP'S BEEN AFTER MY DAUGHTER FOR YEARS.
ALWAYS GIVING HER THE FISH-EYE. I'D EVICT HIM IF THE DAMN LAW WEREN'T IN HIS FAVOR.
NO, IT'S NOT ABOUT MANNY GARCIA...MAYBE WE COULD COME INSIDE AND TALK?

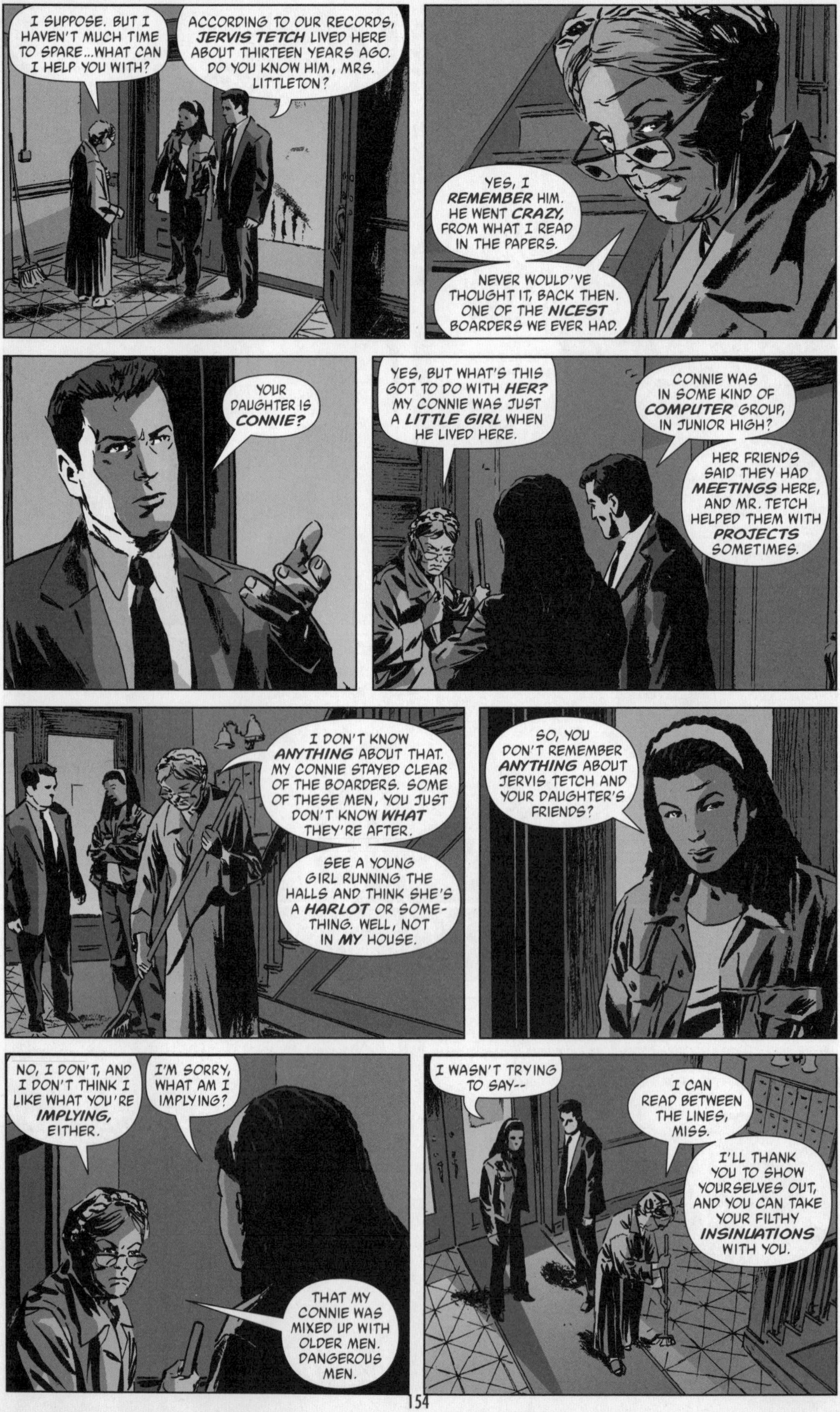
I SUPPOSE. BUT I HAVEN'T MUCH TIME TO SPARE...WHAT CAN I HELP YOU WITH?
ACCORDING TO OUR RECORDS, JERVIS TETCH LIVED HERE ABOUT THIRTEEN YEARS AGO. DO YOU KNOW HIM, MRS. LITTLETON?
YES, I REMEMBER HIM. HE WENT CRAZY, FROM WHAT I READ IN THE PAPERS.
NEVER WOULD'VE THOUGHT IT, BACK THEN. ONE OF THE NICEST BOARDERS WE EVER HAD.
YOUR DAUGHTER IS CONNIE?
YES, BUT WHAT'S THIS GOT TO DO WITH HER? MY CONNIE WAS JUST A LITTLE GIRL WHEN HE LIVED HERE.
CONNIE WAS IN SOME KIND OF COMPUTER GROUP, IN JUNIOR HIGH?
HER FRIENDS SAID THEY HAD MEETINGS HERE, AND MR. TETCH HELPED THEM WITH PROJECTS SOMETIMES.
I DON'T KNOW ANYTHING ABOUT THAT. MY CONNIE STAYED CLEAR OF THE BOARDERS. SOME OF THESE MEN, YOU JUST DON'T KNOW WHAT THEY'RE AFTER.
SEE A YOUNG GIRL RUNNING THE HALLS AND THINK SHE'S A HARLOT OR SOMETHING. WELL, NOT IN MY HOUSE.
SO, YOU DON'T REMEMBER ANYTHING ABOUT JERVIS TETCH AND YOUR DAUGHTER'S FRIENDS?
NO, I DON'T, AND I DON'T THINK I LIKE WHAT YOU'RE IMPLYING, EITHER.
I'M SORRY, WHAT AM I IMPLYING?
THAT MY CONNIE WAS MIXED UP WITH OLDER MEN. DANGEROUS MEN.
I WASN'T TRYING TO SAY--
I CAN READ BETWEEN THE LINES, MISS.
I'LL THANK YOU TO SHOW YOURSELVES OUT, AND YOU CAN TAKE YOUR FILTHY INSINUATIONS WITH YOU.

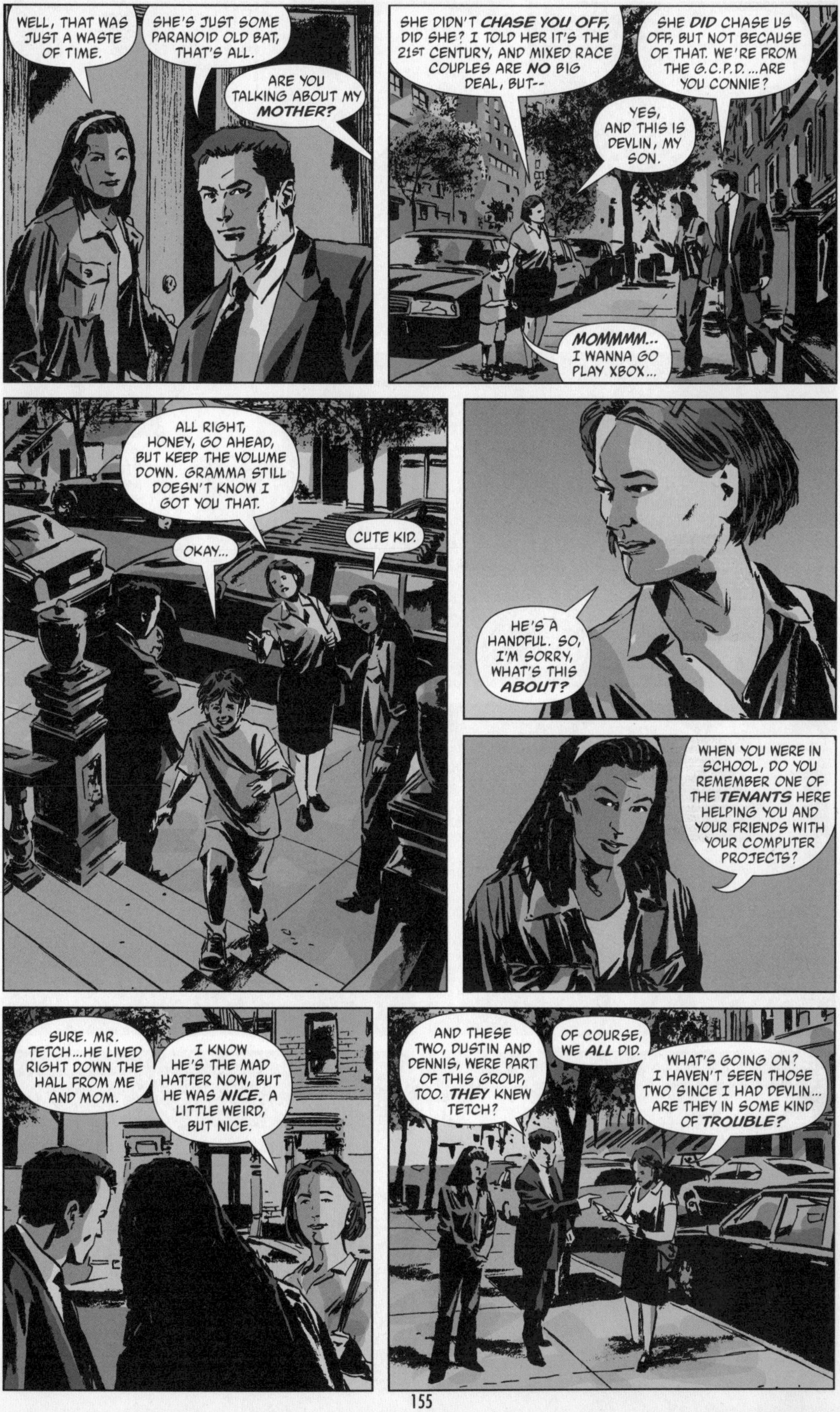
WELL, THAT WAS JUST A WASTE OF TIME.
SHE'S JUST SOME PARANOID OLD BAT, THAT'S ALL.
ARE YOU TALKING ABOUT MY MOTHER?
SHE DIDN'T CHASE YOU OFF, DID SHE? I TOLD HER IT'S THE 21ST CENTURY, AND MIXED RACE COUPLES ARE NO BIG DEAL, BUT--
SHE DID CHASE US OFF, BUT NOT BECAUSE OF THAT. WE'RE FROM THE G.C.P.D. ...ARE YOU CONNIE?
YES, AND THIS IS DEVLIN, MY SON.
MOMMMM... I WANNA GO PLAY XBOX...
ALL RIGHT, HONEY, GO AHEAD, BUT KEEP THE VOLUME DOWN. GRAMMA STILL DOESN'T KNOW I GOT YOU THAT.
OKAY...
CUTE KID.
HE'S A HANDFUL. SO, I'M SORRY, WHAT'S THIS ABOUT?
WHEN YOU WERE IN SCHOOL, DO YOU REMEMBER ONE OF THE TENANTS HERE HELPING YOU AND YOUR FRIENDS WITH YOUR COMPUTER PROJECTS?
SURE. MR. TETCH...HE LIVED RIGHT DOWN THE HALL FROM ME AND MOM.
I KNOW HE'S THE MAD HATTER NOW, BUT HE WAS NICE. A LITTLE WEIRD, BUT NICE.
AND THESE TWO, DUSTIN AND DENNIS, WERE PART OF THIS GROUP, TOO. THEY KNEW TETCH?
OF COURSE, WE ALL DID.
WHAT'S GOING ON? I HAVEN'T SEEN THOSE TWO SINCE I HAD DEVLIN... ARE THEY IN SOME KIND OF TROUBLE?

--KNOW LESS *NOW* THAN WHEN WE GOT UP, MARCUS.

THAT'S WHY I WANT TO TAKE ANOTHER RUN AT TETCH. HE'S HAD US RUNNING IN CIRCLES TODAY AND I, FOR ONE, WANT TO KNOW *WHY*.

MAYBE BECAUSE HE'S INSANE?

NO, HE'S *MESSING* WITH US.

HE KILLED THAT TEAM, AND HE KNEW THE KIDS WHO CHEERED ABOUT IT. SOMETHING MORE IS GOING ON HERE.

HE KNOWS THE *PENGUIN,* TOO.

DON'T THINK I'M NOT GONNA MENTION HIM.

YOU WATCH HATTER'S *EYES* WHEN I DO, TOO. BET HE--

RRTTT-RRTT

WHAT THE HELL IS *GOING* ON?

ESCAPE ATTEMPT! ON LEVEL THREE!

RRTTT-RRTTT-RRTT

TETCH IS ON LEVEL THREE.

OH, HELL...

TTT-RRTTT-RRTTT

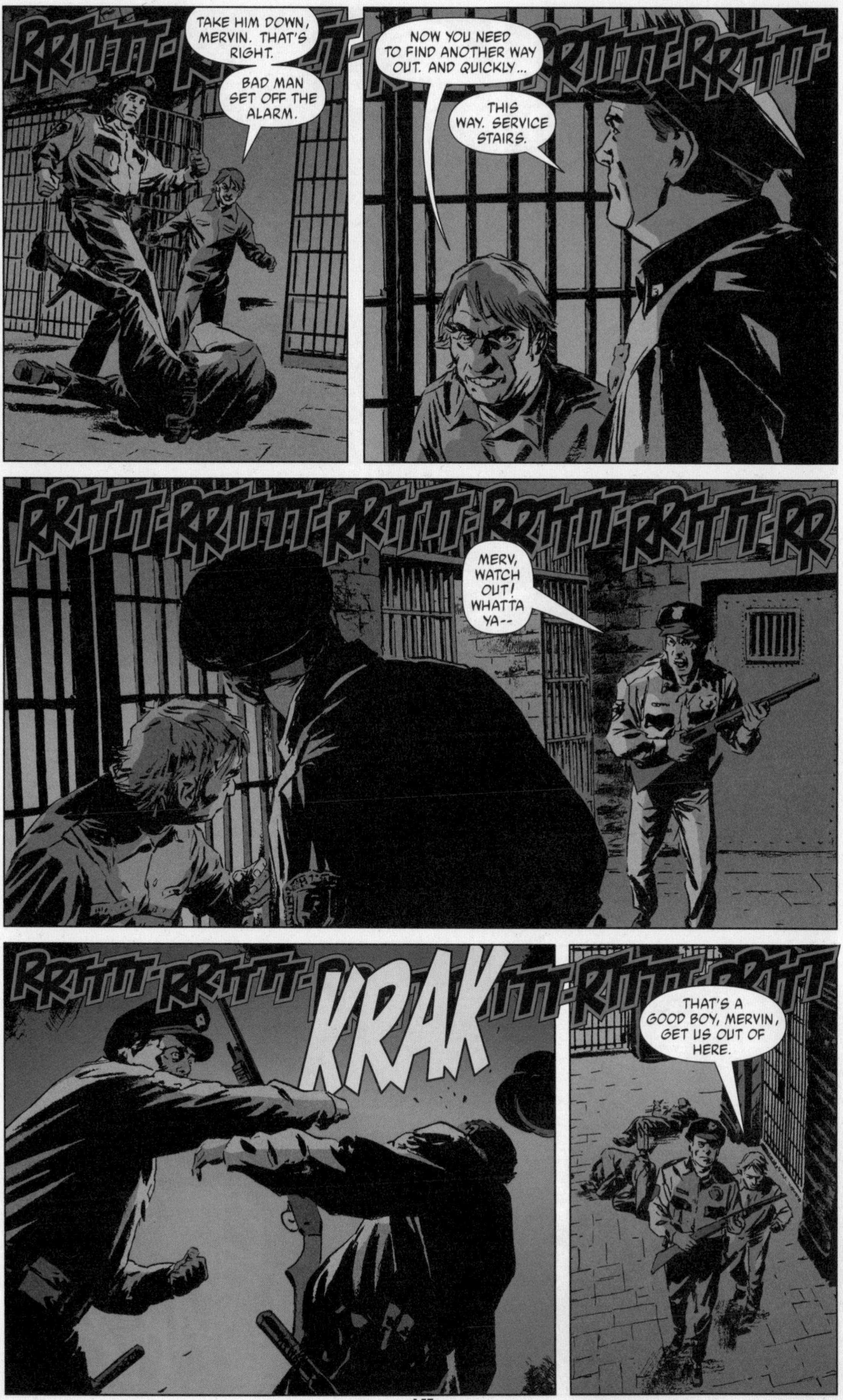
RRTTTT-RRTTTT-
TAKE HIM DOWN, MERVIN. THAT'S RIGHT.
BAD MAN SET OFF THE ALARM.
NOW YOU NEED TO FIND ANOTHER WAY OUT. AND QUICKLY...
THIS WAY. SERVICE STAIRS.
RRTTTT-RRTTTT-
RRTTTT-RRTTTT-RRTTTT-RRTTTT-RRTTTT-RR
MERV, WATCH OUT! WHATTA YA--
RRTTTT-RRTTTT-
KRAK
TT-RTTTT-RRTTTT
THAT'S A GOOD BOY, MERVIN, GET US OUT OF HERE.

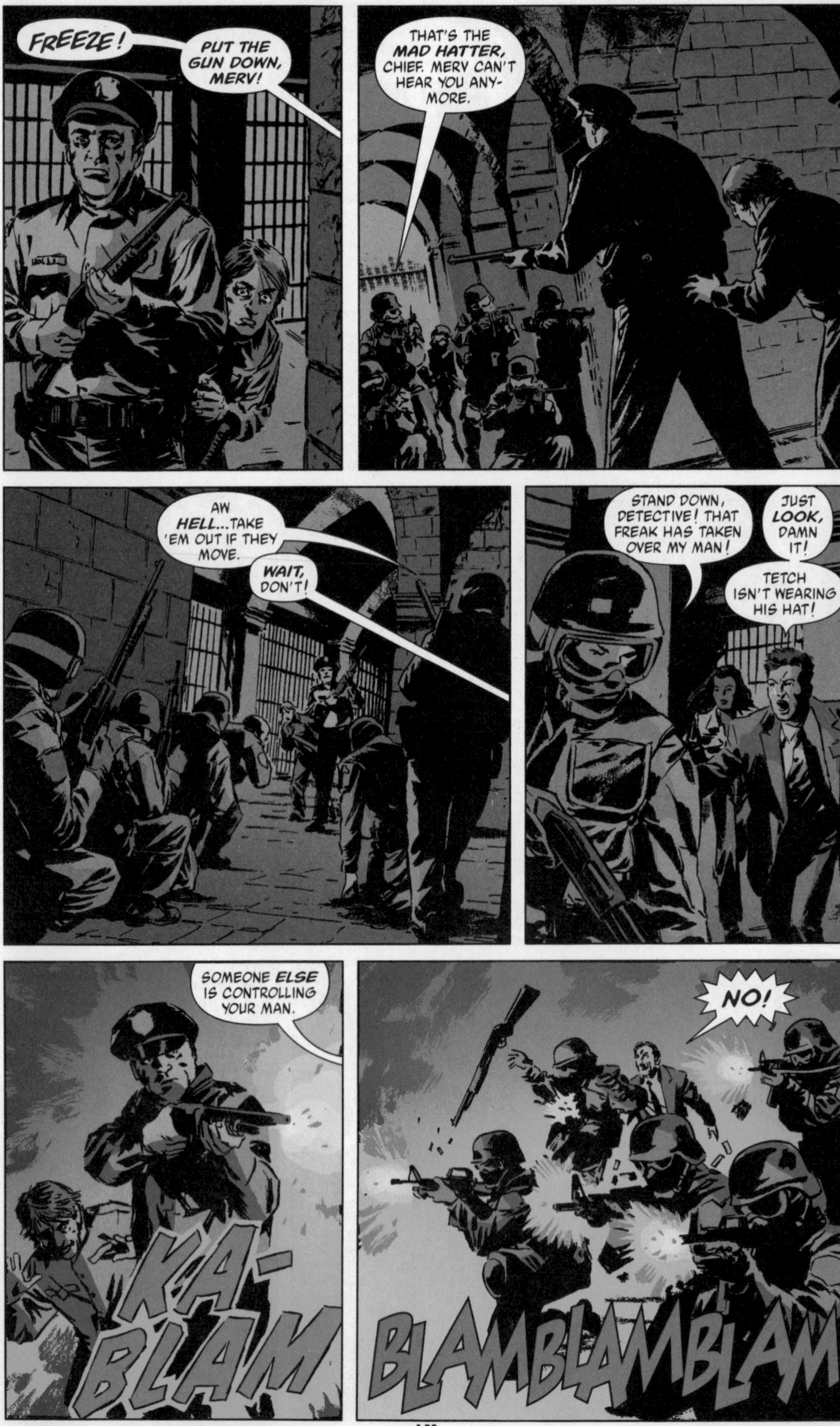

FREEZE!
PUT THE GUN DOWN, MERV!
THAT'S THE MAD HATTER, CHIEF. MERV CAN'T HEAR YOU ANYMORE.
AW HELL...TAKE 'EM OUT IF THEY MOVE.
WAIT, DON'T!
STAND DOWN, DETECTIVE! THAT FREAK HAS TAKEN OVER MY MAN!
JUST LOOK, DAMN IT!
TETCH ISN'T WEARING HIS HAT!
SOMEONE ELSE IS CONTROLLING YOUR MAN.
KA-BLAM
NO!
BLAMBLAMBLAM

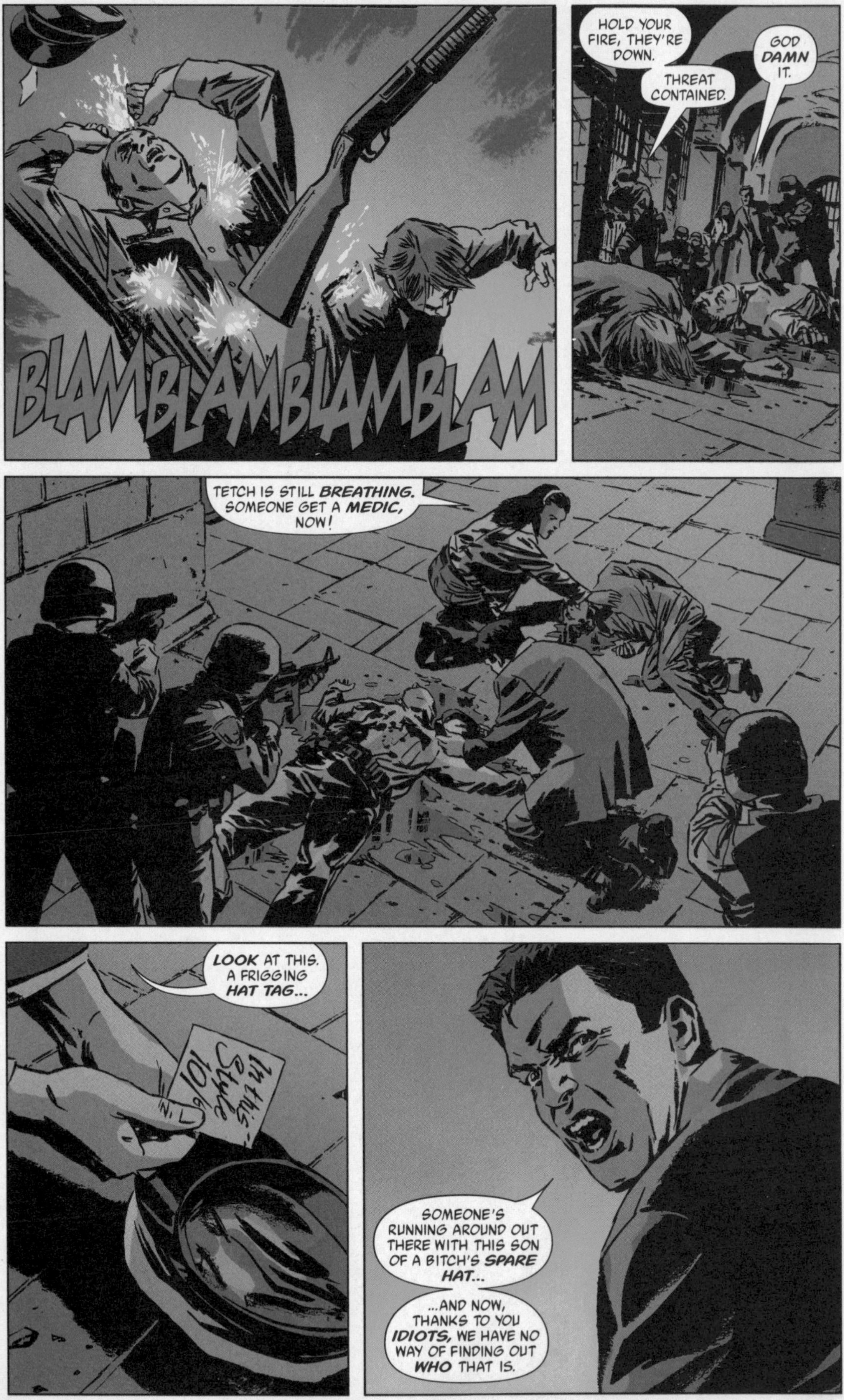
BLAMBLAMBLAMBLAM
HOLD YOUR FIRE, THEY'RE DOWN.
THREAT CONTAINED.
GOD DAMN IT.
TETCH IS STILL BREATHING. SOMEONE GET A MEDIC, NOW!
LOOK AT THIS. A FRIGGING HAT TAG...
In this Style 10/6
SOMEONE'S RUNNING AROUND OUT THERE WITH THIS SON OF A BITCH'S SPARE HAT...
...AND NOW, THANKS TO YOU IDIOTS, WE HAVE NO WAY OF FINDING OUT WHO THAT IS.

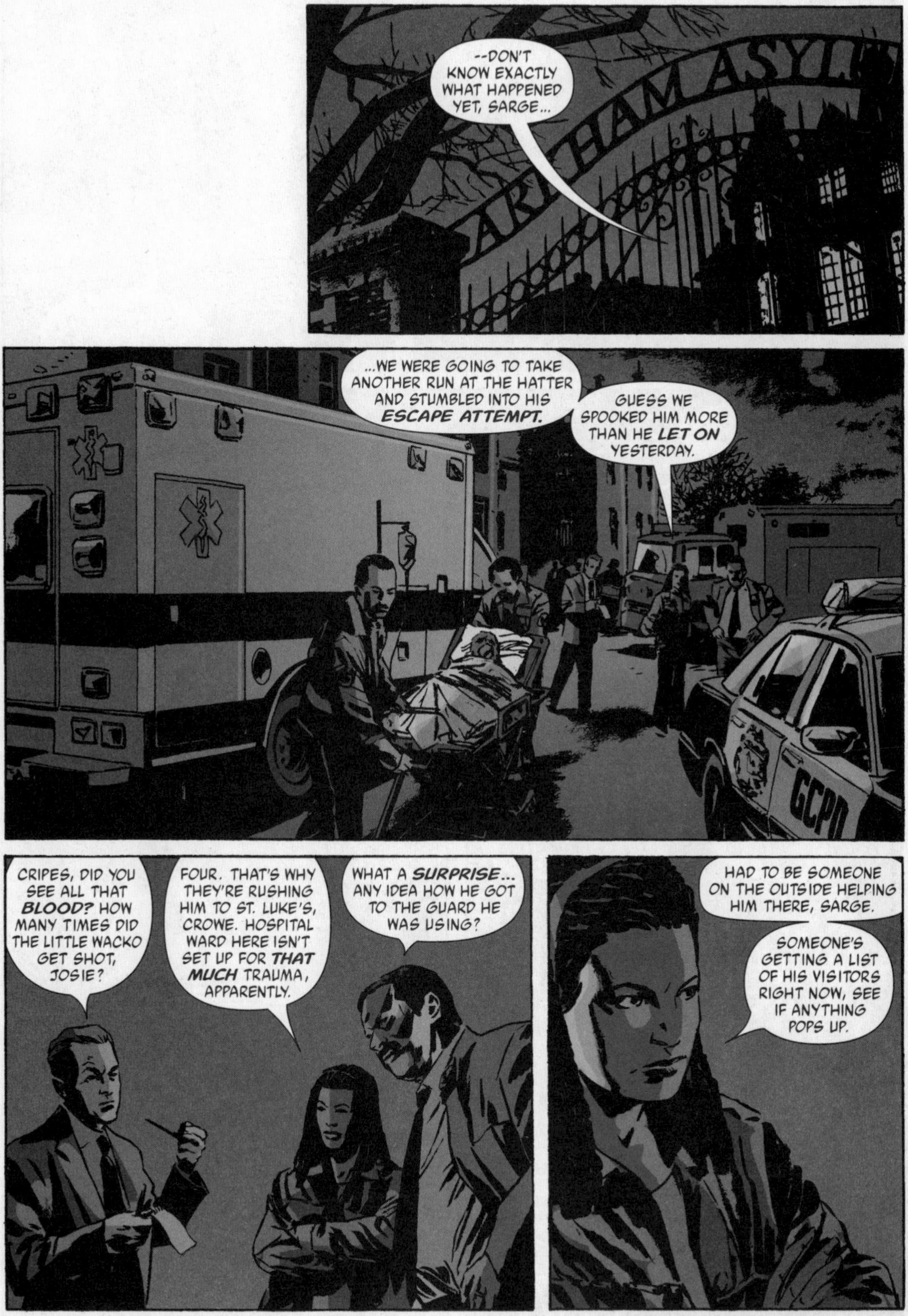

ARKHAM ASYL
--DON'T KNOW EXACTLY WHAT HAPPENED YET, SARGE...
...WE WERE GOING TO TAKE ANOTHER RUN AT THE HATTER AND STUMBLED INTO HIS ESCAPE ATTEMPT.
GUESS WE SPOOKED HIM MORE THAN HE LET ON YESTERDAY.
GCPD
CRIPES, DID YOU SEE ALL THAT BLOOD? HOW MANY TIMES DID THE LITTLE WACKO GET SHOT, JOSIE?
FOUR. THAT'S WHY THEY'RE RUSHING HIM TO ST. LUKE'S, CROWE. HOSPITAL WARD HERE ISN'T SET UP FOR THAT MUCH TRAUMA, APPARENTLY.
WHAT A SURPRISE... ANY IDEA HOW HE GOT TO THE GUARD HE WAS USING?
HAD TO BE SOMEONE ON THE OUTSIDE HELPING HIM THERE, SARGE.
SOMEONE'S GETTING A LIST OF HIS VISITORS RIGHT NOW, SEE IF ANYTHING POPS UP.

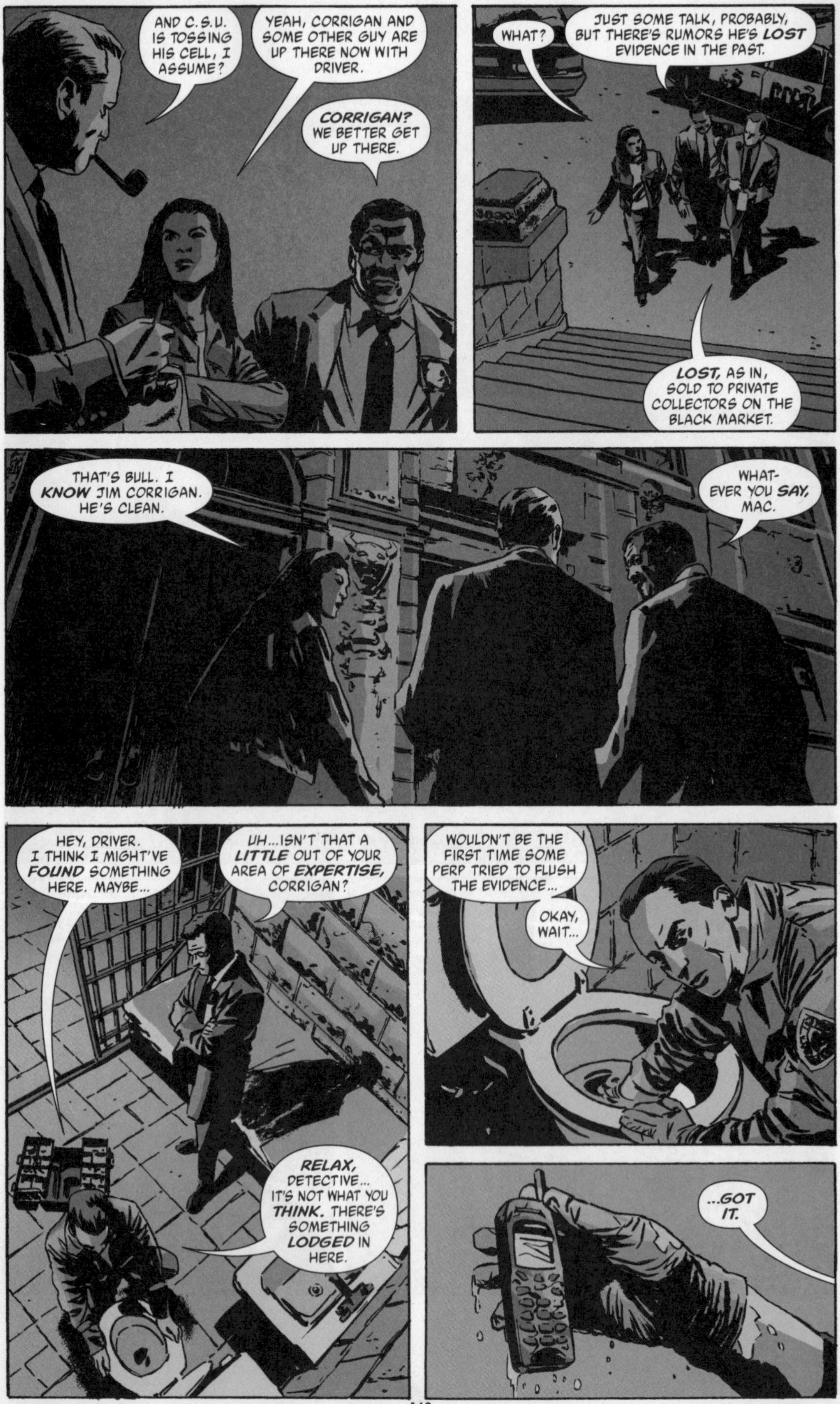
AND C.S.U. IS TOSSING HIS CELL, I ASSUME?
YEAH, CORRIGAN AND SOME OTHER GUY ARE UP THERE NOW WITH DRIVER.
CORRIGAN? WE BETTER GET UP THERE.
WHAT?
JUST SOME TALK, PROBABLY, BUT THERE'S RUMORS HE'S LOST EVIDENCE IN THE PAST.
LOST, AS IN, SOLD TO PRIVATE COLLECTORS ON THE BLACK MARKET.
THAT'S BULL. I KNOW JIM CORRIGAN. HE'S CLEAN.
WHAT-EVER YOU SAY, MAC.
HEY, DRIVER. I THINK I MIGHT'VE FOUND SOMETHING HERE. MAYBE...
UH...ISN'T THAT A LITTLE OUT OF YOUR AREA OF EXPERTISE, CORRIGAN?
RELAX, DETECTIVE... IT'S NOT WHAT YOU THINK. THERE'S SOMETHING LODGED IN HERE.
WOULDN'T BE THE FIRST TIME SOME PERP TRIED TO FLUSH THE EVIDENCE...
OKAY, WAIT...
...GOT IT.

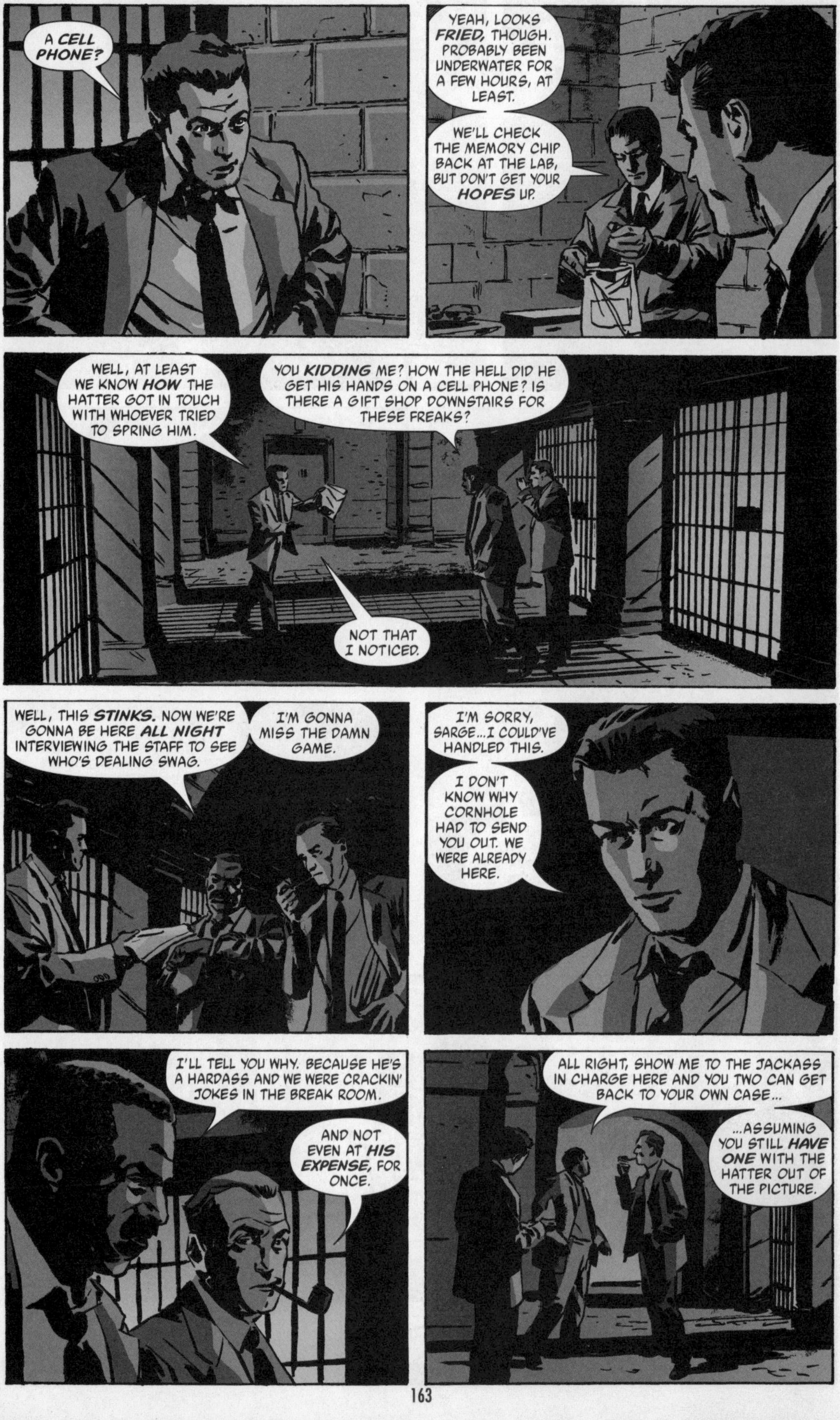
A CELL PHONE?
YEAH, LOOKS FRIED, THOUGH. PROBABLY BEEN UNDERWATER FOR A FEW HOURS, AT LEAST.
WE'LL CHECK THE MEMORY CHIP BACK AT THE LAB, BUT DON'T GET YOUR HOPES UP.
WELL, AT LEAST WE KNOW HOW THE HATTER GOT IN TOUCH WITH WHOEVER TRIED TO SPRING HIM.
YOU KIDDING ME? HOW THE HELL DID HE GET HIS HANDS ON A CELL PHONE? IS THERE A GIFT SHOP DOWNSTAIRS FOR THESE FREAKS?
NOT THAT I NOTICED.
WELL, THIS STINKS. NOW WE'RE GONNA BE HERE ALL NIGHT INTERVIEWING THE STAFF TO SEE WHO'S DEALING SWAG.
I'M GONNA MISS THE DAMN GAME.
I'M SORRY, SARGE...I COULD'VE HANDLED THIS.
I DON'T KNOW WHY CORNHOLE HAD TO SEND YOU OUT. WE WERE ALREADY HERE.
I'LL TELL YOU WHY. BECAUSE HE'S A HARDASS AND WE WERE CRACKIN' JOKES IN THE BREAK ROOM.
AND NOT EVEN AT HIS EXPENSE, FOR ONCE.
ALL RIGHT, SHOW ME TO THE JACKASS IN CHARGE HERE AND YOU TWO CAN GET BACK TO YOUR OWN CASE...
...ASSUMING YOU STILL HAVE ONE WITH THE HATTER OUT OF THE PICTURE.

GOD, DRIVER... ...YOU *SLEEP* HERE LAST NIGHT?

UH, *YEAH,* ACTUALLY. WAITING FOR NEWS ON THAT CELL PHONE LOG.

THEY GET ANYTHING?

MAYBE IT WAS COBBLEPOT TRYING TO COVER HIS OWN $%$*. GET HATTER BACK IN THE REAL WORLD BEFORE HE CAN IMPLICATE HIM.

NAH. THEY'RE NOT GETTING $#*% FROM THAT THING AFTER IT WAS JAMMED IN A TOILET ALL NIGHT. IT'S SHOT.

WELL, THAT'S *MORE* GOOD NEWS.

SO, WHAT DO YOU THINK? WHO'D TETCH CALL TO BUST HIM OUT?

BEEN PONDERING *THAT* ONE ALL MORNING. WONDERING ABOUT BULLOCK'S THEORY A BIT.

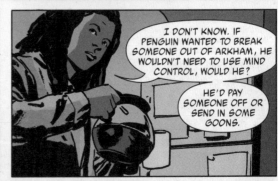

I DON'T KNOW. IF PENGUIN WANTED TO BREAK SOMEONE OUT OF ARKHAM, HE WOULDN'T NEED TO USE MIND CONTROL, WOULD HE?

HE'D PAY SOMEONE OFF OR SEND IN SOME GOONS.

YEAH, GOOD POINT...

UNLESS HE'S TRYING TO KEEP HIMSELF FREE OF SUSPICION AFTER BULLOCK'S DRUNKEN RAMPAGE THE OTHER NIGHT.

IT'S A REACH, STILL.

AND PROBABLY GIVING WAY TOO MUCH CREDIT TO HARVEY BULLOCK'S INSIGHT.

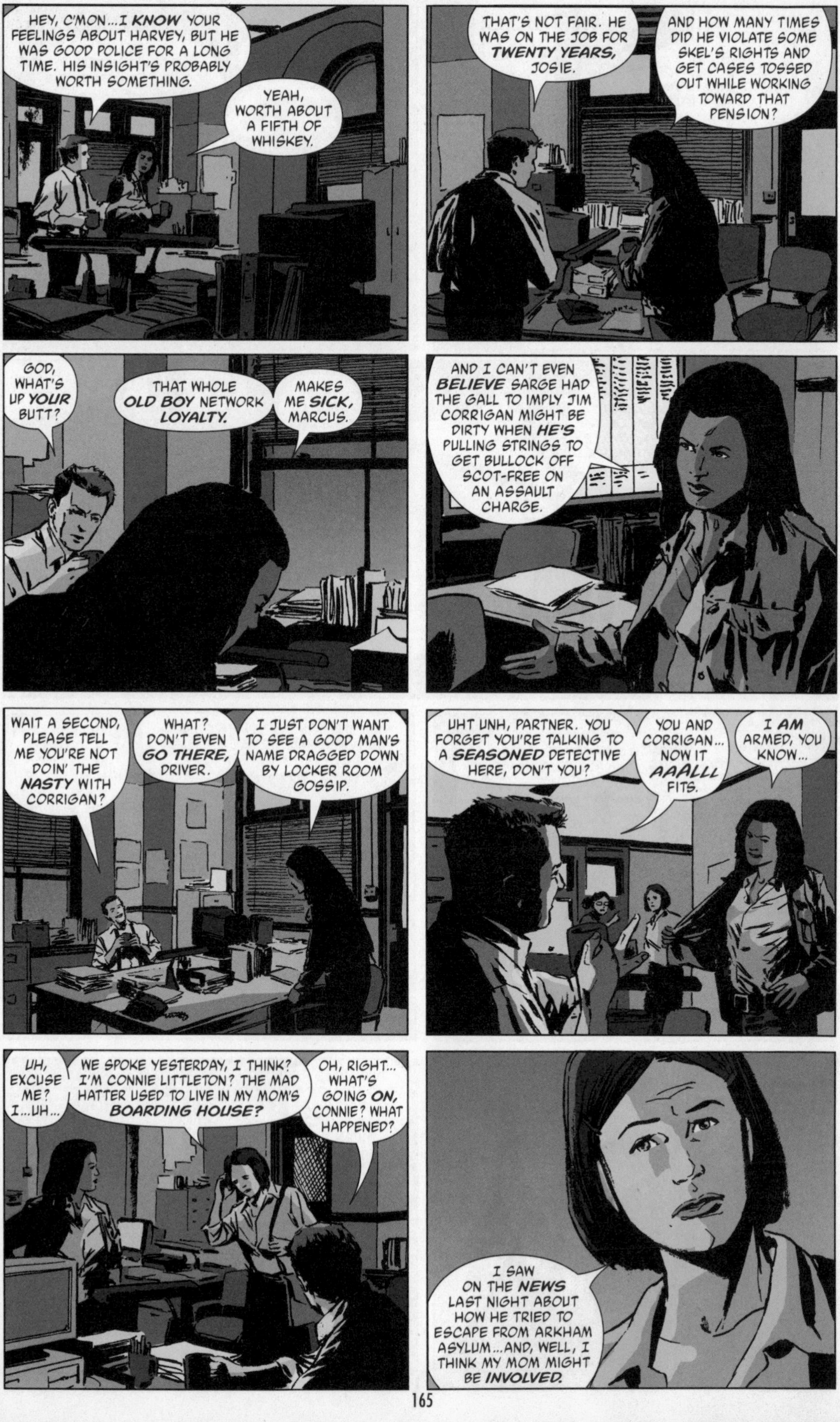
HEY, C'MON...I KNOW YOUR FEELINGS ABOUT HARVEY, BUT HE WAS GOOD POLICE FOR A LONG TIME. HIS INSIGHT'S PROBABLY WORTH SOMETHING.
YEAH, WORTH ABOUT A FIFTH OF WHISKEY.
THAT'S NOT FAIR. HE WAS ON THE JOB FOR TWENTY YEARS, JOSIE.
AND HOW MANY TIMES DID HE VIOLATE SOME SKEL'S RIGHTS AND GET CASES TOSSED OUT WHILE WORKING TOWARD THAT PENSION?
GOD, WHAT'S UP YOUR BUTT?
THAT WHOLE OLD BOY NETWORK LOYALTY.
MAKES ME SICK, MARCUS.
AND I CAN'T EVEN BELIEVE SARGE HAD THE GALL TO IMPLY JIM CORRIGAN MIGHT BE DIRTY WHEN HE'S PULLING STRINGS TO GET BULLOCK OFF SCOT-FREE ON AN ASSAULT CHARGE.
WAIT A SECOND, PLEASE TELL ME YOU'RE NOT DOIN' THE NASTY WITH CORRIGAN?
WHAT? DON'T EVEN GO THERE, DRIVER.
I JUST DON'T WANT TO SEE A GOOD MAN'S NAME DRAGGED DOWN BY LOCKER ROOM GOSSIP.
UHT UNH, PARTNER. YOU FORGET YOU'RE TALKING TO A SEASONED DETECTIVE HERE, DON'T YOU?
YOU AND CORRIGAN... NOW IT AAALLL FITS.
I AM ARMED, YOU KNOW...
UH, EXCUSE ME? I...UH...
WE SPOKE YESTERDAY, I THINK? I'M CONNIE LITTLETON? THE MAD HATTER USED TO LIVE IN MY MOM'S BOARDING HOUSE?
OH, RIGHT... WHAT'S GOING ON, CONNIE? WHAT HAPPENED?
I SAW ON THE NEWS LAST NIGHT ABOUT HOW HE TRIED TO ESCAPE FROM ARKHAM ASYLUM...AND, WELL, I THINK MY MOM MIGHT BE INVOLVED.

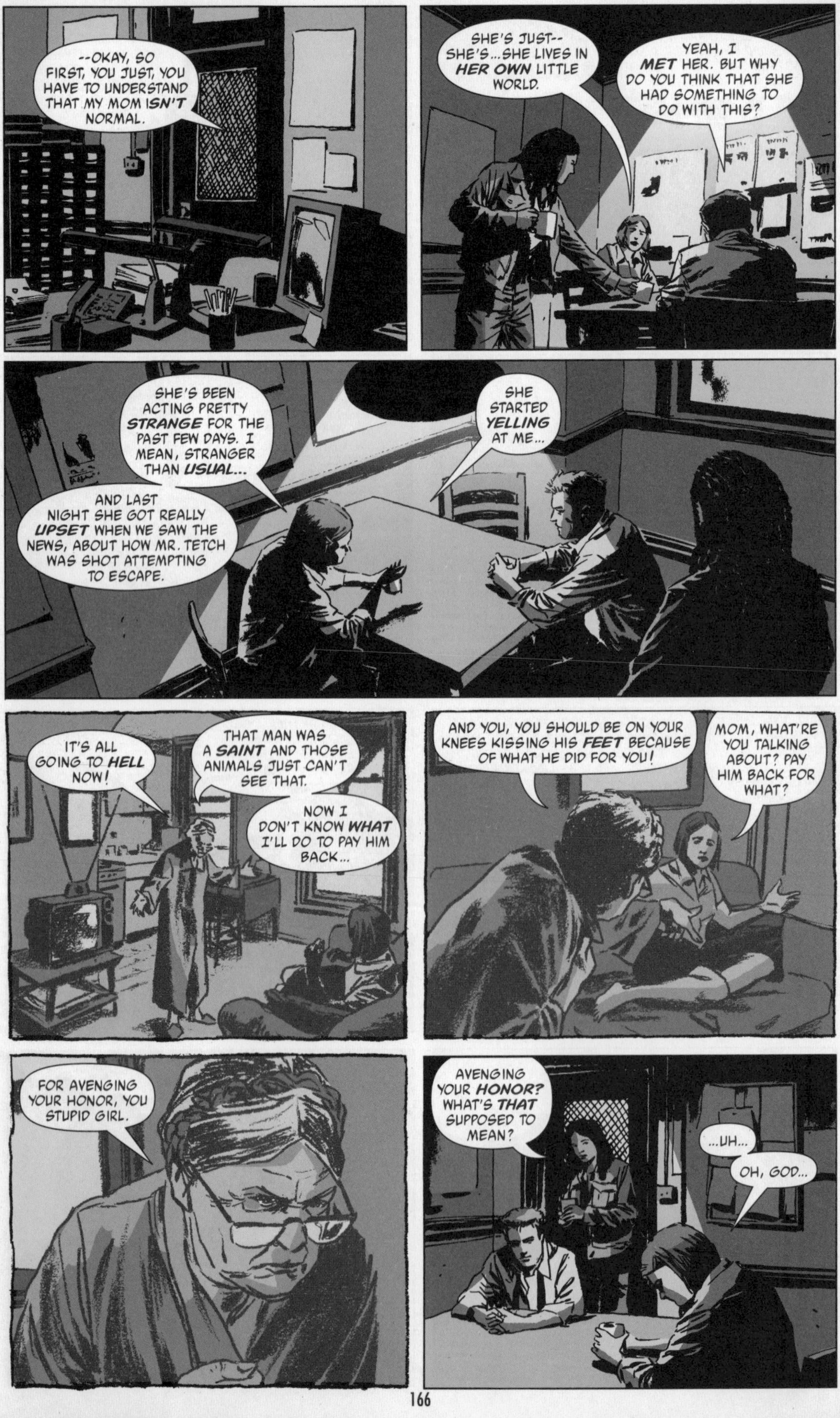
--OKAY, SO FIRST, YOU JUST, YOU HAVE TO UNDERSTAND THAT MY MOM ISN'T NORMAL.
SHE'S JUST-- SHE'S...SHE LIVES IN HER OWN LITTLE WORLD.
YEAH, I MET HER. BUT WHY DO YOU THINK THAT SHE HAD SOMETHING TO DO WITH THIS?
SHE'S BEEN ACTING PRETTY STRANGE FOR THE PAST FEW DAYS. I MEAN, STRANGER THAN USUAL...
AND LAST NIGHT SHE GOT REALLY UPSET WHEN WE SAW THE NEWS, ABOUT HOW MR. TETCH WAS SHOT ATTEMPTING TO ESCAPE.
SHE STARTED YELLING AT ME...
IT'S ALL GOING TO HELL NOW!
THAT MAN WAS A SAINT AND THOSE ANIMALS JUST CAN'T SEE THAT.
NOW I DON'T KNOW WHAT I'LL DO TO PAY HIM BACK...
AND YOU, YOU SHOULD BE ON YOUR KNEES KISSING HIS FEET BECAUSE OF WHAT HE DID FOR YOU!
MOM, WHAT'RE YOU TALKING ABOUT? PAY HIM BACK FOR WHAT?
FOR AVENGING YOUR HONOR, YOU STUPID GIRL.
AVENGING YOUR HONOR? WHAT'S THAT SUPPOSED TO MEAN?
...UH...
OH, GOD...

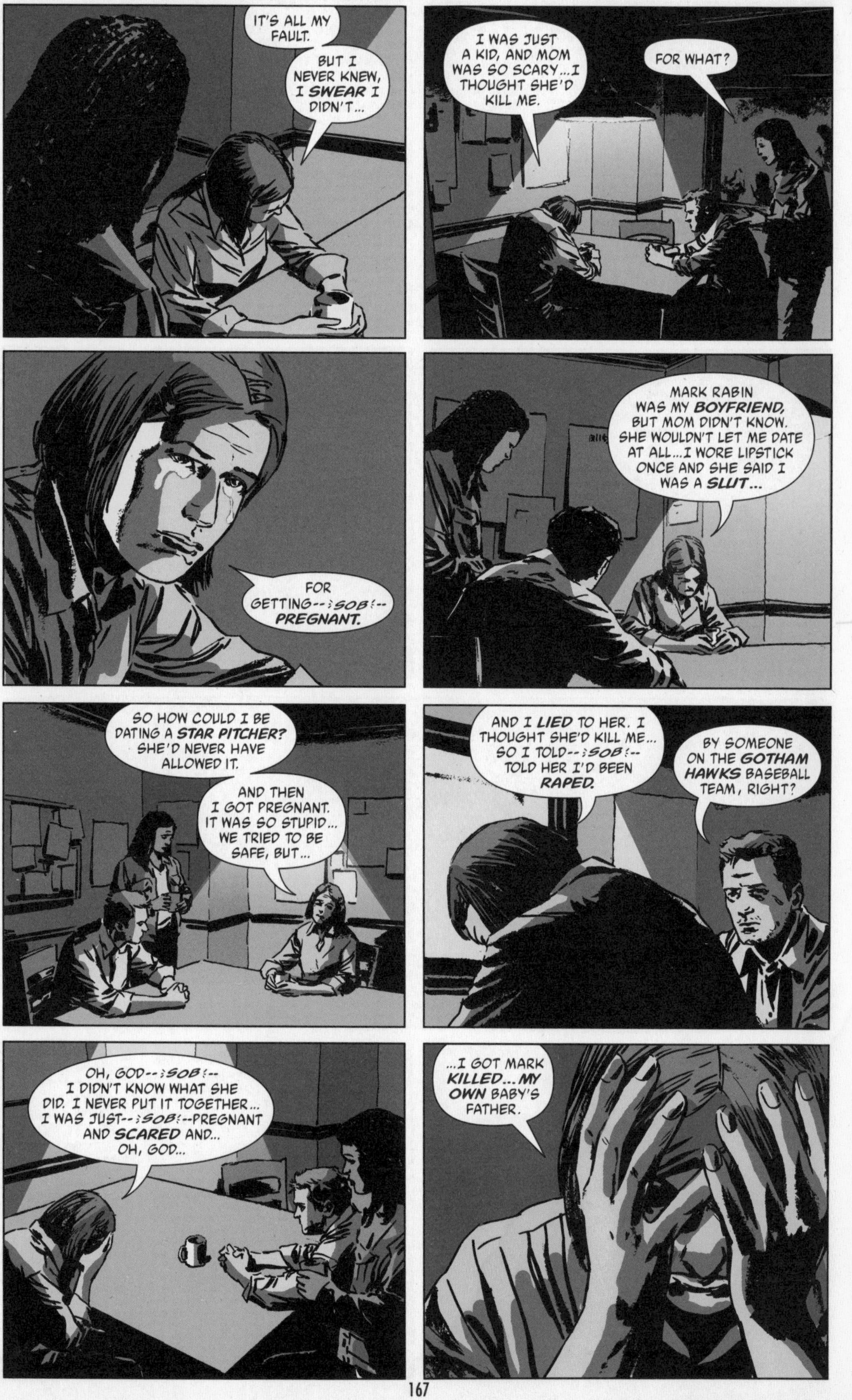
IT'S ALL MY FAULT.
BUT I NEVER KNEW, I SWEAR I DIDN'T...
FOR WHAT?
I WAS JUST A KID, AND MOM WAS SO SCARY...I THOUGHT SHE'D KILL ME.
FOR GETTING--SOB--PREGNANT.
MARK RABIN WAS MY BOYFRIEND, BUT MOM DIDN'T KNOW. SHE WOULDN'T LET ME DATE AT ALL...I WORE LIPSTICK ONCE AND SHE SAID I WAS A SLUT...
SO HOW COULD I BE DATING A STAR PITCHER? SHE'D NEVER HAVE ALLOWED IT.
AND THEN I GOT PREGNANT. IT WAS SO STUPID... WE TRIED TO BE SAFE, BUT...
AND I LIED TO HER. I THOUGHT SHE'D KILL ME... SO I TOLD--SOB--TOLD HER I'D BEEN RAPED.
BY SOMEONE ON THE GOTHAM HAWKS BASEBALL TEAM, RIGHT?
OH, GOD--SOB--I DIDN'T KNOW WHAT SHE DID. I NEVER PUT IT TOGETHER... I WAS JUST--SOB--PREGNANT AND SCARED AND... OH, GOD...
...I GOT MARK KILLED... MY OWN BABY'S FATHER.

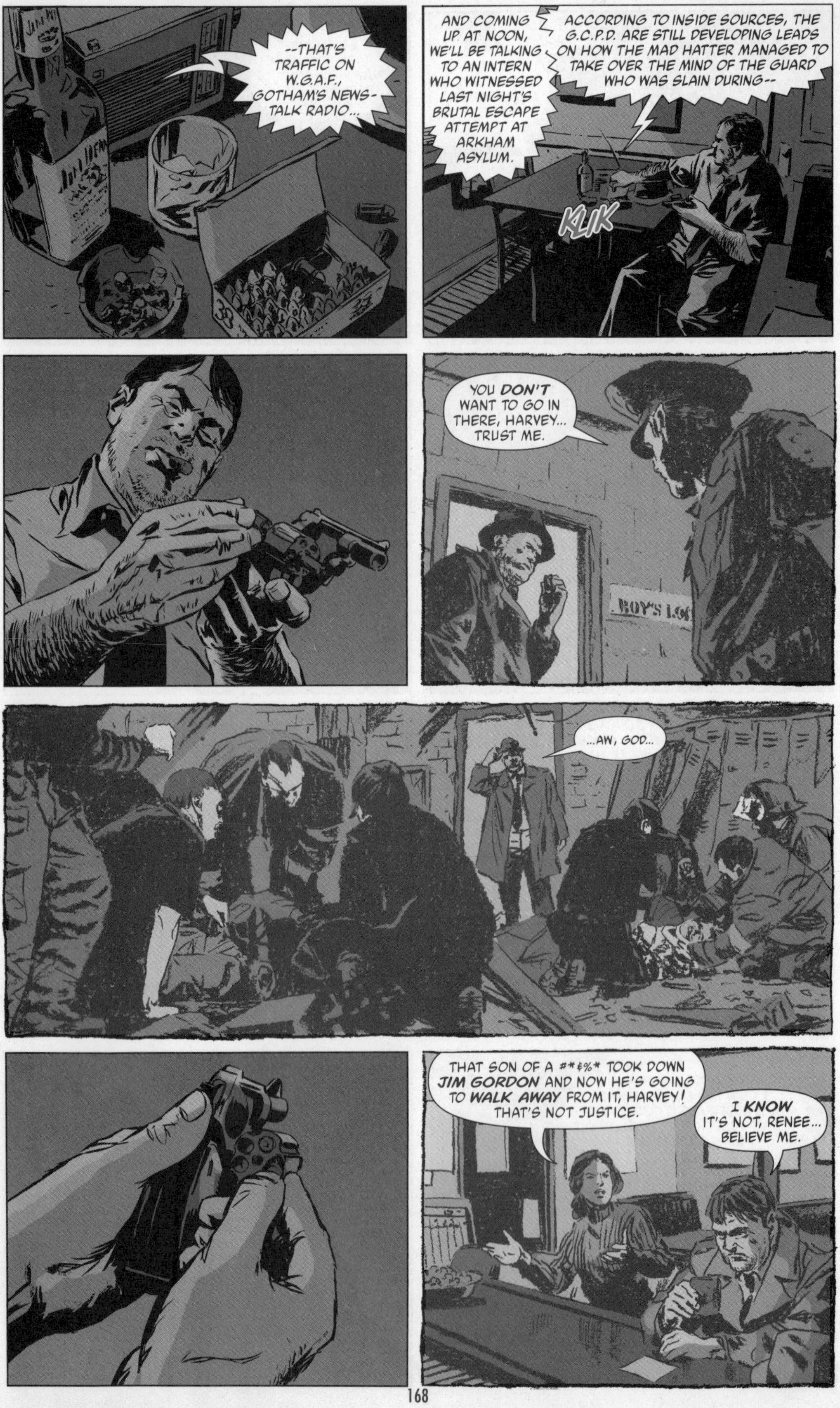
--THAT'S TRAFFIC ON W.G.A.F., GOTHAM'S NEWS-TALK RADIO...
AND COMING UP AT NOON, WE'LL BE TALKING TO AN INTERN WHO WITNESSED LAST NIGHT'S BRUTAL ESCAPE ATTEMPT AT ARKHAM ASYLUM.
ACCORDING TO INSIDE SOURCES, THE G.C.P.D. ARE STILL DEVELOPING LEADS ON HOW THE MAD HATTER MANAGED TO TAKE OVER THE MIND OF THE GUARD WHO WAS SLAIN DURING--
KLIK
YOU DON'T WANT TO GO IN THERE, HARVEY... TRUST ME.
...AW, GOD...
THAT SON OF A #*&%* TOOK DOWN JIM GORDON AND NOW HE'S GOING TO WALK AWAY FROM IT, HARVEY! THAT'S NOT JUSTICE.
I KNOW IT'S NOT, RENEE... BELIEVE ME.

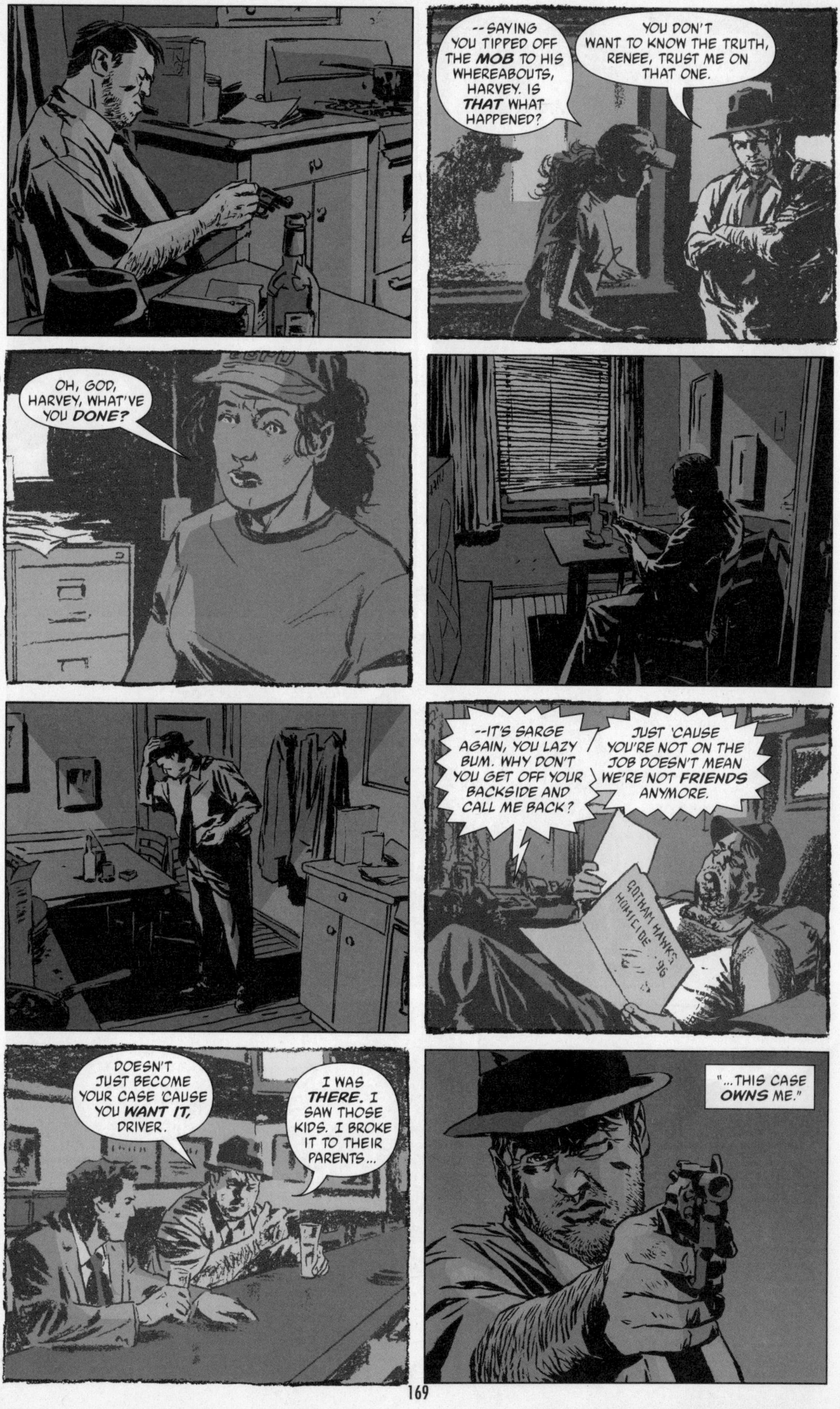
--SAYING YOU TIPPED OFF THE MOB TO HIS WHEREABOUTS, HARVEY. IS THAT WHAT HAPPENED?
YOU DON'T WANT TO KNOW THE TRUTH, RENEE, TRUST ME ON THAT ONE.
OH, GOD, HARVEY, WHAT'VE YOU DONE?
--IT'S SARGE AGAIN, YOU LAZY BUM. WHY DON'T YOU GET OFF YOUR BACKSIDE AND CALL ME BACK?
JUST 'CAUSE YOU'RE NOT ON THE JOB DOESN'T MEAN WE'RE NOT FRIENDS ANYMORE.
GOTHAM HAWKS
HOMICIDE '96
DOESN'T JUST BECOME YOUR CASE 'CAUSE YOU WANT IT, DRIVER.
I WAS THERE. I SAW THOSE KIDS. I BROKE IT TO THEIR PARENTS...
"...THIS CASE OWNS ME."

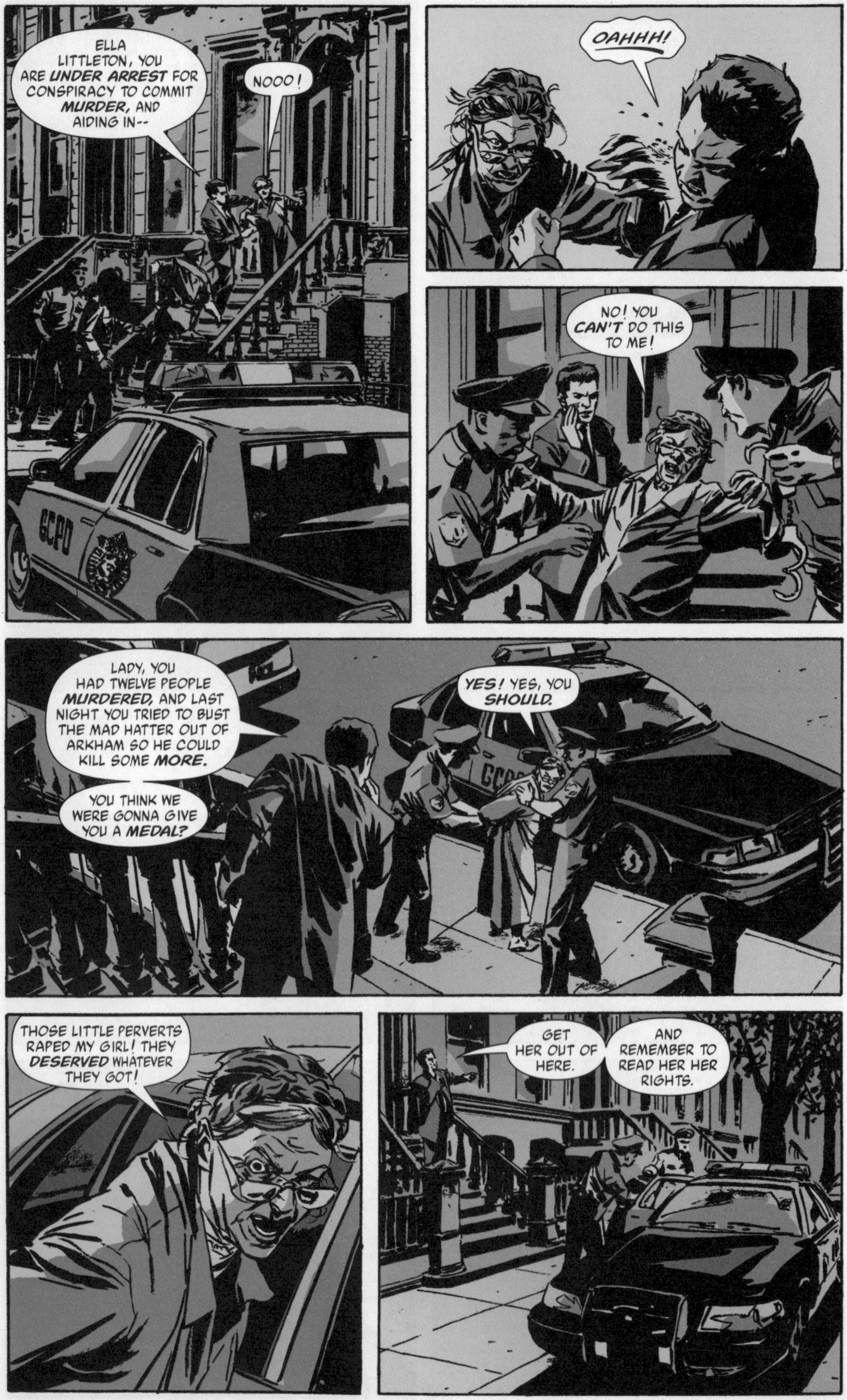
ELLA LITTLETON, YOU ARE UNDER ARREST FOR CONSPIRACY TO COMMIT MURDER, AND AIDING IN--
NOOO!
OAHHH!
NO! YOU CAN'T DO THIS TO ME!
LADY, YOU HAD TWELVE PEOPLE MURDERED, AND LAST NIGHT YOU TRIED TO BUST THE MAD HATTER OUT OF ARKHAM SO HE COULD KILL SOME MORE.
YOU THINK WE WERE GONNA GIVE YOU A MEDAL?
YES! YES, YOU SHOULD.
THOSE LITTLE PERVERTS RAPED MY GIRL! THEY DESERVED WHATEVER THEY GOT!
GET HER OUT OF HERE.
AND REMEMBER TO READ HER HER RIGHTS.

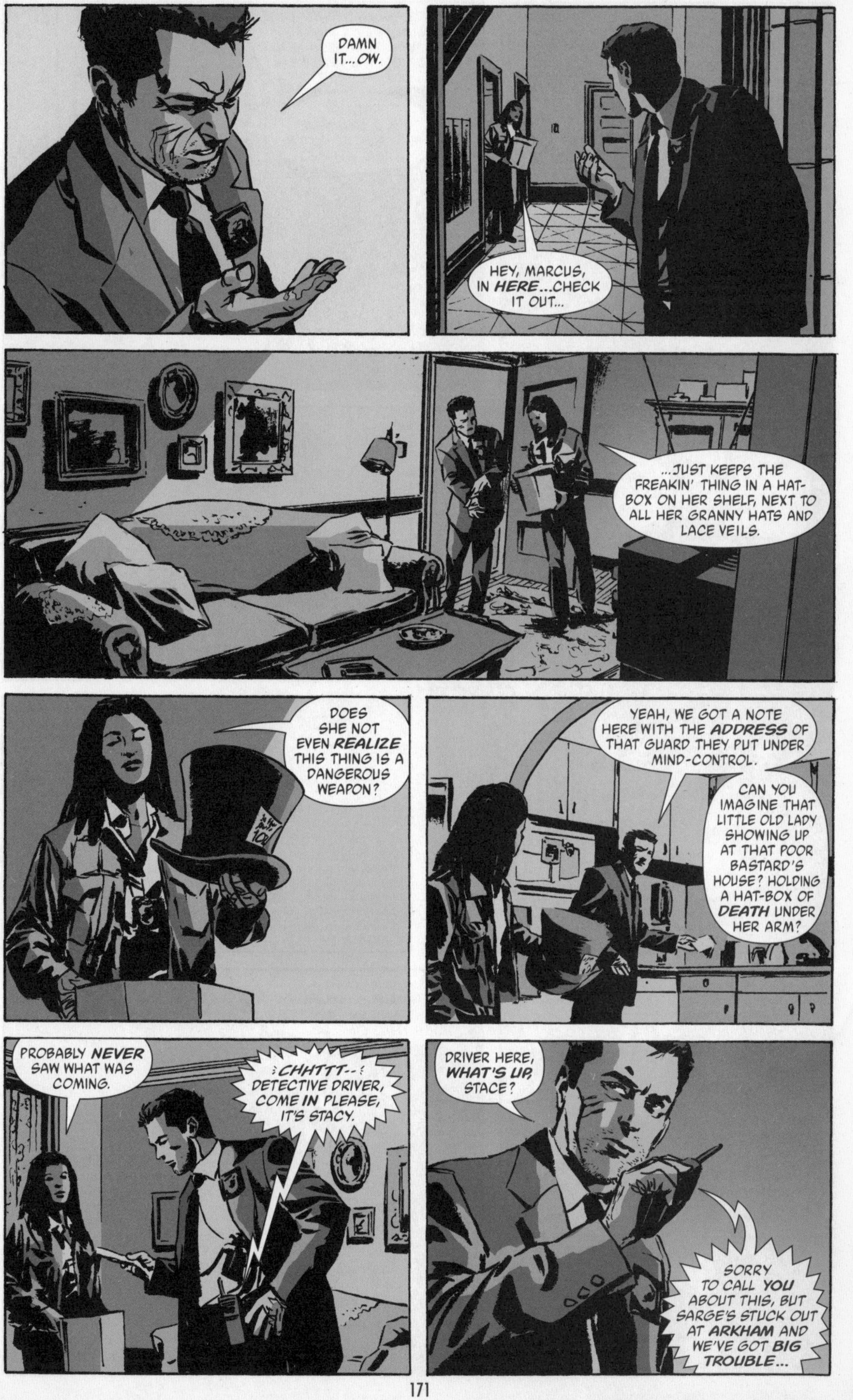
DAMN IT...OW.
HEY, MARCUS, IN HERE...CHECK IT OUT...
...JUST KEEPS THE FREAKIN' THING IN A HAT-BOX ON HER SHELF, NEXT TO ALL HER GRANNY HATS AND LACE VEILS.
DOES SHE NOT EVEN REALIZE THIS THING IS A DANGEROUS WEAPON?
YEAH, WE GOT A NOTE HERE WITH THE ADDRESS OF THAT GUARD THEY PUT UNDER MIND-CONTROL.
CAN YOU IMAGINE THAT LITTLE OLD LADY SHOWING UP AT THAT POOR BASTARD'S HOUSE? HOLDING A HAT-BOX OF DEATH UNDER HER ARM?
PROBABLY NEVER SAW WHAT WAS COMING.
CHHTTT-- DETECTIVE DRIVER, COME IN PLEASE, IT'S STACY.
DRIVER HERE, WHAT'S UP, STACE?
SORRY TO CALL YOU ABOUT THIS, BUT SARGE'S STUCK OUT AT ARKHAM AND WE'VE GOT BIG TROUBLE...

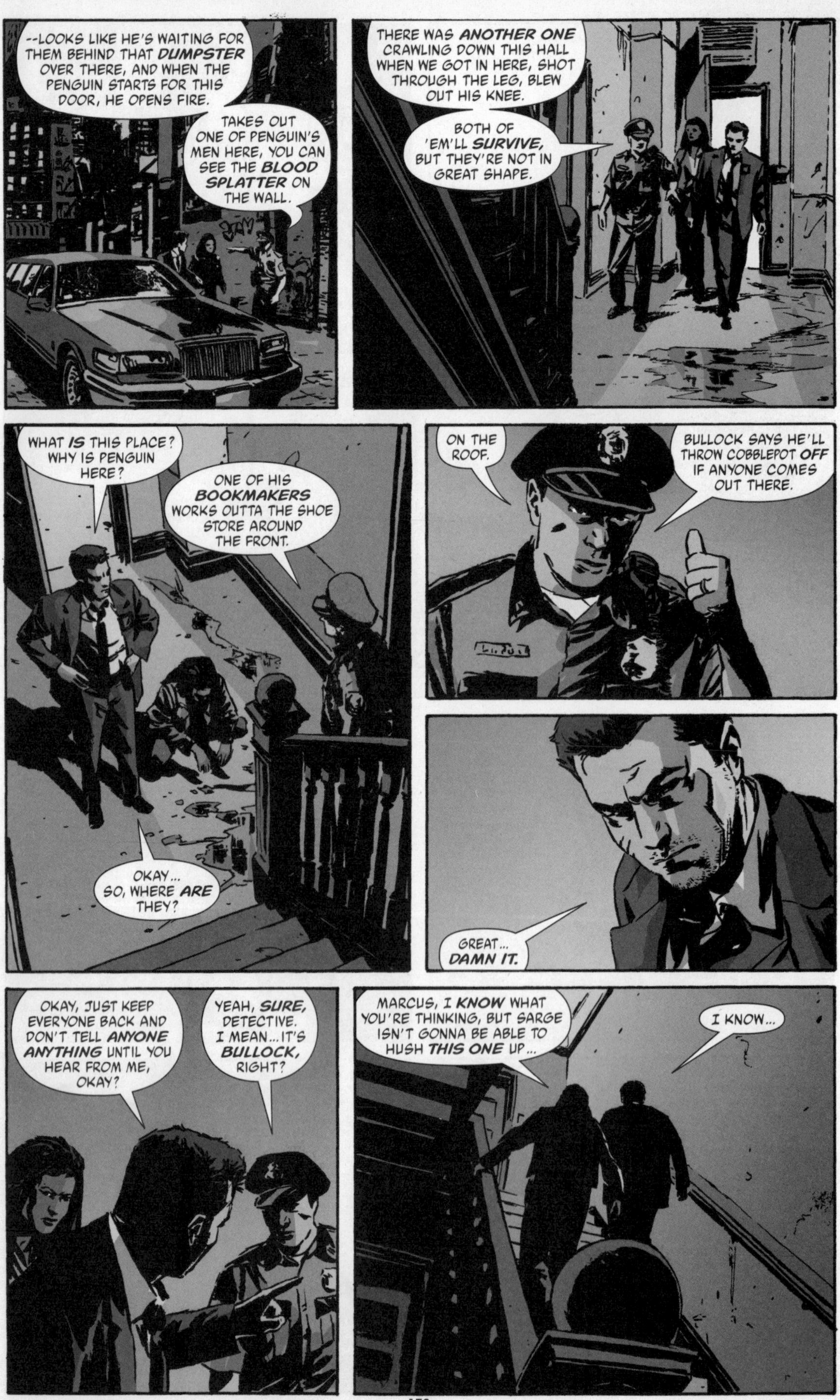
--LOOKS LIKE HE'S WAITING FOR THEM BEHIND THAT DUMPSTER OVER THERE, AND WHEN THE PENGUIN STARTS FOR THIS DOOR, HE OPENS FIRE.
TAKES OUT ONE OF PENGUIN'S MEN HERE, YOU CAN SEE THE BLOOD SPLATTER ON THE WALL.
THERE WAS ANOTHER ONE CRAWLING DOWN THIS HALL WHEN WE GOT IN HERE, SHOT THROUGH THE LEG, BLEW OUT HIS KNEE.
BOTH OF 'EM'LL SURVIVE, BUT THEY'RE NOT IN GREAT SHAPE.
WHAT IS THIS PLACE? WHY IS PENGUIN HERE?
ONE OF HIS BOOKMAKERS WORKS OUTTA THE SHOE STORE AROUND THE FRONT.
OKAY... SO, WHERE ARE THEY?
ON THE ROOF.
BULLOCK SAYS HE'LL THROW COBBLEPOT OFF IF ANYONE COMES OUT THERE.
GREAT... DAMN IT.
OKAY, JUST KEEP EVERYONE BACK AND DON'T TELL ANYONE ANYTHING UNTIL YOU HEAR FROM ME, OKAY?
YEAH, SURE, DETECTIVE. I MEAN... IT'S BULLOCK, RIGHT?
MARCUS, I KNOW WHAT YOU'RE THINKING, BUT SARGE ISN'T GONNA BE ABLE TO HUSH THIS ONE UP...
I KNOW...

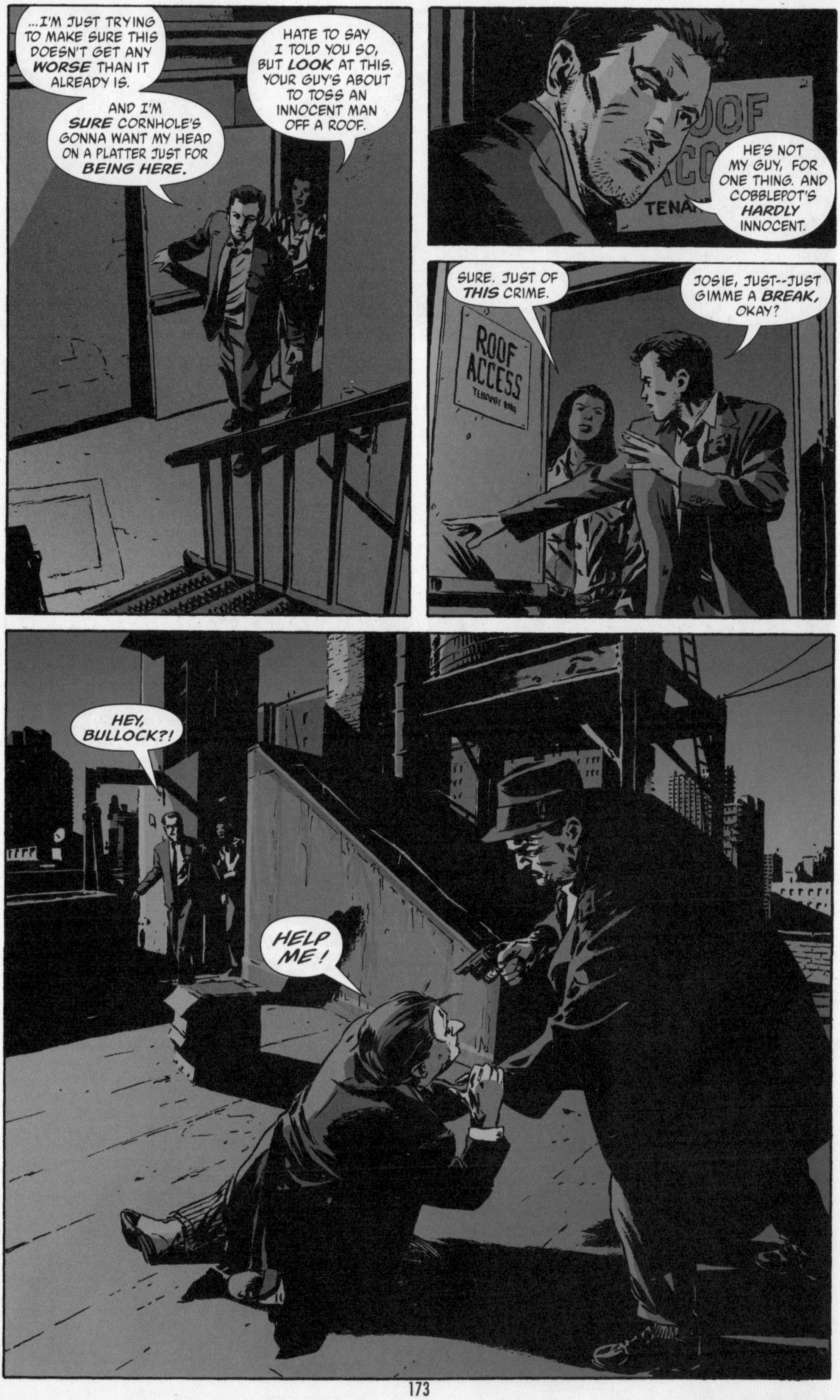
...I'M JUST TRYING TO MAKE SURE THIS DOESN'T GET ANY WORSE THAN IT ALREADY IS.
AND I'M SURE CORNHOLE'S GONNA WANT MY HEAD ON A PLATTER JUST FOR BEING HERE.
HATE TO SAY I TOLD YOU SO, BUT LOOK AT THIS. YOUR GUY'S ABOUT TO TOSS AN INNOCENT MAN OFF A ROOF.
HE'S NOT MY GUY, FOR ONE THING. AND COBBLEPOT'S HARDLY INNOCENT.
SURE. JUST OF THIS CRIME.
ROOF ACCESS
JOSIE, JUST--JUST GIMME A BREAK, OKAY?
HEY, BULLOCK?!
HELP ME!

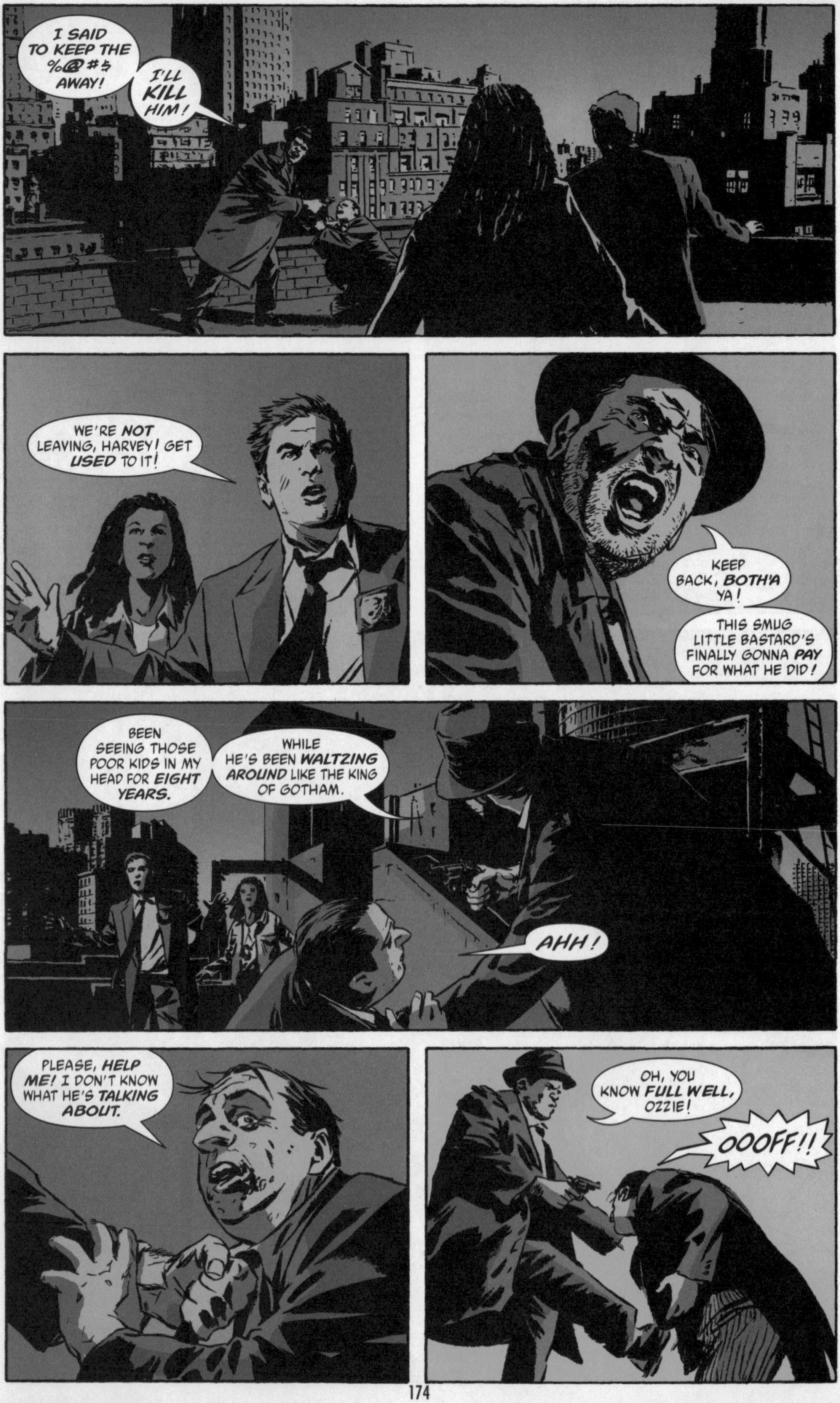
I SAID TO KEEP THE %@#$ AWAY!
I'LL KILL HIM!
WE'RE NOT LEAVING, HARVEY! GET USED TO IT!
KEEP BACK, BOTH'A YA!
THIS SMUG LITTLE BASTARD'S FINALLY GONNA PAY FOR WHAT HE DID!
BEEN SEEING THOSE POOR KIDS IN MY HEAD FOR EIGHT YEARS.
WHILE HE'S BEEN WALTZING AROUND LIKE THE KING OF GOTHAM.
AHH!
PLEASE, HELP ME! I DON'T KNOW WHAT HE'S TALKING ABOUT.
OH, YOU KNOW FULL WELL, OZZIE!
OOOFF!!

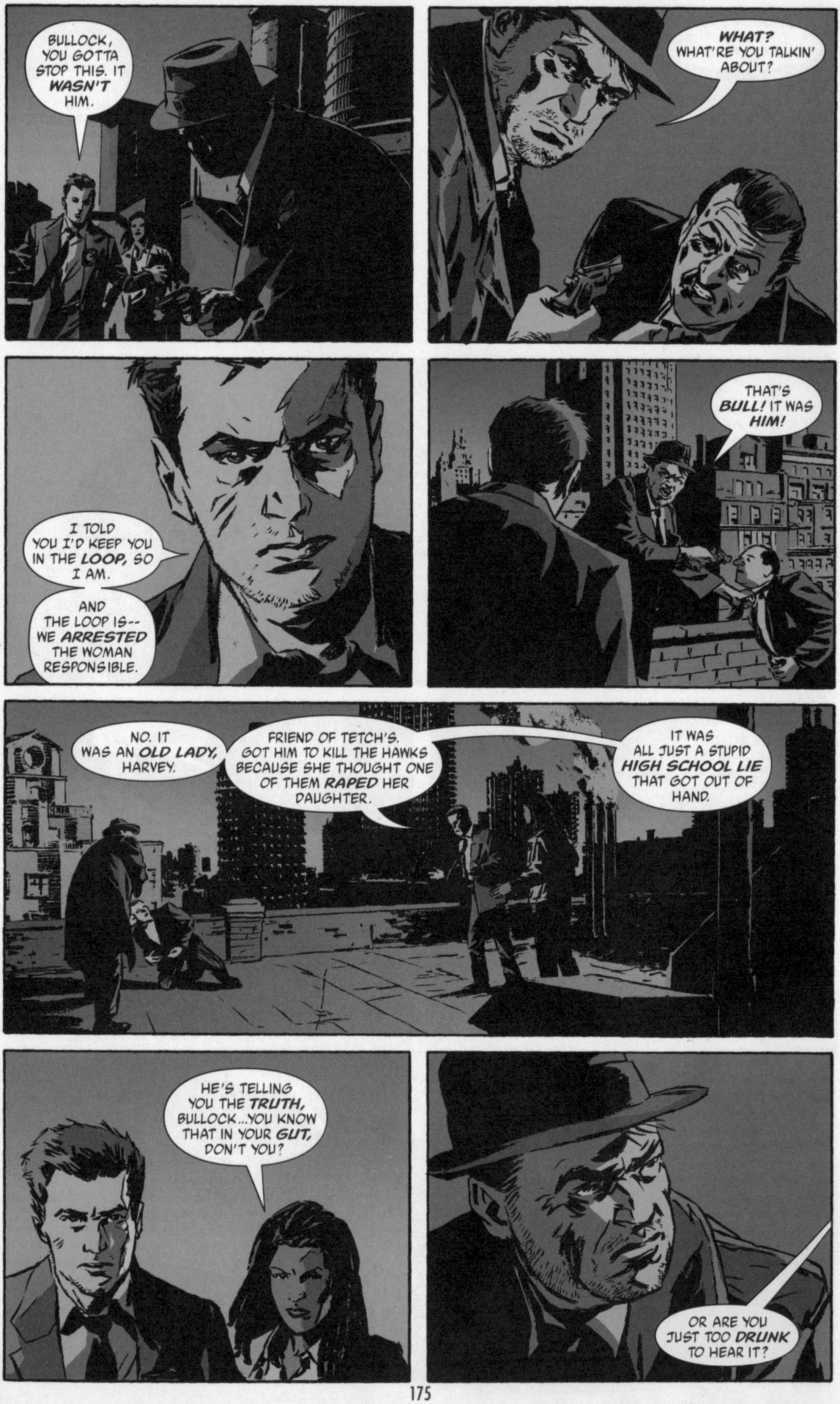

BULLOCK, YOU GOTTA STOP THIS. IT WASN'T HIM.
WHAT? WHAT'RE YOU TALKIN' ABOUT?
I TOLD YOU I'D KEEP YOU IN THE LOOP, SO I AM.
AND THE LOOP IS-- WE ARRESTED THE WOMAN RESPONSIBLE.
THAT'S BULL! IT WAS HIM!
NO. IT WAS AN OLD LADY, HARVEY.
FRIEND OF TETCH'S. GOT HIM TO KILL THE HAWKS BECAUSE SHE THOUGHT ONE OF THEM RAPED HER DAUGHTER.
IT WAS ALL JUST A STUPID HIGH SCHOOL LIE THAT GOT OUT OF HAND.
HE'S TELLING YOU THE TRUTH, BULLOCK...YOU KNOW THAT IN YOUR GUT, DON'T YOU?
OR ARE YOU JUST TOO DRUNK TO HEAR IT?

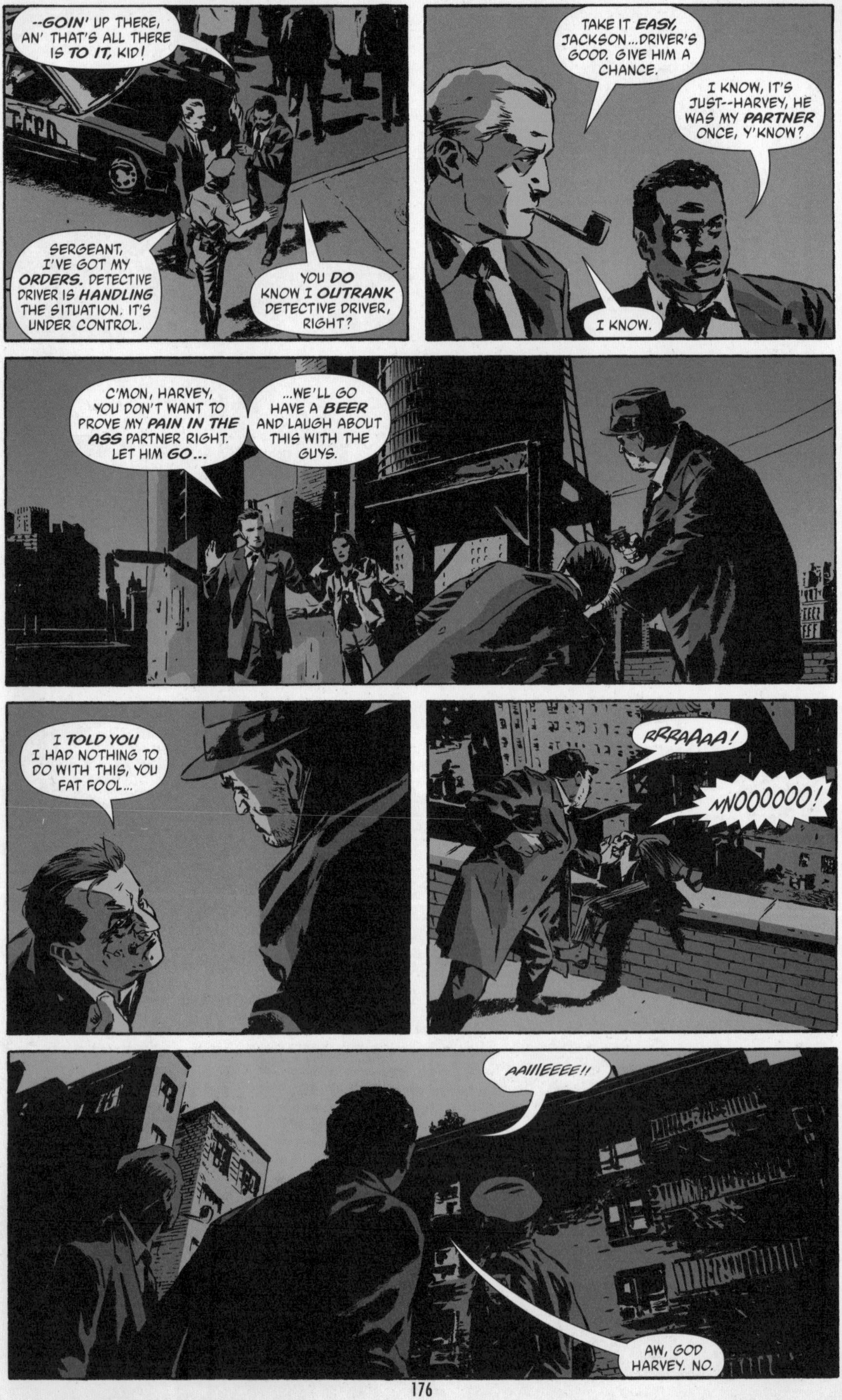
--GOIN' UP THERE, AN' THAT'S ALL THERE IS TO IT, KID!
SERGEANT, I'VE GOT MY ORDERS. DETECTIVE DRIVER IS HANDLING THE SITUATION. IT'S UNDER CONTROL.
YOU DO KNOW I OUTRANK DETECTIVE DRIVER, RIGHT?
TAKE IT EASY, JACKSON...DRIVER'S GOOD. GIVE HIM A CHANCE.
I KNOW, IT'S JUST--HARVEY, HE WAS MY PARTNER ONCE, Y'KNOW?
I KNOW.
C'MON, HARVEY, YOU DON'T WANT TO PROVE MY PAIN IN THE ASS PARTNER RIGHT. LET HIM GO...
...WE'LL GO HAVE A BEER AND LAUGH ABOUT THIS WITH THE GUYS.
I TOLD YOU I HAD NOTHING TO DO WITH THIS, YOU FAT FOOL...
RRRAAAAA!
NNOOOOOO!
AAIIIEEEE!!
AW, GOD HARVEY. NO.

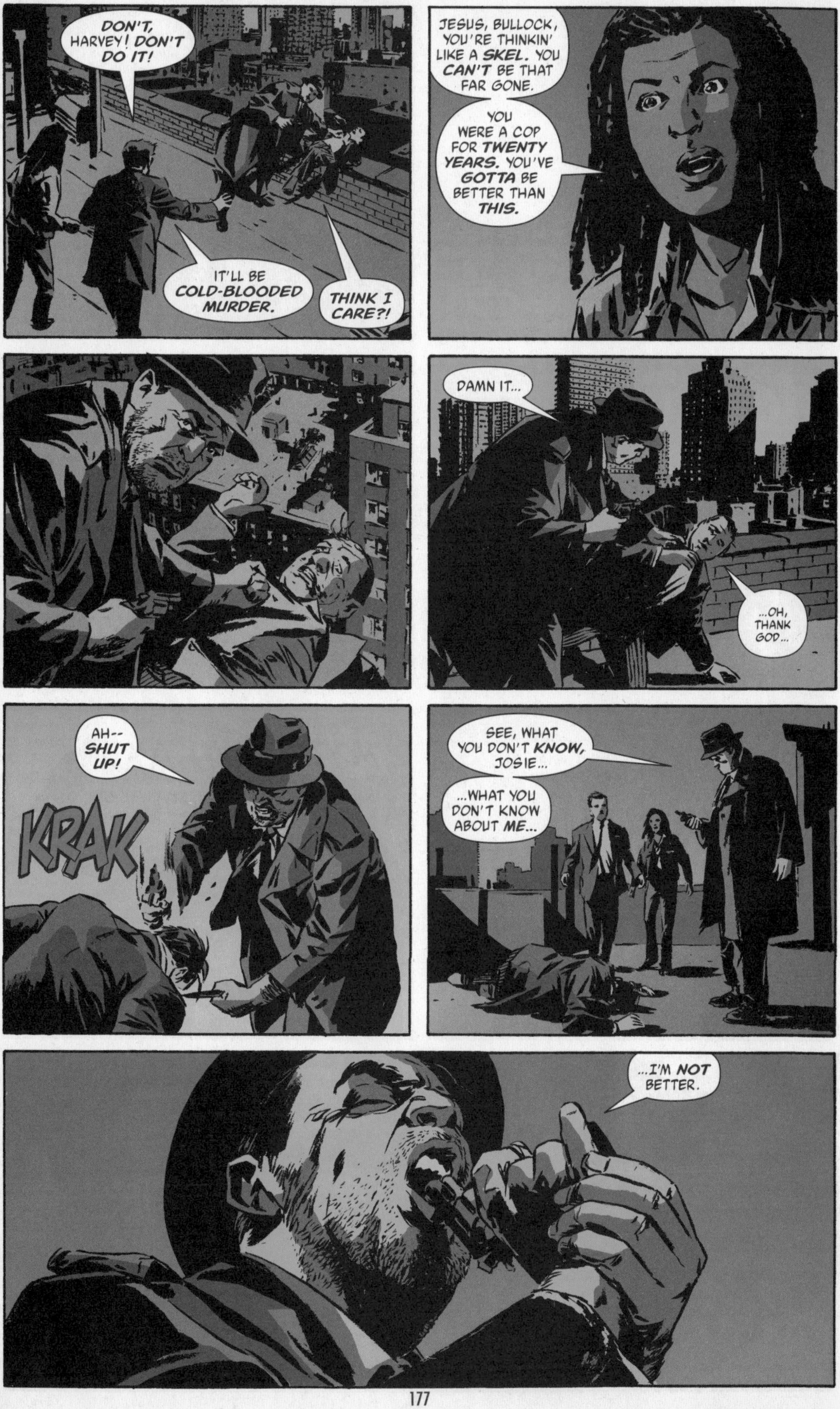
DON'T, HARVEY! DON'T DO IT!
IT'LL BE COLD-BLOODED MURDER.
THINK I CARE?!
JESUS, BULLOCK, YOU'RE THINKIN' LIKE A SKEL. YOU CAN'T BE THAT FAR GONE.
YOU WERE A COP FOR TWENTY YEARS. YOU'VE GOTTA BE BETTER THAN THIS.
DAMN IT...
...OH, THANK GOD...
AH-- SHUT UP!
KRAK
SEE, WHAT YOU DON'T KNOW, JOSIE...
...WHAT YOU DON'T KNOW ABOUT ME...
...I'M NOT BETTER.

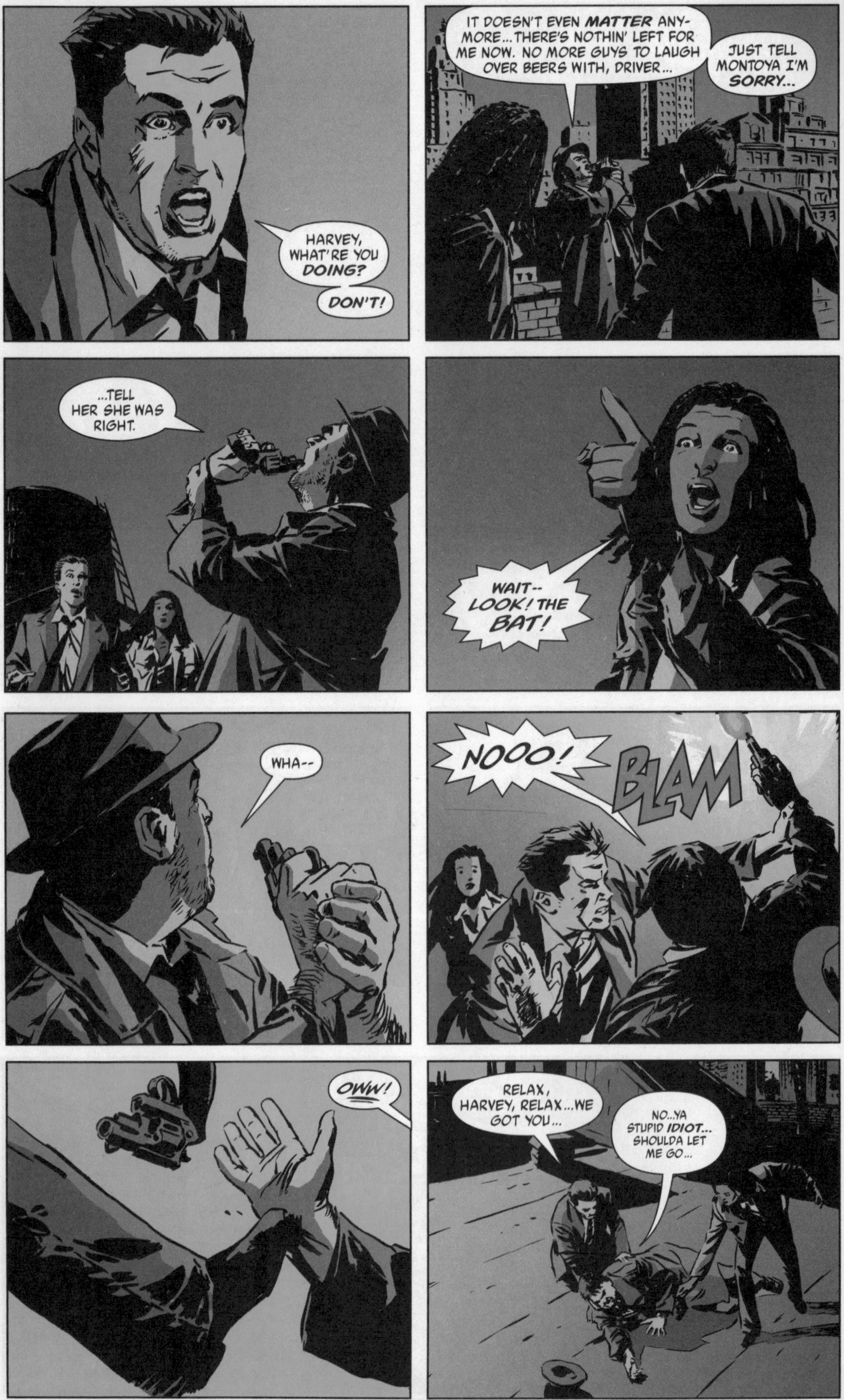
HARVEY, WHAT'RE YOU DOING?
DON'T!
IT DOESN'T EVEN MATTER ANYMORE...THERE'S NOTHIN' LEFT FOR ME NOW. NO MORE GUYS TO LAUGH OVER BEERS WITH, DRIVER...
JUST TELL MONTOYA I'M SORRY...
...TELL HER SHE WAS RIGHT.
WAIT-- LOOK! THE BAT!
WHA--
NOOO!
BLAM
OWW!
RELAX, HARVEY, RELAX...WE GOT YOU...
NO...YA STUPID IDIOT... SHOULDA LET ME GO...

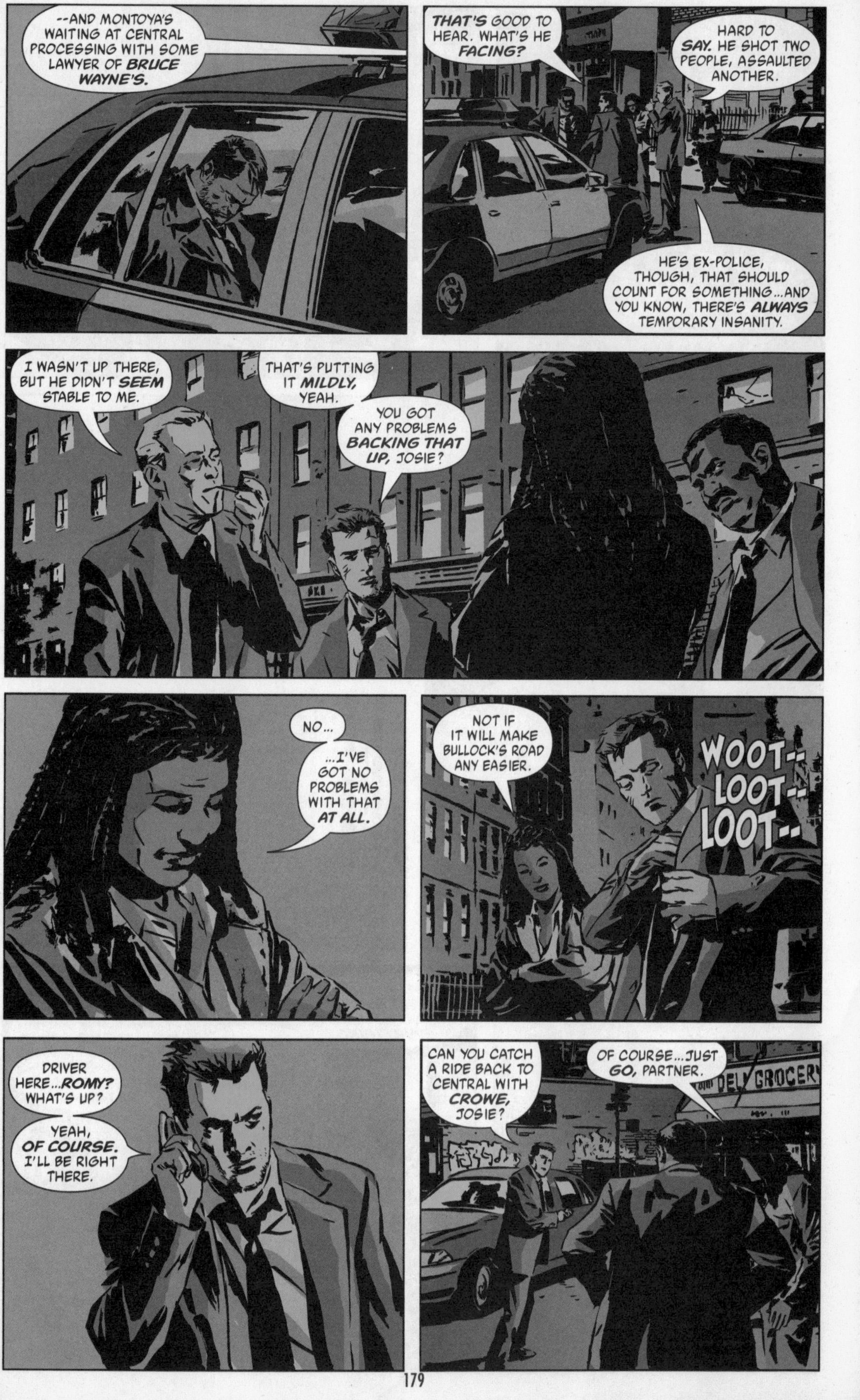
--AND MONTOYA'S WAITING AT CENTRAL PROCESSING WITH SOME LAWYER OF BRUCE WAYNE'S.
THAT'S GOOD TO HEAR. WHAT'S HE FACING?
HARD TO SAY. HE SHOT TWO PEOPLE, ASSAULTED ANOTHER.
HE'S EX-POLICE, THOUGH, THAT SHOULD COUNT FOR SOMETHING...AND YOU KNOW, THERE'S ALWAYS TEMPORARY INSANITY.
I WASN'T UP THERE, BUT HE DIDN'T SEEM STABLE TO ME.
THAT'S PUTTING IT MILDLY, YEAH.
YOU GOT ANY PROBLEMS BACKING THAT UP, JOSIE?
NO...
...I'VE GOT NO PROBLEMS WITH THAT AT ALL.
NOT IF IT WILL MAKE BULLOCK'S ROAD ANY EASIER.
WOOT-- LOOT-- LOOT--
DRIVER HERE...ROMY? WHAT'S UP?
YEAH, OF COURSE. I'LL BE RIGHT THERE.
CAN YOU CATCH A RIDE BACK TO CENTRAL WITH CROWE, JOSIE?
OF COURSE...JUST GO, PARTNER.
DELI GROCERY

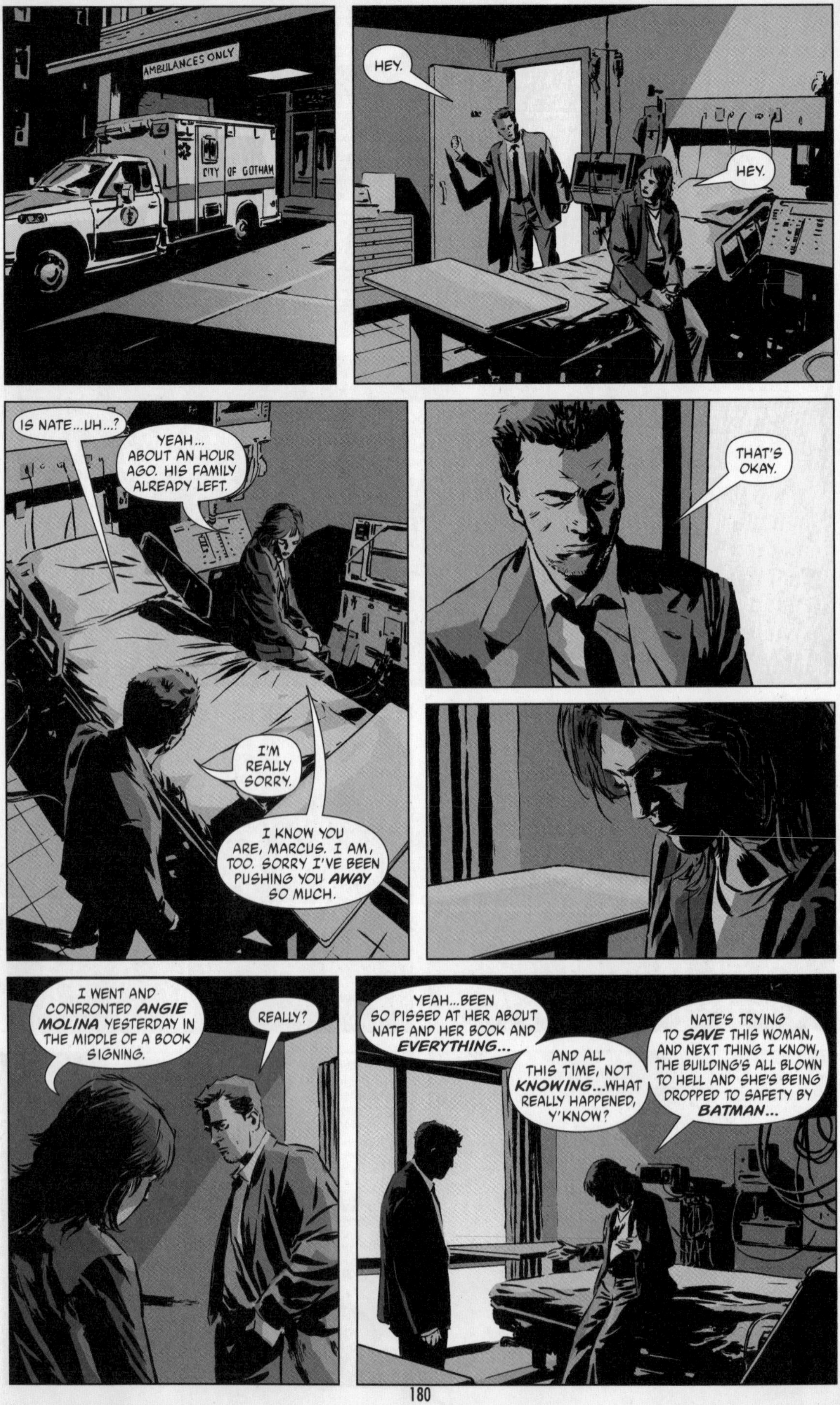
AMBULANCES ONLY
CITY OF GOTHAM
HEY.
HEY.
IS NATE...UH...?
YEAH... ABOUT AN HOUR AGO. HIS FAMILY ALREADY LEFT.
THAT'S OKAY.
I'M REALLY SORRY.
I KNOW YOU ARE, MARCUS. I AM, TOO. SORRY I'VE BEEN PUSHING YOU AWAY SO MUCH.
I WENT AND CONFRONTED ANGIE MOLINA YESTERDAY IN THE MIDDLE OF A BOOK SIGNING.
REALLY?
YEAH...BEEN SO PISSED AT HER ABOUT NATE AND HER BOOK AND EVERYTHING...
AND ALL THIS TIME, NOT KNOWING...WHAT REALLY HAPPENED, Y'KNOW?
NATE'S TRYING TO SAVE THIS WOMAN, AND NEXT THING I KNOW, THE BUILDING'S ALL BLOWN TO HELL AND SHE'S BEING DROPPED TO SAFETY BY BATMAN...

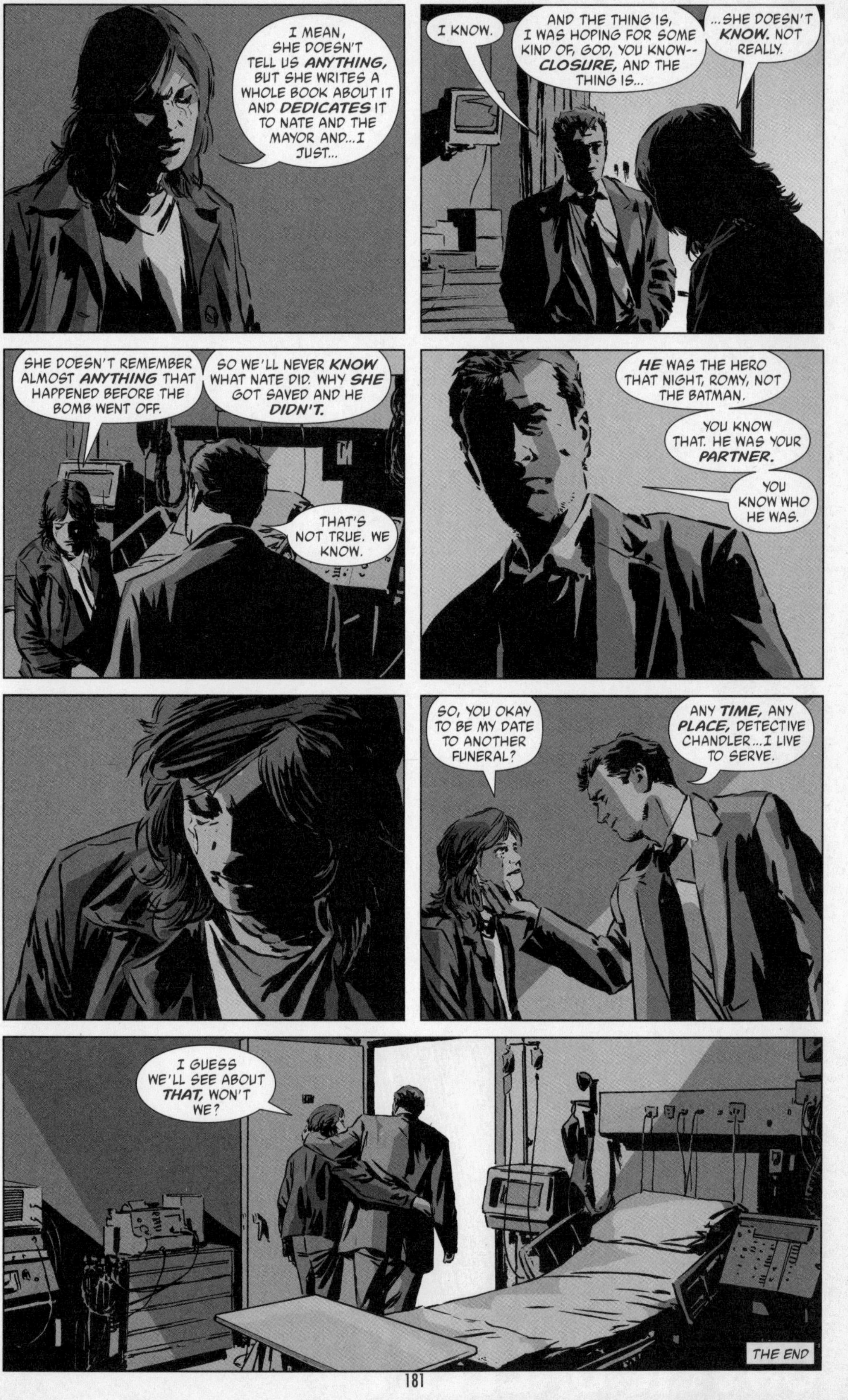
I MEAN, SHE DOESN'T TELL US ANYTHING, BUT SHE WRITES A WHOLE BOOK ABOUT IT AND DEDICATES IT TO NATE AND THE MAYOR AND...I JUST...
I KNOW.
AND THE THING IS, I WAS HOPING FOR SOME KIND OF, GOD, YOU KNOW-- CLOSURE, AND THE THING IS...
...SHE DOESN'T KNOW. NOT REALLY.
SHE DOESN'T REMEMBER ALMOST ANYTHING THAT HAPPENED BEFORE THE BOMB WENT OFF.
SO WE'LL NEVER KNOW WHAT NATE DID. WHY SHE GOT SAVED AND HE DIDN'T.
THAT'S NOT TRUE. WE KNOW.
HE WAS THE HERO THAT NIGHT, ROMY, NOT THE BATMAN.
YOU KNOW THAT. HE WAS YOUR PARTNER.
YOU KNOW WHO HE WAS.
SO, YOU OKAY TO BE MY DATE TO ANOTHER FUNERAL?
ANY TIME, ANY PLACE, DETECTIVE CHANDLER...I LIVE TO SERVE.
I GUESS WE'LL SEE ABOUT THAT, WON'T WE?
THE END

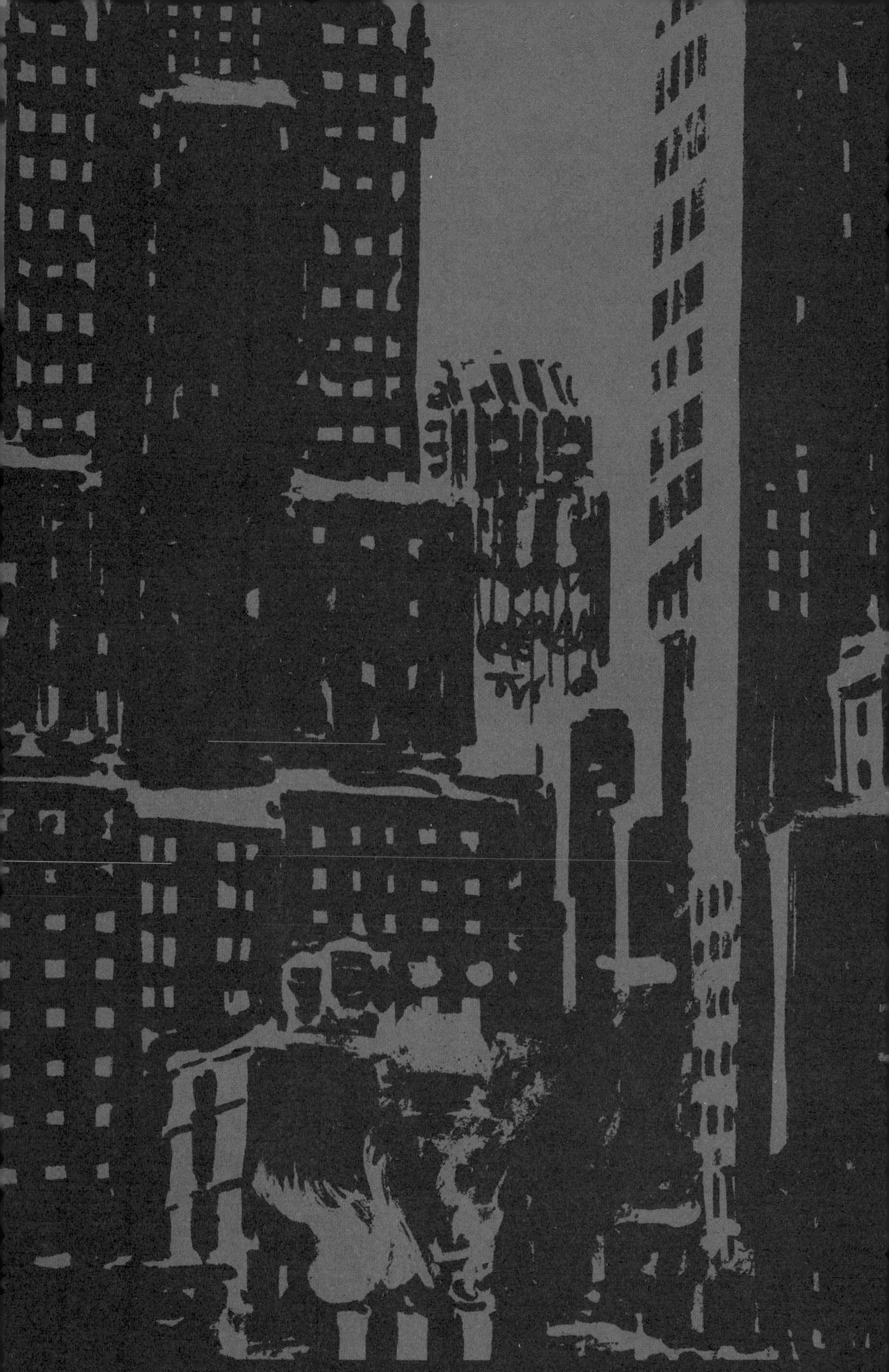

COVER GALLERY

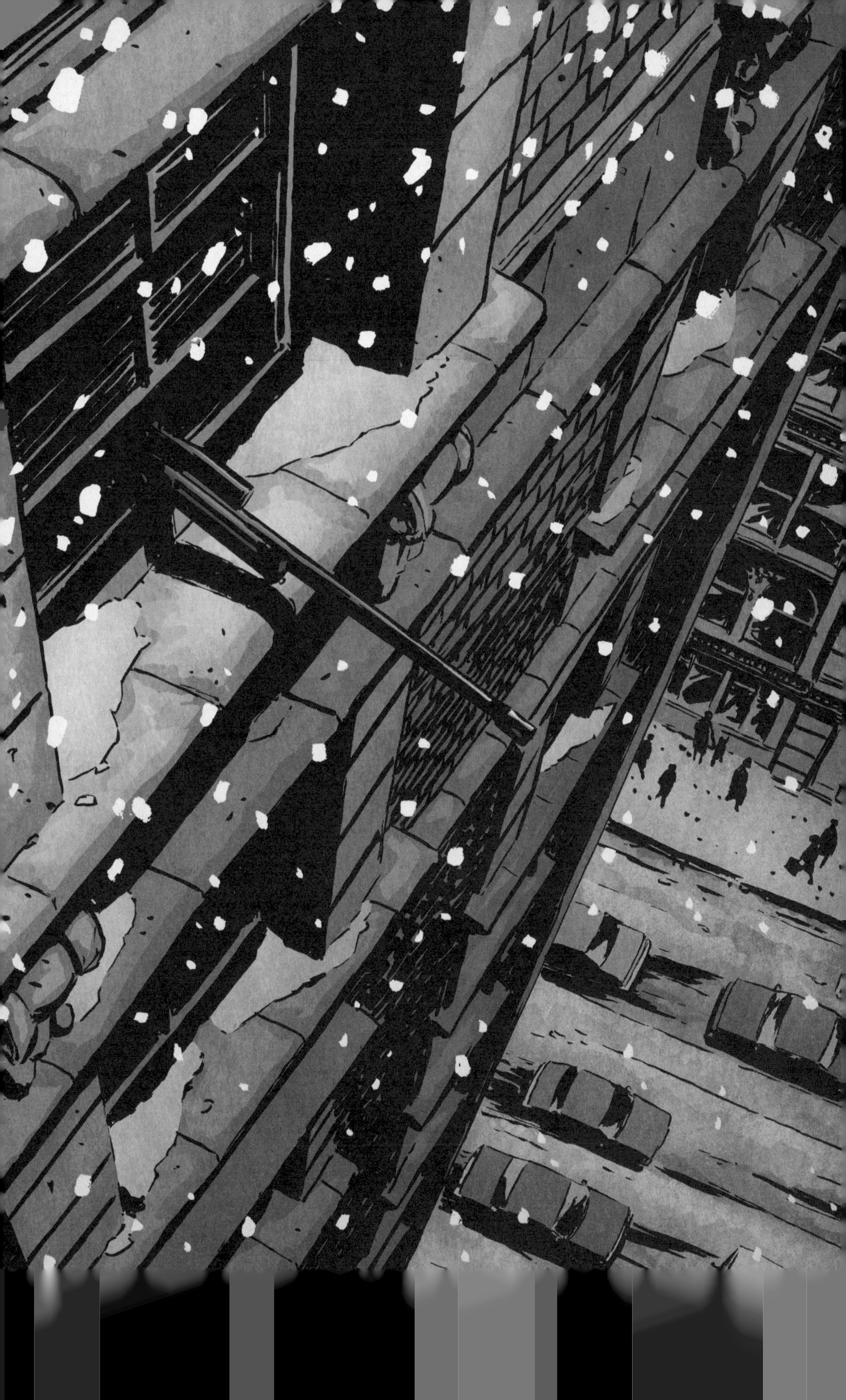

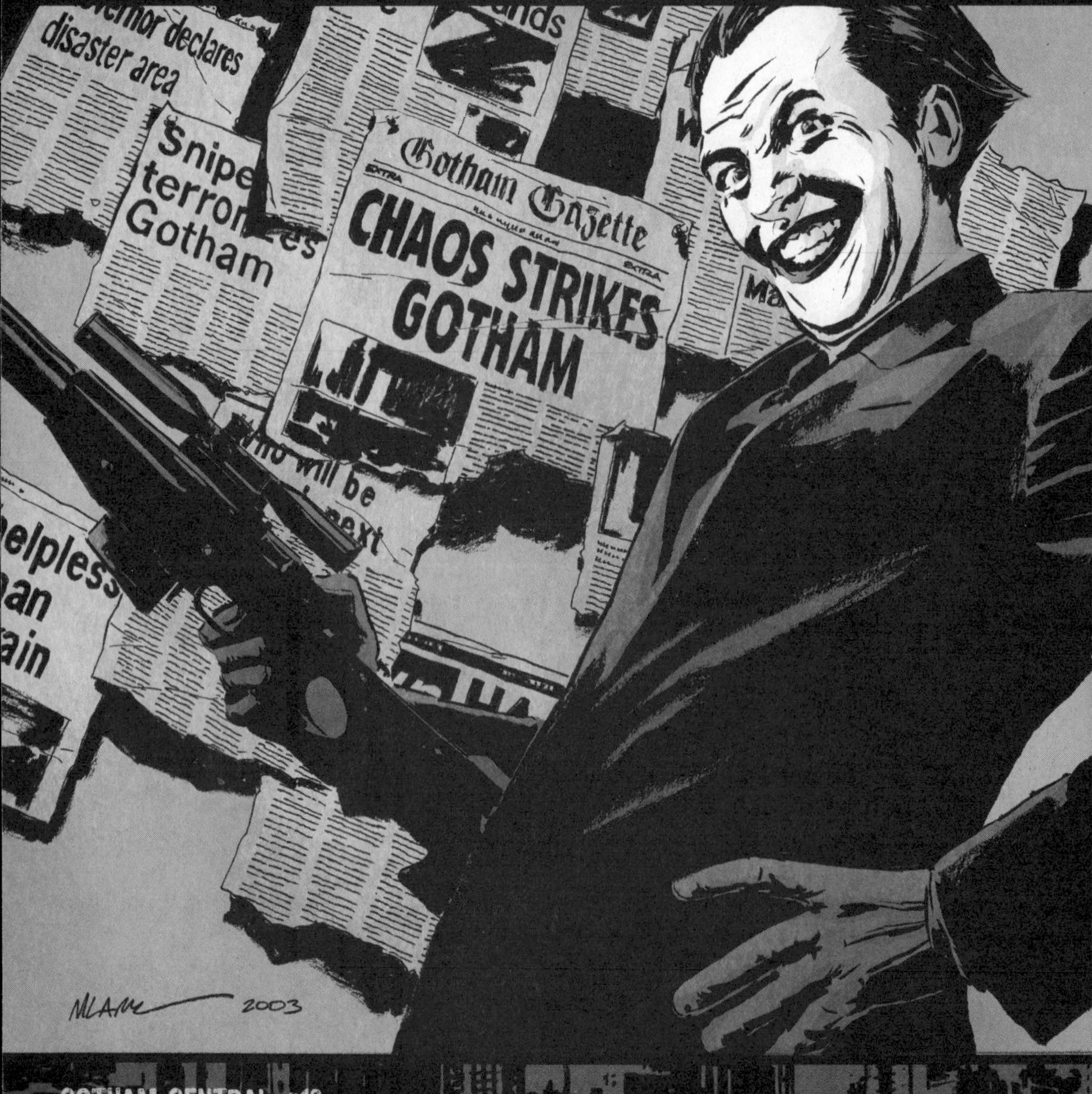
disaster area
Gotham Gazette
CHAOS STRIKES GOTHAM
Gotham
will be
next

GOTHAM CENTRAL #13

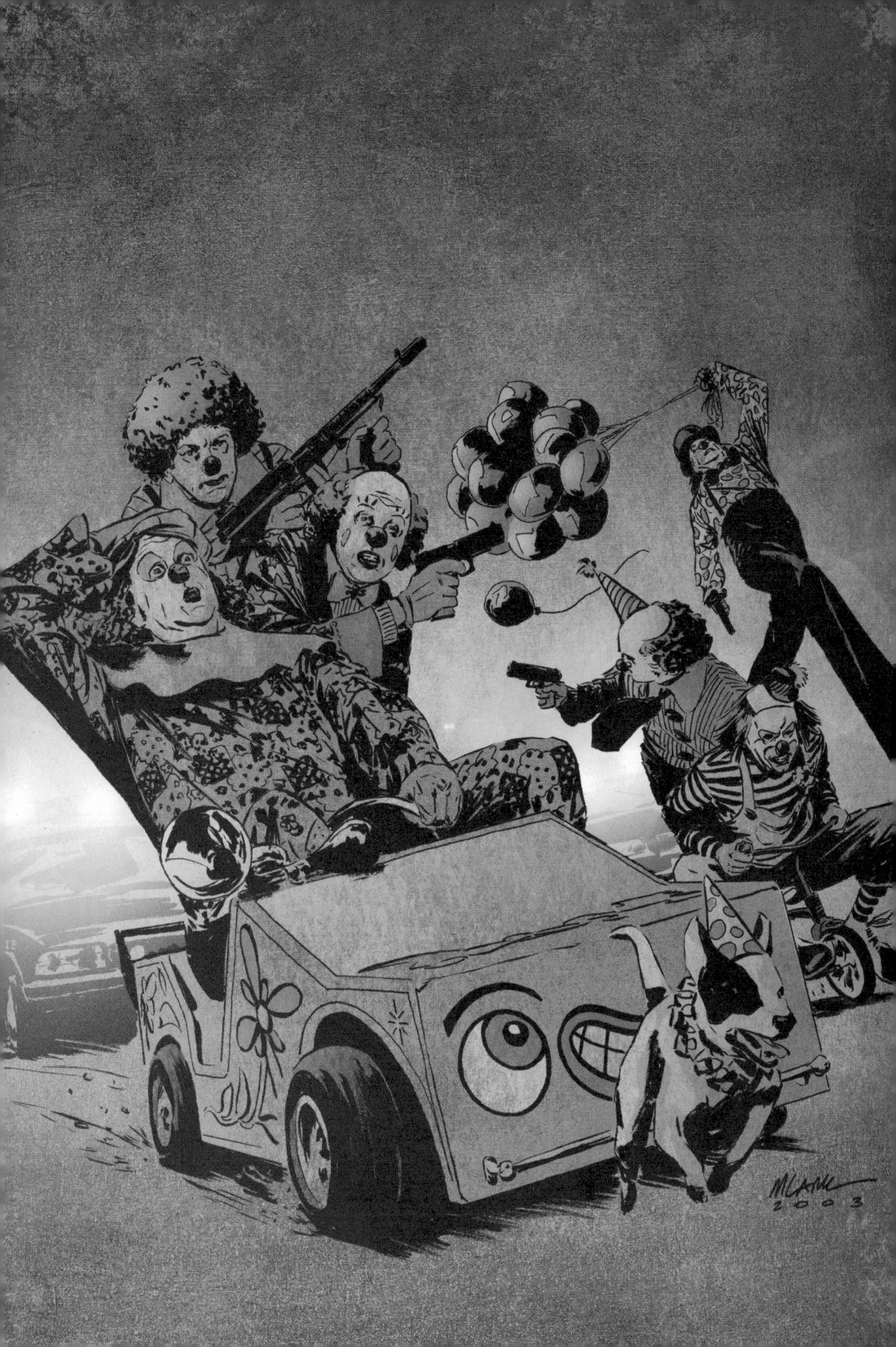

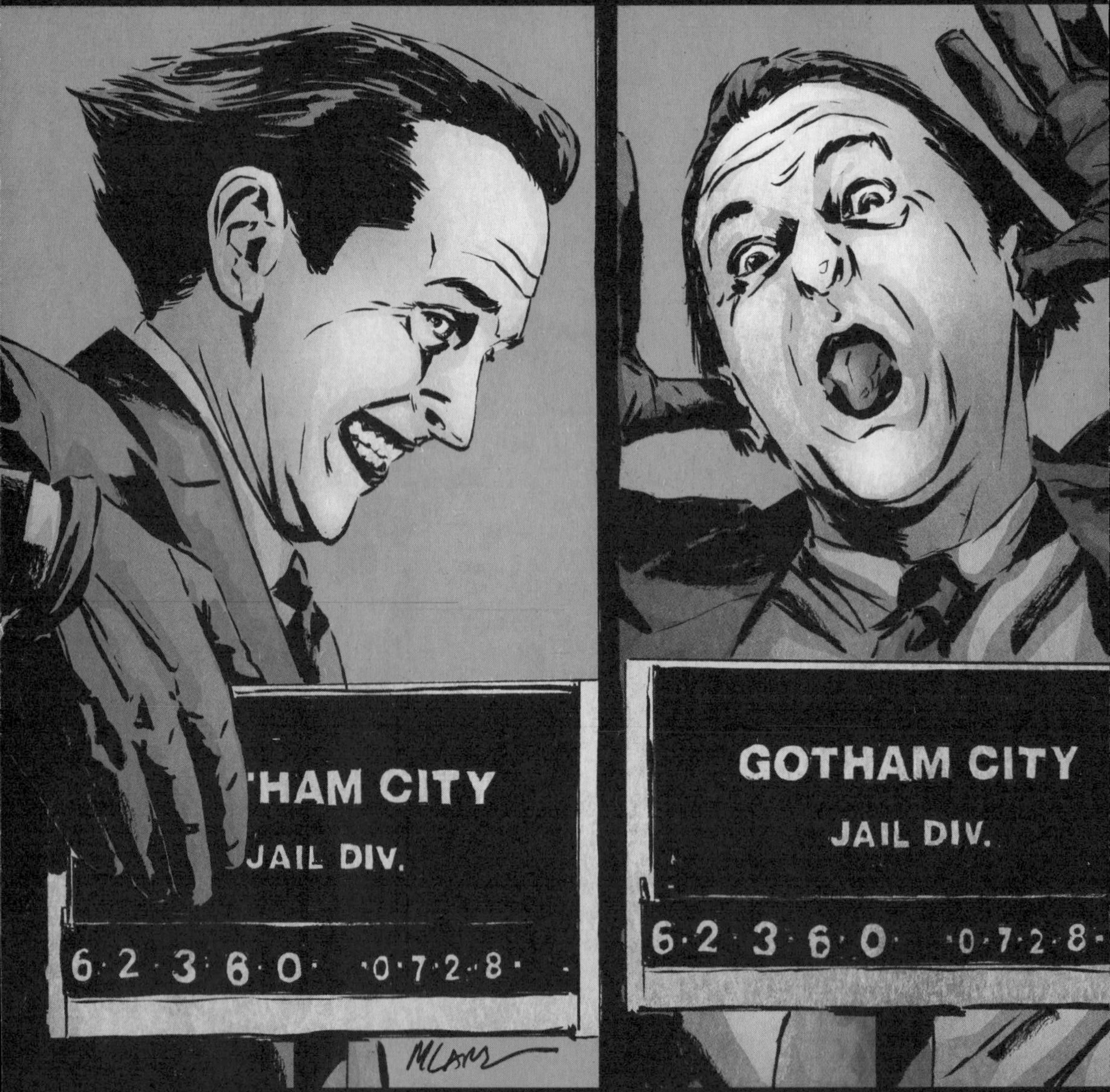
THAM CITY
JAIL DIV.
6·2·3·6·0· ·0·7·2·8·
GOTHAM CITY
JAIL DIV.
6·2·3·6·0· ·0·7·2·8·

GOTHAM CENTRAL #15

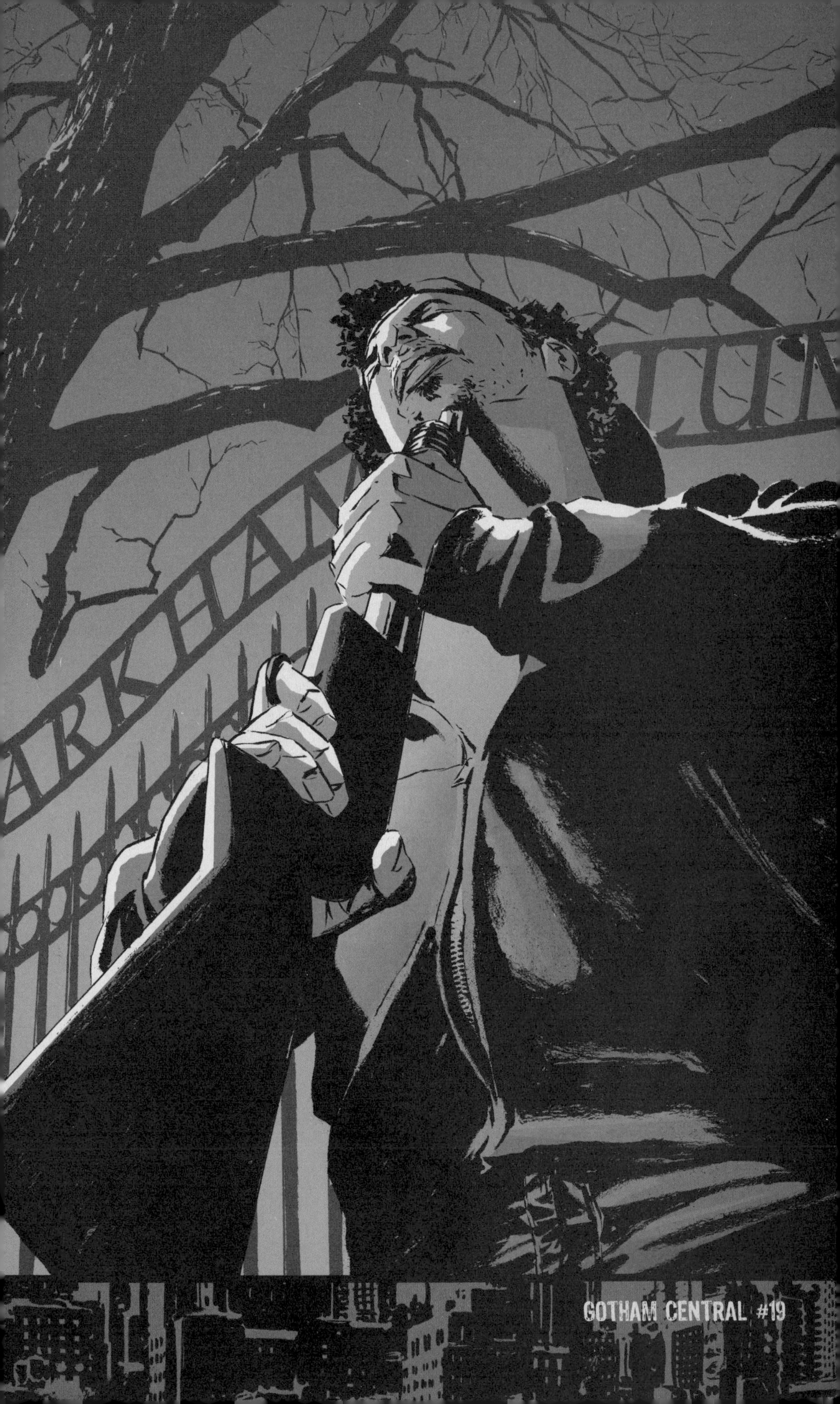
ARKHAM
LUN

GOTHAM CENTRAL #19

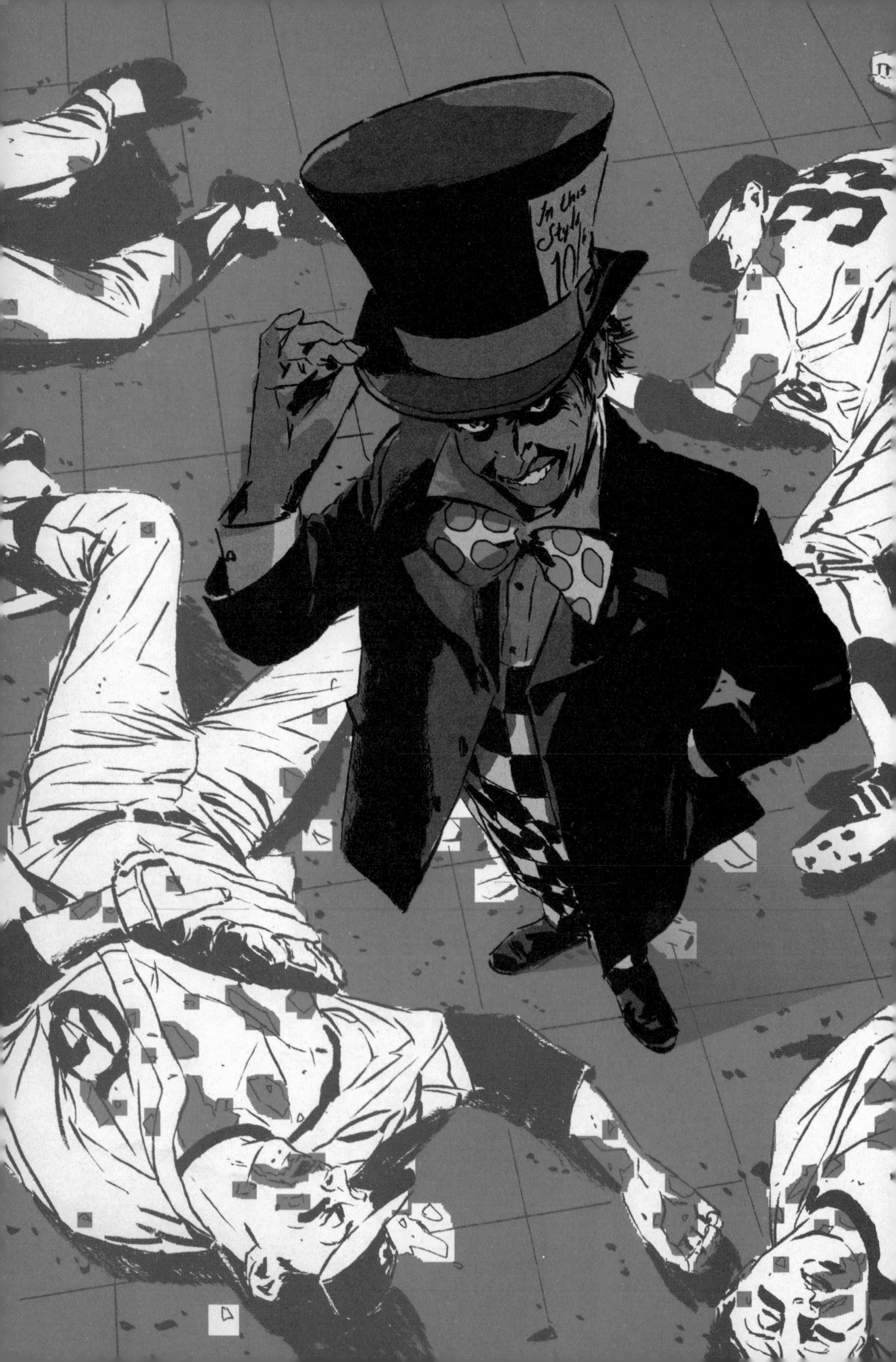
In this Style 10/6

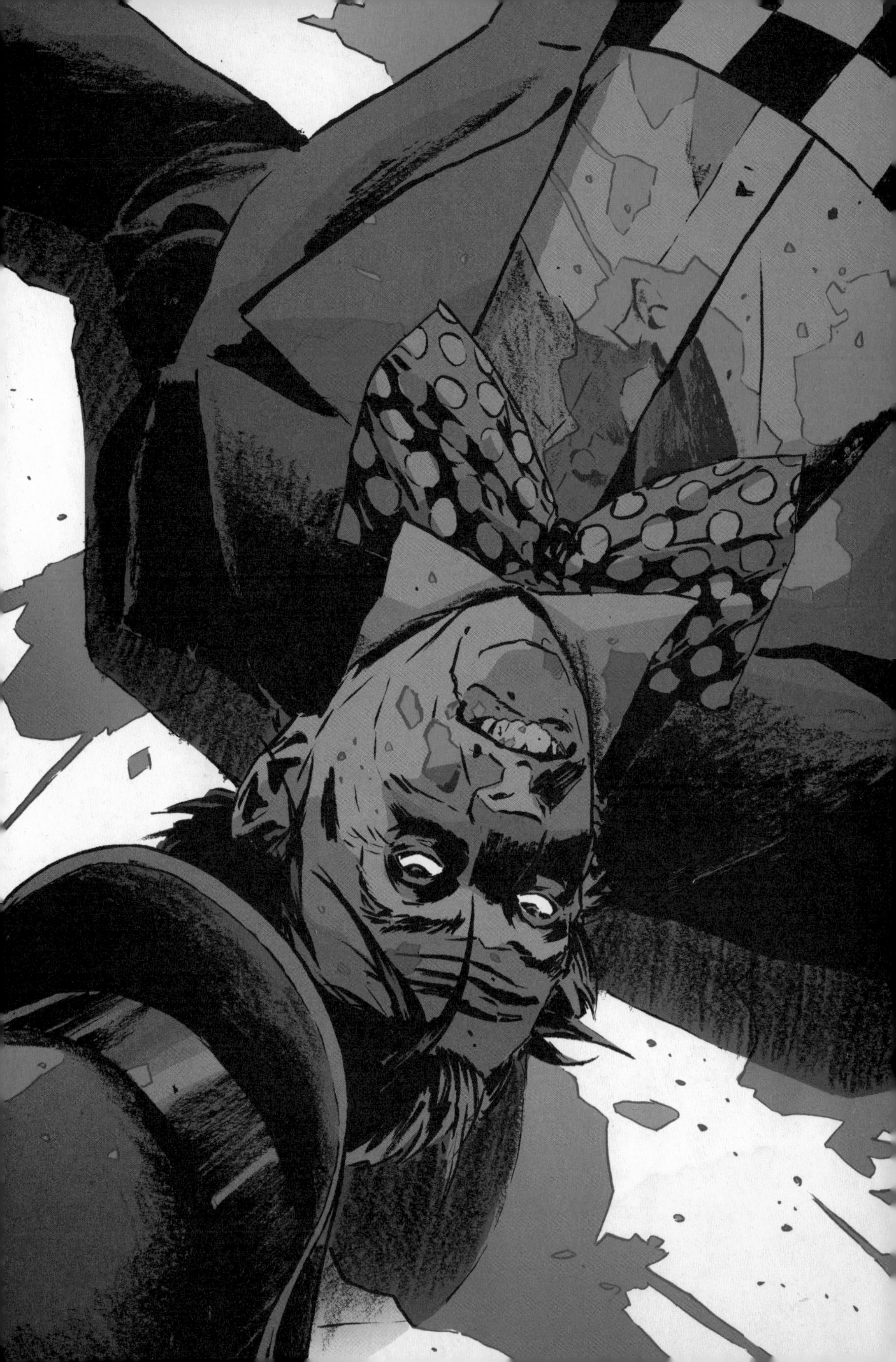

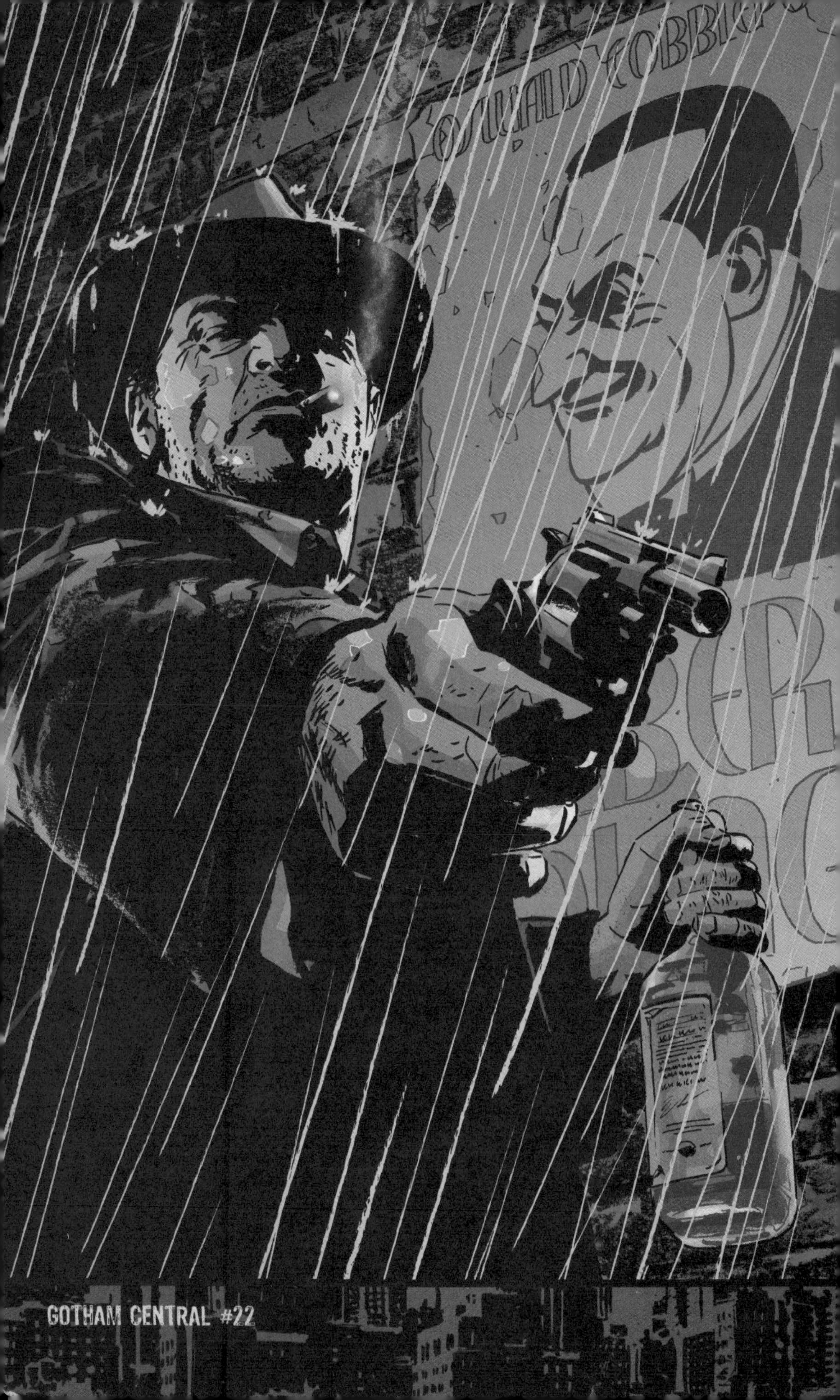

GOTHAM CENTRAL #22